Franchising **& Licensing**

Franchising **& Licensing**

**Two Ways to
Build Your Business**
2nd Edition

Andrew J. Sherman

AMACOM
American Management Association

New York • Atlanta • Boston • Chicago • Kansas City • San Francisco • Washington, D.C.
Brussels • Mexico City • Tokyo • Toronto

This publication is designed to provide accurate and authoritative information in regard to the subject matter covered. It is sold with the understanding that the publisher is not engaged in rendering legal, accounting, or other professional service. If legal advice or other expert assistance is required, the services of a competent professional person should be sought.

Library of Congress Cataloging-in-Publication Data

Sherman, Andrew J.
    Franchising & licensing : two ways to build your business / Andrew J. Sherman. — 2nd ed.
        p.   cm.
    Includes resource directory and index.
    ISBN 0-8144-0450-2
    1. Franchises (Retail trade) — United States.   2. License agreements — United States.   I. Title.
    HF5429.235.U5S54   1999
    658.8'708—dc21   98–41138
                                                                                   CIP

Printing number

10 9 8 7 6 5 4 3 2 1

This book is dedicated with love
to my first franchisee,
Matthew Harris Sherman,
and to my wife,
Judy Joffe Sherman.

I thank them for their never-ending
support and patience.

Contents

Preface to the Second Edition

Much has changed since the first publication of this book in 1991. *Franchising & Licensing: Two Ways to Build Your Business,* now in its fourth printing, has become one of the leading resources for the franchising community. It has been reviewed or referenced in dozens of business publications, used by thousands of franchising executives, referred to by hundreds of business students studying franchising, and read by many professional advisers, both in the United States and abroad.

Despite its many successes, the book needed an overhaul. The Uniform Franchise Offering Circular regulations were significantly changed in 1995, and the regulation of franchising abroad has become more common. The advent of technology has created new challenges and opportunities for franchisors of all sizes and in many different industries. Today's prospective franchisee is wealthier, more sophisticated, and better educated than ever before, thereby leveling the playing field, and has more franchise offerings to choose from than ever before. In fact, strong multiunit franchisees are acquiring franchisors; witness, for example, the purchase of Pollo Tropical by Burger King franchisee Carrols Corp, and the acquisition of Bertucci's by N. E. Restaurant Company. Clearly, the rules of the game have changed.

The impact of technology has also been very significant on franchise communications, especially as many franchisor executive teams shift their strategic focus from sales to support (e.g., getting units open versus keeping them open). In many cases, these management teams have shifted from entrepreneurial to executive leadership and are taking a much more systems-driven approach than previously. In addition, Wall Street has stood up and taken notice of the dynamics of franchising, leading to more initial public offerings and mergers and acquisitions within the franchising community than ever before; that, in turn, has led to the advent of the multiconcept franchisor conglomerates such as Starwood Lodging, The Dwyer Group, Yogen Fruz

International, Servicemaster, Grow Biz International, the International Center for Entrepreneurial Development, and HFS (now Cendant).

Trends in the domestic and international franchising community are moving so fast that by the time this second edition is published, it will probably be time to start working on the third edition. I have had the honor of working with hundreds of franchisors at many different stages of growth and operating in dozens of different industries. This book is dedicated to their continued success and daily commitment to building the strongest possible strategic and mutually beneficial working relationships with their franchisees.

Preface to the First Edition: Current Trends in Franchising

It would be difficult to imagine a day going by in either our personal or business lives during which we did not interact with a franchised business.

On a personal level, we can buy our homes, cars, food, and clothing from franchised stores and offices. We drop off our vehicles in the morning to franchised automobile service centers and our clothing for laundering at franchised dry cleaners. We plan our vacations with franchised travel agencies and enjoy our vacations and recreation at franchised entertainment facilities and health clubs. We can have our children tutored and our pets groomed at franchised offices nationwide.

At the business level, we can contract for temporary help, cleaning services, printing, accounting, computers, automobile rental, corporate travel, video productions, interior design, coffee and tea, catering, courier services, and even rented mailboxes from franchised companies across the country. We can buy our business forms and business supplies from franchised companies and even have our businesses sold by franchisors and franchisees.

The diversity of products and services offered by franchised businesses has enabled the contractual method of marketing and distribution known as franchising to become a powerful force in the U.S. economy. Franchised sales of goods and services at well over 700,000 locations across the country reached nearly $850 billion in 1998.

Franchised businesses now account for well over 8 million jobs in nearly 100 different industries. From a global perspective, nearly 800 franchisors have sold franchises abroad, accounting for over 50,000 overseas locations in markets as diverse as Africa, Japan, Israel, France, and the Caribbean. Clearly, the men and women who make up the franchising community have a lot to be proud of.

How does all of this impact on you, the prospective franchisor, key staff member, adviser, investor, or lender of prospective franchisors and currently growing franchise companies? Maybe your thriving small business should think about franchising as a method of growth and expansion. Or perhaps you should consider life as a subfranchisor, master licensee, or single-unit franchisee as a way to satisfy your entrepreneurial appetite. Or perhaps your role as a service provider or product supplier to franchisors and franchisees qualifies you for membership. But each role requires a fundamental understanding of the business and legal issues affecting the franchise relationship. This knowledge is crucial if you are to prosper in today's competitive marketplace. As you can see, there are many ways to become a member of this dynamic community.

What has made franchising so popular in the United States? From the perspective of the franchisor, franchising represents an efficient method of rapid market penetration and product distribution without the typical capital costs associated with internal expansion. From the perspective of the franchisee, franchising offers a method of owning a business but with a mitigated chance of failure because of the initial and ongoing training and support services offered by the franchisor. From the perspective of the consumer, franchised outlets offer a wide range of products and services at a consistent level of quality and at affordable prices.

There are several trends, some good and some not so good, that will affect the growth of franchising in our economy as we approach the new millennium. Among the more positive developments in franchising are:

♦ The typical franchisee and multiunit developer is smarter and wealthier than ever before—thereby leveling the playing field in both negotiation and enforcement issues.

♦ Franchising has gotten more competitive than ever before. There are an estimated 4,000-plus franchisors in the United States alone. A prospective franchisee may have twenty or more different franchisors to choose from in a given industry niche. Also, more sophisticated companies have looked at franchising.

♦ The Federal Trade Commission (FTC), which regulates franchising at the federal level, has gotten more active in enforcement actions. It brought two times as many actions against noncomplying franchisors in 1995 as it did in all the years since the FTC Rule passed in 1979.

♦ Franchising is being adopted by a series of nontraditional industries—it's not just about fast food and auto services anymore. Growing companies in energy services, healthcare, financial services, and other regulated industries are turning to franchising, raising a host of new legal issues and challenges.

◆ A focus on alternative distribution channels, such as carts, kiosks, satellite units, seasonal units, and in-store units, has raised many structural issues and triggered territorial encroachment issues as franchisors fight for market share.

◆ The International Franchise Association (IFA) opened its doors to membership by franchisees in 1994.

◆ Two new franchisee associations, whose members include franchisees from multiple systems, launched various lobbying efforts at the grassroots levels nationwide.

◆ Franchising has been globalized, with more U.S.-based franchisors than ever launching franchising programs overseas and foreign franchisors penetrating the elusive and competitive U.S. market.

◆ The wide-reaching and controversial Iowa Franchise Practices Act was passed—and subsequently partially repealed because of its unconstitutionality.

◆ Amendments to existing business opportunity laws in states such as Florida, Kentucky, Nebraska, and Utah have enabled states to more closely monitor franchising activities within the states' borders.

◆ There has been an increase in the number of initial public offerings, private placements, and mergers and acquisitions by and among domestic and international franchisors.

◆ There is a new emphasis on the role of the franchisee in the franchisor's decision-making and planning processes through advisory councils, board seats, and better use of telecommunications and computer technologies.

◆ Fortune 500 and multinational conglomerate corporations have entered franchising.

In order to take advantage of the positive aspects of franchising and to reverse the negative trends, current and prospective members of the franchising community need to be aware of—and respect—the key elements of the foundation of a successful franchising program.

A commitment to quality, fairness, and effective communication among franchisors and franchisees should go a long way in reducing disputes among franchisors and franchisees. Current and prospective franchisors must be committed to supporting and servicing the franchises they sell. Franchisors who develop strategic plans that focus on quantity of franchisees and expansion, rather than on quality of franchisees and training, are surely headed for disaster. These franchising management philosophies are emphasized throughout the course of this book.

Franchising & Licensing has been written for two primary audiences: growing businesses considering franchising and companies already engaged in franchising. For the former, this book explains the key management, operational, and legal issues that are involved in building a franchising program. For the latter, this book examines certain issues that are of continuing concern for franchisors at all stages of development, including such topics as protection of intellectual property, litigation, international expansion, executive compensation, mergers and acquisitions, regulatory compliance, and field support.

This book, however, is not limited to these two audiences. Prospective franchisees and area developers should find it helpful not only in gaining insight into the inner workings of a successful franchisor but also in the evaluation of franchise offerings. Professional advisers of all types who work with franchisors and franchisees should find the material contained here useful and helpful in advising their clients.

Franchising & Licensing is divided into five primary parts. Each of the first four addresses the core management and legal issues that are critical in building and maintaining successful franchising programs. Part One, "Management Systems," focuses on the human resources, operations, and quality control concerns that are at the heart of a franchised business. Part Two, "Legal and Strategic Issues," focuses on regulatory and contractual issues, which are of concern to the early-stage and growing franchisor, as well as protection of intellectual property, compliance systems, and dispute management, which are of special concern to the mature and established franchisor. Part Three, "Sales and Marketing Strategies," focuses on domestic and international sales and marketing strategies. And Part Four, "Financial Strategies," focuses on key issues for franchisors at all growth levels, such as capital formation and mergers and acquisitions.

Part Five, "Alternatives to Franchising," explores licensing, joint ventures, distributorships, and multilevel marketing structures, with special focus on the two primary types of licensing: technology licensing and merchandise licencing. Part Five is useful not only for licensing professionals but also for prospective franchisors, who are considering all of the alternative growth-oriented distribution strategies prior to jumping into franchising.

Acknowledgments

The concepts and issues discussed in this book are the result of nearly twenty years' experience in franchising, from both a legal and a business perspective. It would be impossible to thank all of the people with whom I have had the pleasure of working along the way. The support of my many loyal domestic and international clients and my colleagues at Katten Muchin & Zavis deserves special mention.

There are certain individuals whose time, hard work, support, and patience should be acknowledged. I wish to thank Debra Harrison for her assistance on the updates to Chapter 7, Alan Schaeffer for his assistance on the updates to Chapter 5, and Cristin McCabe for her assistance on the updates to Chapter 5. I owe special thanks to my assistant, Samantha Ferrell, who often serves as my right arm, and to our departmental paralegal, Michele Woodfolk, for her word-processing magic, organizational skills, and patience. The Franchising, Licensing and Distribution Department here at Katten Muchin & Zavis makes it happen on a daily basis.

There are also certain well-recognized individuals in the franchising and emerging business communities who have been friends and mentors over the years. For their support, advice, and general friendship, I want to especially thank Bob Gappa at Management 2000, Meg Whittemore at Whittemore Communications, Jerry Darnell at Sterling Optical, John Rogers at Douglas Symes & Brissedon, John Reynolds at the International Franchise Association, Tom Portesy and John Jackel at Franchise Mart Ventures, Verne Harnish of the First Principles Group, Burt Alimansky at Alimansky Capital Group, Dr. Eckhard Flohr of EF*LAW, Greg Matusky at Gregory Communications, John May at New Vantage Partners, Bill Keating at the Dickinson School of Law, Mark Stevens at The Stevens Group, and Steve Marriotti at the National Foundation for Teaching Entrepreneurship.

Ray O'Connell of AMACOM Books was there to provide moral support in pulling this entire project together. He is an excellent orchestrator and sounding board. I also want to thank Mike Sivilli at AMACOM for his skillful editing, and Irene Majuk at AMACOM for her skillful media relations.

Last, but certainly not least, I am grateful to my wife, Judy, and to my son, Matthew, and daughter, Jennifer, who once again sacrificed time with me so that I could complete this manuscript. I couldn't ask for a more supportive family.

Part **One**

Management Systems

The Foundation of Franchising

Over the last three decades, franchising has emerged as a popular expansion strategy for a variety of product and service companies. Recent International Franchise Association (IFA) statistics demonstrate that retail sales from franchised outlets make up nearly 50 percent of all retail sales in the United States, estimated at over $850 billion and employing some 9 million people in 1997. Notwithstanding these impressive figures, franchising as a method of marketing and distributing products and services is really appropriate only for certain kinds of companies. Despite the favorable media attention that franchising has received over the past few years as a method of business growth, it is not for everyone. There are a host of legal and business prerequisites that must be satisfied before any company can seriously consider franchising as an alternative for rapid expansion.

Many companies prematurely select franchising as a growth alternative and then haphazardly assemble and launch the program. Other companies are urged to franchise by unqualified consultants or advisers who may be more interested in professional fees than in the long-term success of the franchising program. This has caused financial distress and failure at both the franchisor and franchisee level and usually results in litigation. Current and future members of the franchising community must be urged to take a responsible view toward the creation and development of their franchising programs.

Responsible franchising starts with an understanding of the strategic essence of the business structure. As Bob Gappe of Management 2000 has always taught, there are three critical components of the franchise system: (1) the brand, (2) the operating system, and (3) the ongoing support provided by the franchisor to the franchisee. The brand creates the demand, allowing the franchisee to initially *obtain* customers. The brand includes the franchisor's trademarks and service marks, its trade dress and decor, and all of the intangible factors that create customer loyalty and build brand equity. The operating system essentially "delivers the promise," thereby allowing the franchisee to maintain customer relationships and build loyalty. The ongoing support and training provide the impetus for growth, giving the franchisee the tools and tips to expand its customer base and build its market share. Responsible franchising also means that the franchisor's management team understands that its role must change. The company must evolve away from *being* an operator to *training* and *supporting* franchisee-operators. This transition from player to coach can be difficult to grasp and presents a real challenge for many early-stage franchisors.

The responsibly built franchise system is one that provides value to its franchisees by teaching them how to get and keep as many customers as possible, who consume as many products and services as possible, as often as possible. In fact, most litigation in franchising revolves around the gap between the *actual* needs of the franchisees to remain competitive in the marketplace and the *reality* of what support the franchisor is capable of providing. The genesis of the disappointment begins during the recruitment phase of the relationship and continues beyond the start-up, as the franchisee struggles to remain competitive *unless* the franchisor delivers on its promises and is committed to providing excellent initial and ongoing training and support.

Reasons for Franchising

There are a wide variety of reasons cited by successful franchisors as to why franchising has been selected as a method of growth and distribution. Through franchising, they are able to:

- Obtain operating efficiencies and economies of scale.
- Increase market share and build brand equity.
- Use the power of franchising as a system to get and keep more and more customers—building customer loyalty.
- Achieve more rapid market penetration at a lower capital cost.
- Reach the targeted consumer more effectively through cooperative advertising and promotion.
- Sell products and services to a dedicated distributor network.
- Replace the need for internal personnel with motivated owner/operators.
- Shift the primary responsibility for site selection, employee training and personnel management, local advertising, and other administrative

concerns to the franchisee, licensee, or joint venture partner with the guidance or assistance of the franchisor.

In the typical franchising relationship, the franchisee shares the risk of expanding the market share of the franchisor by committing its capital and resources to the development of satellite locations modeled after the proprietary business format of the franchisor. The risk of business failure of the franchisor is further reduced by the improvement in competitive position, the reduced vulnerability to cyclical fluctuations, the existence of a captive market for the franchisor's proprietary products and services (as a result of the network of franchisees), and the reduced administrative and overhead costs enjoyed by a franchisor. Figure 1-1 presents some types of franchise relationships.

Figure 1-1. Types of franchise relationships.

TYPES OF FRANCHISEES				
Buy a Job (home-based; low investment)	Sales and Distributorships (product-driven); Routes	Retail Store (business format emphasis)	Management-Driven (multiunit) Larger Territory or Region (manage or lead a team of managers on a permit or district basis; satellite carts, kiosks, etc.)	Financial Investment (large-scale projects—hotels, etc.)
Resources Needed/ Business Acumen Required/etc.				

Lowest ---> Highest

The Key Components of the Relationship

Responsible franchising is the only way that franchisors and franchisees will be able to coexist harmoniously in the twenty-first century. Responsible franchising requires a secure foundation from which the franchising program is launched. In short, the more secure the foundation, the better the chance that the system will be successful. Any company considering franchising as a method of growth and distribution or any individual considering franchising as a method of getting into business must understand the key components of this foundation:

◆ *A proven prototype location* (or chain of stores) that serves as a basis for the franchising program. The store or stores must have been tested, refined, and operated successfully and be consistently profitable. The success of the prototype should not be too dependent on the physical presence or specific expertise of the founders of the system.

◆ *A strong management team* made up of internal officers and directors (as well as qualified consultants) who understand both the particular industry in which the company operates and the legal and business aspects of franchising as a method of expansion.

◆ *Sufficient capitalization* to launch and sustain the franchising program to ensure that capital is available for the franchisor to provide both initial as well as ongoing support and assistance to franchisees. (The lack of a well-written business plan and adequate capital structure is often the principal cause of demise of many franchisors.)

◆ *A distinctive and protected trade identity* that includes federal and state registered trademarks as well as a uniform trade appearance, signage, slogans, trade dress, and overall image.

◆ *Proprietary and proven methods of operation and management* that can be reduced to writing in a comprehensive operations manual, cannot be too easily duplicated by competitors, can maintain their value to the franchisee's over an extended period of time, and can be enforced through clearly drafted and objective quality control standards.

◆ *Comprehensive and structured training programs for franchisees* that integrate all of the latest education and training technologies and that take place both at the company headquarters and on-site at the franchisee's proposed location, at the outset of the relationship and on an ongoing basis. An effective training program teaches system and management know-how as well as creates enthusiasm, instills leadership and confidence, and fosters an endorsement of moral toughness.

◆ *Field support staff* who are skilled trainers and communicators and must be available to visit and assist franchisees periodically as well as monitor quality control standards. Field support staff must be trained to provide all types of services: instructive, directive, and consultative.

◆ *A set of comprehensive legal documents* that reflect the company's business strategies and operating policies. Offering documents must be prepared in accordance with applicable federal and state disclosure laws, and franchise agreements should strike a delicate balance between the rights and obligations of franchisor and franchisee.

◆ *A demonstrated market demand* for the products and services developed by the franchisor that will be distributed through the franchisees. The franchisor's products and services should meet certain minimum quality standards, not be subject to rapid shifts in consumer preferences (e.g., fads), and be proprietary in nature. Market research and analysis should be sensitive to trends in the economy and specific industry, the plans of direct and indirect competitors, and shifts in consumer preferences. It is also important to understand what business you are really in. For example, many of the major oil company franchisors thought that they were in the gasoline business until they realized that they were in the convenience business and quickly jumped into mini-marts, fast food, and quick-service restaurants, either directly or via co-branding.

◆ *A set of carefully developed uniform site selection criteria and architectural standards* that can be readily and affordably secured in today's competitive real estate market.

◆ *A genuine understanding of the competition* (both direct and indirect) that the franchisor will face in marketing and selling franchises to prospective franchisees, as well as the competition the franchisee will face when marketing products and services.

◆ *Relationships with suppliers, lenders, real estate developers, and related key resources* as part of the operations manual and system. These relationships should result in efficiencies throughout the system and cost savings for the franchisees in the form of volume discounts, group-purchasing programs, and cooperative advertising.

◆ *A franchisee profile and screening system* in order to identify the minimum financial qualifications, business acumen, and understanding of the industry that will be required by a successful franchisee.

◆ *An effective system of reporting and record keeping* to maintain the performance of the franchisees and ensure that royalties are reported accurately and paid promptly, and that all other critical sales, marketing, and consumer data are submitted and analyzed on a regular and timely basis.

◆ *Research and development capabilities* for the introduction of new products and services on an ongoing basis to consumers through the franchised network.

◆ *A communications system* that facilitates a continuing and open dialogue with the franchisees and as a result reduces the chances for conflict and litigation within the franchise network. Ongoing communications, meetings, publications, advisory groups, information sharing, and recognition of franchise accomplishments are critical. The use of all current computer, telecommunications, satellite, and audiovisual technology should be employed to enhance and foster franchisor/franchisee communications.

◆ *National, regional, and local advertising, marketing, and public relations programs* designed to recruit prospective franchisees as well as consumers to the sites operated by franchisees.

Strategic Prerequisites to Launching a Franchising Program

The most important strategic prerequisite for the success of any business format franchise system is the operation and management of a successful prototype. This prototype location is where virtually all operating problems are to be resolved, recipes and new products tested, equipment and design decisions made, management and marketing techniques tested, a trade identity and goodwill established, and financial viability proved. The franchisor is selling a tried and tested package to a franchisee, and the contents of that package must be clearly identified prior to sale. *It is irresponsible and potentially in violation of the law to ask someone to part with his or her life savings to invest in a system that is not ready for replication.*

The concept of a system or prescribed business format that is operated according to a uniform and consistent trade identity and image is at the heart of a successful franchising program. Therefore, a prospective franchisor must be able to reduce all aspects of running the business to be franchised into an operations and training manual for use by franchisees in the day-to-day operation of their business. These systems must be adequately and clearly communicated in the initial and ongoing training program. If a company offers services that are highly personalized or a product that is difficult to reproduce, then franchising may not be the most viable alternative for growth because of the difficulty in replicating these systems or products in the operator's manual or in the training program. Similarly, if significant "kinks" in the system have not yet been worked out, it is probably premature to consider franchising. But recognize that one system will *never* be perfect. It will continue to evolve, and there will *always* be room for improvement.

There are a number of other important business and strategic factors that must be considered before franchising. First, franchising should not be viewed as a solution to undercapitalization or as a "get rich quick" scheme. While it is true that franchising is less capital-intensive than is construction of additional company-owned sites, the initial start-up costs for legal, accounting, and consulting fees can be extensive. Second, franchisors must view franchising as the establishment of a series of long-term relationships, and the ongoing success of the company as a franchisor depends on the harmony of these relationships. A field support staff must be built to provide ongoing services to the existing franchisees, as well as to maintain quality control and uniformity throughout the system. New products and services must be developed so that the franchisee can continue to compete with others in its local market. Innovative sales and marketing strategies must be continually developed to attract new customers and retain existing patrons of the franchised outlet. If the franchisor expects the franchisee to continue to make its royalty payment on gross sales each week, then an array of valuable support services must be provided on an ongoing basis to meet the franchisee's changing needs.

Franchising as a Strategic Relationship

Prospective and current franchisors must always bear in mind that first and foremost, franchising is about *relationships*. The franchisor and franchisee knowingly and voluntarily enter into a long-term interdependent relationship, each depending on the other for its success. The exact nature of the franchisor-franchisee relationship has been compared to many others. There are parallels to the relationship between parent and child, between a football coach and the team, between a conductor and the orchestra, and between a landlord and the tenants. The award of the franchise has been compared to the state that grants a driver's license—you may use and renew the privilege of driving, but subject to the rules of the road and the payment of ongoing fees. Like the relationship between franchisor and franchisee, you have the freedom to drive, but not necessarily however or wherever you want. There has been much emphasis in recent years to avoid the "them versus us" mentality and organizational culture with a refocus on the "we" as well as the "and." *The focus of successful and strategic franchising is now on how we can work together for each other's benefit, where the enemy is not each other but rather the competition.* The specific dynamics of the relationship will vary from industry to industry. There are now nearly 100 different industries that have used franchising as a method of growth (industries ranging from car insurance agencies to electric utilities companies to healthcare and financial services).

The financial output of these parties working together can be very powerful in a competitive marketplace. In fact, some say that franchising truly arrived in October 1997 when Warren Buffet, arguably one of the most financially savvy men on the planet, announced that his holding company, Berkshire Hathaway, Inc., agreed to acquire Dairy Queen, with 5,800 franchised outlets worldwide. For years, Buffet had also been one of the largest shareholders of McDonald's, and he hinted that other franchisor acquisitions might be in the near future. Franchising continues to be an alternative growth and acquisition strategy for sophisticated international conglomerates. Companies such as Grand Metropolitan PLC (the British-based owner of Burger King and Haagen-Dazs), Whitman Company (the owner of Midas Muffler and Thrifty Car Rental), Allied Domecq PLC (the British-based owner of Dunkin' Donuts and Baskin-Robbins), and Flagstar Companies, Inc. (the owner of Denny's and El Pollo Loco restaurants) are all active players in the franchising community.

Yes, franchising is about relationships. And like the most sacred of relationships, marriage, if the parties are to stay committed to each other for the long term, then both franchisor and franchisee must respect one another, stay loyal to one another, and each day search for ways to strengthen their bond.

A recent survey seems to indicate that this new focus on the strategic aspects of the relationship seems to be working. While over one-half of marriages in the United States wind up in divorce, nearly 92 percent of the nation's franchisees said they would get married to their franchisor again. In addition, in a recent survey conducted by the Gallup Organization and published by the International Franchise Association Educational Foundation in March 1998, more than nine out of ten (92 percent) of the franchise owners surveyed said they were either very or somewhat successful. Of those who had been in business eleven years or more, 96 percent indicated they were very or somewhat successful.

Gallup surveyed 1,001 U.S. franchisees, nearly eight out of ten of whom owned only one franchised small business. Women accounted for 28 percent, and nearly half of those who responded had a professional or managerial position before purchasing a franchise; nearly two of ten were involved in either services/labor or retail sales. Given the high satisfaction ratings, it is not surprising that nearly two-thirds (65 percent) of the franchise owners said they would purchase the same franchise again if given the opportunity. Of those who wouldn't buy the same franchise again, nearly half (43 percent) said they would consider buying a different one. Nearly two-thirds (64 percent) said they would be less successful if they had tried to open the same type of business on their own and not as part of a franchise system. On average, franchise owners reported annual gross incomes of $91,630. Nearly one of four (24 percent) earned $100,000 or more during the year prior to the survey.

The franchisor who wants its system and franchisee satisfaction ratings to meet or exceed these levels of success must build a culture of honesty, trust, passion, and genuine commitment to long-term success. This often begins in the recruitment process by carefully screening and educating qualified candidates to ensure that your long-term objectives are truly shared and best interests truly aligned. This type of strategy leads to mutually beneficial relationships and significantly decreases the chances of litigation. Of course, some degree of franchisee failure is inevitable, and there are typically two factors at play—one that you can control and one that you often can't. You *can* control the quality of your systems, training, and support tools and innovation of your marketing to help increase the chances of success. Other than through careful screening and continuous monitoring, you *cannot* typically control local market conditions or changes in the franchisee's personal life that may also affect his or her performance.

Curbing the Failure Rate of Early-Stage Franchisors

One of the underlying premises of this book is that successful franchising requires a commitment to building a proper foundation and platform from which to launch and build the franchising program. My mission is to ensure that each reader avoids the mistakes made by the hundreds of franchisors that have failed over the years. That's right, hundreds. Each year since the early 1990s, between seventy-five and one hundred franchisors went out of business. This number represents between 3 and 5 percent of all franchisors operating during those years. Figure 1-2 presents forty of the more common reasons why franchisors fail. Read them carefully and read them often. My goal in writing this book is to mitigate the risk of your company's meeting the same fate in launching and building its franchising program.

Figure 1-2. Forty common reasons why franchisors fail.

1. Lack of adequate control
2. Choice of the wrong consultants
3. Failure to provide adequate support
4. Lack of franchise communications systems
5. Complex and inadequate operations manuals
6. Inability to compete against larger franchisors
7. Disregard for franchise registration and disclosure laws
8. Not joining the International Franchise Association (IFA)
9. Lack of quality control
10. Breakaway franchisees
11. Unworkable economic relationship with franchisees
12. Royalty underpayments/nonpayments by franchisees
13. Lack of effective financial controls
14. Unprotected trademarks
15. Inadequate training program
16. Lack of ongoing research and development
17. Choice of the wrong subfranchisors or multiunit developers
18. Lack of public relations
19. Inadequate relationships with key vendors
20. Premature termination of franchisees
21. Difficulty attracting qualified franchisees
22. Lack of proper disclosure documents
23. An unproven and unprofitable prototype
24. Premature launch into international markets
25. Inadequate site selection criteria
26. Lack of proper screening system for prospective franchisees
27. Lack of business and strategic planning
28. Entrance into oversaturated markets
29. Inexperienced lawyers and accountants
30. Unreasonable pressure to sell franchises
31. Lack of effective compliance systems
32. Operational systems that can be easily duplicated
33. Lack of experienced management
34. Excessive litigation with franchisees
35. Decentralized advertising
36. Unbridled geographic expansion
37. Unprofitable and unhappy franchisees
38. Unwillingness to enforce franchise agreement
39. Improper earnings claims
40. Lack of market research

Understanding the Franchisee of the Year 2000

One way to avoid failure is to understand the profile of today's prospective franchisee. A wide variety of marketing, planning, operational, and strategic decisions can be made by the growing franchisor once certain basic premises are understood. As a general rule, franchisees in today's competitive markets are getting smarter, not dumber. The better educated, better capitalized franchisee is here to stay. As franchising has matured, prospective franchisees have more resources (seminars, media articles, trade shows, IFA programs, etc.) than ever before to turn to for information and due diligence. These new, sophisticated franchisees are very different from their "mom and pop predecessors" of the 1970s and 1980s. This prospect is better trained to ask all the right questions and hire the right advisers in the investigation and franchise agreement negotiation process. These new franchisees are also better heeled and more likely to organize themselves into associations and take action if they are not receiving the required levels of support and assistance. As discussed in Chapter 9, those franchisors who fail to mold their sales and support systems around the characteristics of these new franchisees and who continue to conduct business the old-fashioned way are headed down the road to disaster and litigation.

A Commitment to Being (and Staying) Creative and Competitive

Today's franchisor must have an initial and ongoing commitment to being creative and competitive. Market conditions and technology that affect franchising are changing constantly, and the franchisee of the next millennium expects you to change at the same pace. For example, the ability to adapt your franchising system to allow for growth and market penetration into alternative and nontraditional venues is critical. The more creative and aggressive franchisors in the retail and hospitality industries are always searching for new locations where captive markets may be present—such as airports, hotels, hospitals, highway roadside travel plazas, universities, sports arenas, or military bases—where trends toward outsourcing, the demand for branded products and services, and the desire to enhance the captive customer's experience have all opened up new doors and opportunities for franchising. For example, TCBY, based in Little Rock, Arkansas, has nearly 50 percent of its 3,000 frozen yogurt stores worldwide in these alternative venues. In other cases, franchisors have pursued co-branding strategies to penetrate these new markets, again taking advantage of the trend toward convenience stores, grocery store chains, and gas stations all wanting to provide their patrons with an enhanced customer experience and offer a more comprehensive and integrated solution to their consuming needs. And again, strategies that focus on co-branding and the ability to share costs, positioning the business format to serve as many customer needs as possible, and a commitment to penetrate new market segments at a relative low cost have opened up many doors for the creative and aggressive franchisor who is committed to capturing more market share and serving more and more customers.

2

Operations
and Training

At the heart of any successful franchising program is a prescribed *system* that ensures quality control and consistency throughout the franchise network. In most franchised businesses, the key elements of this system have been developed and fine-tuned in the operation of the franchisor's prototype location. The administration of this system requires effective and comprehensive *documentation* that must be provided to each franchisee, both at the inception of the relationship and on an ongoing basis. It also requires a franchisor's commitment to the integrator of available technologies—the use of computer and telecommunications technologies to provide efficient and effective support to its franchisees on an initial and ongoing basis.

The documentation required to administer the franchise system properly includes:

- Statement of corporate philosophy, policies, and general rules of operations
- Confidential operations and procedures manual
- Local sales, marketing, and public relations kit
- Site selection, architectural, interior design, signage, equipment, and inventory specifications
- Guidelines for financial record keeping and reporting
- Quality control and inspection reports
- Special manuals for subfranchisors and area developers (where applicable)

Depending on the nature of the franchisor's business, many of the required items listed above may be combined into a single confidential operations manual ("the manual"). The manual is the heart and soul of the franchising program, designed to be a resource for the franchisee when the franchisor can't be there. Despite the importance of the manual to the long-term success of the franchising program, many early-stage franchisors experience great difficulty in their attempts to prepare a proper manual. Yet a franchisor unable to properly document and communicate the critical steps of successfully operating the business (often in painstaking detail) is doomed for failure and really has no business getting into franchising in the first place. Franchisors should also take steps to use available computer and communications technologies to support the franchisees. For example, a growing number of franchisors are making their manuals available to franchisees on a security-coded Intranet and sending manual updates and system bulletins via email. Sophisticated franchisees are demanding access to key operational data using this technology.

Guidelines for Preparation of the Manual

Before sitting down to prepare your operations manual, keep in mind the following basic principles and guidelines:

♦ The operations manual is a living, breathing document. Its contents will develop and change as your franchise system develops and changes. Be sure to reserve this level of flexibility in your franchise agreement.

♦ Because it is inevitable that your franchise system will evolve, prepare the manual in a format that is user-friendly and easy to update. For example, a series of three-ring notebooks with tabs for each major heading makes section or page replacements and additions quick and easy, if these updates are not made available electronically.

♦ Assume nothing about the skills and experience of your typical franchisee. The text of the manual should be written at a high-school reading level of comprehension and should anticipate that your franchisee is likely to be a complete novice in your industry. Dry, technical, and difficult-to-use manuals will be ignored by franchisees, and this will cause a breakdown of quality control throughout the system. Be creative in your use of charts and diagrams that may be effective teaching tools and help avoid quality control breakdowns. The more user-friendly it is, the more the manual will actually be used.

♦ No detail should remain unaddressed in the manual. Do not leave any operating discretion in the hands of the franchisee. Everything ranging from preopening procedures to preparation of products to employee discipline must be included. Remember that comprehensiveness in the preparation of your manual provides a certain level of legal protection. Franchisees will not be able to claim, "They never told me how to . . ." in any subsequent litigation if all details are addressed.

◆ The manual must be comprehensive (yet generic) enough to be followed by all franchisees that must run their businesses in a range of different markets and operating conditions. For example, if procedures are different for long stand-alone facilities (as opposed to kiosks within a regional mall), then these expected differences must be included and discussed. If advertising strategies differ in a rural area (as opposed to an inner-city location), then these differences must be anticipated and included within the manual.

◆ The manual should anticipate and answer some of the questions most commonly asked by your franchisees. The more often they need to call you for assistance, the larger the administrative staff (and thus overhead) you need to maintain.

◆ Remember that the manual is confidential and proprietary. As such, it should be treated as a trade secret under the law of intellectual property. Procedures must be developed for protection and care of the manual by each franchisee and its employees. Access should be restricted to those with a "need to know." Remember that the manual is *licensed, not sold* to a franchisee. It remains the property of the franchisor at all times. Special receipts should be developed for providing the manual to franchisees and special forms prepared for ordering replacement manuals.

◆ Avoid the temptation to turn your operations manual into a strategic business plan. Naturally, there should be a section that addresses the franchisor's overall goals, mission, and values. However, the bulk of the manual should teach the franchisee how to perform key tasks and not just be a strategy dissertation.

◆ The manual should at all times be consistent with the representations made in the Uniform Franchise Offering Circular (UFOC), the disclosure document that must be delivered to prospective franchisees under federal and state law, as well as with the specific obligations contained in the franchise agreement. One easy way to find yourself in litigation with your franchisees is through inconsistencies between promises made in the UFOC and actual obligations contained in the manual. (See Figure 2-1.)

Figure 2-1. The relationship between the franchise offering circular and the manual.

It is the modern practice of many franchise lawyers to be rather vague in the preparation of franchise offering circulars and franchise agreements, with common references to information contained in the manual. The rationale here is that amending a manual is far less complicated than amending a registered disclosure document or binding legal agreement. Although I generally advocate this practice, be careful. If the document is too vague, then it will be challenged by the examiners in the registration states. Similarly, if the franchisor attempts to introduce a significant new program, operating procedure, or policy, this may trigger a "material change" that *will* require amendment of the offering circular and perhaps even the franchise agreement itself. See Chapter 5 for a more detailed discussion of the "material change" regulations.

Suggested Outline for the Operations Manual of a Franchisor

An operations manual should encompass virtually every aspect of the business to be operated by the franchisee, from prior to grand opening to the ongoing day-to-day operating procedures and techniques. The following is an outline that has been designed for a typical franchisor in the services business:

Section A: Introduction

1. Foreword/notice of proprietary and confidential information
2. Acknowledgment
3. History of the franchisor
4. The franchisor's management team
5. The franchisor's obligations to the franchisees (an overview)
6. The franchisee's obligations to the franchisor and the system (an overview)

Section B: Timetable for Opening the Franchised Office

A comprehensive timetable that the franchisee is to follow, beginning the date that the franchise agreement is signed to the first date that business will be conducted and beyond

Section C: Pre-Opening Obligations and Procedures

1. Architectural, engineering, interior design, and site construction specifications
2. Minimum requirements for utilities, ventilation, etc.
3. Signage
   a. General information
   b. Description and explanation of signs to be used, interior and exterior
   c. Dimensions, specifications, etc.
4. Ordering and receiving fixtures, supplies, equipment, and inventory
5. Building the management team: managers, employees, and professional advisers
6. Application for licenses, permits, utilities, insurance, and bonding
7. Lease review and negotiations
8. Community involvement, trade groups, charities, chambers of commerce, etc. (pre- and post-opening)
9. Recommended reference books on small business management

Section D: Office Policies

1. Image, decor, and theme
2. Quality standards of services
3. Pricing policies and fee structure
4. Service and courtesy to clients
5. Handling typical complaints and problems
6. Employee appearance (uniforms) and hygiene
7. Hours of operation

Section E: Office Operation and Maintenance

1. General housekeeping
2. Basic duties of personnel: office manager, sales staff, employees, etc.
3. Daily office: opening procedure and checklists
4. Daily office: closing procedure
5. Daily, weekly, and monthly reports
6. Self-inspection
7. Health and safety standards
8. Rest rooms

9. Pest control
10. Parking lot care and management (where applicable)
11. Alarms, locks, and keys
12. Emergency procedures

Section F: Equipment, Computer System, Inventory, and Supplies

1. Equipment, inventory, and supply list for a typical franchised office
   a. Specifications
   b. Approved vendors
   c. Repair and maintenance (equipment only)
2. Operation and management of the franchisor's proprietary database
3. Approved vendors for equipment, inventory, and supplies

Section G: Administration

1. Personnel: job chart, position descriptions, hiring, qualifications and interviewing, application form, checking references, hours, shifts, timekeeping, vacancies, sick pay, time off, training, payroll taxes, laws concerning employees, rules of conduct for employees, bulletin boards, and required notices
2. Record keeping and accounting
3. Collections and accounts receivable management
4. Accounts payable management
5. Recruitment and training
6. Quality control
7. Group insurance policies

Section H: Sales Promotion

1. Grand-opening promotion plans (with timetable)
2. General ongoing promotion: newspaper, radio, direct mail, advertising cooperatives, and community groups
3. Special promotions: franchisee referral programs, customer referral premiums, etc.
4. Public relations
5. Use of public figures
6. Use of coupons and direct-marketing mailers
7. Group discounts and promotions
8. Maintaining high visibility in the community

9. Understanding and analyzing local demographic statistics and trends

Section I: Protection of Trademarks and Trade Secrets

1. Trademark usage and guidelines
2. Examples of trademark misuse
3. Care and protection of trade secrets
4. Use and care of the operations manual
5. Key employee nondisclosure agreements
6. Protection of proprietary computer software and manuals

Section J: Preparation of Reports to the Franchisor

1. Guidelines and requirements
2. Examples of forms

Section K: Guidelines for Transfer of a Franchise

1. Requirements
2. Sample forms and notices

Section L: Corporate Structure and Financing

1. Required corporate structure
2. The franchisor and franchisee as independent parties
3. Financing and loan applications
4. Financing alternatives

Drafting the Operations Manual: Selected Topics

The preparation of a comprehensive operations manual is truly an art. No level of attention or detail can be ignored. For example, most franchisors might assume (and for good reason) that a typical franchisee would know how to prepare a peanut butter and jelly sandwich. Yet there are many levels of detail that need to be addressed if the old-fashioned PB&J sandwich were a staple on the franchisor's menu, such as:

- ◆ What type of peanut butter? Chunky or smooth? Any particular brand?
- ◆ What flavor jelly? Grape? Apricot? Strawberry? May a customer choose?
- ◆ How many ounces of peanut butter per sandwich? Of jelly?

◆ What type of bread? White? Wheat? Rye? May a customer choose?

◆ The bread served toasted or untoasted? If toasted, using what type of oven? How long should the bread be in the oven?

◆ The sandwich served with condiments? Pickles? Potato chips? Coleslaw? How much of each condiment?

◆ How is the sandwich to be served? What type of packaging?

◆ What are the suggested price ranges for the sandwich? Does the condiment selected affect the price? What other products should be recommended to the customer when the sandwich is ordered?

Now multiply the answers to these questions by the number of issues that must be addressed in order for the franchisee to properly operate the specific franchised business, and you begin to get a feel for the level of detail required. For example, the operations manual of a temporary services franchisor should emphasize hiring and recruiting techniques, sales training, interviewing and screening methods, development of referrals, fee structure, use and protection of the proprietary computer system and database, public relations, and administrative management.

The specific organization and content of each manual varies from franchisor to franchisor and from industry to industry. Naturally, the manual of a fast-food operation may have a more detailed section on sewage, plumbing, food preparation, inventory controls, and lavatory facilities than would that of a services-driven business.

Consider the level of detail contained in these sample provisions in Figure 2-2 dealing with garbage, refuse, and rodent control for a fast-food franchisor.

(text continues on page 26)

Figure 2-2. Sample operations manual provisions concerning garbage and refuse.

Containers

◆ Garbage and refuse shall be kept in durable, easily cleanable, insect-proof and rodent-proof containers that do not leak and do not absorb liquids. Plastic bags and wet-strength paper bags may be used to line these containers, and they may be used for storage inside the food service establishment.

◆ Containers used in food preparation and utensil washing areas shall be kept covered after they are filled.

- Containers stored outside the establishment, and dumpsters, compactors, and compactor systems, shall be easily cleanable; provided with tight-fitting lids, doors, or covers; and kept covered when not in actual use. In containers designed with drains, drain plugs shall be in place at all times, except during cleaning.
- There shall be a sufficient number of containers to hold all the garbage and refuse that accumulate.
- Soiled containers shall be cleaned at a frequency to prevent insect and rodent attraction. Each container shall be thoroughly cleaned on the inside and outside in a way that does not contaminate food, equipment, or utensils, and detergent or steam shall be provided and used for washing containers. Liquid waste from compacting or cleaning operations shall be disposed of as sewage.

Storage

- Garbage and refuse on the premises shall be stored in a manner to make them inaccessible to insects and rodents. Outside storage of unprotected plastic bags or wet-strength paper bags or baled units containing garbage or refuse is prohibited. Cardboard or other packaging material not containing garbage or food wastes need not be stored in covered containers.
- Garbage refuse storage rooms, if used, shall be constructed of easily cleanable, nonabsorbent, washable materials; shall be kept clean; shall be insect-proof and rodent-proof; and shall be large enough to store the garbage and refuse containers that accumulate.
- Outside storage areas or enclosures shall be large enough to store the garbage and refuse containers that accumulate and shall be kept clean. Garbage and refuse containers, dumpsters, and compactor systems located outside shall be stored on or above a smooth surface of nonabsorbent material such as concrete or machine-laid asphalt that is kept clean and maintained in good repair.

Disposal

- Garbage and refuse shall be disposed of often enough to prevent the development of odor and the attraction of insects and rodents.
- Where garbage or refuse is burned on the premises, it shall be late matter in accordance with law. Areas around incineration shall be clean and orderly.

(continues)

Figure 2-2. *(continued)*

Reasoning

◆ Proper storage and disposal of garbage and refuse are necessary to minimize the development of odors, to prevent such waste from becoming an attraction and harborage or breeding place for insects and rodents, and to prevent the soiling of food preparation and food service areas. Improperly handled garbage creates nuisance conditions, makes housekeeping difficult, and may be a possible source of contamination of food, equipment, and utensils.

Examples of Violations

◆ Garbage stored in unprotected plastic bags outside of building
◆ Lid on outside garbage storage container left open
◆ Refuse containers not cleaned frequently
◆ Drain plugs missing on dumpster-type storage units
◆ Outside refuse area not kept clean and neat
◆ Outside garbage cans and dumpster-type storage unit set on unpaved area

Discussion

◆ Complying with each section of the manual makes compliance with other sections much less a task. An excellent example of this interrelationship are the requirements of this section easing compliance with the following sections on insect and rodent control. Note some of the specific requirements of these paragraphs:

  ◆ Storage of garbage and refuse in plastic bags is approved for inside the restaurant building, but not outside.
  ◆ Provide hot water, detergent, or steam for washing containers.
  ◆ Dumpsters or containers must be located on a nonabsorbent slab of concrete or blacktop, preferably some distance away from the establishment doors so as not to entice vermin into the establishment.
  ◆ Indoor garbage and refuse storage rooms must be insect- and rodent-proof.
  ◆ Cardboard or other packaging material not containing garbage or food wastes need not be stored in covered containers.

Insect and Rodent Control

General Requirements

Effective measures intended to minimize the presence of rodents, flies, cockroaches, and other insects on the premises shall be utilized. The premises shall be kept in such condition as to prevent the harborage or feeding of insects or rodents.

Openings

Openings to the outside shall be effectively protected against the entrance of rodents. Outside openings shall be protected against the entrance of insects by tight-fitting, self-closing doors; closed windows; screening; controlled air currents; or other means. Screen doors shall be self-closing, and screens for windows, doors, skylights, transoms, intake and exhaust air ducts, and other openings to the outside shall be tight-fitting and free of breaks. Screening material shall not be less than sixteen mesh to the inch.

Reasoning

Insects and rodents are capable of transmitting diseases to humans by contamination of food and food-contact surfaces. Because insects require food, water, and shelter, action must be taken to deprive them of these necessities.

Examples of Violations

- ◆ Front/back door of restaurant propped open for prolonged period
- ◆ Screening on doors and windows in poor repair
- ◆ Evidence of recent rodent activity
- ◆ Outside doors not self-closing or tight-fitting

Discussion

A restaurant cannot keep both pests and customers. One or the other must go. And there can be no doubt as to which is more expendable. There is no place for pests in the facility. Your pest control measures may include:

- ◆ Mechanical means such as the use of screen and screening materials, traps, electric screens, and even "air curtains"
- ◆ Chemical means such as the use of sprays, repellents, baits, and other insecticides

(continues)

Figure 2-2. *(continued)*

◆ Preventive measures such as cleanup campaigns, proper storage techniques, and other measures related to sanitation and good housekeeping

A proper warning: Prevent contamination by pests without introducing contamination by pesticide. A number of federal regulations cover the handling, use, storage, and disposal of pesticides. Be aware of these regulations if you are conducting your own control program.

If you select a pest control company, be certain it is knowledgeable and competent. The following guidelines are offered in choosing a reliable pest control company and ensuring quality service:

◆ Reach a complete understanding with a company before work starts or a contract is signed. Find out what the pests are, what will be done, over how long a period of time, and what results can be expected at what cost.

◆ Be sure you know what is and isn't guaranteed. Be sure the company will back up its work.

◆ Ask about how the technician who will serve your food service operation has been trained. There are numerous home study courses as well as frequent seminars and training courses run by associations and universities.

◆ Ask your fellow operators for the name of the company they are currently using or may have used in the past. Find out if they were happy and satisfied with the service.

◆ Seek value from the pest control company you hire. Don't just look at the price.

◆ Pests of concern to the food service operation may generally be placed in three classes:

1. Insect pests, including roaches, ants, flies, and pantry pests
2. Rodent pests, including mice and rats
3. Pest birds, including pigeons, starlings, and sparrows

Another critical area for a fast-food operation that must be addressed in a detailed manner is the management of relationships with vendors. Franchisees in the fast-food business are likely to have daily contact with food suppliers and sundry vendors; weekly contact with uniform and linen supply companies, equipment maintenance and service companies, trash collectors, vending machine dealers, and pest control companies; and periodic contact with insurance agents, sign makers, security system installers, locksmiths, plumbers, and cash register equipment companies. It is incumbent on the franchisor to develop quality control criteria and specifications for the selection and approval of these vendors. The mechanics of the vendor approval process should be reviewed by legal counsel in order to consider all applicable principles of antitrust law. Qualification standards must be carefully developed, clearly communicated, and reasonably enforced throughout the franchise system. Nepotism, greed, and the failure to approve qualified suppliers are causes of constant conflict between franchisors and franchisees, as discussed in Chapter 8.

Who Should Prepare the Manual?

There is often an issue, particularly among early-stage franchisors, as to who should prepare the manual. Perhaps the best solution is for the franchisor's management team to work closely with a truly experienced consulting firm. This creates a balance between the substance of the manual being reflective of the franchisor's operational policies and the quality of the technical and explanatory writing that an experienced consultant can bring to the table. If the manual is written only by the franchisor's management team, then there is a high likelihood that critical areas may be omitted or that there is a lack of the technical skills needed to write a document that properly conveys useful information at a level that all users of the manual can grasp. On the other hand, if the manual is prepared only by the consultant without proper input from the franchisor, then the end product is likely to be generic and not truly reflective of the operational success factors that drive the franchisor's system.

Designing Effective Training Programs

A properly designed training program is one that does an effective job on an initial and ongoing basis for preparing the franchisee for the "real world." This is a world that includes the pre-opening steps and challenges, the logistics of grand opening, the steps necessary to manage and motivate your employees, the procedures for dealing with an angry customer, the tips for negotiating with a difficult vendor, the tips for building a profitable and sustainable business, and the strategies for handling a fierce competitor. This is the world that the franchisee must face day in and day out, and this is the world that your operations manual as well as initial and ongoing training programs must address. A well-designed training program seeks to *educate* (rather than dictate) franchisees on how to build a successful business, *confirms* and *defines* the role of each party in building the business, *develops* the skills for effective leadership and business planning, and *reinforces* the importance of the franchisor's brands, mission, and system compliance. An effective training program also instills and encourages teamwork by and between the franchisor and franchisee as well as by and among the franchises.

For a food business, franchisees must learn how to prepare every item on the menu—not from behind a desk but inside a real training kitchen. They must understand employee hiring, promotion and termination techniques, purchasing, product handling, key financial management ratios, cost controls, store design and construction, and advertising and marketing. Business education skills must be coupled with technical and operational instruction in the trenches. Role playing and field training must be a critical part of the training program. The training materials must be effective and the instructors knowledgeable both in their fields and as quality instructors and coaches. The training program should incorporate appropriate technologies where appropriate—such as interactive CD-ROMs, training videos, Electronic Data Interchange (EDI), electronic ordering and inventory control programs (POS systems)—and have skilled scoring and evaluation techniques, with a final exam to determine eligibility to open a store. The ongoing training should also provide the franchisees with goals and benchmarks for measuring and evaluating their own financial or operational performance for each of their units. These results can then be disseminated throughout the system to reduce costs and increase productivity.

Training and education in a franchise system can be a lot more than an instructor standing up in front of a group of attendees, lecturing with viewgraphs or slides. In this Information Age as we approach the new millennium, technology can be used to enhance the learning process, as well as to deliver the actual training materials. Technology can be used to improve your training and education programs as follows:

◆ To reduce administrative and delivery costs, including travel for instructors and students and the need for fewer instructors

◆ To enhance the effectiveness and flexibility of the learning process

◆ To demonstrate your company's commitment to integrate available technology into training and support programs

◆ To reduce replication costs for printing and distribution of training materials (e.g., a CD-ROM disk weighs a lot less than five bulky spiral notebooks)

Interactive systems are more responsive to the learning needs of the franchisee. According to Daniel Grunberg at ChainWave Systems in Lexington, Massachusetts, studies have shown that interactive systems greatly improve the learning process because they hold the franchisee's attention more effectively. The most widely used method for producing a training course is to put it on videotape. Although this is an easy-to-duplicate medium that people can access with just a VCR, its drawbacks are the lack of interactivity and easy search capability. The following are some of the new technologies that can be used to enhance the training process:

◆ CD-ROMs (the same size as music CDs) can be used to hold video and computer software. About thirty minutes of video can be placed on a single CD-ROM, depending on the resolution. The great advantage of a CD-ROM is that it can be made interactive. The cost of producing copies of a CD-ROM is relatively low, about $1 each in quantities of 2,000.

◆ DVD is a relatively new technology that was originally developed to replace videotapes for distribution of movies to consumers. Over two hours of video can be stored on a single disk. The same types of education and training software can be placed on a DVD disk as a CD-ROM, with more capacity per disk. Of course, fewer users currently have compatible equipment, and at the moment that equipment is more expensive. But it might be worth exploring if you have some video-intensive instructional material.

◆ The Internet is fast becoming a popular way to deliver instructional material. Sometimes called distance learning, it allows people, wherever they are located, to access the materials. With the speeds of most users' current Internet access, this is not a great way to deliver lengthy video sequences, but it may be perfect for your franchise system otherwise. You can quickly modify and update materials without incurring additional reproduction costs, as you would with CD-ROM or DVD. Users can access the material instantly from anywhere in the world for the cost of their local Internet access. These technologies can also be used to build a private electronic community or an Intranet, where news, tips, system updates, and other useful information can be shared for the benefit of all the franchisees in the system.

Once you determine the mix of appropriate technology, traditional classroom learning, and field support that will make up the bulk of your initial training program, the next step is to plan your agenda. The actual agenda for the training program must now be disclosed as part of the franchisor's obligations in Item 11 of the UFOC. A portion of a sample training agenda from the UFOC of a restaurant franchisor appears in Figure 2-3.

Figure 2-3. A portion of a sample training agenda from the UFOC of a restaurant franchisor.

Franchisees Training Agenda Topics to Be Covered	Instructional Material	Hours of Classroom Training	Hours of on-the-Job Training	Instructor
Opening	Manual	8	16	See Note 1
Closing	Manual	2	6	See Note 1
Open Prep	Manual	2	6	See Note 1
Open Prep/Fry	Manual	2	6	See Note 1
Close Fry	Manual	0	8	See Note 1
Swing Dish	Manual	2	6	See Note 1
Open Broiler	Manual	2	6	See Note 1
Close Broiler	Manual	0	8	See Note 1
Open Window	Manual	0	8	See Note 1
Swing Window	Manual	0	8	See Note 1
Close Window	Manual	0	8	See Note 1
Swing Host/Hostess	Manual	2	6	See Note 1
Open Host/Hostess	Manual	0	8	See Note 1
Open Server	Manual	2	6	See Note 1
Close Server	Manual	2	6	See Note 1
Swing Server	Manual	2	6	See Note 1
Out of House/Human Resource	Manual	8	0	See Note 1
Managers and the Law	Manual	8	0	See Note 1
Management Shift/Follows (5 A.M. and P.M. Shifts Floor Supervision; Standard Responsibilities)	Manual	0	80	See Note 1
Final Validation	Manual	4	0	See Note 1

As discussed at the outset of this chapter, training transcends the initial session provided at the outset of the relationship and must be delivered on an ongoing and continuous basis. An effective training program recognizes that learning is a process and not an event, and it builds in tools for reinforcement accordingly. The franchisor must be committed to using its field support staff as well as available technology—such as software applications, videoconferencing, electronic bulletin boards, and satellite technology—to communicate "best practices," system changes and updates, customer service and retention, employee relations and turnover, operational tips, technical expertise on existing as well as newly introduced products and services, key financial data, industry trends, and other key information on a periodic basis. The importance of business planning skills must also be taught and reinforced during the initial and ongoing training program. The franchisee's ability to draft and refine a basic business plan, a long-range strategic plan, a detailed sales proposal, or even a thirty-day action plan is critical.

Even the "mega-players" in the software industry are recognizing the need and importance of this technology. In 1997, Microsoft introduced a special application of its Intranet and Extranet business process automation software for the franchising community. The software was designed to meet the information and communications needs of the typical franchisor in keeping its franchisees well-trained and informed on an ongoing basis.

This software application, called Microsoft Solution Providers, enables franchisors and their franchisees to increase productivity, efficiency, and cost savings by automating all information sharing and distribution processes currently delivered through conventional distribution methods. An Extranet provides secure, external access to an Intranet. Franchisors can even take the technology further by customizing to meet their needs as a franchise organization. The whole idea is to communicate smarter and faster and at a lower cost. Some of the benefits offered by this software are as follows:

♦ It reduces costs associated with internal and external business transactions, such as paper materials and printing and postage, as well as saving time.

♦ It enhances communication and information distribution capabilities, enabling franchisors and franchisees to easily search and browse large databases and bulletin boards containing the latest news and information from all aspects of the company, including sales, marketing, human resources, legal, and finance. By implementing Intranet applications, franchises are empowered to seek out and access the information they need most. Franchisees also receive ongoing syndicated content feeds specific to their industry.

◆ It streamlines business processes, such as report generation, order placement, fulfillment, personnel information, and database management.

◆ It provides secure, interactive communication between corporate headquarters and franchisees through the use of Internet tech-nology such as chat forums. With an Intranet, franchisors and franchisees have instant access to the latest resources and information, twenty-four hours a day, seven days a week. Franchisees are able to increase interaction with customers and increase sales during business hours, with the option of handling administrative operations such as product ordering and sales tracking.

The solution offered by Microsoft Solution Providers addresses the issues of openness, scalability, and reliability. Microsoft, along with the software product teams, works with franchisors to develop, implement, and support a customized Intranet and Extranet solution. Microsoft Solution Providers uses the Microsoft Solutions Platform of products as building blocks for customized solutions and offers various value-added services, such as integration, consulting, software customization, development of turnkey applications, technical training, and support. These electronic communities should be driven by software that has the following functional capabilities and applications:

◆ Survey generation
◆ Document libraries (operator's manuals, marketing resources, etc.)
◆ Organizational and staff directory
◆ Events/marketing calendar
◆ News and views (current events, industry trends, etc.)
◆ Collaboration (resource and idea sharing among the franchisees, productivity tracking, etc.)
◆ Training (interactive and distance learning, reference materials, etc.)
◆ Software libraries (version control, updates, training, etc.)
◆ Inventory controls (supply ordering, group purchasing, etc.)

The development of custom software or automated financial systems is another area where franchisor/franchisee communications and training can be strengthened. Many franchisors have had custom software developed for their franchisees to provide tools for financial management, logistics and operations, sales training, personnel management, credit and collections management, customer relations and follow-ups, proposal writing, or business planning. The most common example is a point-of-sale (POS) system. These systems have multiple advantages that originate from automating the input of financial transactions so that daily, weekly, monthly, and annual reports can be generated. These reports can then be analyzed, providing information about performance to assist the franchise system—both franchisors and franchisees—in planning, marketing, and sales strategies.

A POS system collects and stores data about transactions and sometimes controls decisions made as a part of a transaction (e.g., validating a credit card). These were the first computerized information systems. POS systems are based on detailed models of how the transaction should be processed. Most contain enough structure to enforce rules and procedures for work done by franchisees. Some POS systems bypass clerks entirely and totally automate transactions.

Franchising companies normally use real-time processing POS systems. Once data for the transaction have been collected and validated, the POS stores the data in a standard format for later access by others. These reliable data assist management in more effectively evaluating and assisting franchise owners. Franchisees also request comparisons with each other to understand their individual strengths and weaknesses and compare themselves to the average and top peers. These technologies can also be used to enhance interactions with customers and increase sales. Franchisors are developing technology that enables their franchisees to conduct business with their customers online, whether they are ordering a meal or providing specifications for a complex printing order.

Information generated from a POS system can also improve a franchisee's bottom line. Aside from the time savings of automated reporting, POS systems provide the potential for increased information sharing among franchisees. For instance, if one franchisee observes that another outlet is more successful than he is in selling a specific product or service, he can contact the franchise owner to find out the reasons behind the success to learn how to improve his own store's performance.

3

Developing System Standards and Enforcing Quality Control

Many owners of growing companies fear that the decision to franchise will result in the loss of quality control over the operations and management of their business. In reality, there are a variety of vehicles available to franchisors for maintaining the level of quality that they and their consumers have come to expect. A well-planned franchising or licensing program includes a wide variety of system standards, training methods, and operational manuals to establish quality control guidelines as well as a carefully assembled field support staff to educate franchisees and enforce the franchisor's quality control guidelines.

To succeed, a franchise system demands quality control. A system that does not maintain and enforce an effective quality control strategy is not likely to survive in the competitive marketplace. The licensor of a trademark has an obligation under federal trademark laws to control the quality of the products and services offered in connection with the trademark. Thus, by establishing and enforcing quality control standards, a franchisor not only ensures uniformity of quality but also satisfies an obligation imposed by the federal Lanham Act upon the owner of a trademark. Failure to monitor and control the operations of a franchisee/licensee could result in a "statutory abandonment" of the franchisor's rights in the trademark because it may no longer distinguish a particular product or service from those offered by others in the market. Therefore, the trademark laws provide a *justification* and basis for the implementation of reasonable controls over franchisees/licensees in all aspects of the business format.

Developing and Enforcing System Standards

The glue holding the typical franchise system together consists of the uniform policies, procedures, and specifications that must be followed by all franchisees. These rules and regulations, typically found in the operations manual, must be (1) *carefully planned* and developed by the franchisor; (2) *clearly articulated* by the franchisor to the franchisees, both initially and on an ongoing basis; (3) *accepted* by the network of franchisees as being understood and reasonable; (4) *consistently applied;* and (5) *rigidly enforced* by the franchisor, typically through its field support staff. Obviously, the development of uniform standards is of little utility unless there are systems in place for monitoring and enforcing these standards, as well as penalties for noncompliance with the standards, which are typically found in the franchise agreement.

Compliance with quality control standards requires mutual respect by and among the franchisor and all of its franchisees. The franchisor must be reasonable and resist the temptation to "go hog-wild" in the development and enforcement of system standards. The franchisee must understand that reasonable standards are in the best interests of all franchisees in the network. Franchisees typically have a "love-hate" relationship with system standards. On the one hand, they love reasonable standards that result in happy consumers and weed out noncomplying franchisees. On the other hand, they detest standards that are unattainable, vaguely communicated, and arbitrarily or too rigidly enforced.

System standards, which are prescribed in the operations manual and other written and electronic communications from the franchisor, are deemed to be part of the franchise agreement under the contract law doctrine of incorporation by reference. System standards dictate, among other things:

◆ The required and authorized products and services to be offered and sold
◆ The manner in which the franchisee may offer and sell these products and services (including product preparation, storage, handling, and packaging procedures)
◆ The required image and appearance of facilities, vehicles, and employees
◆ Designated and approved suppliers and supplier approval procedures and criteria
◆ Types, models, and brands of required operating assets (including equipment, signs, furnishings, furniture, and vehicles) and supplies (including food ingredients, packaging, and the like)
◆ Use and display of the trade and service marks
◆ Sales, marketing, advertising, and promotional programs and the materials and media used in these programs
◆ Terms and conditions of the sale and delivery of items that the franchisee acquires from the franchisor and its affiliates

◆ Staffing levels and training
◆ Days and hours of operation
◆ Participation in market research and testing and product and service development programs
◆ Payment, point-of-sale, and computer systems
◆ Reporting requirements
◆ Insurance requirements
◆ Other operational rules

These standards that a franchisor implements at the beginning and during the course of the franchisee relationship, and the franchisor's willingness and ability to enforce those standards systemwide, usually determine the success of the franchise system. It is essential that system standards be communicated to franchisees in well-organized and understandable formats.

The obvious dilemma from the list set forth above is that many of these system standards are moving targets. They can and do change as technology and market conditions change, and franchisors must be able to modify the system standards without seeking an addendum to the franchise agreement every time a modification to the system is necessary. The franchisor must build a culture where change is inevitable, expected, and warmly embraced by the franchisee—right at the start of the relationship. Changes to the system must be viewed as a positive evolution of the business format, not as a burden. To accomplish this, however, there must be a culture of trust: The franchisee wants to be assured that these changes are reasonable and necessary. If the change involves new products and services, the franchisee wants to be assured that adequate market research went into the development of these new concepts and that they are not the whimsical or harebrained idea of the franchisor's founder. Most franchisors build a certain degree of flexibility into their franchise agreements to allow the peaceful implementation of system changes, such as the clause set forth below.

Over the course of the relationship, there are periodic events and trends that can trigger change, such as new competitive conditions, a change in territorial policies, technological innovations, the loss of a key supplier, the introduction of alternative locations, or a merger or acquisition. In other cases, the change may be to rectify deficiencies in existing franchise agreements, particularly those relating to system change. These events may require the franchisor's consent and/or execution of the franchisor's "then-current" form of franchise agreement, which may include broader "change" language. For example, a franchisor might condition the sale of a franchised unit, or the renewal of the term of the franchise agreement, upon an upgrade of the refurbishment of the franchised unit to the franchisor's then-current design criteria. In addition, a franchisor might condition the opening of additional units by the franchisee upon the franchisee's agreement to comply with these new policies for its existing franchised units and/or an agreement to comply with some specific element of change in the system. These opportunities may, however, be limited by existing franchise agreement language and the scope or the required upgrade. A sample clause providing the flexibility of the franchisor to modify the system standards from time to time might look like this:

> You may acknowledge and agree that the development and operation of your Store in accordance with the mandatory specifications, standards, operating procedures, and rules we prescribe for the development and operation of [ABC] stores (the "System Standards") are the essence of this Agreement and essential to preserve the goodwill of the Marks and all [ABC] stores. Therefore, you agree that, at all times during the term of this Agreement, you will develop, maintain, and operate the Store in accordance with each and every System Standard, as periodically modified and supplemented by us at our discretion during the term of this Agreement. Among the aspects of the development and operation of franchised [ABC] stores that we may regulate through the System Standards are the following:

> 1. Design, layout, decor, appearance, and lighting; periodic maintenance and cleaning; replacement of obsolete or worn-out improvements, equipment, furniture, furnishings, and signs; periodic painting, redecorating, and remodeling and the frequency of such painting, redecorating, and remodeling; use of signs, banners, graphics, emblems, lettering, and logos; and periodic modification of the Store in accordance with our plans, specifications, and directions at such time or times as we require

> 2. Types, models, and brands of required or authorized equipment, furniture, furnishings, signs, and other products, materials, and supplies

> 3. Requirements for stocking, storing, and rotating an inventory of products for resale of such types and formats and in such packages as we may prescribe and other specifications relating to inventory practices and product mix

> 4. Designated or approved suppliers (including us and our affiliates) of equipment, furniture, furnishings, signs, inventory, and other products, materials, and supplies

We may from time to time modify System Standards, and such modifications may obligate you to invest additional capital in the Store and/or incur higher operating costs, but such modifications will not alter your fundamental status and rights under this Agreement. System Standards may accommodate regional or local variations or other factors as we determine. Although we may require you to refurbish the Store (including changes in signage, floor covering, wall covering, and other decor features except for fixtures) to conform with System Standards, we will not require such refurbishing more often than once every five (5) years. You agree that System Standards prescribed from time to time in the Confidential Operating Manual, or otherwise communicated to you in writing, will constitute provisions of this Agreement as if fully set forth in this Agreement. All references to this Agreement include all System Standards as periodically modified.

Methods for Enforcing Quality Control and System Standards

There are many methods a franchisor may use to ensure certain levels of quality are maintained that help distinguish the franchisor's products and services from those of its competitors. This chapter examines the use of (1) the franchise agreement, (2) field support personnel to establish, ensure, and maintain quality control, (3) initial and ongoing training programs, (4) operations manuals, (5) approved supplier programs, and (6) tying arrangements. The limitations imposed by law with respect to the controls that may be imposed upon a franchisee/licensee are also explored.

Field Support Staff and Quality Control

Many franchisors view their field support personnel as necessary for providing franchisees with the ongoing support and assistance the franchisor is obligated to provide under its franchise agreement. While ongoing support is an important component of the role of field support personnel, franchisors may overlook the important role a well-assembled field support staff can play in ensuring that franchisees maintain the franchisor's quality control and uniform system standards. These two components of the role of field support staff should be carefully considered by current and prospective franchisors.

For the early-stage franchisor, it is not difficult to make periodic visits to each franchisee for the purpose of providing support and assistance, ensuring compliance with quality control guidelines, and listening to franchisees' questions and concerns. This becomes more of a challenge as the franchisor's network of franchisees continues to grow and spread throughout the country, which makes it impossible for the franchisor to offer the same level of tender love and care (TLC) to its franchisees. This growth could have an adverse impact on the quality of the products and services offered by the franchise system. Developing and training a field support staff that can continue to provide TLC and ensure compliance with quality control standards when there are 500 franchisees, at the same level provided when the franchisor had 5 franchisees, will help the franchisor's system succeed and prosper.

◆ *Ongoing support and assistance.* Most franchisors undertake to provide franchisees with some level of ongoing support and assistance. A field support staff is generally assembled for this purpose. A franchisor's ability to duplicate the level of success and quality offered by its prototype facility is in the hands of the field support staff.

For this reason, field support personnel should be carefully selected and trained. To ensure consistency, each member of the field support team should receive *exactly the same types and levels of training.* They should know the intricacies of the franchise business, be sensitive to the needs and concerns of franchisees, and be diplomatic in their dealings with franchisees. The information provided to the franchisees should be accurate and consistent. If there are differences in the interpretation of a particular standard or role among various members of the field support staff nationwide, then the standard itself may be considered waived or even abandoned. If there is no consistency in the enforcement and communication of standards, then they will be viewed as not being standards at all, and this will lose consumer goodwill, dilute the franchisor's trademarks and proprietary system, and occasion litigation and lowered franchisee morale.

It is important for field support personnel to be able to recognize and satisfy the ongoing needs of franchisees, using a positive management philosophy, motivation techniques, good communication, and innovative franchisee programs. If field support personnel are successful in maintaining good relationships with franchisees, franchisees will be motivated to comply with the necessary controls established by the franchisor for the operation of the business. Maintaining a good relationship with franchisees is accomplished through conducting regular regional and national meetings, providing retraining programs and periodic seminars that focus on various areas of interest to franchisees, offering management consulting services, and maintaining routine telephone and personal contact.

♦ *Meetings and seminars.* Regional and national meetings should be used, among other things, as a forum for franchisees to voice their concerns and questions. The franchisor should take all franchisee questions, concerns, and criticisms seriously and directly address each by (1) offering immediate comfort and suggestions at the meeting, (2) addressing problems raised in newsletters or follow-up bulletins after the meeting, and (3) conducting interviews one-on-one with the franchisee(s) who raised such concerns. The ability of the franchisor's field support personnel to address such concerns and offer franchisees comfort and/or solutions is critical to the viability of the franchisor's system. The franchisor must, at all times, be perceptive to the needs and concerns of its franchisees and capable of providing meaningful, realistic, and practical solutions.

Seminars that focus on a particular aspect of the operation of the franchise business should be conducted on a regular basis. The franchisor's field support staff should play an important role in developing these seminars. Through personal contacts with franchisees, they can offer insight into appropriate topics for seminars and identify essential issues that franchisees would find beneficial. Seminars can be excellent tools to both educate and motivate franchisees.

♦ *Training and retraining programs.* The franchisor must carefully develop a training program that covers all of the topics of concern to franchisees. The initial training program must be comprehensive and informative, covering topics such as management and operation of a business, preparation of products and/or provision of services, quality control, personnel management, advertising and marketing, bookkeeping and reporting, use of trademarks, maintaining the confidential nature of trade secrets, legal obligations, and customer relations. In developing an initial training program, franchisors must be mindful that many franchisees have never owned or operated a business. For this reason, adequate initial training and ongoing assistance and support are crucial to the success of the franchisees and the franchisor. The most effective training programs combine old-fashioned, personal, hands-on support with the appropriate use of high-tech training tools. Both components must be utilized in the training program, and neither is a substitute for the other. Marketing topics should not necessarily predominate the training session. Franchisees must be taught not only how to bring in the business but also how to deliver the products and services once the customer is in the door.

Franchisors should also consider implementing retraining programs for franchisees who need continuous reinforcement of the franchisor's business format, standards, and guidelines. Retraining should be recommended (or required) for franchisees who continually fail in one or more identifiable areas of the operation of the franchise business. For example, a franchisee has continually failed to provide the franchisor with all of the required monthly, quarterly, and annual reports mandated by the franchise agreement. The franchisor's field support personnel have worked with the franchisee several times to correct the deficiency; however, the problem has not been resolved. Field support personnel report to the franchisor that the franchisee is (1) unfamiliar with the reporting requirements and forms, (2) not accustomed to the computer-generated accounting system, and (3) willing to learn and comply but slow. This franchisee may have good intentions and may just need some additional training and attention in learning the financial aspects of the business. He or she should, therefore, be allowed (or required) to attend a retraining program that focuses on accounting, reporting, record keeping, and other financial matters. If the franchisor's field support personnel continually report the same franchisee deficiencies for a group of franchisees, then the franchisor may want to reevaluate that portion of its training program to determine its overall effectiveness. The field support visit to the franchisee's site should be viewed as a quality control enforcement check as well as a tutoring and assistance session for troubled franchisees.

◆ *Management consulting services.* Some franchisees have problems that cannot be resolved with the periodic assistance of field support personnel. For this reason, some franchisors offer management consulting services to franchisees at an hourly rate. While this is a more costly means of resolving a franchisee's problems, it may be the only way to identify and deal with them. If a consultant (usually someone who is part of the field support staff) is on-site for one to two weeks, the franchisee's deficiencies can be more quickly and accurately identified. Once problems are identified, the consultant can suggest methods and techniques for resolving them, assist in the implementation, and, to a certain extent, monitor the results. Management consulting services should be offered to franchisees only if the franchisor truly has the personnel and expertise to provide meaningful services. In addition, the rates charged for consulting services should be reasonable so as not to be perceived by the franchisee as merely a money-making vehicle for the franchisor.

◆ *Personal and telephone contact.* Field support personnel are notorious for their regular monthly visits to the franchise location, inspections, unexpected visits, and telephone calls. These are the traditional and most effective methods for providing on-site field support and quality control inspections of franchisees. If, however, a visit by the field support staff is viewed as an intrusion (or even as spying) on the franchisee's ability to operate his or her business independently, then the franchisor has not succeeded in establishing a good relationship with its franchisees. It is difficult to balance the franchisee's desire for independence with the franchisor's need for quality control. If an appropriate balance is not found, franchisees may become resentful and resist the franchisor's necessary controls, thus creating an unnecessarily tense and hostile relationship. The field support staff is primarily responsible for striking the appropriate balance between the interests of the franchisees and those of the franchisor. It is therefore critical that the franchisor use care in the hiring and training of its field support personnel.

The personal visit to a franchisee's operating location by a field support person offers the best opportunity for establishing the appropriate relationship and striking that balance of interests. The franchisor should put together a staff large enough to cover the entire network on a regular basis, such as once per month. If the staff is "spread too thin," it will not be able to conduct timely follow-up visits to check on the franchisee's progress with certain problems. In addition, if a field support person is responsible for visiting too many franchisees, he or she is less likely to remember each franchisee's problems and concerns, which may make it more difficult to establish and maintain the necessary rapport between the franchisor's staff and the franchisee.

The field support representative should set aside enough time to prepare for each visit (see Figure 3-1) and time to summarize the meeting soon afterward. These details may be overlooked if the franchisor's field support staff is overloaded. A franchisee can recognize an unprepared representative and certainly won't appreciate the inconvenience and waste of time this is likely to create. Each field support person typically develops his or her own style and each franchisee has different needs, but this is no excuse for straying from the uniform system standards that must be continuously communicated to the franchisees.

Figure 3-1. Preparing for the site visit.

- ◆ Send confirmation of the visit, including an agenda of things franchisee should have prepared (unless the visit is intended to be a random "surprise" for enforcement and monitoring purposes).
- ◆ Contact the franchisee to get input for developing the agenda.
- ◆ Identify staff members needed for meetings, and secure time for them during the visit.
- ◆ Evaluate the franchisee's sales data and reports.
- ◆ Review the report from the last visit.
- ◆ Check on timeliness of royalty and other payments to the franchisor.
- ◆ Develop goals for the visit.

The visit itself should be carefully orchestrated and always include (1) follow-up on goals set during last meeting, (2) walk-through inspection, (3) training (usually in an area of weakness or a newly introduced service, product, method, or technique), (4) identification of the franchisee's successes and weaknesses, (5) establishment of goals to be met by the next visit, (6) identification of the franchisee's needs and concerns, (7) talks with employees and customers, and (8) reinforcement of quality control guidelines.

Inspections of the franchisee's facility should be conducted in accordance with a standardized checklist developed by the franchisor. A point-scoring method is typically used for such evaluations. Field support personnel should be required to report the results of these evaluations to the franchisor within a specified time frame. All reports should note both deficient and outstanding quality performance.

Except for certain major infractions, which there is no effective means of correcting (these typically result in immediate notice of termination under the franchise agreement), franchisees should be given the opportunity to cure or correct defaults or deficiencies. The field representative should be responsible for (1) offering guidance to the franchisees on ways to correct the cited deficiencies and (2) following up with franchisees to see that deficiencies have been corrected. Typically, a franchisee is given thirty days to correct deficiencies unless the deficiency cannot be corrected within this time period.

- ◆ *Unannounced visits and test customers.* Field visits and inspections should occur on a regular basis. A recent study conducted by the International Franchise Association (IFA) indicates that most franchisors conduct monthly field calls and that a large number of franchisors also conduct such calls on a quarterly, bimonthly, or semiannual basis. In addition to regularly scheduled visits, field personnel should conduct periodic surprise/unannounced visits and inspections. Many franchisees may be put off by unannounced inspections, viewing them as an infringement on their independence. For this reason, the field personnel should carefully orchestrate surprise inspections. Franchisees should be informed from the start that an imminent inspection should have no effect on the standards, service, products, cleanliness, or other aspects of their business operation. The field person should be viewed as "just another customer," grading and judging the same way customers do. The difference is that the field person goes behind the scenes to check aspects of the business that create the product and service. The inspection is designed to help the franchisee improve its performance. An unsatisfied customer won't return; the field person, on the other hand, helps the franchisee identify and correct any problems.

Franchisors often discover that adjacent franchisees establish a network to inform other franchisees that the field support person is in the area. As a franchise system grows, the communications network makes it more and more difficult to conduct *truly* surprise visits. Nonetheless, such visits should continue to be used as part of the franchisor's quality control program.

Test customers can be used as an alterative or supplement to surprise visits by field personnel. Generally, the franchisor hires people unfamiliar to its franchisees to act as customers for the purpose of evaluating the franchisee's performance in the areas of customer relations, product and service quality, and cleanliness. To achieve the best results, test customers should not identify themselves as such and should report to the field person with detailed observations. Later, the field support person who usually deals with the franchisee should make an announced visit for the purpose of discussing the observations of the test customer. Maintaining the anonymity of test customers (1) prevents franchisees from alerting other area franchisees that a surprise inspection is likely and (2) puts the franchisee on notice that any customer could in fact be a "test customer" sent by the franchisor.

◆ *Team approaches to field support.* Some franchisors have developed a team approach toward providing field support and enhancing system standards. For example, at Cost Cutters Family Hair Care, each new franchisee is assigned a service team made up of one person from four key departments: marketing, education/operations, finance, and product/distribution. Teams and franchise owners meet yearly to develop goals and action plans to meet them. Progress is tracked monthly. In addition, Cost Cutters revisits each new shop at forty-five days, six months, and one year. The focus is on troubled areas during the follow-up visits. Some franchisors have also developed formal mentoring programs, designed to match new franchisees with veteran ones. Veteran franchisees talk at least once a week with new franchisees during their critical first ninety days in business.

Beyond formal training and support programs, many leading franchisors are also focused on being accessible and responsive and treating their franchisees as partners. Follow-up training can also include town-hall meetings, such as one-day sessions, held two times a year. In addition, an operators exchange group, formed and run by franchisees with twenty or more stores, can draw together members three times a year to discuss issues geared to larger franchisees.

The Development of Enforcement Systems

As a general rule, the franchisor has an obligation to develop system standards and procedures that are reasonable and attainable. Once developed, the standards and procedures should be clearly communicated and uniformly enforced. The enforcement must be neither too loose nor too rigid. If the penalties for noncompliance are too loose, the franchisor will be viewed as a toothless lion that neither intends nor has the power to insist on compliance. If the enforcement is too rigid, the standards will be resented and disregarded, resulting in litigation and poor franchisee morale throughout the network.

Many times, the enforcement strategy adopted depends on the franchisor's own stage of growth. For example, a gentle rap on the knuckles (in lieu of an actual termination) may be more prudent early on in the franchisor's own development because of the impact of a dispute at this stage. The costs of litigation, the perception of actual and prospective franchisees, and the nature of the infraction should all be considered. If a "quasi-acquiescence" policy of enforcement is adopted by the younger franchisor, then issues of waivers and laches should be discussed with legal counsel. As the franchisor grows and matures, it becomes easier to rigidly enforce system standards and apply significant penalties for noncompliance because the threat of termination becomes a more powerful deterrent.

The franchisor should consider the following general factors in determining how to proceed against a franchisee in noncompliance with system standards:

1. Whether the franchisee in question has a "high profile" within the system
2. The exact nature of the franchisee's infraction(s)
3. The current condition and stability of the franchisor's industry
4. The availability of a replacement franchisee for this specific site
5. The quality of the training program and operations manual in the area where the infractions have occurred
6. The existence of any potential counterclaims by the franchisee
7. The quality of the evidence gathered by the field support personnel to prove the incidents of noncompliance
8. The reaction of the other franchisees within the system to the enforcement action
9. The geographic location of the franchisee in question

The penalties that may be applied by the franchisor to the noncomplying franchisee include a formal warning, a written notice of default, a threat of termination, an actual termination, damages or fines, a forced sale or transfer, or a denial of a benefit, such as eligibility for participation in a new program. Support for those penalties must be found in the franchise agreement or must be separately negotiated.

The courts have recognized that in some cases it will be necessary for the franchisor to take legal action against a franchisee who fails to follow system standards in order to protect the franchisor's intellectual property. For example, in *Adcom Express, Inc. et al. v. EPK, Inc.,* No. 92-10829 [Trade Cases 1995-96] Bus. Fran. Guide (CCH) ¶ 10,685 (4th Dist. Minn. Apr. 12, 1995), the court upheld a franchisor's termination of its California franchisee for refusing to use the franchisor's New York franchisee for deliveries in the New York territory in breach of a material provision of the franchise agreement. The court relied on the Adcom franchise agreement provision, which gave the franchisor discretion to terminate the franchise upon default and also provided that "good cause for termination means any breach of any material provision of the Franchise Agreement or any intentional, repeated or continuous breach of any provision of the Agreement . . . without the [franchisor's] consent." The court stated that there was "no doubt" that requiring a franchisee in the freight forwarding business to use other franchisees in the system for deliveries is a material provision of the franchise agreement. In *Great Clips, Inc. v. Levine,* Civ. No. 3-90-211 [Trade Cases 1992-93] Bus. Fran. Guide ¶ 70,930 (D. Minn. June 16, 1993), a franchisee was permanently enjoined from continuing to violate its franchise agreement by departing from the franchisor's single-price, even-dollar haircut policy.

In another case, *Novus de Quebec v. Novus Franchising, Inc.*, Civ. No. 4-95-702 [Trade Cases 1995-96] Bus. Fran. Guide ¶ 10,823 (D. Minn. Dec. 5, 1995), an auto glass repair franchisor terminated its area developer for "failure to comply with the uniformity and quality standards" in the franchise agreement and for failure to cooperate with an audit inspection as required under the agreement. The area developer also had awarded franchises to franchisees of competing franchise systems after the franchisor had already rejected them as suitable candidates. The district court rejected the area developer's request for an injunction to prevent termination of the license, citing the area developer's "total disregard for the spirit and philosophy behind the Novus System and for the goodwill associated with the Novus Marks and System."

Another case where a franchisee's noncompliance with the franchisor's system was determined to cause irreparable harm to the franchise system and its marks was *Burger King Corp. v. Stephens,* 1989 WL 147557 (E.D. Pa.), where the court granted Burger King's request for an injunction to force a franchisee to cease operating where the franchisee had violated Burger King's operating standards and Burger King was thus "[unable] to [e]nsure the maintenance of high quality service that the trademarks represented, [thereby] causing irreparable injury to the franchisor's business reputation and goodwill." Other examples where courts have protected franchisors and licensors from possible damage to their marks by franchisees or licensees include *Cottman Transmission Systems, Inc. v. Melody,* 851 F.Supp. 660 (E.D. Pa. 1994) (continued use of marks by a terminated franchisee could cause irreparable harm by loss of consumer faith and confidence); *Jiffy Lube International, Inc. v. Weiss Brothers, Inc.,* 834 F.Supp. 683 (D. N.J. 1993) (unauthorized use of franchisor's trade dress and marks enjoined because a continuing infringement would cause irreparable harm); *Star Houston, Inc. v. Texas Dept. of Transportation and Saab Cars U.S.A., Inc.,* 957 S.W. 2d 102, 109 (App. Tex. 1997) (dealer's refusal to participate in new signage program was a material breach constituting good cause for termination). As these cases illustrate, a franchisor's efforts to apply quality control that ensures consistency in the licensed products and services offered under the given marks protect the value (i.e., goodwill) of a franchisor's intellectual property.

Other Methods of Enforcing Quality Control Standards in a Franchise System

♦ *Operations manuals and training programs.* The franchisor usually provides the franchisee with a comprehensive operations manual, which is generally reviewed for the first time at the initial training session for owners and managers of the franchise business. These manuals and training programs instruct the franchisee on all aspects of operating and managing the business within the quality control standards established by the franchisor. The operations manual should set forth in a clear and concise fashion the minimum levels of quality to be maintained in all aspects of the business, from cleanliness to customer service to recipes to employee relations. These standards should be taught and reinforced throughout the training program.

◆ *Architectural/engineering plans and drawings.* In most types of franchised businesses, uniformity of physical appearance is imperative. The franchisor often provides detailed architectural drawings and engineering plans, both as a service to franchisees and as a method of protecting quality control. These plans reinforce the importance of a consistent image in the minds of consumers, who may be looking for the "golden arches" or "orange roof" in their search for a familiar place to eat along the highway. Plans may include specifications for signage, counter design, display racks, paint colors, HVAC systems, lighting, interior decoration, or special building features.

◆ *Trade dress.* Trade dress, which consists of all the design and interior features of your system thereby distinguishing you from your competitors (e.g., signage, decor, uniforms), is also a method of enforcing quality control and design standards. The leading case on the protection of a franchisor's trade dress is *Taco Cabana International, Inc. v. Two Pesos, Inc.,* 932 F.2d 1113 (5th Cir. 1991), affirming a jury's finding that Taco Cabana had a protectable trade dress that was inherently distinctive, and that consumers might likely confuse or associate Taco Cabana with a competitor restaurant that had infringed on Taco Cabana's trade dress. The court explained that "an owner may license its trade dress and retain proprietary rights if the owner maintains adequate control over the quality of goods and services that the licensee sells with the mark or dress."

◆ *Site selection assistance.* The top three priorities for the success of a franchisee's business have often been cited as "location, location, and location." Many franchisors assist franchisees in selecting a proper site for their franchise business and even assist in lease negotiations and supervision of construction. Such efforts not only help to ensure the franchisee's success but also provide an additional basis for maintaining quality control in terms of minimum parking requirements, traffic patterns, minimum/maximum square footage, demographics of the local market, and prevention of market saturation.

◆ *Intranets and technology.* Modern franchisors are also turning to Intranets, videoconferencing, and related communications and computer technologies as a way to enforce systems standards, provide support, and monitor quality control. The diverse technologies available for use in Intranets include email, Web browsers, groupware, Java, streaming audio and video, "push" technology, and countless other Web-based software applications.

The enforcement of quality control and system standards can be accomplished by publishing product, service, and marketing information that can then be accessed easily and inexpensively by each franchisee in the system, and by designated, password-controlled individuals within a franchisee organization, using public telecommunications networks. Outside contractors and suppliers also can be given limited access to the Intranet, to facilitate their interaction with the system.

An Intranet can also provide a secure central point for collecting financial information, in order to track financial performance and maintain financial controls. Intranets also can permit authorized external users, such as suppliers, shareholders, and analysts, to have limited access to certain financial data, in order to build better relationships through timely, accurate communications. Other finance and accounting applications on an Intranet can be used specifically for company-owned operations, such as budgeting, payroll, expense reports, cash management, and online banking. Intranets also can be used to replace the "centralized cash registers" and other forms of legacy systems, for greater control over franchisee operations. The addition of a secure transaction processing feature to an Intranet could also be used to facilitate inventory management, as well as to further enhance cash management, reporting, and other controls.

◆ *National or uniform advertising programs.* Advertising and promotion of the franchise business on a local and national level is an essential part of virtually all franchise systems. If the franchisees are left on their own to develop advertising and promotional materials for local television, radio, and newspapers, the system does not send out a uniform message about the products and/or services offered by the franchise network. In addition, franchisors do not have control over the quality and content of the advertising materials used by franchisees. Franchisees may not be knowledgeable of the laws prohibiting unfair or deceptive advertising and trade practices. Thus, without the franchisor's guidelines, they are more likely to stumble into trouble, diminishing the goodwill the franchisor has worked hard to build. For this reason, a centralized advertising program, engineered by the franchisor's in-house staff or an outside advertising agency, develops newspaper, television, and radio advertisements for use by franchisees in their local markets, helping the franchisor maintain a certain minimum level of quality in advertising. Moreover, this centralized advertising program should include a franchisor review and approval process for advertisements developed by franchisees.

◆ *Approved supplier program.* The franchisee needs a wide variety of raw materials, office and business supplies, equipment, foodstuff, and services in order to operate the franchise business. The level of control that the franchisor is entitled to exercise over the acquisition of these supplies and materials varies, depending on the nature of the franchise business and the extent to which such goods are propriety. Franchisors may be prohibited, under certain circumstances, from forcing a franchisee to buy all equipment and supplies from them or their designated sources.

The franchisor does, however, have a right to establish objective performance standards and specifications to which alternate suppliers and their products or services must adhere. Such standards are justifiable for the purpose of ensuring a certain minimum standard of quality.

In establishing an approved supplier or vendor certification program, the franchisor should carefully develop procedures for the suggestion and evaluation of alternative suppliers proposed by the franchisee. The standards by which a prospective supplier is evaluated should be clearly defined and reasonable. This evaluation should be based upon:

1. Ability to produce the products or services in accordance with the franchisor's standards and specifications for quality and uniformity
2. Production and delivery capabilities and ability to meet supply commitments
3. Integrity of ownership (to ensure that association with the franchisor would not be inconsistent with the franchisor's image or damage its goodwill)
4. Financial stability

5. Familiarity of the proposed supplier with the franchise business
6. Negotiation of a satisfactory license agreement to protect the franchisor's trademarks

The franchisor should always reserve the right to disapprove any proposed supplier that does not meet these standards. In addition, an approved supplier should be removed from the list of suppliers if, at any time, it fails to maintain these standards. Other reasonable standards, applicable in the franchisor's industry, may also be adopted.

Special Legal Issues Affecting Exclusive Supplier and Vendor Certification Programs

For certain highly proprietary aspects of the franchise business such as the "secret sauce," the franchisor typically has the authority to require the franchisee to purchase those products *exclusively* from the franchisor or from a supplier designated and approved by the franchisor. This is known as a tying arrangement. Not all tying arrangements are permitted under applicable antitrust laws. Proposed tying programs continue to be one of the greatest sources of conflict and litigation between franchisors and franchisees. This section discusses how and when a franchisor can legally require its franchisees to purchase products solely from the franchisor (or from a specific supplier, which may or may not be affiliated with the franchisor). It also examines the limitations on the franchisor's right to impose a tying arrangement and discusses other limitations on the franchisor's controls over franchisees.

Federal antitrust law identifies a tying arrangement as an arrangement whereby a seller refuses to sell one product (the tying product, the actual franchise system) unless the buyer also purchases another product (the tied product—food products or ingredients, for example). Such arrangements are perceived as posing an unacceptable risk of "stifling competition" and as a general matter are not favored by the courts.

One of the critical factors examined by the courts in determining whether a particular transaction or set of purchase terms constitutes an unlawful tying arrangement is a tie-in between *two separate and distinct products or services* that are readily distinguishable in the eyes of the consumer, whereby the availability of the tying product is conditioned on the purchase of the tied product.

For example, in a case involving Kentucky Fried Chicken Corp. (KFC), the court discussed the distinction between two separate products unlawfully tied together by a seller and two interrelated products that are justifiably tied together. In that case, Marion-Kay, a manufacturer and distributor of chicken seasoning, counterclaimed against KFC, alleging unlawful tying of its KFC franchises to the purchase of its own special KFC seasoning exclusively from two designated distributors. The court found that the alleged tying product (the KFC franchise) and the alleged tied product (the chicken seasoning) were not two separate products tied together unlawfully. Rather, the court stated that the use of the KFC trademarks and service marks by franchisees is so interrelated with the KFC chicken seasoning that *no person could reasonably find that the franchise and the seasoning are two separate products.*

In the Kentucky Fried Chicken case, the court recognized *the need* and *the right* of a franchisor to require its franchisees to purchase certain products from the franchisor directly or from its designated sources *if* those products are *so* intimately related to the intellectual property licensed to the franchisee as to be necessary for the purpose of maintaining the quality of the product identified by the trademark. The crucial inquiry is into the relationship between the trademark and the product allegedly tied to it. In a similar case involving Baskin-Robbins franchisees, the court found that the trademark licensed to the Baskin-Robbins franchisees was inseparable from the ice cream itself and concluded that the trademark was therefore utterly dependent upon the perceived quality of the product it represented. If the trademark serves *only* to identify the tied product, there can be no illegal tie-in because the trademark and the quality of the product it represents are so inextricably interrelated in the mind of the consumer as to preclude any finding that the trademark is a separate product.

The crucial distinction is between a *product-driven franchise system* (distribution system), where the trademark represents the end product marketed by the system, and *a business format system,* in which there is generally only a remote connection between the trademark and the products the franchisees are compelled to purchase. In a product-driven system, a tying arrangement is more likely to be upheld because the products being tied to the purchase of the franchise are an integral part of the franchisor's system and are intimately related to the trademarks being licensed to the franchisee.

A *business format franchise* is usually created merely to implement a particular business system under a common trade name. The franchise outlet itself is generally responsible for the production and preparation of the system's end product or service. The franchisor merely provides the trademark and, in some cases, also provides the supplies used in operating the franchised outlet and producing the system's products. Under a distribution system, the franchised outlet serves merely as a conduit through which the trademarked goods of the franchisor flow to the ultimate consumer. Generally, these goods are manufactured by the franchisor or by its licensees according to detailed specifications.

In a related case involving the Chicken Delight franchise system, the tied products imposed on the franchisees were commonplace paper products and packaging goods neither manufactured by the franchisor nor uniquely suited to the franchised business. Under the business format franchise system, the connection between the trademark and the products the franchisees are compelled to purchase were remote enough that the trademark, which simply reflects the goodwill and quality standards of the enterprise it identifies, *may be considered as separate* from the commonplace items that are tied more closely to the trademark's actual use.

Therefore, in order for tying arrangements to be looked upon favorably, the court must find that the tied products are uniquely related to the franchise system and *intimately related to the trademarks being licensed to franchisees.* Thus, the purchase of certain products, which are sold by franchisees under the franchisor's trademarks and are highly proprietary and an integral part of the system, may be restricted by designating certain suppliers (even if that supplier is the franchisor) and maintaining strict product specifications.

On the other hand, it is unlikely that restrictions on the purchase of supplies such as forms, service contracts, business cards, and signage would be upheld as a valid tie-in because these items, although an integral part of the system, are not uniquely suited to the system or intimately related to the trademarks licensed to the franchisees. Furthermore, as more fully discussed below, a restriction on the purchase of these supplies could not be justified if less restrictive alternatives are available that would yield the same level of quality control. In the case of these "commonplace" supplies, a court could find that providing strict specifications for the quality and uniformity of supplies and allowing franchisees to obtain the approval of other suppliers for these items would be less restrictive and thus the favored method of ensuring quality and uniformity.

Justification for Certain Types of Tying Arrangements

An otherwise illegal tying arrangement may, under appropriate circumstances, be justified by a franchisor and upheld by a court. One such justification recognized by the courts is a tying arrangement necessary to preserve the distinctiveness, uniformity, and quality of a franchisor's products in connection with the license of the franchisor's trademarks.

In the case of a franchisor who grants a license to its franchisees to use its trademarks, the franchisor (licensor) owes an affirmative duty to the public to ensure that in the hands of the licensee, the trademark continues to represent what it purports to represent. If a licensor relaxes quality control standards by permitting inferior products under a licensed mark, this may well constitute a misuse or even statutory abandonment of the mark. Courts have qualified what would appear to be a level of absolute discretion being vested in the franchisor by stating that not all means of achieving and maintaining quality control are justified. Rather, they have held that a restraint of trade can be justified only in the absence of less restrictive alternatives.

If specifications of the type and quality of the products to be used by the franchisee are sufficient to ensure the high standards of quality and uniformity the franchisor desires to maintain, then this less restrictive alternative must be utilized in lieu of requiring the franchisee to purchase those products only from the franchisor. If specifications for a substitute would require such detail that they could not be supplied (i.e., they would divulge trade secrets or be unreasonably burdensome), then protection of the trademarks may warrant the use of what would otherwise be an illegal tying arrangement.

Whether or not such a tying arrangement is unlawful depends on whether or not the franchisor can successfully demonstrate that restricting the franchisee to sources of approved suppliers, to the exclusion of other potential sources, is necessary and justified in order to ensure product distinctness, uniformity, and quality. For example, in *Ungar v. Dunkin' Donuts of America, Inc.* (D. Pa. 1975), the court denied the franchisor's motion for summary judgment of an unlawful tying claim, holding that a requirement that franchisees purchase supplies from approved sources might have constituted an unlawful tying arrangement in view of allegations that the approved supplier system was merely a vehicle for payment of kickbacks and the franchisor was unwilling to approve new suppliers, despite their ability to meet specifications. Similarly, in *Midwestern Waffles, Inc. v. Waffle House, Inc.*, 734 F.2d 705 (11th Cir. 1984), the court held that a franchisor's requirement that franchisees purchase equipment and vending services from approved sources could constitute a *per se* illegal tying arrangement because, although an approved source requirement was not by itself illegal, if franchisees were coerced into purchasing equipment from companies in which the franchisor had an interest, then the illegal tie could exist.

In another example where the tying arrangement was rejected, *Siegel v. Chicken Delight, Inc.*, 448 F.2d 43 (9th Cir. 1991), the court held that a franchisor's trademark and licenses were separate and distinct items from its packaging, mixes, and equipment that purportedly were essential components of the franchise system. The court explained that in determining whether an aggregation of separable items should be regarded as one or more items for tie-in purposes in normal cases of sales, the function of the aggregation must be analyzed, and questions such as cost savings and whether items involved are normally sold or used must be addressed. "In franchising, it is not what articles are used but how they are used that gives the system and its end product entitlement to trademark protection."

In *William Cohen & Son, Inc. dba Quality Foods v. All American Hero, Inc.*, 693 F.Supp. 201 (D. N.J. 1988), the issue of whether the franchisor's requirement that its franchisees purchase all of their supplies of marinated steak sandwiches from an affiliate company amounted to a per se illegal tying of the sandwich meat portions to the grant of restaurant franchises could not be decided on summary judgment. Similarly, in *Carpa, Inc. v. Ward Foods, Inc.*, 536 F.2d 39 (5th Cir. 1976), a seafood restaurant franchisor unlawfully tied the purchase of design fixtures, equipment, and food products to the use of its trademark where franchisees were required to pay large surcharges to the franchisor for approved items.

More recently, several courts have again recognized the business justification standard as an appropriate defense to an allegation that a franchisor is involved in an illegal tying arrangement. In 1987, the U.S. Court of Appeals held that a U.S. importer of German automobiles was justified in requiring its dealers to purchase all of their replacement parts from the importer as a condition of their securing a franchise to sell the automobiles in order to secure quality control, to protect goodwill, and to combat "free-riding" dealers. The court was satisfied with the substantial evidence to support the importer's assertion that the tie-in was used to ensure quality control in view of the fact that the importer purchased 80 percent of its parts from German manufacturers and subjected parts purchased from other manufacturers to an *elaborate and rigorous inspection procedure.*

On August 27, 1997, the U.S. Court of Appeals for the Third Circuit affirmed a lower court ruling dismissing antitrust claims against Domino's Pizza brought by an association of Domino's Pizza franchisees. The case, known as *Queen City Pizza, Inc. v. Domino's Pizza, Inc.*, 1997 WL 526213 (3d Cir. 1997), involved an allegation by the plaintiffs that Domino's Pizza had monopolized the sale of ingredients and supplies to its franchisees and had engaged in illegal tying and exclusive dealing arrangements in violations of Sections 1 and 2 of the Sherman Act. The lower court had ruled that all of the plaintiffs' antitrust claims failed because Domino's Pizza could not as a matter of law possess market power in ingredients and supplies sold to its franchisees. In dismissing the Sherman Act claims, the lower court concluded that whatever market power Domino's Pizza might have had over its franchisees arose out of its franchise agreement. The Court of Appeals held that

Domino's-approved ingredients and supplies sold to Domino's Pizza franchisees could *not* be a relevant product market for antitrust purposes. The court stated that a relevant product market includes all reasonably interchangeable products available to consumers (i.e., pizza stores) for the same purpose. Since ingredients and supplies sold by Domino's Pizza to its franchisees were comparable to (and reasonably interchangeable with) ingredients and supplies available from other suppliers and used by other pizza companies, these items could not be a separate market for antitrust purposes.

Whether a legally recognizable justification exists to warrant a tying arrangement ultimately depends on (1) the licensor's legitimate need to ensure quality control, (2) the availability of "less restrictive means" to achieve protection of the quality control, and (3) whether the alleged "tied product" is truly proprietary in nature. The relationship between the trademark and the product must be sufficiently intimate to justify the tie-in on grounds of quality control, uniformity, and protection of goodwill. More importantly, a tie-in otherwise justified in the name of quality control will not be upheld if less restrictive means are available for ensuring quality and uniformity.

There is a continuous struggle between the antitrust laws that generally disfavor tying arrangements and the trademark laws that impose a duty upon the owner of a trademark to monitor the use of the mark by licensees to ensure that the licensor's standards of quality are maintained and that the licensee's use of the mark is consistent with the licensor's intentions.

Quality Control and the Field Staff

The franchisor's quality control program that is, for the most part, administered by the field support staff is the front line of defense for the franchisor's trademarks. Field support personnel are responsible for enforcing the franchisor's quality control standards and for reporting field conditions to the franchisor. Quality control strategies developed by top management may be misguided if the information gathered and reported by field support personnel is not accurate. The franchisor should, therefore, closely monitor its field support personnel and replace those who are lenient, arbitrary, or inconsistent.

In a large system, the field support staff is typically the only contact the franchisee has with the franchisor. It is therefore essential that all members of the field support staff possess those qualities necessary to create and maintain a good relationship with franchisees while at the same time reinforcing the franchisor's necessary standards. A properly administered quality control program provides the franchisor with a method for policing franchisees that achieves positive results and uniformity throughout the franchise system. By establishing, maintaining, and enforcing high standards of quality, all parties, including the franchisee, benefit. Thus, the importance of quality control should be properly explained to franchisees (initially at training) and reinforced on an ongoing and consistent basis by field support personnel.

The role of field support staff does not end with the enforcement of quality control standards. Often, field personnel act as troubleshooters in helping franchisees improve their business. In emergency situations, they may even step in as operating manager. For this reason, the franchisor's field personnel should be well educated in the intricacies of operating the franchise business. They should be able to handle any situation that may arise. They will be looked to as leaders and should be comfortable in that role. Above all, field support personnel should be good listeners and communicators.

Pricing as a Quality Control Enforcement Tool

Until recently, virtually all types of vertical price restraints were viewed by the courts as per se illegal, thereby giving franchisors the power to *suggest* prices but not the ability to set prices. In November 1997, the U.S. Supreme Court reversed thirty years of case law by holding that vertical *maximum* price fixing arrangements were no longer per se illegal under Section 1 of the Sherman Act, but, rather, such maximum price fixing arrangements were now to be evaluated under a "rule of reason" standard. Under this standard, a maximum price fixing agreement is illegal only if it "imposes an unreasonable restraint on competition, taking into account a variety of factors, including specific information about the relevant business, its condition before and after the restraint was imposed, and the restraint's history, nature and effect," *State Oil v. Kahn*, 118 S.Ct. 275 (1997).

The facts in *Kahn* involved a gasoline station operator who leased the station from State Oil Company and whose agreement required Kahn to buy gasoline from State Oil at a suggested retail price less a specified margin. The agreement also required that any profit Kahn earned as a result of charging customers more than the suggested retail price be rebated to State Oil. When Kahn was being evicted after falling behind on his lease payments, he sued State Oil for preventing him from raising his prices, asserting vertical maximum price fixing in violation of Section 1 of the Sherman Act. The *Kahn* court did not change the law on minimum price fixing arrangements, however, and such arrangements are still per se illegal. The result of *Kahn* is that a supplier or franchisor must now determine whether the imposition of maximum prices somehow restrains trade unreasonably. If it does not, then such a pricing strategy may be legally acceptable.

While minimum price fixing is per se illegal, at least one court has held that setting price points without either a floor or ceiling may be permitted. In *Great Clips, Inc. v. Levine*, 1993 WL ¶ 76,623 (D. Minn. 1993), the court found that Great Clips's even-dollar, single-price restrictions did not violate the Sherman Act. The Great Clips pricing policy required franchisees to charge an even-dollar price (e.g., $7, $8, $9) but did not set that price. Great Clips also required franchisees to post a single price for haircuts on its price board. Great Clips did allow franchisees to offer discounts from the even-dollar price, however, but only on twenty-one days out of every three months. This restriction was imposed to ensure compliance with certain consumer fraud regulations, according to Great Clips. Franchisees were also permitted to offer coupons through direct mail and print media.

The *Great Clips* court explained that the even-dollar, single-price restriction was not anticompetitive because Great Clips franchisees were free to set the price within the restricted pricing structure. Even the imposition of the "three weeks per three months" discount policy did not violate the Sherman Act, the court explained, because franchisees had many ways to set their prices without violating the franchise agreement. The court noted Great Clips's "legitimate and important interests in how the franchise is run," and that Great Clips's marketing strategy was procompetitive because it would stimulate interbrand competition, and that must be the focus of the inquiry, 1991 WL ¶ 322975 7 (D. Minn. 1991).

Suggested resale prices have long been recognized as a form of manufacturer/supplier price maintenance that does not violate antitrust laws. Problems sometimes do arise, however, where steps are taken to force dealers or retailers to observe "suggested" prices. On the other hand, a manufacturer/supplier is free to refuse to sell to a distributor/retailer who refuses to sell at the suggested price. The inquiry typically focuses on coercion by the manufacturer.

The *Great Clips* court addressed the practice of offering discounts and coupons in the context of examining the franchisor's control over the retail prices of its franchisees. The court explained the general rule that pricing restrictions such as those imposed by Great Clips will not be per se illegal even though they may affect the franchisee's prices because such restrictions do not directly limit the franchisee's freedom to independently establish its prices. In the Great Clips system, the court noted, the franchisees were free to establish discounts and special events pricing. The court noted that even though Great Clips further limited its franchisees' pricing practices with the three-week/three-month discount limitation, the franchisees remained free to coupon through such means as "direct mail promotions, return customer coupons, newspaper advertisements, flyer distributions, radio offers and business discounts through paycheck stuffers," among others. Thus, as long as Great Clips did not actually specify the prices to be charged, the even-dollar, single-price policy, *together with the franchisee's ability to offer discounts and coupons on a limited basis,* was not per se an unreasonable restraint of trade in violation of the Sherman Act and, in the court's view, did not ultimately constitute an unreasonable restraint.

If a franchisor chooses to restrict the use of coupons, discounts, and rebates, that indirect price restriction policy would not by itself be a violation of the Sherman Act. The anticoupon policy in conjunction with specified price points, however, would be problematic based on the analysis in *Great Clips,* which allows certain indirect restrictions, such as the even-dollar and/or single-price policies, so long as the franchisee retained flexibility and independence in setting prices. The combination of these pricing restrictions would appear to cross the line from reasonable to unreasonable under *Great Clips.*

Under *Kahn,* a franchisor has some flexibility in setting *maximum* resale prices of the products sold by its franchisees, provided the franchisor can justify its policy for imposing what might be argued is an anticompetitive restriction. If a franchisor wishes to impose maximum prices, it should document this policy as necessary in order to compete effectively and set forth all the reasons demonstrating that this policy does not unreasonably restrain trade. Even after *Kahn,* however, the prices set may be only a ceiling, not a floor. This means that the franchisor may not set specific retail prices since this is akin to setting minimum prices, which remains per se illegal.

In addition, a franchisor may rely on the *Great Clips* decision for the ability to establish a pricing policy providing for even-dollar pricing or single-price requirements, as long as no minimum is set. The franchisor may also choose to restrict its franchisees from offering coupons or discounts. At the same time, however, *Great Clips* dictates that such anticoupon policies in conjunction with even-dollar pricing restrictions would constitute an antitrust violation.

Part **Two**

Legal and Strategic Issues

4

Regulatory Issues

The offer and sale of a franchise is regulated at both the federal and state level. At the federal level, the Federal Trade Commission (FTC) in 1979 adopted its trade regulation rule 436 (the "FTC Rule"), which specifies the minimum amount of disclosure that must be made to a prospective franchisee in any of the fifty states. In addition to the FTC Rule, over a dozen states have adopted their own rules and regulations for the offer and sale of franchises within their borders. Known as the registration states, they include most of the nation's largest commercial marketplaces, such as California, New York, and Illinois. These states generally follow a more detailed disclosure format, known as the Uniform Franchise Offering Circular (UFOC).

The UFOC was originally developed by the Midwest Securities Commissioners Association in 1975. The monitoring of and revisions to the UFOC are now under the authority of the North American Securities Administrators Association (NASAA). Each of the registration states has developed and adopted its own statutory version of the UFOC. The differences among the states should be checked carefully by both current and prospective franchisors and their counsel, as well as individuals considering the purchase of a franchise opportunity.

A new version of the UFOC was adopted by NASAA in April 1993 and approved by the FTC in December 1993. As of January 1, 1995, the registration states had approved the new UFOC and mandated its use for filings in their states. The new UFOC Guidelines ("Guidelines") require that the offering circular be written in plain English. Disclosures must be made "clearly, concisely and in a narrative form that is understandable by a person unfamiliar with the franchise business" and should not contain technical language, repetitive phrases, or "legal antiques."

A Brief History of Franchise Registration

The laws governing the offer and sale of franchises began in 1970, when the state of California adopted its Franchise Investment Law. Shortly thereafter, the FTC commenced its hearings to begin the development of the federal law governing franchising. After seven years of public comment and debate, the FTC adopted its trade regulation rule, which is formally titled "Disclosure Requirements and Prohibitions Concerning Franchising and Business Opportunity Venture," on December 21, 1978, to be effective October 21, 1979. Many states followed the lead of California, and as of late 1998, there were sixteen states that regulate franchise offers and sales.

The states that require full registration of a franchise offering prior to the "offering" or selling of a franchise are California, Illinois, Indiana, Maryland, Minnesota, New York, North Dakota, Rhode Island, South Dakota, Virginia, and Washington. Although Illinois is still regarded as a "registration state," in June 1998, it passed significant changes to its Franchise Disclosure Act, which involves one initial registration effective within twenty-one days after filing unless the attorney general's office rejects the filing due to failure to meet UFOC guidelines. One filing must still meet certain Illinois-specific filing requirements.

Other states that regulate franchise offers include Hawaii, which requires filing of an offering circular with the state authorities and delivery of an offering circular to prospective franchisees; Michigan and Wisconsin, which require filing of a "Notice of Intent to Offer and Sell Franchises"; Oregon, which requires only that presale disclosure be delivered to prospective investors; and Texas, which requires the filing of a notice of exemption with the appropriate state authorities under the Texas Business Opportunity Act.

Among other things, the FTC Rule requires that every franchisor offering franchises in the United States deliver an offering circular (containing certain specified disclosure items) to all prospective franchisees (within certain specified time requirements). The FTC has adopted and enforced its rule pursuant to its power and authority to regulate unfair and deceptive trade practices. The FTC Rule sets forth the minimum level of protection that shall be afforded to prospective franchisees. To the extent that a "registration state" offers its citizens a greater level of protection, the FTC Rule will not preempt state law. There is no private right of action under the FTC Rule; however, the FTC itself may bring an enforcement action against a franchisor that does not meet its requirements. Penalties for noncompliance have included asset impoundments, cease and desist orders, injunctions, consent orders, mandated rescission or restitution for injured franchisees, and civil fines of up to $10,000 per violation.

The FTC Rule regulates two types of offerings: (1) *package and product franchises* and (2) *business opportunity ventures*. The first type, package and product franchises, involves three characteristics: (1) the franchisee sells goods or services that meet the franchisor's quality standards, in cases where the franchisee operates under the franchisor's trademark, service mark, trade name, advertising, or other commercial symbol designating the franchisor ("Mark") that are identified by the franchisor's Mark; (2) the franchisor exercises significant assistance in the franchisee's method of operation; and (3) the franchisee is required to make payment of $500 or more to the franchisor or a person affiliated with the franchisor at any time before to within six months after the business opens.

Business opportunity ventures also involve three characteristics: (1) the franchisee sells goods or services that are supplied by the franchisor or a person affiliated with the franchisor; (2) the franchisor assists the franchisee in any way with respect to securing accounts for the franchisee, securing locations or sites for vending machines or rack displays, or providing the services of a person able to do either; and (3) the franchisee is required to make payment of $500 or more to the franchisor or a person affiliated with the franchisor at any time before to within six months after the business opens.

Relationships covered by the FTC Rule include those within the definition of a "franchise" and those represented as being within the definition when the relationship is entered into, regardless of whether, in fact, they are within the definition. The FTC Rule exempts (1) fractional franchises, (2) leased department arrangements, and (3) purely verbal agreements. The FTC Rule excludes (1) relationships between employer/employees and among general business partners, (2) membership in retailer-owned cooperatives, (3) certification and testing services, and (4) single trademark licenses.

As previously stated, the FTC Rule requires franchisors offering franchises in the United States to deliver an offering circular containing certain specified disclosure items. The disclosure document required by the FTC Rule must include information on the twenty subjects listed in Figure 4-1.

Figure 4-1. Topics to address in the FTC disclosure document.

1. Identifying information about the franchisor
2. Business experience of the franchisor's directors and key executives
3. The franchisor's business experience
4. Litigation history of the franchisor and its directors and key executives
5. Bankruptcy history of the franchisor and its directors and key executives
6. Description of the franchise
7. Money required to be paid by the franchisee to obtain or commence the franchise operation
8. Continuing expenses to the franchisee in operating the franchise business that are payable in whole or in part to the franchisor

(continues)

Figure 4-1. *(continued)*

9.　A list of persons, including the franchisor and any of its affiliates, with whom the franchisee is required or advised to do business

10.　Realty, personalty, services, and so on that the franchisee is required to purchase, lease, or rent, and a list of any person with whom such transactions must be made

11.　Description of consideration paid (such as royalties or commissions) by third parties to the franchisor or any of its affiliates as a result of franchisee purchases from such third parties

12.　Description of any franchisor assistance in financing the purchase of a franchise

13.　Restrictions placed on a franchisee's conduct of its business

14.　Required personal participation by the franchisee

15.　Termination, cancellation, and renewal of the franchise

16.　Statistical information about the number of franchises and their rate of termination

17.　Franchisor's right to select or approve a site for the franchise

18.　Training programs for the franchisee

19.　Celebrity involvement with the franchise

20.　Financial information about the franchisor

The information must be current as of the completion of the franchisor's most recent fiscal year. In addition, a revision to the document must be promptly prepared whenever there has been a material change in the information contained in the document. The FTC Rule requires that the disclosure document must be given to a prospective franchisee at the earliest of (1) the prospective franchisee's *first personal meeting* with the franchisor, (2) *ten business days* prior to the execution of a contract, or (3) *ten business days* before the payment of money relating to the franchise relationship. In addition to the disclosure document, the franchisee must receive a copy of all agreements that it will be asked to sign at least *five business days* prior to the execution of the agreements. A business day is any day other than Saturday, Sunday, or the following national holidays: New Year's Day, Presidents' Day, Memorial Day, Independence Day, Labor Day, Columbus Day, Veterans Day, Thanksgiving, and Christmas.

The timing requirements described above apply nationwide and preempt any lesser timing requirements contained in state laws. The ten-day and five-day disclosure periods may run concurrently, and sales contacts with the prospective franchisee may continue during those periods. (See Figure 4-2.)

Figure 4-2. Time frame for disclosing prospective franchisee and collecting money in accordance with U.S. guidelines.

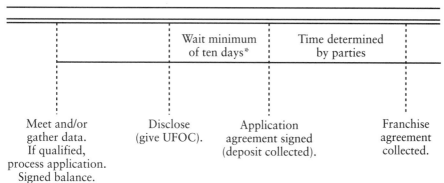

	Wait minimum of ten days*	Time determined by parties	
Meet and/or gather data. If qualified, process application. Signed balance.	Disclose (give UFOC).	Application agreement signed (deposit collected).	Franchise agreement collected.

*The prospective franchisee cannot be contacted within the ten-day (cooling-off) period.

It is an unfair or deceptive act or practice within the meaning of Section 5 of the FTC Act for any franchisor or franchise broker:

1. To fail to furnish prospective franchisees, within the time frame established by the Rule, with a disclosure document containing information on twenty different subjects relating to the franchisor, the franchise business, and the terms of the franchise agreement
2. To make any representations about the actual or potential sales, income, or profits of existing or prospective franchisees except in the manner set forth in the Rule
3. To fail to furnish prospective franchisees, within the time frame established by the Rule, with copies of the franchisor's standard form of franchise agreement and copies of the final agreements to be signed by the parties
4. To fail to return to prospective franchisees any funds or deposits (such as down payments) identified as refundable in the disclosure document

The New SBA Central Registry of Franchise Systems

Although there are no registration requirements at the Federal Trade Commission level, the Small Business Administration (SBA) did create in

1998 a central registry of eligible franchise systems to accomplish its twin objectives of eliminating:

1. Unnecessary review of franchise agreements and documents that creates lengthy processing delays by the SBA when a franchisee candidate applies for a loan
2. Inconsistent decisions among different SBA field offices regarding the same franchise system

In 1997, the SBA approved 3,708 loans to franchisees with a total principal amount of $978,509,000. The SBA also reported that it approved more than 11,900 loans to franchisees in 1,166 different franchise systems over the period from 1994 to 1997. Historically, the typical transaction involves a franchisee that is unable to obtain financing on reasonable terms through normal lending channels and thus requires a loan guarantee from the SBA to obtain such financing. The process of obtaining such a loan guarantee has resulted in delays as well as conflicting policies and interpretations among different SBA field offices regarding the same franchise system. The Eligibility Guidelines set forth substantive criteria for determining whether a franchise system qualifies for SBA loan guarantees to the system's franchisees. The Eligibility Guidelines include restrictions on the franchisor's control of the franchisee's business; the franchisor's default, termination, and renewal rights and the franchisor's right to approve transfers.

Eligibility Guidelines

The Eligibility Guidelines provide standards for screening each system based on five major criteria and loan conditions that must be met during the term of the SBA-guaranteed loan:

1. Control. The franchisor may not control its franchisee to the point that the franchisee does not have the independent right to both profit from its efforts and bear the risk of loss commensurate with ownership. However, the franchisor may still impose quality controls with respect to the operations of the franchised business. The franchisor may not:

   ◆ Set the franchisee's net profit from the franchised business.
   ◆ Prescribe or strictly control the right of its franchisee to withdraw increases in the net worth of the franchised business.
   ◆ Manage the daily operations of the franchised business for an extended period of time.

◆ Hire, fire, or otherwise directly control its franchisee's employees.
◆ Require its franchisee to deposit all revenues into an account which franchisor controls, or from which the franchisor must consent to withdrawals.

2. *Leasing from franchisor.* The franchisor may not terminate any real estate unless an uncured default has occurred under the terms of the real estate lease or the franchise agreement.

3. *Renewal.* The terms of the renewal agreement offered to the franchisee may not be less favorable to the franchisee than either (a) the terms of the franchisor's then-current form of franchise agreement or (b) the renewal terms offered by the franchisor to other comparable renewing franchisees.

4. *Transfer.* The franchisee must be free to transfer its interest in the franchised business at any time to a franchisee meeting the franchisor's qualifications. Consent must not be unreasonably withheld or delayed.

5. *Default and termination.* The franchise agreement must identify:

◆ All events of default
◆ Those events of default which will constitute the basis for termination of the franchise agreement
◆ The written notice of termination of each default
◆ Defaults which are grounds for automatic termination and for which there is no opportunity to cure and for all other defaults
◆ The time for cure which the franchisor will give for all other defaults

During the term of the SBA guaranteed loan, the franchisor may terminate the franchise agreement only for automatic terminations and uncured defaults. A series of cured defaults within a specified period of time, chronic deficiencies, or repeated violations can be considered an "uncured" default, if identified clearly as such in the franchise agreement.

Other Loan Conditions

The franchise agreement's term must be at least equal to the term of the SBA-guaranteed loan. If the franchisee leases or subleases the premises of the franchised business from the franchisor, the lease term must be equal to the loan term. The SBA will carefully evaluate and weigh the credit implications if a lease that is a sublease does not include an option for the franchisee to lease directly from the landlord if the franchisor defaults, rejects, disavows, or is unable to perform.

The franchisor is to give the lender or CDC (Community Development Corporation) and SBA, during the loan term, the same notice and opportunity to cure a default under a franchise agreement or lease that is given to the franchisee under the document. The franchisor must give the franchisee, lender or CDC, and SBA access to its pertinent books and records, if the franchisor does any of the following:

- Provides billing and collection services.
- Controls accounts receivable.
- Accepts payments from franchisee's customers or third-party payors.
- Services the franchisee's accounts.

Once a franchisor has been deemed eligible, franchisees requesting SBA financial assistance need to provide only a one-page certification from one franchisor stating that the contract is the same as the form, which is approved in the registry, thereby eliminating the need for local SBA office renewal and delays in the processing of the loan. For additional information, visit the Website at www.franchiseregistry.com or the Website for the IFA at www.franchise.org, which includes news, events, resources, and a wide variety of information about the franchising community.

State Franchise Laws

The goal of the FTC Rule is to create a minimum federal standard of disclosure applicable to all franchisor offerings and to permit states to provide additional protection as they see fit. Thus, while the FTC Rule has the force and effect of federal law and, like other federal substantive regulations, preempts state and local laws to the extent that these laws conflict, the FTC has determined that the Rule will not preempt state or local laws and regulations that either are consistent with the Rule or, even if inconsistent, would provide protection to prospective franchisees equal to or greater than that imposed by the Rule.

Examples of state laws or regulations that would not be preempted by the Rule include state provisions requiring the registration of franchisors and franchise salespersons, state requirements for escrow or bonding arrangements, and state-required disclosure obligations set forth in the Rule. Moreover, the Rule does not affect state laws or regulations that regulate the franchisor/franchisee relationship, such as termination practices, contract provisions, and financing arrangements.

Definitions Under State Law

Each state franchise disclosure statute has its own definition of a "franchise," which is similar to, but not the same as, the definition set forth in the FTC Rule. If the proposed relationship meets this definition, then the franchisor must comply with the applicable registration and disclosure laws.

There are four major types of state definitions of a franchise or business opportunity. They consist of:

1. Majority state definition. In the states of California, Illinois, Indiana, Maryland, Michigan, North Dakota, Oregon, Rhode Island, and Wisconsin, a franchise is defined as having three essential elements:

   ◆ A franchisee is granted the right to engage in the business of offering, selling, or distributing goods or services under a marketing plan or system prescribed in substantial part by a franchisor.
   ◆ The operation of the franchisee's business is substantially associated with the franchisor's trademark or other commercial symbol designating the franchisor or its affiliate.
   ◆ The franchisee is required to pay a fee.

2. Minority state definition. The states of Hawaii, Minnesota, South Dakota, and Washington have adopted a somewhat broader definition of franchise. In these states, a franchise is defined as having the following three essential elements:

   ◆A franchisee is granted the right to engage in the business of offering or distributing goods or services using the franchisor's trade name or other commercial symbol or related characteristics.
   ◆ The franchisor and franchisee have a common interest in the marketing of goods or services.
   ◆ The franchisee pays a fee.

3. New York definition. The state of New York has a unique definition. Under its law, a franchisee is defined by these guidelines:

   ◆ The franchisor is paid a fee by the franchisee.
   ◆ Either the franchisee's business is essentially associated with the franchisor's trademark, or the franchisee operates under a marketing plan or system prescribed in substantial part by the franchisor.

4. *Virginia definition.* The Commonwealth of Virginia also has its own definition of a franchise, which stipulates that:

♦ A franchisee is granted the right to engage in the business of offering or distributing goods or services at retail under a marketing plan or system prescribed in substantial part by a franchisor.
♦ The franchisee's business is substantially associated with the franchisor's trademark.

Virginia and New York have definitions that are broad in certain respects. Virginia does not have a fee element to its definition. New York requires a fee but specifies either association with franchisor's trademark or a marketing plan prescribed by the franchisor. Therefore, in New York no trademark license is required for a franchise relationship to exist. However, the regulations in New York exclude from the definition of a franchise any relationship in which a franchisor does not provide significant assistance to or exert significant controls over a franchisee.

Guidelines for Determining What a Franchise Is: Is the Relationship Fish or Fowl?

Every year, I am asked by a few clients to advise them on how to structure a relationship that avoids the definition of a "franchise" under federal or state laws. The first question I ask is "Why?" in order to find out the legal and strategic reasons they might have for wanting to avoid the need to comply with these laws. Most answers fall into one of the following categories:

♦ An overseas franchisor who is uncomfortable with concepts of disclosure that may not be required in his or her country of origin
♦ A midsize or large company that feels that (as a pioneer) its industry is not ready for or will react adversely to the kinds of controls that a franchise relationship typically implies
♦ A company that has an aspect of its past that it would prefer not to be disclosed, which raises other legal problems (there may also be a case of an individual offer who has an aspect of his/her past that he/she would prefer not to be disclosed)
♦ A small company concerned with the perceived costs of preparing

and maintaining the legal documents
 ◆ The real or perceived belief that by becoming a franchisor the company somehow increases its chances of being sued (a myth I usually try to debunk)
 ◆ Some other specific circumstances or myth or fear that the company's management team has toward franchising

Before dealing with the parameters developed by the courts and regulatory authorities over the years that provide some (but not complete) insight as to which relationships will be considered a franchise and which will not, we usually try to solve the client's problem with creative thinking and structural alternatives. For example, under the first example given in the list above, a foreign franchisor may want to set up a new subsidiary in lieu of disclosing the parent company's (usually privately held) financial statements. If the subsidiary is properly capitalized and certain other specific conditions met, the confidentiality of the parent company's data may be preserved. Under the second example given above, we have often created the "non-franchise franchisor," which is a company that has essentially agreed to prepare and provide a UFOC even though the details of its relationships are in a regulatory gray area. This way the franchisor appeases the regulators but also placates the industry participants who may be more comfortable with a "strategic partner" or "licensee" designation than a franchisor-franchisee relationship.

If the company still insists on avoiding compliance with these laws, then we go through an exercise of determining from a cost-benefit analysis which leg of the "three-legged stool" it will agree to sacrifice. In today's brand-driven environment, the willingness to license the system without the brand to avoid the trademark license leg has not been very popular. Similarly, in an economy where "cash flow is king," most of these clients have not been willing to waive the initial franchise fee or wait over six months for their financial rewards. And the age-old trick of "hiding" the franchise fee in a training program or initial inventory package was figured out by the regulators a long time ago. So it is often the third leg of the stool, the one that is most difficult to interpret, where the creative structuring must take place.

The courts and the federal and state regulators have not provided much clear guidance as to the *degrees* of support or the *degrees* of assistance that will meet the definition and those which will not. The mandatory use of an operating system or marketing plan will meet the third element of the test, but what if the use of the system is optional? What if the plan or system is not very detailed and provides lots of room for discretion by the franchisee without penalty for adopting the plan or system to meet local market conditions? And if you choose this path, does allowing this degree of discretion and flexibility sacrifice your ability to maintain quality control? In addition, a competitive environment where most growing companies are trying to provide *more and more* support and assistance (as well as exercise more controls) to their partners in the distribution channel, would providing less than the norm just to avoid the definition of a "franchise" really make sense? These legal and strategic decisions should not be made hastily without the long-term implications properly analyzed.

FTC Analysis

The term *franchise* is defined in Section 436.2(d) of the FTC Rule. There are three key components to this definition: (1) The franchisee's goods and/or services are to be offered and sold under the franchisor's trademarks, (2) the franchisee is required to make a minimum $500 payment to the franchisor, and (3) the franchisor exercises significant control of, or provides significant assistance to, the franchisee's method of operation. Each of these components is outlined below.

- *Trademark.* This element is satisfied when the franchisee is given the right to distribute goods or services under the franchisor's trademark or service mark.
- *Required payment.* This element is met if a franchisee is required to pay the franchisor at least $500 as a condition of obtaining the franchise or of commencing operations. Payments made at any time prior to or within six months after commencing operations will be aggregated to determine if the $500 threshold is met. The payments may be required by the franchise agreement, an ancillary agreement between the parties, or by practical necessity (such as required supplies that are available only from the franchisor).
- *Significant control and assistance.* The key to this element is that the control or assistance must be significant. According to the *Final Guides to the Franchising and Business Opportunities Ventures Trade Regulation Rule* (the "Final Guides"), published by the Federal Trade Commission, the term *significant* "relates to the degree to which the franchisee is dependent upon the franchisor's superior business expertise." The *Final Guides* states that the dependence on the business expertise of the fran-

chisor may be conveyed by the franchisor's controls over the franchisee's methods of operation or by the franchisor's furnishing assistance to the franchisee in areas related to methods of operations. The presence of any one of the following types of control or assistance may suggest the existence of "significant control or assistance" sufficient to satisfy this prong of the definition of a franchise:

Types of Control	*Types of Assistance*
Site approval	Formal sales, repair, or
Site design/appearance	business training
requirements	Establishing accounting systems
Dictating hours of operation	Furnishing management,
Production techniques	marketing, or personnel advice
Accounting practices	Site selection assistance
Personnel policies/practices	Furnishing detailed
Required participation in, or	operations manual
financial contribution to,	
promotional campaigns	
Restrictions on customers	
Restrictions on sales area or location	

There is a wide variety of strategic questions and structural issues to consider when conducting this analysis. Among them:

◆ Do we anticipate the relationship to be short-term or long-term? Are we just dating or really serious about getting married?
◆ Are we ready to sacrifice the ability to build brand awareness and increase the value of other intangible assets on our balance sheet in a brand-driven competitive environment?
◆ Are we prepared to deliver the level and the quality of training and support that is typically implied and expected in the franchisor-franchisee relationship?
◆ Will we be converting or keeping in place existing distributors, sales representatives, or other components of the current distribution channel? How will the franchising program *truly* differ?
◆ In considering the operational dynamics of the proposed relationship, how interdependent do we really need or want to be? Are you truly inextricably intertwined with synergistic and shared goals, or would a more casual commitment suffice? Would a joint venture or

strategic partnering relationship adequately suffice? (See Chapters 16 and 18.)

◆ To what extent will training, support, marketing, and other key functions truly be uniform and centralized? Or will a more flexible system suffice?

◆ Could you "unbundle" the license of the intellectual property being offered, making items an optional menu of support and services rather than making them mandatory and integrated?

◆ If you choose to operate in the gray area and without a UFOC, how comfortable are you and your management team with living with the possibility of a regulatory investigation and/or a systemwide rescission offer if the relationship is subsequently deemed to be a franchise? How comfortable are you with this strategy if your company is publicly traded?

◆ To what extent will market conditions dictate that you maintain control over the product mix, warranty policies, discounting policies, etc., or the need to conduct quality control audits or make pricing suggestions?

Again, you don't want to emasculate key strategic aspects of the program merely to avoid compliance with federal and state franchise laws. Remember that the courts and the regulators are likely to examine the "totality of the relationship," with an emphasis on reality and practice, rather than the written word of the contract or offering materials. For example, if you take the position that the support services are optional but, in practice, 99 percent of your franchisees have elected to use and pay for them, then the reality of the situation will probably prevail. If the marketing plan or operating system is prescribed in substantial part by you in practice, and there will be adverse consequences to the other party if these procedures and standards are not followed, whether or not your agreement says so, then you will have difficulty supporting your position that you are not a franchise. Although a "community of interest" is not generally a term that provides much insight, here are some factors directly considered by the court in arriving at this determination:

◆ The franchisor's advertising claims to prospective franchisees that a successful marketing plan is available

◆ The contemplation of nationwide or areawide distribution on an exclusive or semiexclusive basis, possibly with multiple levels of jurisdiction (such as regional and location distributorships and arrangements) designed to establish uniformity of prices and marketing terms

◆ Reservation of control by the franchisor over matters such as customer terms and payments, credit practices, and warranties and representations made to customers

◆ The franchisor's rendering of collateral services to the franchisee

◆ Any prohibition or limitation on the franchisee's sale of competitive or noncompetitive products

◆ A requirement that the franchisee observe the franchisor's direction or obtain the franchisor's approval for site selection, trade names, advertising, signs, appearance of the franchisee's business premises, fixtures and equipment used in the business, employee uniforms, hours of operation, housekeeping procedures, etc.

◆ The franchisor's implementation of its requirements regarding the conduct of the business by inspection and reporting procedures

◆ The franchisor's right to take corrective measures that may be at the franchisee's expense

◆ Comprehensive advertising or other promotional programs, especially if the programs identify the location of the franchisee and if the franchisee's advertising or promotional activities require the franchisor's approval

◆ Grant of an exclusive territory, and the sale of products or services at bona fide wholesale prices

◆ Percentage discounts (although insubstantial), and mutual advertising and soliciting by the franchisor and the franchisee

◆ Volume discounts attained by a system of distributors and subdistributors, and mutual advertising

◆ Use of the franchisor's confidential operating manuals or forms by the franchisee, and mutual opportunity of profit

◆ Grant of an exclusive patent and an exclusive territory, and a training program for which the franchisor receives payment from the franchisee

◆ Required purchases from the franchisor, an exclusive territory, franchisor-supplied advertising, the provision of leads to the franchisee, and prohibitions on selling competitive products

◆ The franchisor's selection of locations, and required purchases through the franchisor

◆ Performance of services devised by the franchisor, franchisor-approved forms, mutual service of customers, franchisor approval of the franchisee's presentations, and mutual financial benefit

◆ The franchisee's production of products under the franchisor's patent, technical assistance, training, the franchisee's ability to subfranchise, and required record keeping

◆ The franchisor's selection of locations, the franchisee's purchase of product from the franchisor for regularly serviced accounts, and required record keeping

Preparing the Disclosure Document: Choosing the Appropriate Format

In many ways, the choice of the appropriate format for the franchisor's franchise offering circular is difficult and complex because the requirements of the FTC Rule, the UFOC Guidelines, and the particular state laws must all be coordinated. The format selection process is a decision regarding the *form* in which the disclosure is made but is not a choice of which law shall govern. Even if the UFOC format is selected, the federal laws governing the timing of the delivery of the disclosure document, the restrictions on the use of earnings claims, and the penalties available to the FTC for noncompliance still apply.

Depending on the targeted markets selected by the company, most franchisors have elected to adopt the UFOC format in the preparation of their disclosure documents. Because many registration states do not accept the FTC Rule format (even though the FTC has endorsed the UFOC format), it is simply more cost-effective to have only one primary document for use in connection with franchise offers and sales. If the franchisor will be limiting its marketing activities to states that do *not* have registration statutes, then the FTC Rule format may offer certain advantages. For example, the FTC Rule format generally requires less information than the UFOC format does in the areas of training and personnel of the franchisor, the litigation history of the franchisor (the FTC Rule requires a seven-year history while the UFOC format requires a ten-year history), history of termination and nonrenewals (the FTC, one year; the UFOC, three years), bankruptcy history (the FTC, seven years; the UFOC, ten years), and sanctions under Canadian law (required by the UFOC but not the FTC). The FTC Rule also requires less stringent disclosure regarding the refundability of payments made by the franchisee.

The FTC Rule format may also be easier for the early-stage franchisor to satisfy because it allows for a three-year phase-in period for the use of audited financials. Under the UFOC format, audited financials are required from the onset, and if the financial condition of the franchisor is weak, then many state administrators will impose costly escrow and bonding procedures or require personal (or parent company for a subsidiary) guaranties of performance. In some registration states, a financially weak franchisor will be denied registration until its condition improves. Early-stage franchisors that are grossly undercapitalized, have a negative net worth, or may have suffered significant recent operating losses should be prepared for an uphill battle with the state franchise examiners before approval will be granted.

Preparing the Disclosure Document Under UFOC Guidelines

The UFOC format of franchise disclosure consists of twenty-three categories of information that must be provided by the franchisor to the prospective franchisee at least ten business days prior to the execution of the franchise agreement. Because this format has been adopted by many states as a matter of law, franchisors may not change the order in which information is presented, nor may any of the disclosure items be omitted in the document. In addition, many sections of the UFOC must be a mirror image of the actual franchise agreement (and related documents) that the franchisee will be expected to sign. There should be no factual or legal inconsistencies between the UFOC and the franchise agreement.

With the implementation of the new UFOC Guidelines in 1995, one of the most noticeable differences found in the new format is that charts and tables replace the narrative format in many key sections such as: Item 6: Other Fees; Item 9: Franchisee's Obligations; Item 10: Financing; the section on Training in Item 11: Franchisor's Obligations; Item 17: Renewal, Termination, Transfer, and Dispute Resolution; and Item 20: List of Franchise Outlets.

A description of the information required by each disclosure item of the UFOC follows.

Cover
Page   Old Version
           NASAA has sought to create a generic cover page by moving state-specific information to Item 23 (Receipt) or to exhibits to the offering circular. Information moved off the cover page includes state-mandated language regarding offering circular delivery requirements and related disclaimers, addresses of administrators, and the list of registered agents, subfranchisors, and franchise brokers. The new Guidelines mandate disclosure of certain risk factors. A franchisor must use prescribed language to disclose as a risk that its franchise agreement includes an out-of-state form and/or choice of law provision. Additional risk factor disclosures may be required by state regulators.

New Version
[No significant changes.]

Item 1:   Old Version
The Franchisor and Any Predecessors. This first section of the UFOC
is designed to inform the franchisee as to the historical background
of the franchisor and any of its predecessors. The franchisor's corporate and trade name, form of doing business, principal headquarters, state and date of incorporation, prior business experience, and
current business activities all must be disclosed in this section. The
franchisor must also disclose the nature of the franchise being
offered and its qualifications for offering this type of business. This
includes a general description of the business operations to be conducted by the franchisee, the length of time that the franchisor has
offered franchises for such businesses, and a discussion of the competition that the franchisee will face in similar lines of business.

New Version
The Franchisor, Its Predecessors and Affiliates. Under the new
Guidelines, franchisors must now identify themselves by using "we,"
initials, or two words of reference. "Franchisors" and "Franchisee"
are not to be used. The entities for which disclosure must be made
are expanded to included franchisor's affiliates. The number of years
of the franchisor's predecessors is reduced from fifteen to ten.
Agents for service of process may be disclosed in Item 1, Item 23
(Receipt), or an exhibit to the offering circular. In addition, franchisors must disclose, in general terms, "any regulations specific to
the industry in which the franchise business operates." Regulations
that are applicable to businesses generally need not be disclosed.

Item 2:   Old Version
Identity and Business Experience of Persons Affiliated With the
Franchisor; Franchise Brokers. This section requires disclosure of the
identity of each director, trustee, general partner (where applicable),
and officer or manager of the franchisor who will have significant
responsibility in connection with the operation of the franchisor's
business or in the support services to be provided to the franchisee.
The principal occupation of each person listed in Item 2 for the past
five years must be disclosed, including dates of employment, nature
of the position, and the identity of the employer. The identity and

background of each franchise broker (if any) authorized to represent the franchisor must also be disclosed in this item.

New Version
Business Experience. Other than the title of the item, no significant changes were made.

Item 3: Old Version
Litigation. A full and frank discussion of any litigation, arbitration, or administrative hearings affecting the franchisor, its officers, directors, or sales representatives over the past ten years should be included in this section. The formal case name, location of the dispute, nature of the claim, and the current status of each action must be disclosed. Item 3 does not require disclosure of all types of litigation but rather focuses on specific allegations and proceedings that would be of particular concern to the prospective franchisee.

New Version
Litigation. Under the Guidelines, the entities that must be made are expanded to include the franchisor's predecessors and those affiliates that sell franchises under the franchisor's principal trademark. The types of litigation that must be disclosed are expanded to include securities law violations. The franchisor is now expressly required to disclose litigation that is "material" even if the nature of the claims does not fall within the types of claims specifically listed. "Ordinary routine litigation incidental to the business" is not to be considered material. Litigation is deemed "ordinary routine" if it "ordinarily results from the business and does not depart from the normal kind of actions in the business." In addition, the new Guidelines clarify that settlement of an action does not diminish its materiality if the franchisor "agrees to pay material consideration or agrees to be bound by obligations which are materially adverse to its interests."

Item 4: Old Version
Bankruptcy. This section requires the franchisor to disclose whether the company or any of its predecessors, officers, or general partners have, during the past fifteen years, been adjudged bankrupt or reorganized due to insolvency. The court in which the bankruptcy or reorganization proceeding occurred, the formal case title, and any material facts and circumstances surrounding the proceeding must be disclosed.

New Version

Bankruptcy. Under the new Guidelines, the entities for which disclosure is required are expanded to include all affiliates of the franchisor. In addition, the number of years for which disclosure regarding bankruptcy must be made is reduced from fifteen to ten.

Item 5: Old Version

Franchisee's Initial Franchise Fee or Other Initial Payment. The initial franchise fee and related payments to the franchisor upon execution of the franchise agreement must be disclosed in this section. The manner in which the payments are made, the use of the proceeds by the franchisor, and whether or not the fee is refundable in whole or in part must be disclosed.

New Version

Initial Franchise Fee. Under the new Guidelines, the franchisor must disclose all payments to the franchisor or its affiliates for goods and services that the franchisee will receive *prior to opening the franchise*. Previously, the Guidelines limited disclosure to initial fees and payments charged to the franchisee upon signing the franchise agreement. If the initial franchise fee is not uniform, the franchisor must disclose the formula or range of initial fees received by it in the most recent fiscal year prior to the application date. In addition, the new Guidelines delete the current requirement that the franchisor disclose how initial fees will be applied or used.

Item 6: Old Version

Other Fees. Any other initial or recurring fee payable by the franchisee to the franchisor or any affiliate must be disclosed and the nature of each fee fully discussed, including but not limited to royalty payments, training fees, audit fees, public offering review fees, advertising contributions, mandatory insurance requirements, transfer fees, renewal fees, lease negotiation fees, and any consulting fees charged by the franchisor or an affiliate for special services. The amount, time of the payment, and refundability of each type of payment should be disclosed.

New Version

Other Fees. Under the new Guidelines, the disclosure of "other fees" must be in tabular form. A "remarks" column or footnotes may be used to elaborate on the information about the fees disclosed in the table. In addition, if fees are paid to a franchisee cooperative, the franchisor must disclose the voting power of its outlets in the cooperative. Further, the range of any fees imposed by that cooperative must be disclosed if the franchisor's outlets have controlling voting power.

Item 7:   Old Version
Franchisee's Initial Investment. Each component of the franchisee's initial investment that the franchise is required to expend in order to open the franchised business must be estimated in this section, usually in chart form, regardless of whether such payments are made directly to the franchisor. Real estate, equipment, fixtures, security deposits, inventory, construction costs, working capital, accounting and legal fees, license and permit fees, and any other costs and expenditures should be disclosed. The disclosure should include to whom such payments are made, under what general terms and conditions, and what portion, if any, is refundable. The following statement must appear at the end of Item 7: "There are no other direct or indirect payments in conjunction with the purchase of the franchise."

New Version
Initial Investment. Under the new Guidelines, the disclosure must be made in a prescribed tabular form. A payment must be disclosed if it is required to be paid during the "initial phase" of the business. The guidelines instruct that "a reasonable time for the initial phase of the business is at least three months or a reasonable period of the industry." The Guidelines also require disclosure of additional funds required during the initial phase and the factors, basis, and experience upon which the franchisor bases his/her calculation.

Item 8:   Old Version
Obligations of the Franchisee to Purchase or Lease From Designated Sources. Any obligation of the franchisee to purchase goods, services, supplies, fixtures, equipment, or inventory that relates to the establishment or operation of the franchised business from a source designated by the franchisor should be disclosed. The terms of the purchase or lease as well as any minimum-volume purchasing requirements must be disclosed. If the franchisor will or may derive direct or indirect income based on these purchases from required sources, then the nature and amount of such income must be fully

disclosed. Remember that such obligations must be able to withstand the scrutiny of the antitrust laws.

New Version

Restrictions on Sources of Products. Under the new Guidelines, disclosure requirements contained in Items 8 and 9 of the old guidelines were consolidated. In addition to disclosing whether the franchisor or its affiliates will or may derive revenue or material consideration as a result of franchisee's required purchases or leases, the franchisor must also disclose the estimated proportion of these required purchases and leases to all purchases and leases by the franchisee of goods and services necessary to establish and operate the franchise. The franchisor must disclose whether there are any purchasing or distribution cooperatives serving its system. The franchisor must disclose, based on the immediately preceding year's financial statements, its: (1) total revenues, (2) revenues derived from required purchases and leases of products and services, (3) and percentage of total revenues from such required purchases and leases. If the franchisor's affiliates also sell or lease products or services to the franchisee, the franchisor must also disclose the percentage of the affiliates' revenues derived from these sales or leases. Any fees required for approval of a new supplier must also be disclosed. In addition, the franchisor must disclose whether it offers the franchisee inducements, such as renewal or additional franchises, for purchasing goods or products from designated or approved sources.

Item 9:   Old Version

Obligations of the Franchisee to Purchase or Lease in Accordance With Specifications or From Approved Suppliers. All quality control standards, equipment specifications, and approved supplier programs that have been developed by the franchisor and must be followed by the franchisee must be disclosed under this item. The criteria applied by the franchisor for approving or designating a particular supplier or vendor must be included. A detailed discussion of these standards and specifications need not be actually set forth in the UFOC; rather, a summary discussion of the programs with reference to exhibits or confidential operations manuals is sufficient. Finally, any income derived by the franchisor in connection with the designation of an approved supplier, or as a result of an approved supplier being an affiliated corporation, must be disclosed.

New Version
Franchisee's Obligations. The disclosure items contained in Item 9 are entirely new. The franchisors must set forth the franchisee's obligations in prescribed tabular form with regard to twenty-four specific categories. The table must cite the relevant sections of both the franchise agreement and offering circular.

Item 10: Old Version
Financing Arrangements. In this section, the franchisor must disclose the terms and conditions of any financing arrangements offered to the franchisee either by the franchisor or any of its affiliates. The exact terms of any direct or indirect debt financing, equipment or real estate leasing programs, operating lines of credit, or inventory financing must be disclosed. If any of these financing programs is offered by an affiliate, then the exact relationship between the franchisor and the affiliate must be disclosed. Terms that may be detrimental to the franchisee upon default, such as a confession of judgment, waiver of defenses, or acceleration clauses, must be disclosed in this item of the UFOC.

New Version
Financing. Under the new Guidelines, the terms and conditions of "indirect offers of financing" made to franchisees must be disclosed. An "indirect offer of financing" includes: (1) a written arrangement between the franchisor, or its affiliate, and a lender for the lender to offer financing to the franchisee; (2) an arrangement in which the franchisor or its affiliate receives benefits from a lender for franchisee financing; and (3) the franchisor's guarantee of a note, lease, or obligation of the franchisee. A franchisor is permitted, but not required, to make disclosure in tabular form. A franchisor must disclose the annual percentage rate of interest (APR) charged for financing, computed in accordance with Sections 106–107 of the Consumer Protection Credit Act, 15 U.S.C. If the APR varies depending on when the financing is issued, the franchisor must disclose the APR as of a disclosed recent date. The franchisor must also disclose to the franchisee the consequences of any default of its obligations, including operation of any cross-default provisions, acceleration of amounts due, and payment of court costs and attorney's fees. In addition, a franchisor must include in the offering circular specimen copies of any financing documents.

Item 11: <u>Old Version</u>

<u>Obligations of the Franchisor; Other Supervision, Assistance, or Services</u>. This section is one of the most important to the prospective franchisee because it discusses the initial and ongoing support and services provided by the franchisor. Each obligation of the franchisor to provide assistance must be cross-referenced to the specific paragraph of the franchise agreement where the corresponding contractual provision may be found. Most services offered by the franchisor fall into one of two categories: initial or continuing services. Initial support includes all services offered by the franchisor prior to the opening of the franchised business, such as the provision of architectural or engineering plans, construction supervision, personnel recruitment, site selection, pre-opening promotion, and acquisition of initial inventory. The location, duration, content, and qualifications of the franchisor's staff responsible for conducting the training program offered by the franchisor must be discussed in some detail. Any assistance provided by the franchisor that it is not contractually bound to provide must also be disclosed in Item 11. Similar disclosures should be made for the continuing services to be offered by the franchisor once the business has opened, such as ongoing training, advertising and promotion, bookkeeping, inventory control, and any products to be sold by the franchisor to the franchisee.

<u>New Version</u>

<u>Franchisor's Obligations</u>. Under the new Guidelines, a franchisor must disclose only those pre-opening obligations that it is contractually required to provide to the franchisee. Pre-opening assistance that the franchisor intends to provide, but which it is not contractually bound to provide, may not be included. Accordingly, this disclosure must begin with the following sentence: "Except as listed below, the franchisor need not provide any assistance to you." The franchisor must make comprehensive disclosures regarding advertising, including: (1) the type of media in which the advertising may be distributed; (2) whether the media coverage is local, regional, or national in scope; (3) the source of the advertising (e.g., in-house or advertising agency); (4) the conditions under which the franchisee is permitted to use his/her own advertising; and (5) if applicable, the manner in which the franchisee advertising council operates and advises the franchisor. Franchisors must make specific disclosures regarding local or regional advertising cooperatives, including: (1) how the area

and/or membership of the cooperative is defined; (2) how the franchisee's contributions to the cooperative are calculated; (3) who is responsible for administration of the cooperative; (4) whether cooperatives must operate from written governing documents and whether the documents are available for review by the franchisee; (5) whether cooperatives must prepare annual or periodic financial statements and whether such statements are available for review by the franchisee; and (6) whether the franchisor has the power to form, change, dissolve, or merge cooperatives. Franchisors must disclose information about advertising funds they administer, including: (1) the basis upon which franchisor-owned outlets contribute to the fund; (2) whether a franchisee contributes at a uniform rate; and (3) the percentages of the funds spent on production, media placement, administrative, and other expenses. A franchisor must also disclose whether it is obligated to advertise in the area in which the franchise is to be located and the percentage of funds used for advertising that is principally a solicitation for the sale of franchises. The franchisor is required to disclose whether the franchisee must buy or use electronic cash registers or computer systems. If there is such a requirement, the franchisor must describe in nontechnical language: (1) the hardware components; (2) the software program; and (3) whether such hardware and software are proprietary property of the franchisor, an affiliate, or a third party. If the hardware or software is not proprietary, the franchisor must disclose: (1) whether the franchisee has any contractual obligation to upgrade or update the equipment, and if so, any limitations on the frequency and cost of such obligation; (2) how it will be used in the franchise; and (3) whether the franchisor has any independent access to information or data in the system. The new Guidelines expand disclosure regarding site selection.

Item 12: Old Version

Exclusive Area or Territory. The exact territory or exclusive area, if any, to be granted by the franchisor to the franchisee should be disclosed, as well as the right to adjust the size of this territory in the event that certain contractual conditions are not met, such as the failure to achieve certain performance quotas. The right of the franchisor to establish company-owned units or to grant franchises to others within the territory must be disclosed. A detailed description and/or map of the franchisee's territory should be included as an exhibit to the franchise agreement.

New Version

Territory. In addition to disclosing whether it has established or may establish additional franchised or company-owned outlets that may compete with the franchisee's outlets, the franchisor must disclose whether it has established or may establish "other channels of distribution" under its mark. The franchisor must disclose the conditions under which it will approve the relocation of a franchise or the establishment of additional franchises. In addition, a franchise must disclose whether it or an affiliate operates or has plans to operate another chain or channel of distribution *under a different trademark* to sell goods or services that are similar to those offered by the franchise. If the franchisor operates competing systems, it must also disclose the methods it will use to resolve conflicts between them regarding territory, customers, and franchisor support. If the principal business address of the competing system is the same as the franchisor's, it must also disclose whether it maintains separate offices and training facilities.

Item 13: Old Version

Trademarks, Service Marks, Trade Names, Logotypes, and Commercial Symbols. It has often been said that the trademark is at the heart of a franchising program. Therefore, the extent to which the franchisor's trade identity (trademarks, logos, slogans, etc.) have been protected should be disclosed, including whether or not these marks are registered at either the federal or state level, or whether there are any limitations of infringement disputes involving the marks or related aspects of the trade identity. The rights and obligations of the franchisor and franchisee in the event of a trademark dispute with a third party must also be disclosed.

New Version

Trademarks. Under the new Guidelines, franchisors need to disclose only the *principal* trademarks, rather than all the trademarks, to be licensed to the franchisee. In addition, the franchisor no longer needs to disclose state trademark filings. If a principal trademark is not federally registered, the franchisor must include a statement that "by not having a Principal Register federal registration for a trademark, the franchisor does not have certain presumptive legal rights granted by registration."

Item 14: Old Version

Patents and Copyrights. Any rights in patents or copyrights that are material to the operation and management of the franchised business should be described in the same detail as required by Item 13.

New Version

Patents, Copyrights, and Proprietary Information. Under the new Guidelines, if the franchisor claims proprietary rights in confidential information or trade secrets, it must disclose the general subject matter of its proprietary rights and the terms and conditions under which they may be used by the franchisee.

Item 15: Old Version

Obligation of the Franchisee to Participate in the Actual Operation of the Franchised Business. The franchisor must disclose in this item whether or not absentee ownership and management will be permitted in connection with the operation of the franchised business. If direct participation is required by the franchisee, then the extent of such participation must be disclosed. If the franchisee may hire a manager to operate the franchised business, then the franchisor must disclose any mandatory employment terms or equity ownership requirements.

New Version

Obligation to Participate in the Actual Operation of the Franchised Business. Under the new Guidelines, the franchisor is required to disclose obligations arising from its practices, personal guarantees, and confidentiality or noncompetition agreements.

Item 16: Old Version

Restrictions on Goods and Services Offered by Franchisee. In this section the franchisor must disclose any special contractual provisions or other circumstances that limit either the types of products and services the franchisee may offer or the types or location of the customers to whom the products and services may be offered.

New Version

Restrictions on What the Franchisee May Sell. Other than the title of the item, no significant changes were made.

Item 17: <u>Old Version</u>

<u>Renewal, Termination, Repurchase, Modification, and Assignment of the Franchise Agreement and Related Information</u>. This item is typically the longest section of the UFOC and also of great importance to the prospective franchisee. The term of the franchise agreement, the conditions to renewal, the grounds upon which the franchise agreement may be terminated, the conditions under which the franchise agreement may be assigned, and the rights of the heirs of the franchisee upon death must all be disclosed in this section. Specific events of default, as well as any notice provisions and opportunities to cure defaults that will be provided by the franchisor to the franchisee, must be defined. Obligations of the franchisee following termination, such as covenants against competition or against the use of proprietary information, must be disclosed. Finally, the conditions under which the franchise agreement may be modified either by the franchisor or franchisee must be discussed in this item.

<u>New Version</u>

<u>Renewal, Termination, Transfer, and Dispute Resolution</u>. Under the new Guidelines, the disclosures may no longer be satisfied by restating provisions of the franchise agreement and, instead, must be presented in a prescribed tabular form. The table must contain abbreviated summaries regarding twenty-three specific categories with references to relevant sections of the franchise agreement. Preceding the table, the offering circular must state: "This table lists important provisions of the franchise and related agreements. You should read these provisions in the agreements attached to this offering circular."

Item 18: <u>Old Version</u>

<u>Arrangements With Public Figures</u>. Any compensation or benefit given to a public figure in return for an endorsement of the franchise and/or products and services offered by the franchisee must be disclosed. The extent to which the public figure owns or is involved in the management of the franchisor must also be disclosed. The right of the franchisee to use the name of the public figure in its local promotional campaign and the material terms of the agreement between the franchisor and the public figure must also be included in this item.

<u>New Version</u>

<u>Public Figures</u>. The new Guidelines clarify that disclosure is required

only if a public figure endorses or recommends an investment in the franchise to prospective franchisee's rights to use the names of public figures who are featured in consumer advertising or other promotional efforts.

Item 19: <u>Old Version</u>

<u>Actual, Average, Projected, or Forecasted Franchise Sales, Profits, or Earnings</u>. If the franchisor is willing to provide the prospective franchisee with sample earnings claims or projections, they must be discussed in Item 19.

<u>New Version</u>

<u>Earnings Claims</u>. Other than the title of the item, no significant changes were made.

Item 20: <u>Old Version</u>

<u>Information Regarding Franchises of the Franchisor</u>. A full summary of the number of franchises sold, number of operational units, and number of company-owned units must be broken down in Item 20, usually in tabular form, including an estimate of franchise sales for the upcoming fiscal year that are broken down by state. The names, addresses, and telephone numbers of franchisees should be included in this item. In addition, the number of franchisees terminated or not renewed (voluntary and involuntary), and the cause of termination or nonrenewal, must be broken down for the previous three years of operations.

<u>New Version</u>

<u>List of Franchise Outlets</u>. The new Guidelines significantly expand this disclosure. With the exception of the list of franchise names, addresses, and telephone numbers, the franchisor must disclose all information required by this item in tabular form. The franchisor must disclose the number of franchised and company-owned outlets sold, opened, and closed in its system as of the close of each of its last three fiscal years. Operational outlets must be listed separately from those not opened, and disclosure must be provided on a state-by-state basis. The franchisor may limit its disclosure of the franchisee's names, addresses, and telephone numbers to those franchised outlets in the state in which the franchise offering is made if there are one hundred outlets in such state. If there are

fewer than one hundred in the state, the franchisor must disclose the names, addresses, and telephone numbers of franchised outlets from contiguous states and, if necessary, the next closest states until at least one hundred are listed. For the three-year period immediately before the close of its most recent fiscal year, the franchisor must disclose the number of franchised outlets that have: (1) had a change in "controlling ownership interest"; (2) been canceled or terminated; (3) not been renewed; (4) been reacquired by the franchisor; (5) or otherwise ceased to do business in the system. The franchisor must disclose the last known home address of every franchisee who has had an outlet terminated, canceled, or not renewed or who otherwise voluntarily or involuntarily ceased to do business under the franchise agreement during the most recently completed fiscal year end or who has not communicated with the franchisor within ten weeks of the application date. In addition, the franchisor must disclose information about company-owned outlets that are substantially similar to its franchised outlets. The same table may be used for both franchised and company-owned outlets so long as the data regarding each are set out in a distinct manner.

Item 21: Old Version
Financial Statements. A full set of financial statements prepared in accordance with generally accepted accounting principles must be included in Item 21 as part of the disclosure package to be provided to a franchisee. Most registration states require that the statements be audited, with limited exceptions for start-up franchisors. The balance sheet provided should have been prepared as of a date within ninety days prior to the date that the registration application is filed. Unaudited statements may be used for interim periods. A franchisor with a weak financial statement may be required to make special arrangements with the franchise administrator in each state for the protection of a prospective franchisee.

New Version
Financial Statements. Under the new Guidelines, the franchisor must include its balance sheet for the last two fiscal years. As under the previous Guidelines, disclosures of statements of operations, stockholders' equity, and cash flow are required for the franchisor's last

three fiscal years. If the most recent balance sheet and statement of operations are as of a date more than ninety days before the application date, the franchisor must also include an unaudited balance sheet and statement of operations for a period falling within ninety days of the application. If the franchisor does not have audited financial statements for its last three fiscal years, it may provide either: (1) an audited financial statement for its last fiscal year and, if the audit is not within ninety days of the application date, an unaudited balance sheet and income statement for a period falling with ninety days of application; or (2) an unaudited balance sheet as of the date within ninety days of the application and an audited income statement from the start of its fiscal year through the date of the audited balance sheet.

Item 22: Old Version

Franchise Agreement and Related Contracts. A copy of the franchise agreement as well as any other related documents to be signed by the franchisee in connection with the ownership and operation of the franchised business must be attached as exhibits to the UFOC.

New Version

Contracts. Other than the title of the item, no significant changes were made.

Item 23: Old Version

Acknowledgment of Receipt. The last page of the UFOC is a detachable document that is executed by the prospective franchisee acknowledging receipt of the offering circular.

New Version

Receipt. The new Guidelines require the franchisor to provide two copies of the receipt in the offering circular: one to be kept by the prospective franchisee and the other to be returned to the franchisor. The franchisor must disclose the name, principal business address, and telephone number of any subfranchisor or franchise broker offering the franchise in the state. The receipt must contain an itemized listing of all exhibits to the offering circular. If not previously disclosed in Item 1, the franchisor must disclose the name(s) and address(es) of its agent(s) authorized to receive service of process.

The Mechanics of the Registration Process

Each of the registration states has slightly different procedures and requirements for the approval of a franchisor prior to offers and sales being authorized. In all cases, however, the package of disclosure documents is assembled,
consisting of an offering circular, franchise agreement, supplemental agreements, financial statements, franchise roster, mandated cover pages, acknowledgment of receipt, and the special forms that are required by each state, such
as corporation verification statements, salesperson disclosure forms, and consent to service of process documents. (See Figure 4-3.) The specific requirements of each state should be checked carefully by the franchisor and its
counsel. Initial filing fees range from $250 to $500, with renewal filings usually ranging from $100 to $250.

Figure 4-3. Data to gather when implementing a franchising program.

The FTC and the registration states have adopted regulations that dictate the
contents of the franchise offering circular. The disclosure requirements range
from history of the company and its principals (including litigation and bank-
ruptcies) to a detailed description of the terms of the franchise agreement to be
executed by the franchisee. The mandatory contents of the franchise offering
circular will, therefore, provide an appropriate starting point for a new franchisor in developing its franchising program.

1. *Information regarding the company and its principals.* The following information should be provided with respect to the company and its principals:

   ◆ Give history of the company's operations and business. Identify
     any predecessors and/or affiliated companies.
   ◆ Describe the market to be serviced by franchisees. The descrip-
     tion will include information about general or specific markets
     to be targeted, whether the market is developed or developing,
     and whether the business is seasonal. In addition, general infor-
     mation about industry-specific laws and regulations must be
     included, along with a description of the competition.
   ◆ Identify all of the company's directors, principal officers, and other
     executives who have management responsibility in connection
     with the operation of the company's business. As to each, provide
     a summary of their job history for at least the past five years.
   ◆ Identify and describe all litigation in which the company, its offi-

cers, and its directors are involved or have previously been involved.

   ◆ Identify and describe any and all bankruptcy proceedings involving the company, its officers, and its directors.

2. *Initial fees.* The offering circular must disclose all payments a franchisee is required to make to the franchisor before opening the franchised business. This will include the initial franchise fee and any other pre-opening purchases/leases from the franchisor. Before determining the initial franchise fee, you may want to compare the fees charged by competitors. The fee may be expressed as a single amount for all franchisees, or it may be a range of amounts, based on criteria you specify. In addition, you will need to provide information on any plans for allowing the fee to be paid in installments, and whether the fee will be refundable under certain conditions. The disclosure should also discuss the allocation of the initial franchise fees collected by the franchisor. For example, fees are often used to cover administrative and legal costs associated with the franchise offer, as well as to fund initial training programs and other pre-opening assistance provided by the franchisor.

3. *Royalty.* The royalty rate and method of payment must be determined. Again, a comparison of competitors' royalty structures may be helpful. The royalty formula (e.g., percentage of gross sales), payment frequency, and refundability must be disclosed.

4. *Advertising fund.* Will you require franchisees to contribute to a regional or national advertising fund? Typically, advertising fund contributions are based on the same formula and made with the same frequency as royalty payments. If such a fund is contemplated, you need to discuss the fund's objectives, administration, and participants (company-owned stores?). *Note*: All fees collected for the advertising fund *must* be used for that purpose.

5. *Other fees paid to franchisor.* The offering circular must identify all other fees that a franchisee is required to pay to the franchisor, or to the franchisor's affiliate, including fees collected on behalf of third parties. Typically, these fees include ongoing training/consultant fees and expenses, real property and equipment leases, required supply purchases, transfer fees, renewal fees, and audit fees.

6. *Initial investment.* The offering circular must include a chart detailing all costs necessary to begin operation of the franchised business and to operate the business during the first three months (or some other initial phase more appropriate for the industry), including the costs of furniture, equipment, supplies, inventory, leasehold improvements, rent security, utilities, advertising, insurance, licenses, and permits. (Note that the "initial

(continues)

Figure 4-3. *(continued)*

phase" is not the equivalent of a "break-even point.") Many of the cost items will be stated in a low-high range, rather than a specific amount.

7. *Sources for products and services.* What products and services must franchisees purchase: (a) only from the franchisor or its affiliates? (b) only from approved suppliers? (c) only in accordance with the franchisor's specifications? Will the franchisor derive any revenue from these purchases? For example, if there are proprietary items that must be purchased from you or a particular designated supplier, then this needs to be disclosed in the offering circular.

8. *Franchisee's obligations.* The franchisee's principal obligations under the franchise agreement are disclosed in a chart referencing twenty-four specific obligations. The chart also serves as a cross-reference for franchisees between the offering circular and the franchise agreement. The list attached as Exhibit A details the specific franchisee obligations that must be addressed in this chart.

9. *Financing.* Will the franchisor or its affiliates offer any direct or indirect financing arrangements to franchisees? Indirect financing includes guarantying franchisee loans and facilitating arrangements with lenders. If so, then the terms of the loan must be disclosed.

10. *Franchisor's obligations.* These obligations are broken down into two categories: obligations performed before the franchised business opens, and ongoing obligations:

    ◆ *Pre-opening obligations.* How will the franchisor assist franchisees (if at all) in locating a site for the business or in developing the site so that it is suitable for the operation of the franchised business? Will the franchisor hire and/or train franchisees' employees?

    ◆ *Ongoing obligations.* What assistance (if any) will the franchisor provide with: (a) developing/improving the franchised business, (b) operating problems encountered by franchisees, (c) administrative, bookkeeping, and inventory control procedures? Specific details about the franchisor's advertising program and any computer systems or cash registers required to be used in the business must be provided.

In addition, a training program must be developed that will be offered to franchisees and/or the franchisees' managers. The training program should encompass instruction in the operation and management of a franchised business as well as instruction in the areas of advertising, marketing, personnel management, bookkeeping, inventory control, and any other issues unique to the operation of the franchised business. In connection with the training program, the following must also be determined:

a. Who will bear the costs for said training?
b. Who will pay the transportation, lodging, and other miscellaneous expenses associated with training?
c. How many people will be required to attend training, and who will be required to attend (i.e., the franchisee, franchisee's manager, franchisee's employees)?
d. If additional designees of the franchisee attend, will there be a charge?
e. Where will training be held, and what is the length of said training?
f. When will franchisee and its managers/employees be required to complete the training program (i.e., how many weeks prior to the opening of the center)?

The franchisor's training program must be described in detail, including information regarding the location, duration, and a general outline of the training program. What topics will be covered? What materials will be used? Who are the instructors? Is training mandatory?

11. *Territory.* Will franchisees be granted an exclusive territory? Will there be conditions on exclusivity? Will franchisees be subject to performance standards?
12. *Franchisee participation.* Are franchisees required to participate personally in the direct operation of the franchised business?
13. *Restrictions on goods and services.* Are there any restrictions or conditions on the products that the franchisee may sell? For example, is the franchisee obligated to sell only those products approved by the franchisor?
14. *Renewal, termination, transfer, dispute resolution:*

   ◆ *Term and renewal.* What will be the term of the franchise agreement? Will the franchisees be able to renew the agreement, and if so, under what conditions? Will a fee be charged? Under what conditions may the franchisor terminate the agreement? Under what conditions (if any) may the franchisees terminate the agreement?
   ◆ *Termination.* What obligations are imposed on franchisees after the franchise agreement is terminated or expires? Will the fran-

(continues)

Figure 4-3. *(continued)*

chisees be bound by a noncompete agreement? Will the noncompete agreement restrict the franchisees' activities during and after
the term of the agreement? What obligations (if any) are imposed
on the franchisor after termination or expiration of the agreement?

♦ *Transfer.* May franchisees assign or transfer the franchise agreement? If so, under what conditions? Will a fee be charged? Will
the franchisor have a right of first refusal to purchase the franchised business before it can be transferred or sold to a third
party?

♦ *Dispute resolution.* How and where will disputes be settled? (For
example, must disputes be arbitrated? Will the arbitration or litigation take place in the city/state of_____?)

Please note that some state laws limit the franchisor's ability to enforce
these provisions of the franchise agreement.

15. *Public figures.* Will any public figure be involved in promoting or managing the franchise system?

16. *Earnings claims.* Do you intend to include an earnings claim in the offering
circular?

17. *List of outlets.* Although there are currently no franchisees, information
about any company-owned stores must be disclosed, including the locations
of these stores over the last three years and projections about the number of
additional stores to be opened in the next fiscal year and their locations.

18. *Financial statements.* The financial statements required will differ depending upon which legal entity is selected to serve as the franchisor. If the franchisor is a newly established corporation or LLC, then it will at least need
to include opening financial statements (i.e., an audited balance sheet).

EXHIBIT A
FRANCHISEE OBLIGATIONS

a.   Site selection and acquisition/lease
b.   Pre-opening purchases/leases
c.   Site development and other pre-opening requirements
d.   Initial and ongoing training
e.   Opening
f.   Fees
g.   Compliance with standards and policies; operating manual

h. Trademarks and proprietary information
i. Restrictions on products/services offered
j. Warranty and customer service requirements
k. Territorial development and sales quotas
l. Ongoing product/service purchases
m. Maintenance, appearance, and remodeling requirements
n. Insurance
o. Advertising
p. Indemnification
q. Owner's participation/management/staffing
r. Records and reports
s. Inspection and audits
t. Transfer
u. Renewal
v. Postermination obligations
w. Noncompetition covenants
x. Dispute resolution

The first step is for counsel to "custom tailor" the UFOC format to meet the special requirements or additional disclosures required under the particular state regulations. Once the documents are ready and all signatures have been obtained, the package is filed with the state franchise administrator, and a specific franchise examiner (usually an attorney) is assigned to the franchisor. The level of scrutiny applied by the examiner in reviewing the offering materials varies from state to state and from franchisor to franchisor. The sales history, financial strength, litigation record, reputation of legal counsel, time pressures and workload of the examiner, geographic desirability of the state, and the general reputation of the franchisor will have an impact on the level of review and the timetable for approval. Franchisors should expect to see at least one "comment letter" from the examiner requesting certain changes or additional information as a condition of approval and registration. The procedure can go as quickly as six weeks or as slowly as six months, depending on the concerns of the examiner and the skills and experience of legal counsel.

The initial and ongoing reporting and disclosure requirements vary from state to state. For example, the filing of an amendment to the offering circular is required in the event of a "material change" (discussed in greater detail in Chapter 5); however, each state has different regulations as to the definition of a material change. Similarly, although all registration states require the annual filing of a renewal application or annual report, only Maryland requires that quarterly reports be filed. When advertising materials are developed for use in attracting franchisees, they must be approved in advance by all registration states except Virginia and Hawaii. (See the discussion of advertising material requirements in Chapter 5.) All franchise registration states except Virginia require the filing of salesperson disclosure forms. California, Illinois, New York, and Washington require their own special forms. It is critical that the franchisor's legal compliance officer stay abreast of all of these special filing requirements.

One interesting and potentially complex legal issue raised by the growth of the Internet is whether a franchisor's general home page, which may include information about the offer and sale of a franchise to prospective franchisees, constitutes an "offer" as that term is defined by a given registration state. If yes, then a franchisor must register its offering circular in that state before making its Website available nationwide. As of the date of publication of this book, at least one registration state (Indiana) has issued an administrative policy interpretation, which clarifies that one mere offer via the Internet does *not* trigger the need to register in Indiana, provided that if an Indiana resident shows interest in a franchise promoted on the Internet, then one franchisor (already registered in Indiana) must inform the franchisee that the offer is not yet available in Indiana or register prior to making a formal offer. It is likely that other registration states will adopt a similar policy in late 1998 or 1999.

5

Compliance

The development of an in-house legal compliance program and the designation of a legal compliance officer is *a necessity, not a luxury,* for the growing franchisor operating in today's litigious society. In all likelihood, the compliance staff will be "pitted against" the sales and marketing staff, with ongoing conflict and tension between the need to market aggressively and the need to market legally. An attitude and a philosophy of teamwork must be fostered early on in order to avoid such tension within the company. There must be a commitment from day one to only sell franchises within the bounds of the law and to maintain complete and comprehensive compliance files. (See Figure 5-1 for contents of a typical compliance file.) The compliance file should contain information about the initial meeting with the prospect to the execution of the franchise agreement to the termination of the relationship and beyond. The timing and content of the first few contacts with a prospective franchisee are the most critical in proper compliance. It is often in a franchisor's best interests to implement self-imposed disclosure timing guidelines for its sales and marketing personnel. (See Figure 5-2 for sample guidelines.) These record-keeping requirements and timing guidelines will often seem burdensome but will also go a long way in protecting the company in the event of a subsequent dispute with the franchisee or in connection with a federal or state regulatory investigation.

Figure 5-1. A typical compliance file.

Here are the contents of a typical compliance file that must be established and maintained by the compliance staff:

1. Acknowledgment of receipt of offering circular
2. Completed applicant questionnaire
3. Executed deposit agreement (if used)
4. Copy of the check for initial deposit

(continues)

Figure 5-1. *(continued)*

    5. Copy of executed franchise agreement

    6. Area development agreement (where applicable)

    7. Inventory purchase agreement (where applicable)

    8. Option for assignment of lease

    9. Mandatory addendum to lease

  10. Receipt for manuals

  11. Written consent of board of directors of franchisee

  12. Proof of insurance

  13. Franchisor's written approval of site

  14. Franchisee's certification of receipt of all licenses, permits, and bonds

  15. Franchisee's written notice of commencement of construction

  16. Franchisor's approval of the opening of the franchised business

  17. Copy of franchisee's lease

  18. Certification of completion of basic training

  19. All ongoing correspondence between franchisor and franchisee (post-opening)

  20. Inspection reports

  21. Notices of default

Figure 5-2. Disclosure timing guidelines.

Following are timing and content guidelines for the proper and efficient disclosure of prospective franchisees, formulated by an existing franchisor to ensure compliance as well as to ensure that only properly qualified candidates receive disclosure.

Step 1: Inquiry/Mild Scrutiny

Ask four to five basic questions, such as:

1. How did you hear of the opportunity?
2. Tell me about your current situation.
3. What other opportunities are you considering?
4. What is your timetable?
5. Do you understand that our opportunity requires $____ in readily available capital?

Step 2: Send Brochure/Application

1. Send application to obtain more detailed information on location, etc.
2. If not registered, *stop here.*
3. If registered *and* prospective franchisee meets personal qualifications, then go on to Step 3.

Step 3: Visit

1. Present characteristics of franchisor's success.
2. Conduct basic discussion of opportunity.
3. Determine if prospective franchisee has access to sufficient advisers.
4. If still a candidate, present UFOC, starting the ten-day period of required disclosure.

Step 4: Second Meeting

1. Further questions and/or closing.
2. Execution of documents, receipt of check.

A compliance program means more than careful record keeping. A well-planned compliance system requires initial and ongoing training for the franchisor's sales and marketing personnel, the development of special forms and checklists, a management philosophy and compensation structure that rewards compliance and discourages noncompliance, a system for monitoring all registration and renewal dates, custom-tailored verbal scripts and video presentations that must be used and strictly followed by the sales personnel, the development of a compliance manual and periodic policy statements, special approval and renewal process for the award of new franchises, and a periodic random and "unannounced" inspection of the franchise sales and compliance files in order to ensure that procedures are being followed. The success of the compliance program should not be made dependent on outside legal counsel but rather should be a priority for the franchisor's management team.

No compliance system is 100 percent perfect in preventing franchise law violations. Human nature forces a franchise sales representative to "stretch the truth a little" if he or she has not had a sale in months and faces the loss of a job or a home. Human error may result in a Maryland resident being disclosed with a New York offering document because the wrong package was hastily pulled off the shelf. The franchisor's ability to devote sufficient resources for the compliance program, select the right person as the compliance officer, and foster a positive attitude toward compliance among the sales staff will all affect the success or failure of the compliance program.

The franchise compliance officer must be selected carefully and charged with the responsibility of implementing the compliance program and enforcing its procedures. The officer serves as the in-house clearinghouse for franchise files and information, as well as the liaison with outside legal counsel. The compliance officer must gain (and maintain) the respect of the sales and marketing personnel or the system will fail. This will be achieved only if a senior executive within the company assumes responsibility for disciplining those who have an apathy toward compliance.

Special Topics in Compliance: Earnings Claims

One classic catch-22 in franchising is the desire of a prospective franchisee to know what it is likely to earn as a franchise owner and the strict rules governing the use of "earnings claims" in a sales presentation to a prospect. In the early days of franchising, there was much abuse in this area, with salespersons jotting down projections "on the back of a cocktail napkin" in order to induce the prospect to buy a franchise. Eventually, federal and state regulators caught on to these potentially deceptive practices and developed strict regulations for the use of an earnings claim.

An earnings claim is defined under the law as any information given to a prospective franchisee by, on behalf of, or at the direction of a franchisor or its agent, from which a specific level or range of actual or potential sales, costs, income, or profit from franchised or nonfranchised units may be easily ascertained. Earnings claims may include a chart, table, or mathematical calculation presented to demonstrate possible results based upon a combination of variables (such as multiples of price and quantity to reflect gross sales). An earnings claim must include a *description of its factual basis* and the *material assumptions underlying its preparation and presentation.*

The catch-22 was created by the original strictness of these rules. Prospective franchisees wanted to know what they were likely to earn, and franchisors wanted to tell them, but many franchisors could not meet the strict standards contained in the federal and state regulations. Others feared that the earnings claim would be misused or misunderstood by the prospect and only come back to haunt them in subsequent litigation. As a result, the majority of franchisors did not provide prospective franchisees with earnings claims primarily because:

- ◆ The detailed substantiation requirements of federal and state law made compliance difficult and expensive, *especially for early-stage franchisors.*
- ◆ Many franchisors feared that the documents would "come back to haunt them" in subsequent disputes with disgruntled or disappointed franchisees.
- ◆ Differences between the geographic location, actual performance, and number of units in the system made it difficult to have a sufficient foundation from which to compile the earnings information.

Pressures from members of the franchise community resulted in certain changes to the rules affecting earnings claims in 1987, which were designed to provide greater flexibility in franchise sales and marketing practices. The primary reasons cited for the changes, aside from "political" pressures, included the following: (1) efforts by start-up and early-stage franchisors to sell franchises had been severely restricted; and (2) sophistication had grown (education, net worth, professional advisers, etc.) among prospective franchisees who wanted and needed to know what to expect financially when buying a franchise.

Amendments to the earnings claim disclosure rules under Item 19 of the Uniform Franchise Offering Circular (UFOC) were unanimously adopted by the North American Securities Administrators Association (NASAA) on November 21, 1986. The changes liberalized the rules governing earnings claims provided by franchisors to prospective franchisees. On June 9, 1987, the Federal Trade Commission (FTC) approved for its disclosure format the amendments to Item 19 that were adopted by NASAA. The FTC permitted use of either the old version of Item 19 or the new version through December 31, 1988. As of January 1, 1989, the commission allows use of only the new version to comply with the Item 19 earnings claim disclosure requirements. The new Item 19 is entitled Earnings Claims. It has been adopted by every state regulating disclosure and registration except the state of New York, which, for the most part, has retained the old Item 19 disclosure requirements with its own variations and legends.

Special Topics in Compliance: Material Changes

As the franchise system grows, the franchisor is likely to experience a wide variety of challenges that may result in significant changes to the corporate structure, franchise program, financial statements, or relationships with its franchisees. When these significant structural or program changes occur, they must be disclosed to the prospective franchisee through an update to the UFOC. The laws that dictate how and when these updates must be made are commonly referred to as the "material change" regulations.

The determination of what constitutes a "material change" can be difficult, and federal and state law provide for a significant degree of discretion. For example, the term *material change* is defined by the FTC as "any fact, circumstance, or set of conditions which has a substantial likelihood of influencing a reasonable franchisee or a reasonable prospective franchisee in the making of a significant decision relating to a named franchise business or which has any significant financial impact on a franchise or prospective franchisee."

With respect to the timing of offering circular amendments, it is important to keep in mind the danger of continuing to grant franchises with knowledge of a material event or change that may require disclosure. The longer an amendment is deferred, the greater the risk that sales made prior to the amendment will be challenged as illegal or be subject to rescission, which essentially grants the franchisee an "option" rather than a binding and enforceable franchise agreement. Amendments filed to the disclosure document in registration states will cause a short delay in the ability of the franchisor to offer and sell franchises in that or those states. However, the cost of this delay should be viewed as minor compared to the benefits of a "legal" sale.

Examples of Material Changes

The following list provides examples of facts and circumstances that have been considered by federal and state franchise regulators to constitute a material change:

1. A change in any franchise or other fee charged, or significantly increased costs of developing or operating a franchised outlet.
2. The termination, closing, failure to renew, or repurchase of a significant number of franchises. Whether the number is significant depends on the number of franchises in exis-

tence and whether the area in which the above occurred is the same area in which new franchises will be offered, except where specific state regulations define what constitutes a significant number (e.g., Hawaii and New York).

3. A significant *adverse* change in any of the following:

   ◆ The obligations of the franchisee to purchase items from the franchisor or its designated sources
   ◆ Limitations or restrictions on goods or services that the franchisee may offer to its customers
   ◆ The obligations to be performed by the franchisor
   ◆ The key terms of the franchise agreement
   ◆ The franchisor's financial situation, resulting in a 5 percent or greater change in net profits or losses in any six-month period
   ◆ The services or products offered to consumers by the franchisees of the franchisor
   ◆ The identity of persons affiliated with the franchisor and any franchise brokers
   ◆ The current status of the franchisor's trade or service marks

4. Any change in control, corporate name, state of incorporation, or reorganization of the franchisor.

5. A significant change in status of litigation or administrative matters that have been disclosed in the UFOC. In addition, a franchisor should be alert to provide for the addition of any new claims or counterclaims that have been filed against the franchisor that may need to be disclosed.

6. Any recent developments in the market(s) for the products or services sold by the franchisees that could increase competition or create operating problems for franchisees.

7. A change in the accuracy of earnings claims information (if applicable) disclosed.

Compliance in the Nonregistration States

According to Section 436.2(n) of the Federal Trade Commission Trade Regulation Rule relating to disclosure requirements and prohibitions concerning franchising and business opportunity ventures, the terms *material,* *material fact,* and *material change* include any fact, circumstance, or set of conditions that has a substantial likelihood of influencing a reasonable franchisee or a reasonable prospective franchisee in the making of a significant decision relating to a named franchise business or that has any significant financial impact on a franchisee or prospective franchisee. According to the FTC's interpretative guide to this rule, the disclosure document must be promptly updated, on at least a quarterly basis, whenever a material change occurs in the information contained in the disclosure document. The material change disclosure may be attached to the UFOC as an addendum.

Compliance in the Registration States

The following overview shows how each of the registration states handles the filing and registration of a material change.

California

California is a registration state that requires a franchisor to promptly notify the Commissioner of Corporations, in writing, by an application to amend the registration, of any material change in the information contained in the application as originally submitted, amended, or renewed.

Hawaii

Hawaii is a registration state that requires a franchisor to file with the Director a copy of the offering circular as amended to reflect any material event or material change at least seven days before a sale of a franchise is made. "Material event" or "material change" includes, but is not limited to, the following:

1. The termination, closing, or failure to renew during any three-month period of:

   ◆ The greater of 1 percent or five of all franchises of a franchisor or subfranchisor regardless of location
   ◆ The lesser of 15 percent or two of the franchises of a franchisor or subfranchisor located in Hawaii

2. Any change in control, corporate name, or state of incorporation, or reorganization of the franchisor, whether or not the franchisor or its parent, if the franchisor or sub-

franchisor is a subsidiary, is required to file reports under Section 12 of the Securities Exchange Act of 1934.

3. The purchase by the franchisor of in excess of 5 percent of its existing franchises during any three-month period on a continuous basis.

4. The commencement of any new product, service, or model line involving, directly or indirectly, additional investment by any franchisee or the discontinuation or modification of the marketing plan or system of any product or service of the franchisor where the total sales from such product or service exceeds 20 percent of the gross sales of the franchisor on an annual basis.

Illinois

Illinois is currently a registration state that requires a franchisor to promptly file with the Administrator an amended disclosure statement reflecting any "material change," defined as follows:

A change in information contained in the disclosure statement is material within the meaning of the Act if there is a substantial likelihood that a reasonable prospective franchisee would consider it significant in making a decision to purchase or not purchase the franchise. Without limitation, examples of changes that could be material include:

1. Any increase or decrease in the initial or continuing fees charged by the franchisor.

2. The termination, cancellation, failure to renew, or reacquisition of a significant number of franchises since the most recent effective date of the disclosure statement.

3. A change in the franchisor's management.

4. A change in the franchisor's or franchisee's obligations under the franchise or related agreements.

5. A decrease in the franchisor's income or net worth.

6. Limitations or significant prospective limitations regarding sources of supply that are known to or should reasonably be anticipated by the franchisor.

7. Additional litigation or a significant change in the status of litigation including:

◆ The filing of an amended complaint alleging or involving violations of any franchise law, fraud, embezzlement, fraudulent conversion, restraint of trade, unfair or deceptive practices, misappropriation of property, or breach of contract.

◆ The entry of any injunctive or restrictive order relating to the franchise; or the entry of any injunction under any federal, state, or Canadian franchise securities, antitrust trade regulation, or trade practice law.

◆ The entry of a judgment that has or would have any significant financial impact on the franchisor. Such a judgment is considered to have significant financial impact if it equals 15 percent or more of the current assets of the franchisor and its subsidiaries on a consolidated basis.

8. The reincorporation of the franchisor or its merger into a corporation other than the registrant. In a merger where the surviving corporation changes its name to that of the original registrant, the material change has still occurred.

Indiana

Indiana is a registration state that requires a franchisor to promptly notify the Indiana Securities Commissioner of any material change in the information contained in an effective registration by filing an application to amend the registration. Such an amendment to an effective registration is effective five days after the date the amendment is filed. However, the Securities Commissioner has not defined what shall be considered a material change. Therefore, the definition used in nonregistration states should be consulted in preparing amendments to the offering circulars registered in Indiana.

Maryland

Maryland is a registration state that requires a franchisor to promptly file an application for amendment of the registration statement with the Securities Commissioner in the Office of the Attorney General in the event of any "material event" or "material change," which includes, but is not limited to, the following:

1. The termination, in any manner, of more than 10 percent

of the franchises of the franchisor that are located in the
state during any three-month period

2. The termination, in any manner, of more than 5 percent of
all franchises of the franchisor regardless of location during any three-month period

3. A reorganization of the franchisor

4. A change in control, corporate name, or state of incorporation of the franchisor

5. The commencement of any new product, service, or model
line requiring, directly or indirectly, additional investment
by any franchisee

6. The discontinuation or modification of the marketing plan
or system of any product or service of the franchisor that
accounts for at least 20 percent of the annual gross sales of
the franchisor

Michigan

Michigan is a registration state that requires a franchisor to file with the
Department of the Attorney General promptly in writing any change in the
notice as originally submitted or amended.

Minnesota

Minnesota is a registration state that requires a franchisor with a registration
in effect to notify the Commissioner of Commerce in writing within thirty
days of any material change in the information on file with the Commissioner
by an application to amend the registration. "Material event" or "material
change" includes, but is not limited to, the following:

1. The termination, closing, or failure to renew by the franchisor during any consecutive three-month period after
registration of 10 percent of all franchises of the franchisor,
regardless of location, or 10 percent of the franchises of
the franchisor located in the state of Minnesota

2. Any change in control, corporate name, or state of incorporation, or reorganization of the franchisor

3. The purchase by the franchisor during any consecutive
three-month period after registration of 10 percent of its
existing franchises, regardless of location, or 10 percent of

its existing franchises in the state of Minnesota

4. The commencement of any new product, service, or model line involving, directly or indirectly, an additional investment in excess of 20 percent of the current average investment made by all franchisees or the discontinuation or modification of the marketing plan or marketing system of any product or service of the franchisor where the average total sales from such product or service exceed 20 percent of the average gross sales of the existing franchisees on an annual basis

5. Any change in the franchise fees charged by the franchisor

6. Any significant change in:

    ◆ The obligations of the franchisee to purchase items from the franchisor or its designated sources
    ◆ The limitations or restrictions on the goods or services the franchisee may offer to its customer
    ◆ The obligations to be performed by the franchisor
    ◆ The franchise contract or agreement, including all amendments thereto

New York

New York is a registration state that requires a franchisor to promptly notify the New York State Department of Law, by application to amend its offering, of any material changes in the information contained in the prospectus as originally submitted or amended. As used in New York, the term "material change" includes, but is not limited to:

1. The termination, closing, or failure to renew, during a three-month period, of the lesser of ten or 10 percent of the franchises of a franchisor, regardless of location

2. A purchase by the franchisor in excess of 5 percent of its existing franchises during six consecutive months

3. A change in the franchise fees charged by the franchisor

4. Any significant adverse change in the business condition of the franchisor or in any of the following:

    ◆ The obligations of the franchisee to purchase items from the franchisor or its designated sources

◆ Limitations or restrictions on the goods or services the franchisee may offer to its customers
◆ The obligations to be performed by the franchisor
◆ The franchise contract or agreements, including amendments thereto
◆ The franchisor's accounting system resulting in a 5 percent or greater change in its net profit or loss in any six-month period
◆ The service, product, or model line

5. Audited financial statements of the preceding fiscal year

North Dakota

North Dakota is a registration state that requires a franchisor to promptly notify the Securities Commissioner, in writing, by an application to amend the registration, of any material change in the information contained in the application as originally submitted, amended, or renewed. Although North Dakota is a registration state, the Commissioner of Securities has not defined what shall be considered a material change. Therefore, the definition used in nonregistration states should be consulted in preparing amendments to the offering circulars registered in North Dakota.

Oregon

While Oregon is a registration state, the Director of the Department of Insurance and Finance has not defined what shall constitute a material change, and therefore the definition used in the nonregistration states should be consulted.

Rhode Island

Rhode Island is a registration state that requires a franchisor to promptly notify the Director of Business Regulation in writing, by an application to amend the registration, of any material change in the information contained in the application as originally submitted, amended, or renewed. The Director has not defined what constitutes a material change, and therefore the definition used in the nonregistration states should be consulted.

South Dakota

South Dakota is a registration state that requires franchisors with a registration in effect to notify the Director in writing within thirty days after the occurrence of any material change in the information on file with the Director of the Division of Securities by an application to amend the registration. The Director has not defined the term "material change," and therefore the definition used in the nonregistration states should be consulted.

Virginia

Virginia is a registration state that requires the franchisor to amend the effective registration filed at the Commission upon the occurrence of any material change. Virginia defines "material change" to include any fact, circumstance, or condition that would have a substantial likelihood of influencing a reasonable prospective franchisee in making a decision related to the purchase of a franchise.

Washington

Washington is a registration state that requires a supplemental report to be filed as soon as reasonably possible (and in any case before the further sale of any franchise) if a material adverse change occurs in the condition of the franchisor or subfranchisor or any material change occurs in the information contained in its offering circular. Because the terms "material adverse change" and "material change" are not defined, the definition of material change used in nonregistration states should be consulted.

Wisconsin

Wisconsin is a registration state that requires a franchisor to amend its registration in writing with the Division of Securities within thirty days after any material event that affects a registered franchise by an application to amend the registration statement. As defined in Wisconsin, the terms "material event" and "material change" include, but are not limited to, the following:

1. The termination, closing, or failure to renew during any three-month period of (1) the greater of 1 percent or five of all franchises of a franchisor regardless of location or (2) the lesser of 15 percent or two of the franchises of a franchisor located in the state of Wisconsin.

2. Any change in control, corporate name, or state of incorporation, or reorganization of the franchisor, whether or not the franchisor or its parent, if the franchisor is a subsidiary, is required to file reports under Section 12 of the Securities Exchange Act of 1934.

3. The purchase by the franchisor in excess of 5 percent of its existing franchises during any three-month period on a running basis.

4. The commencement of any new product, service, or model line involving, directly or indirectly, additional investment by any franchisee or the discontinuation or modification of the marketing plan or system of any product or service of the franchisor where the total sales from such product or service exceed 20 percent of the gross sales of the franchisor on an annual basis.

5. An adverse financial development involving the franchisor or the franchisor's parent company, controlling person, or guarantor of the franchisor's obligations. In this paragraph, *adverse financial development* includes, but is not limited to either:

   ◆ The filing of a petition under federal or state bankruptcy or receivership laws
   ◆ A default in payment of principal, interest, or sinking fund installment on indebtedness that exceeds 5 percent of total assets that is not cured within thirty days of the default

Special Topics in Compliance: Advertising Regulations

Certain states have enacted laws that regulate the use of advertising by a franchisor that is directed at prospective franchisees. Many of these states require the filing and approval of these advertising and marketing materials prior to their use. Below is a discussion of those states with special provisions that must be built into the overall compliance program.

◆ *California.* No advertisement offering a franchise may be published in California unless a true copy of the advertisement has been filed in the office of the California Commissioner of Corporations at least three business days prior to the first publication or unless such advertisement has been exempted by rule of the Commissioner. In addition, all advertising must contain the following legend (in not less than ten-point type):

THESE FRANCHISES HAVE BEEN REGISTERED UNDER THE FRANCHISE INVESTMENT LAW OF THE STATE OF CALIFORNIA. SUCH REGISTRATION DOES NOT CONSTITUTE APPROVAL, RECOMMENDATION OR ENDORSEMENT BY THE COMMISSIONER OF CORPORATIONS NOR A FINDING BY THE COMMISSIONER THAT THE INFORMATION PROVIDED HEREIN IS TRUE, COMPLETE AND NOT MISLEADING.

♦ *Illinois.* In June of 1998, Illinois repealed its requirement for the filing of advertising materials.

♦ *Indiana.* A copy of any advertising the franchisor intends to use in Indiana must be filed in the Office of the Indiana Securities Commissioner at least five days prior to the first publication of such advertising.

♦ *Maryland.* A franchisor may not publish any advertisement offering a franchise unless the advertisement (in duplicate) has been filed with the Securities Commissioner in the Office of the Attorney General at least seven business days before the first publication of the advertisement. An advertisement may not be used unless and until it has been cleared for use by the Division of Securities.

♦ *Michigan.* The Michigan Department of the Attorney General may by rule or order require an advertisement to be filed that is addressed or intended to be distributed to prospective franchisees, as well as any other sales literature or advertising communication having the same purpose.

♦ *Minnesota.* The franchisor must file one true copy of any advertisement proposed for use in Minnesota with the Office of the Commissioner of Commerce at least five business days before the first publication thereof. If not disallowed by the Commission within five business days from the date filed, the advertisement may be published.

♦ *New York.* All sales literature must be submitted to the New York Department of Law at least seven days prior to its intended use. The franchisor must verify, in writing submitted with the sales literature, that it is not inconsistent with the filed prospectus. All sales literature must contain the following statement (in easily readable print) on the cover of all circulars, flyers, cards, letters, and other literature intended for use in New York:

> This advertisement is not an offering. An offering can only be made by a prospectus filed first with the Department of Law of the State of New York. Such filing does not constitute approval by the Department of Law.

In all classified-type advertisements, not more than five inches long and no more than one column of print wide, and in all broadcast advertising thirty seconds or less in duration, the following statement may be used in lieu of the statement provided above:

> This offering is made by prospectus only.

◆ *North Dakota.* The franchisor must file a true copy of any advertisement proposed for use in the state with the Office of the Commissioner of Securities at least five business days before the first publication.

◆ *Oklahoma.* All sales literature and advertising must be filed with the Administrator and approved prior to use. A filing shall include the sales literature and advertising package, a review fee of $25, and a representation by the seller that reads substantially as follows:

> I,_____, hereby attest and affirm that the enclosed sales literature or advertising package contains no false or misleading statements or misrepresentations of material facts and that all information contained therein is in conformity with the most recent disclosure document relating to the particular business opportunity offered thereby on file with the Administrator.

◆ *Rhode Island.* No advertisements may be published in Rhode Island unless a true copy of the advertisement and required filing fee have been filed in the Office of the Director of Business Regulations at least five business days prior to its first publication.

◆ *South Dakota.* The franchisor must file two true copies of any advertisement offering a franchise subject to the registration requirements of South Dakota law with the Office of the Director of the

Division of Securities at least three business days prior to the first publication.

◆ *Washington.* The franchisor must file one true copy of any advertisement offering a franchise subject to the registration requirements of Washington law with the Office of the Director of Licensing at least seven days before publication.

6

Structuring Franchise Agreements, Area Development Agreements, and Related Documents

The principal document that sets forth the binding rights and obligations of each party to the franchise relationship is known as the franchise agreement. The franchise agreement contains the various provisions binding on the parties for the life of their relationship and therefore must maintain a delicate balance of power. On one hand, the franchisor must maintain enough control in the franchise agreement to enforce uniformity and consistency throughout the system, yet at the same time be flexible enough to anticipate changes in the marketplace and modifications to the franchise system and to meet the special considerations or demands resulting from the franchisee's local market conditions.

The franchise agreement can and should reflect the business philosophy of the franchisor and set the tenor of the relationship. A well-drafted franchise agreement reflects the culmination of literally thousands of business decisions and hundreds of hours of strategic planning, market research, and customer testing. The length, term, and complexity of the franchise agreement will (and should) vary from franchisor to franchisor and from industry to industry. Many start-up franchisors make the critical mistake of "borrowing" terms from a competitor's franchise agreement. Such a practice can be detrimental to the franchisor and the franchisee because the agreement will not accurately reflect the actual dynamics and financial realities of the relationship.

Early-stage franchisors should resist the temptation to copy from the franchise agreement of a competitor or to accept the "standard form and boilerplate" from an inexperienced attorney or consultant. The relationship between the franchisor and franchisee is far too complex to accept such compromise in the preparation of such a critical document.

There is a wide variety of drafting styles and practices among those attorneys who regularly practice in the area of franchise law. Some franchise lawyers prefer to "roll everything" into a single agreement (which can result in quite a behemoth), while others prefer to address the equipment leases, product purchasing requirements, personal guaranty, site development obligations, security interests, options for assignment of leases, and other key aspects of the relationship in "supplemental agreements" that are separate from the actual franchise agreement. The advantage to this latter approach, which I have come to appreciate over the years, is that the franchisee and its counsel are not overwhelmed (or intimidated) by the complexity and depth of a single document. This chapter examines the key elements of a basic franchise agreement and then turns to some of the various supplemental agreements that further define the long-term rights and obligations of the franchisor and franchisee. Figure 6-1 presents some initial general tips for the negotiation of franchise agreements.

Figure 6-1. Tips for the negotiation of franchise agreements.

There are two distinct philosophies among franchise marketing representatives: "No negotiations" represents the disciplined camp of representatives who fear reprimand from the franchisor's sales director and outside legal counsel, and "everything's negotiable" represents the camp whose representatives fear the wrath of their spouses if there is no sales commission revenue to pay the monthly mortgage. Neither camp represents the proper approach in franchise sales and franchise agreement negotiation. The franchise agreement is not to be presented as a "contract of adhesion." It is within the human nature of the prospective franchisee (and its legal counsel) to request and expect some degree of negotiation of the franchise agreement. This must be balanced against the need for both uniformity and consistency throughout the franchise system as well as the material change rules (which trigger an amendment to the offering circular) as discussed in Chapter 5. Certain states, such as New York and California, have developed strict regulations that govern the negotiations of franchise agreements. Each request by the prospective franchisee to modify a key term of the franchise agreement should be carefully considered from an economic and quality control perspective, as well as be reviewed by franchise counsel in order to identify potential legal problems and disclosure obligations.

Key Elements of the Basic Single-Unit Franchise Agreement

Regardless of size, stage of growth, industry dynamics, or specific trends in the marketplace, all basic single-unit franchise agreements should address the key topics discussed below.

◆ *Recital.* The recital or preamble of the franchise agreement essentially sets the stage for the discussion of the contractual relationship. This section provides the background information regarding the development and ownership of the proprietary rights of the franchisor that are being licensed to the franchisee. The preamble should always contain at least one recital specifying the obligation of the franchisee to operate the business format in strict conformity with the operations manual and quality control standards provided by the franchisor.

◆ *Grant, term, and renewal.* The typical initial section of the franchise agreement is the grant of a franchise for a specified term. The length of the term is influenced by a number of factors including market conditions, the franchisor's need to periodically change certain material terms of the agreement, cost of the franchise and the franchisee's expectations in relation to start-up costs, length of related agreements necessary to the franchisee's operations such as leases and bank loans, and anticipated consumer demand for the franchised goods and services. The renewal rights granted to a franchisee, if included at all, will usually be conditioned upon the franchisee being in good standing (e.g., no material defaults by the franchisee) under the agreement. Other issues that must be addressed in any provisions regarding renewal include renewal fees, obligations to execute the "then current" form of the franchise agreement, and any obligations of the franchisee to upgrade its facilities to the "latest" standards and design. The franchisor's right to relocate the franchisee, adjust the size of any exclusive territory granted, or change the fee structure should also be addressed.

◆ *Legal status of franchisee.* This section seeks to establish and confirm the arms-length legal relationship between the franchisor and franchisee, confirming the parties are not acting in the legal capacity or role of employer and employee, principal and agent, general partners, or any other status that might imply to a governmental agency or some disgruntled third party that the franchisor is anything but a licensor of intellectual property from a liability perspective. This section also attempts to avoid the characterization of the franchisee as an employee or an agent because such may make termination more difficult (in terms of the enforcement of covenants against competition, minimum notice requirements, and even the possible mandatory payment of a severance compensation) in certain countries.

◆ *Rights granted.* The franchisor grants the franchisee the right to use the intellectual property developed by the franchisor. The specific components of the intellectual property are articulated to the franchisee and its advisers, thereby defining the franchisee's expectations regarding the "value-added" to be provided by the franchisor and the scope of the license (e.g., by clarifying what is intended and what is not) and by serving as a type of due diligence for the franchisee and its advisers, evaluating the franchisor's level of preparedness for the challenges and demands of the local market.

The scope of the rights to be granted is often quite broad (though advisers to the franchisor will often say that it is wise to "underpromise" and "overdeliver" in this area) and typically includes a set of trademarks and service marks, trade dress (signage, counter design, uniforms, special design features, etc.), the know-how (usually codified in the operations manual, the initial training program, and the ongoing training and support programs), ongoing technical assistance and access to resources, and the right to manufacture or distribute the franchisor's proprietary products and/or branded merchandise.

◆ *Territory.* The size of the geographic area granted to the franchisee by the franchisor must be specifically discussed in conjunction with what exclusive rights, if any, will be granted to the franchisee with respect to this territory. These provisions address whether the size of the territory is a specific radius, city, or county and whether the franchisor will have a right to either operate company-owned locations and/or grant additional franchises within the territory. Some franchisors designate a specific territory within which market research indicates that a given number of locations could be successful without market oversaturation, and then sell that exact number of franchises, without regard to specific location selected within the geographic area. Any rights of first refusal for additional locations, advertising restrictions, performance quotas relating to territory, and policies of the franchisor with regard to territory are addressed in this part of the franchise agreement.

◆ *Site selection.* The responsibility for finding the specific site for the operation of the franchised business rests either with the franchisor or franchisee. If the franchisee is free to choose its own site, then the franchise agreement will usually provide that the decision is subject to the approval of the franchisor. Some franchisors provide significant assistance in site selection in terms of marketing and demographic studies, lease negotiations, and securing local permits and licenses, especially if a "turnkey" franchise is offered. Site selection, however, can be the most difficult aspect of being a successful franchisee, and as a result most franchisors are reluctant to take on full responsibility for this task contractually. For additional protection and control, some franchisors insist on becoming the landlord to the franchisee through a mandatory sublease arrangement once an acceptable site has been selected. A somewhat less burdensome method of securing similar protection is to provide for an automatic assignment of the lease to the franchisor upon termination of the franchise.

◆ *Services to be provided by the franchisor.* The franchise agreement should clearly delineate which products and services will be provided to the franchisee by the franchisor or its affiliates, both in terms of the initial establishment of the franchised business ("pre-opening obligations") and any continuing assistance or support services provided throughout the term of the relationship ("post-opening services"). The pre-opening obligations generally include a trade secret and copyright license for the use of the confidential operations manual, recruitment and training of personnel, standard accounting and bookkeeping systems, inventory and equipment specifications and volume discounts, standard construction, building and interior design plans, and grand opening promotion and advertising assistance. The quality and extent of the training program is clearly the most crucial pre-opening service provided by the franchisor and should include classroom as well as on-site instruction. Post-opening services provided to the franchisee on a continuing basis generally include field support and troubleshooting, research and development for new products and services, development of national advertising and promotional campaigns, and the arrangement of group purchasing programs and volume discounts.

◆ *Supplying of the products.* In most product-driven franchise systems, there is one or more proprietary products that are manufactured or controlled by the franchisor. The franchisee is under an affirmative duty to purchase these products, either for resale to the customers of the franchisee (such as ice cream) or for use by the franchisee in the delivery of the services (such as the use of proprietary cleaning materials in a home or commercial cleaning service franchise). In most jurisdictions, and subject to applicable antitrust and commercial laws, the franchisor is under a contractual or implied duty to deliver these products on a timely, high-quality basis at a reasonable price. Naturally, in a service-driven franchise system where the franchise relationship does not create a distribution channel for the franchisor's proprietary products, these provisions may not be necessary.

♦ *Franchise, royalty, and related fees payable to the franchisor and reporting.* The franchise agreement should clearly set forth the nature and amount of fees that will be payable to the franchisor by the franchisee, both initially and on a continuing basis. The initial franchise fee is usually a nonrefundable lump sum payment due upon execution of the franchise agreement. Essentially, this fee is compensation for the grant of the franchise, the trademark and trade secret license, pre-opening training and assistance, and the initial opening supply of materials, if any, to be provided by the franchisor to the franchisee.

A second category of fees is the continuing fee, usually in the form of a specific royalty on gross sales. This percentage can be fixed or be based on a sliding scale for different ranges of sales achieved at a given location. Often minimum royalty payment will be required, regardless of the franchisee's actual performance. These fees should be payable weekly and submitted to the franchisor together with some standardized reporting form for internal control and monitoring purposes. A weekly payment schedule generally allows the franchisee to budget for this payment from a cash flow perspective and provides the franchisor with an early warning system if there is a problem, as well as allowing the franchisee to react before the past due royalties accrue to a virtually uncollectible sum.

The third category of recurring fees is usually in the form of a national cooperative advertising and promotion fund. The promotional fund may be managed by the franchisor, an independent advertising agency, or even a franchisee association. Either way, the franchisor must build a certain amount of control over the fund into the franchise agreement in order to protect the company's trademarks and ensure consistency in marketing efforts.

Other categories of fees payable to the franchisor may include the sale of proprietary goods and services to the franchisee, consulting fees, audit and inspection fees, lease management fees (where the franchisor is to serve as sublessor), and renewal or transfer fees.

The obligations of the franchisee to provide periodic weekly, monthly, quarterly, and annual financial and sales reports to the franchisor should also be addressed in the franchise agreement.

◆ *Quality control.* A well-drafted franchise agreement always includes a variety of provisions designed to ensure quality control and consistency throughout the franchise system. Such provisions often take the form of restrictions on the franchisee's sources of products, ingredients, supplies, and materials, as well as strict guidelines and specifications for operating procedures. These operating procedures will usually specify standards of service, trade dress and uniform requirements, condition and appearance of the facility, hours of business, minimum insurance requirements, guidelines for trademark usage, advertising and promotional materials, accounting systems, and credit practices. Any restrictions on the ability of the franchisee to buy goods and services or requirements to purchase from a specific source should be carefully drafted within the perimeters of applicable antitrust laws. If the franchisor is to serve as the sole supplier or manufacturer of one or more products to be used by the franchisee in the day-to-day operation of the business, then such exclusivity must be justified by a product that is truly proprietary or unique.

◆ *Insurance, record keeping, and other related obligations of the franchisee.* The franchise agreement should always address the minimum amounts and types of insurance that must be carried by the franchisee in connection with its operation of the franchised businesses. Typically the franchisor is named as an additional insured party under these policies. Other related obligations of the franchisee that must be set forth in the franchise agreement include the keeping of proper financial records (which must be made available for inspection by the franchisor upon request); the obligation to maintain and enforce quality control standards with its employees and vendors; the obligation to comply with all applicable employment laws, health and safety standards, and related local ordinances; the duty to upgrade and maintain the franchisee's facilities and equipment; the obligation to continue to promote the products and services of the franchisor; the obligation to reasonably process requests by patrons for franchising information; the obligation not to produce goods and services that do not meet the franchisor's quality control specifications or that may be unapproved for offer at the franchisee's premises (such as video games at a fast-food restaurant or X-rated material at a bookstore); the obligation not to solicit customers outside its designated territory; the obligation of the franchisee personally to participate in the day-to-day operation of the franchised business (required by many but not all franchisors); and the general obligation of the franchisee to refrain from any activity that may reflect adversely on the reputation of the franchise system.

◆ *Protection of intellectual property and covenants against competition.* The franchise agreement should always contain a separate section on the obligations of the franchisee and its employees to protect against misuse or disclosure of the trademarks and trade secrets being licensed. The franchisor should provide for a clause that clearly sets forth that the trademarks and trade names being licensed are the exclusive property of the franchisor and that any goodwill is established to the sole benefit of the franchisor. It should also be made clear that the confidential operations manual is "on loan" to the franchisee under a limited use license, and that the franchisee or its agents are prohibited from the unauthorized use of the trade secrets both during and after the term of the agreement. To the extent that such provisions are enforceable in local jurisdictions, the franchise agreement should contain covenants against competition by a franchisee, both during the term of the franchise agreement and following termination or cancellation.

◆ *Termination of the franchise agreement.* One of the most important sections of the franchise agreement is the section discussing how a franchisee may lose its rights to operate the franchised business. The various "events of default" should be carefully defined and tailored to meet the needs of the specific type of business being franchised. Grounds for termination can range anywhere from the bankruptcy of a franchisee to failure to meet specified performance quotas or strictly abide by quality control standards. Certain types of violations will be grounds for termination, while other types of default will provide the franchisee with an opportunity for cure. This section should address the procedures for notice and opportunity to cure, as well as the alternative actions that the franchisor may pursue to enforce its rights to terminate the franchise agreement. Such clauses must be drafted in light of certain state regulations that limit franchise terminations to "good cause" and have minimum procedural requirements. The obligations of the franchisee upon default and notice of termination must also be clearly spelled out, such as the duty to return all copies of the operations manuals, pay all past-due royalty fees, and immediately cease using the franchisor's trademarks.

◆ *Miscellaneous provisions.* As with any well-prepared business agreement, the franchise agreement should include a notice provision, a governing law clause, severability provisions, an integration clause, and a provision discussing the relationship of the parties. Some franchisors may want to add an arbitration clause, a "hold harmless" and indemnification provision, a reservation of the right to injunctions and other forms of equitable relief, specific representations and warranties of the franchisee, attorney's fees for the prevailing party in the event of dispute, and even a contractual provision acknowledging that the franchisee has reviewed the agreement with counsel and has conducted an independent investigation of the franchise and is not relying on any representations other than those expressly set forth in the agreement.

An Overview of Some Sample Supplemental Agreements Commonly Used in Franchising

In addition to the franchise agreement, there is a wide variety of other contracts that may be necessary to govern the rights and the obligations of the franchisor and franchisee. These include:

◆ *General release.* The general release should be executed by all franchisees at the time of renewal of their franchise agreement and/or at the time of a transfer of the franchise agreement or their interest in the franchised business. The document serves as a release by the franchisee of the franchisor from all existing and potential claims that the franchisee may have against the franchisor. In recent years, however, some courts have restricted the scope of the release if it is executed under duress or where its effect will run contrary to public policy.

◆ *Personal guaranty.* For a wide variety of tax and legal purposes, many franchisees want to execute the franchise agreement in the name of a closely held corporation that has been formed to operate the franchised business. Under the circumstances, it is highly recommended that each shareholder of the franchise corporation be personally responsible for the franchisee's obligation under the franchise agreement. A sample personal guaranty, specially designed for multiple shareholders, is found in Figure 6-2.

Figure 6-2. Sample personal guaranty for multiple shareholders.

In consideration of, and as an inducement to, the execution of the foregoing Franchise Agreement ("Agreement") dated _____, ___, 19___ by Franchisor, each of the undersigned Guarantors, as shareholders of XYZ corporation, agrees as follows:

1. The Guarantors do hereby jointly and severally unconditionally guarantee the full, prompt, and complete performance of the Franchisee under the Agreement of all the terms, covenants, and conditions of the Agreement, including without limitation the complete and prompt payment of all indebtedness to Franchisor under the Agreement and any revisions, modifications, and amendments thereto (hereinafter collectively referred to as the "Agreement"). The word indebtedness is used herein in its most comprehensive sense and includes without limitation any and all advances, debts, obligations, and liabilities of the Franchisee, now or hereafter incurred, either voluntarily or involuntarily, and whether due or not due, absolute or contingent, liquidated or unliquidated, determined or undetermined, or whether recovery thereof may be now or hereafter barred by any statute of limitation or is otherwise unenforceable.

2. The obligations of the Guarantors are independent of the obligations of Franchisee and a separate action or actions may be brought and prosecuted against the Guarantors, or any of them, whether or not actions are brought against the Franchisee or whether the Franchisee is joined in any such action.

3. If the Franchisee is a corporation or partnership, Franchisor shall not be obligated to inquire into the power or authority of the Franchisee or its partners or the officers, directors, or agents acting or purporting to act on the Franchisee's behalf and any obligation or indebtedness made or created in reliance upon the exercise of such power and authority shall be guaranteed hereunder. Where the Guarantors are corporations or partnerships, it shall be conclusively presumed the Guarantors and the partners, agents, officers, and directors acting on their behalf have the express corporations or partnerships and that such corporations or partnerships have the express power to act as the Guarantors pursuant to this Guaranty and that such action directly promotes the business and is in the interest of

such corporations or partnerships.

4. Franchisor, its successors, and assigns, may from time to time, without notice to the undersigned (a) resort to the undersigned for payment of any of the liabilities, whether or not it or its successors have resorted to any property securing any of the liabilities or proceeded against any other of the undersigned or any party primarily or secondarily liable on any of the liabilities; (b) release or compromise any liability of any of the undersigned hereunder or any liability of any party or parties primarily or secondarily liable on any of the liabilities; and (c) extend, renew, or credit any of the liabilities for any period (whether or not longer than the original period); alter, amend, or exchange any of the liabilities; or give any other form of indulgence, whether under the Agreement or not.

5. The undersigned further waives presentment, demand, notice of dishonor, protest, nonpayment, and all other notices whatsoever, including without limitation: notice of acceptance hereof; notice of all contracts and commitments; notice of the existence or creation of any liabilities under the foregoing Agreement and of the amount and terms thereof; and notice of all agreement or otherwise, and the settlement, compromise, or adjustment thereof.

6. In the event any dispute between the Franchisor and the Guarantors cannot be settled amicably, the parties agree said dispute shall be settled in accordance with the Commercial Rules of the American Arbitration Association. The Arbitration shall be held at the Franchisor's headquarters in [*franchisor's headquarters*]. The undersigned agrees to pay all expenses paid or incurred by Franchisor in attempting to enforce the foregoing Agreement and this Guaranty against Franchisee and against the undersigned and in attempting to collect any amounts due thereunder and hereunder, including reasonable attorneys' fees if such enforcement or collection is by or through an attorney-at-law. Any waiver, extension of time, or other indulgence granted from time to time by Franchisor or its agents, successors, or assigns, with respect to the foregoing Agreement, shall in no way modify or amend this Guaranty, which shall be continuing, absolute, unconditional, and irrevocable.

7. This Guaranty shall be enforceable by and against the respective administrators, executors, successors, and assigns of the Guarantors and the death of a Guarantor shall not terminate the liability of such Guarantor or limit the liability of the other Guarantors hereunder.

8. If more than one person has executed this Guaranty, the term "the undersigned," as used herein shall refer to each such person, and the liability of each of the undersigned hereunder shall be joint and several and primary as sureties.

(continues)

Figure 6-2. *(continued)*

IN WITNESS WHEREOF, each of the undersigned has executed this Guaranty under seal effective as of the date of the foregoing Agreement.

_____
Signature

_____
Printed Name

_____
Home Address

_____
Home Telephone

_____
Business Address

_____
Business Telephone

_____
Date

◆ *Sign lease agreement.* There is a wide variety of reasons why a franchisor may want to separately lease the signage bearing its trademarks to the franchisee. Aside from the additional rental income, the sign lease should contain cross-default provisions that allow the franchisor to immediately remove the signs upon termination of the franchisee. The sign lease agreement sets forth the specific rental terms and conditions to which the franchisee is bound. A sample sign lease agreement is found in Figure 6-3.

(text continues on page 135)

Figure 6-3. Sample sign lease agreement.

SIGN LEASE AGREEMENT

THIS AGREEMENT made this day of _____, by and between FRANCHISOR, a corporation organized under the laws of the State of _____, with its principal offices at [*address of headquarters*] (hereinafter referred to as "Franchisor"); and with its principal offices at _____ (hereinafter referred to as "Franchisee").

WITNESSETH:

WHEREAS, on _____, ___, 19___, Franchisor and Franchisee entered into a written Franchise Agreement by the terms of which Franchisee has been licensed to operate a ["Center"] to be operated in accordance with Franchisor's System and Proprietary Marks at the premises located at and has a valid lease for possession of, or has title to, said premises for that purpose; and

WHEREAS, the Franchisee is desirous of leasing certain building, window, and street signage (collectively "the Signage") for advertising and identifying the Center from the Franchisor for use at the Center.

NOW, THEREFORE, in consideration of the mutual covenants herein contained, it is mutually agreed as follows:

1. *Lease of Signs.* Franchisor hereby leases and rents Franchisee the Signage (which is more particularly described in Appendix "A" attached hereto and incorporated herein by this reference). The Signage shall be erected and used only at the premises of and in the operation of the Center as described herein.

2. *Title to Signs.* The parties acknowledge and agree that title to the Signage leased under this Agreement is in the Franchisor and the Signage shall always remain the property of Franchisor or its successors, assignees, or designees herein.

3. *Security Deposit and Rental.* Franchisee shall pay a security deposit of ___ Dollars ($___) to Franchisor, as collateral to secure the care and maintenance of the Signage, upon the execution of this Agreement. Franchisee shall thereafter pay to the Franchisor as and for rent for the use of the Signage ___ Dollars ($___) per year, payable monthly in advance, the first payment of ___ Dollars ($___) to be made upon delivery of the Signage and each subsequent payment shall be made not later than the tenth day of each month thereafter together with any and all payments due to Franchisor pursuant to said Franchise Agreement. Any default in the payment of rent for the Signage shall be treated in the same manner as a default in the payment of franchise or royalty fees, except that the remedy provided in Paragraph Six (6) or Nine (9) below shall be in addition to and not in lieu of any other remedy available to the Franchisor under any other document for such default in payment of fees or royalties.

(continues)

Figure 6-3. *(continued)*

4. *Term.* The term of this Agreement shall commence at the time that the Signage is installed and shall continue for such period of time as Franchisee shall maintain and operate a Center at the premises described herein.

5. *Installation and Maintenance.* All Signage shall be installed by Franchisee at its expense pursuant to the plans and specifications of Franchisor. Franchisee shall not remove the Signage without first receiving written permission from Franchisor. Franchisee shall secure the necessary public permits and private permission to install all Signage. Franchisee shall pay the cost, if any, of such permits and shall comply with all laws, orders, and regulations of federal, state, and local authorities. Franchisee shall be responsible for all repair and maintenance of the Signage as may be required from time to time and as may be specified by Franchisor. Franchisee shall pay all taxes and assessments of any nature that may be assessed against or levied upon the Signage before the same become delinquent.

6. *Right of Entry and/or Repossession.* If, for any reason, Franchisee should be in default of its obligations hereunder, its obligations under the Franchise Agreement, its obligations under the lease of the premises described herein, or any stipulation executed by Franchisee, Franchisor shall have the right to enter upon the premises of the Center at any hour to take possession of the Signage leased hereunder without liability therefor. Franchisee agrees that Franchisor shall not be required to obtain prior permission to enter upon the premises and remove the Signage. Franchisee hereby grants Franchisor the limited power of attorney to obtain an order and judgment in Franchisor's behalf in any court of competent jurisdiction that orders and authorizes the entry of Franchisor on the premises and the removal of the Signage. Franchisee further agrees that if Franchisor is forced to resort to this procedure by any interference with the Franchisor's rights hereunder or for any other reason, Franchisee shall pay all attorneys' fees and other costs associated with Franchisor's obtaining such order and judgment on its behalf. Franchisee further agrees to reimburse Franchisor for any costs or expenses incurred in connection with any such removal or detachment. Franchisee shall be liable and hereby assumes responsibility for any damage done to the building, premises, or the Signage as a result of the removal thereof.

7. *Repairs.* The Franchisee shall keep the Signage in the same condition as when delivered and shall make all necessary repairs in order to maintain such condition. The Franchisee shall be responsible for any damage to the Signage and shall pay the Franchisor at Franchisor's option the current replacement cost of the Signage if destroyed or the cost of repairing the damage. If the Franchisee shall fail to make any necessary repairs, Franchisor shall have the right to repair the Signage on the premises, or off the premises if Franchisor resorts to its repossession under Paragraph Six (6) for the purpose of repairing the Signage. Franchisee shall pay to the Franchisor the cost of such repairs or the current replacement cost, to be paid in one lump sum along with the next royalty payment that becomes due under the Franchise Agreement. Franchisee agrees that his rental fee obligations under Paragraph Two (2) for the term hereof shall continue even though the Signage is damaged or destroyed. Franchisee shall not make any alterations or additions to the Signage without the prior written consent of Franchisor.

8. *Transfers or Encumbrances.* Franchisee shall not pledge, loan, mortgage, or part with possession of the Signage or attempt in any other manner to dispose of or remove the Signage from the present location or suffer any liens or legal process to be incurred or levied thereupon.

9. *Default.* The occurrence of any of the following shall constitute an event of default hereunder:
   (a) Failure of Franchisee to pay when due any installment of rent hereunder or any other sum herein required to be paid by Franchisee; and
   (b) Franchisee's failure to perform any other covenant or condition of this Agreement or the Franchise Agreement or any stipulations thereunder.

   Any default hereunder shall constitute and be considered a default of the Franchise Agreement, wherefor Franchisor shall be entitled to the enforcement of any and all rights under said Franchise Agreement or this Agreement.

10. *Warranties and Insurance.* Franchisor, upon written request of Franchisee, shall assign and transfer to Franchisee without recourse all assignable or transferable manufacturer's warranties, if any, which Franchisor may have with respect to the Signage. Franchisee agrees and acknowledges that Franchisor has made no representations or warranties, either express or implied, with respect to the Signage. Franchisee hereby assumes any and all risk and liability for the Signage

(continues)

Figure 6-3. *(continued)*

including but not limited to the possession, use, operation, and maintenance thereof; injuries or death to person; and damage to property however arising or damage or destruction of the Signage however arising therefrom. Franchisee, at its own expense, shall carry adequate liability insurance coverage on the Signage, naming the Franchisor and Franchisee as named insureds, affording protection from and against damages, claims, and expenses however caused and shall provide Franchisor a copy of said insurance policy upon request.

11. *Return.* Upon termination of this Agreement, the Franchisee shall at its own expense return the Signage to the Franchisor at the Franchisor's place of business in the same condition as when received, less ordinary wear and tear. If Franchisee fails to return the Signage, the Franchisor may, by his agents, take possession of the Signage, with or without process of law, and for this purpose may enter upon any premises of the Franchisee without liability and remove all or any of the Signage in the manner provided in Paragraph Six (6) above. Franchisee shall pay to Franchisor and any third parties all costs and expenses incurred in connection with such removal.

12. *Joint Liability; Gender.* If there be more than one person comprising the party designated as Franchisee, then all reference in this Agreement shall be deemed to refer to each such person jointly and severally, and all such persons shall be jointly and severally liable hereunder. Words of any gender used in this Agreement shall be construed to mean corresponding words of any other gender, and words in the singular number shall be construed to mean corresponding words in the plural, when the context so requires.

13. *Successors.* All terms and conditions of this Agreement shall be binding upon the successors, assignees, and legal representatives of the respective parties hereto.

IN WITNESS WHEREOF, the parties, intending to be legally bound hereby, have signed this Agreement and affixed their seals on the day and year above written.

WITNESS: FRANCHISOR:

_____   _____

                                              FRANCHISEE:

_____   _____

◆ *Site selection addendum to the franchise agreement.* A site selection addendum to the franchise agreement should be executed at the time that a *specific site* within the geographic area established in the franchise agreement has been secured for the retail unit. The addendum will modify the initial designation of the territory initially agreed to at the time the franchise agreement is signed.

◆ *Option for assignment of lease.* The option for assignment of lease agreement provides the franchisor with the option, exercisable upon the termination of the franchisee for any reason, to be substituted as the tenant under the franchisee's lease with its landlord for the premises on which the franchisee's center is located.

◆ *Employee noncompetition and nondisclosure agreement.* This agreement should be executed by all employees of the franchisee. This agreement ensures that all information disclosed to said employees will be kept confidential and also imposes noncompetition restriction on employees of the franchisee.

◆ *Acknowledgment of receipt of franchise offering circular and franchise agreement.* This document should be executed at the time that the franchisor releases a franchise offering circular and franchise agreement to a prospective franchisee for his or her review and consideration. It serves as an acknowledgment of receipt and notifies prospective franchisees that the documents remain the property of the franchisor and contain trade secrets that are confidential and must be treated as such.

◆ *Special disclaimer.* This document should be initialed and signed by the franchisee at the time of closing. It serves as a written acknowledgment that no earnings claims, representations, or warranties not contained in the offering circular have been made by the franchisor or relied upon by the franchisee. It also serves as an acknowledgment that the proper offering circular and related documents were provided to the franchisee on a timely basis.

◆ *Inventory purchase agreement.* The inventory purchase agreement defines the rights and obligations between the franchisor and the franchisee with respect to the purchase of certain items of inventory, supplies, and other items available for purchase through the franchisor or its affiliates. A sample inventory purchase agreement is found in Figure 6-4.

(text continues on page 140)

Figure 6-4. Sample inventory purchase agreement.

INVENTORY PURCHASE AGREEMENT

THIS AGREEMENT is made and entered into this _____ day of _____ by and between [*name of franchisor*], an _____ corporation, (the "Franchisor"), and _____ (the "Purchaser").

W I T N E S S E T H:

WHEREAS, Franchisor has attained prominence in the industry and through its techniques and methods has developed numerous products;

WHEREAS, Purchaser entered into a Franchise Agreement with Franchisor, on _____, 19___ by the terms of which Purchaser as Franchisee has been granted the right and license to operate a (the "Center");

WHEREAS, Purchaser is obligated by the terms of the Franchise Agreement to purchase certain merchandise, products, and other supplies (the "Products") solely from Franchisor or its approved suppliers;

WHEREAS, Purchaser has agreed to maintain Franchisor's uniformly high standards of quality for its products and services, which Purchaser acknowledges to be critical to the Franchisor's positive image and the protection of Franchisor's goodwill, and which, if not maintained, would result in irreparable harm to the Franchisor and the Purchaser; and

WHEREAS, Purchaser desires to purchase from Franchisor and Franchisor desires to sell to Purchaser certain merchandise, products, and supplies to be used in connection with its operation of the Center.

NOW, THEREFORE, in consideration of the mutual promises, covenants, and conditions contained herein and for other good and valuable consideration, the receipt and sufficiency of which is hereby acknowledged, the parties agree as follows:

1. *Orders.* Orders for Products placed by Purchaser with Franchisor shall be subject to acceptance by Franchisor and Franchisor reserves the right to wholly or partially accept or reject any order placed by Purchaser. Franchisor also reserves the right to limit the amount of credit it will extend to Purchaser, to suspend shipments, to make shipments only after all prior orders shipped to Purchaser have been paid in full, to make shipments on a cash in advance or C.O.D. basis or on any other terms that Franchisor in its discretion deems to be appropriate.

2. *Price.* Franchisor agrees to sell the Products to Purchaser at the prices set forth in the Price Schedule attached hereto as Exhibit A and incorporated herein by this reference. The Price Schedule may be changed by Franchisor from time to time in the normal course of business. Any lists of suggested retail prices that Franchisor may provide to Purchaser for the sale of the Products to its customers shall be nothing more than suggested prices. Purchaser shall be free to set its prices for resale as it sees fit. Franchisor, in its sole discretion, shall make price adjustments in accordance with then current market conditions.

3. *Payments.* Purchaser shall submit full payment for its orders and all shipping and handling charges at the time that said order is submitted to the Franchisor in accordance with the Price Schedule attached as Exhibit A, which may be amended from time to time by the Franchisor. Purchaser agrees to pay Franchisor for all orders pursuant to Franchisor's then current payment terms and policies, which terms and policies may be changed by Franchisor from time to time in its sole discretion without incurring any liability to Purchaser.

4. *Security Interest.* In order to secure prompt payment of all amounts due to Franchisor hereunder, the Purchaser grants Franchisor a security interest in Purchaser's accounts receivable, contract rights, inventory, equipment, fixtures, personal property, and all other assets whether now owned or hereafter acquired. Purchaser agrees to execute a Security Agreement and such financing statements as may be required under the Uniform Commercial Code in order to secure Franchisor's interest in the aforementioned assets of Purchaser.

5. *Delivery.* Franchisor understands that time is of the essence in the fulfillment of orders submitted by Purchaser and will make a good faith effort to fill all orders in a timely manner. Franchisor shall not be responsible for delays or failures in manufacture or delivery, due to any cause beyond its control.

6. *Warranties.* Franchisor hereby assigns to Purchaser, when such assignment may be made, each and every warranty for Products manufactured or supplied by others which is provided to Franchisor. Franchisor makes no other warranty of any nature concerning the Products supplied to Purchaser. FRANCHISOR MAKES NO OTHER WARRANTY, EXPRESSED, STATUTORY, OR IMPLIED, INCLUDING ANY WARRANTY OF FITNESS FOR A PARTICULAR PURPOSE OR WARRANTY OF MERCHANTABILITY. FRANCHISOR

(continues)

Figure 6-4. *(continued)*

SHALL HAVE NO OTHER LIABILITY NOR DOES IT AFFIRM ANY REPRESENTATION BEYOND THE DESCRIPTION SET FORTH HEREIN OR ON THE LABEL OF ANY PRODUCT. Franchisor may, at its option, issue a credit to the Purchaser for damaged or defective merchandise provided that the Purchaser returns said merchandise to Franchisor in accordance with its standards and procedures for the return of merchandise. Franchisor will issue said credit upon receipt of the damaged or defective merchandise from Purchaser. Franchisor shall not be liable for incidental, consequential, or other damages suffered by the Purchaser due to defective products.

7. *Term.* The term of this Agreement shall be the same as the term of the Franchise Agreement dated _____, 19___, by and between Purchaser and Franchisor including all renewal terms. Upon termination or expiration of this Agreement, the Purchaser must return to Franchisor, within seven (7) days, any Products in the Purchaser's possession that have been provided on a consignment basis or that have been shipped to Purchaser by Franchisor for which payment has not been received.

8. *Waiver.* The failure of either party to enforce at any time of the provisions hereof shall not be construed to be a waiver of such provisions or of the right of any party thereafter to enforce any such provisions.

9. *Assignment.* This Agreement and the rights hereunder are not assignable by Purchaser and the obligations imposed on Purchaser are not delegatable without the prior written consent of Franchisor.

10. *Modification.* No renewal hereof, or modification or waiver of any of the provisions herein contained, or any future representation, promise, or condition in connection with the subject matter hereof, shall be effective unless agreed upon by the parties hereto a signed writing.

11. *Independent Contractor.* This Agreement shall not be construed so as to characterize Purchaser as an agent, legal representative, joint venturer, partner, employee, or servant of Franchisor for any purpose whatsoever; and it is understood between the parties hereto that the Purchaser shall be an independent contractor and in no way shall Purchaser, its officers, directors, agents, or employees be authorized to make any contract, agreement, warranty, or representation on behalf of Franchisor or to create any obligation, express or implied, on behalf of Franchisor.

12. *Guaranty of Franchisee's Shareholder.* All shareholders of the Purchaser hereby undertake to guarantee the performance by the Purchaser of any and all obligations imposed upon the Purchasers under this Agreement.

13. *Notices.* Any and all Notices required or permitted under this Agreement shall be in writing and shall be personally delivered or mailed by certified or registered mail, return receipt requested, to the respective parties at the addresses set forth below, unless and until a different address has been designated by a written Notice to the other party. Notice by mail shall be deemed received five (5) days after deposit with the United States Postal Service.

14. *Entire Agreement.* This instrument contains the entire agreement between the parties. This Agreement supersedes and is in lieu of all existing agreements or arrangements between the parties relating to the Products heretofore sold or delivered to Purchaser, and with respect to any fair trade agreement that may be in existence as of the effective date hereof.

15. *Execution of Documents.* Purchaser agrees to execute any and all documents or agreements and to take all action as may be necessary or desirable to effectuate the terms, covenants, and conditions of this Agreement.

16. *Binding Effect.* This Agreement shall be binding upon the parties hereto, their heirs, executors, successors, assigns, and legal representatives.

17. *Severability.* If any provision of this Agreement or any part thereof is declared invalid by any court of competent jurisdiction, such act shall not affect the validity of this Agreement and the remainder of this Agreement shall remain in full force and effect according to the terms of the remaining provisions or part provisions hereof.

18. *Remedies.* The rights and remedies created herein shall be deemed cumulative and no one of such rights or remedies shall be exclusive at law or in equity of the rights and remedies that Franchisor may have under this Agreement or otherwise.

19. *Attorney's Fees.* If any action is instituted by any party to enforce any provision of this Agreement, the prevailing party shall be entitled to recover all reasonable attorneys' fees and costs incurred in connection therewith.

20. *Construction.* This agreement shall be governed by and construed in accordance with the laws of the State of _____.

(continues)

Figure 6-4. *(continued)*

IN WITNESS WHEREOF, the parties hereto have caused this Purchase Agreement to be executed on the day and year first above written.

ATTEST   FRANCHISOR:

                                                  By: _____
_____

Secretary
[corporate seal and notary signature]

ATTEST   PURCHASER:

                                                  By: _____
_____

Secretary
[corporate seal and notary signature]

◆ *Assignment of franchise agreement or franchised business.* This agreement is executed at the time of an assignment by a franchisee of its rights, title, and interest in the franchise agreement or the franchised business. It serves as the formal assignment agreement as well as a consent to the assignment by the franchisor and imposes certain obligations upon the franchisee (assignor) and the assignee.

◆ *Addendum to lease agreement regarding assignment.* This addendum is executed at the time of closing. It contains various provisions that must be contained in the franchisee's lease agreement for the premises on which the franchised business is located.

◆ *Special consulting agreement.* This agreement should be used in the event that the franchisor intends to provide special support services to a franchisee or assume interim control of a franchisee's facility in the event of death or disability of the franchisee.

Area Development Agreements and Subfranchising

Most franchises are sold to individual owner/operators who will be responsible for managing a single site in accordance with the franchisor's business format and quality control standards. Thus far, this chapter has addressed the context of the single-unit franchisee. However, a recent trend in franchising has been the sale of "multiple-unit franchises" to more aggressive entrepreneurs who will be responsible for the development of an entire geographic region.

The two primary types of multiple-unit franchises are (1) *subfranchisors,* who act as independent selling organizations that are responsible for the recruitment and ongoing support of franchisees within their given region, and (2) *area developers,* who have no resale rights but rather are themselves directly responsible for meeting a mandatory development schedule for their given region. There is a wide variety of variations on these two principal types of multiple-unit franchises. For example, some franchise relationships that are initially single units wind up as multiple-unit owners through the use of option agreements or rights of first refusal. Other franchisors have experimented with codevelopment rights among adjacent franchisees of a nearby territory, franchises coupled with management agreements (under circumstances where the franchisee deserves to be more passive), equity participation by franchisors in franchisees (and vice versa), employee ownership of franchisor-operated units, and codevelopment rights between the franchisor and franchisee.

As a general rule, the inclusion of multiple-unit franchises in a franchisor's development strategy allows for even more rapid market penetration and fewer administrative burdens. Often the franchisee demands the right to develop and operate multiple units. However, a wide range of legal and strategic issues must be addressed when multiple-unit franchises are included in the overall franchising program.

Structuring Area Development Agreements

The key issues in structuring an area development agreement usually revolve around the size of the territory, fees, the mandatory timetable for development, and ownership of the units. The franchisor usually wants to reserve certain rights and remedies in the event that the franchisee defaults on its development obligations. The area developer must usually pay an umbrella development fee for the region, over and above the individual initial fee that is to be due and payable as each unit becomes operational within the territory. The amount of the fee varies, depending on factors such as the strength of the franchisor's trademarks and market share, the size of the territory, and the term (and renewal) of the agreement. This development fee is essentially a payment to the franchisor that prevents the franchisor from offering any other franchises within that region (unless there is a default). Sample key provisions of the area development agreement are found in Figure 6-5.

(text continues on page 146)

Figure 6-5. Selected key provisions from a typical area development agreement.

A. *Recitals*

WHEREAS, Franchisor, as the result of the expenditure of time, skill, effort, and money, has developed and owns a unique system (hereinafter, the "System"), in connection with the development, and operation of _____ (the "Franchised Business" or "Center");

WHEREAS, the distinguishing characteristics of the System include, without limitation, unique _____ techniques; technical assistance and training in the operation, management, and promotion of the Franchised Business; specialized bookkeeping and accounting methods; and advertising and promotional programs, all of which may be changed, improved, and further developed by Franchisor;

WHEREAS, Franchisor is the owner of certain rights, title, and interest in the trade name, trademark, and service mark and such other trade names, trademarks, and service marks as are now designated (and may hereafter be designated by Franchisor in writing) as part of the System (hereinafter referred to as the "Proprietary Marks");

WHEREAS, Franchisor continues to develop, expand, use, control, and add to its Proprietary Marks for the benefit and exclusive use of itself and its franchisees in order to identify for the public the source of products and services marketed thereunder and to represent the System's high standards of quality and service;

WHEREAS, Area Developer desires to obtain the exclusive right to develop, construct, manage, and operate a series of Centers within the marketing territory specified hereunder as the "Designated Marketing Territory" (a geographic map of which is attached hereto as Exhibit "A") under the System and Proprietary Marks, as well as to receive the training and other assistance provided by Franchisor in connection therewith; and

WHEREAS, Area Developer understands and acknowledges the importance of Franchisor's uniformly high standards of quality and service and the necessity of operating the Centers in strict conformity with Franchisor's quality control standards and specifications.

B. *Grant*

1. Franchisor hereby grants to Area Developer the right and license to develop, construct, operate, and manage_____ (_____) Centers in strict accordance with the System and under the Proprietary Marks within the marketing territory ("Designated Marketing Territory") as described in Exhibit "A" attached hereto. Each Center shall be operated according to the terms of the individual Franchise Agreement with respect thereto.

2. If the Area Developer complies with the terms of this Agreement, the Development Schedule, and the individual Franchise Agreement for each Center, then Franchisor will not franchise or license others, nor will it itself directly or indirectly develop, own, lease, construct, or operate in any manner, any Centers in the Designated Marketing Territory during the term hereof.

3. This Agreement is not a franchise agreement and Developer shall have no right to use in any manner the Proprietary Marks of Franchisor by virtue hereof.

C. *Development Fee*

Area Developer shall pay to Franchisor a nonrefundable development fee of X Thousand Dollars ($X,000) per Center to be developed by Area Developer, which shall be paid upon execution of this Agreement, which fee shall be fully earned by Franchisor in consideration of its execution of the Agreement and its services and forbearance in offering franchises in the Designated Marketing Territory that is the subject of this Agreement. With respect to all Centers to be developed under this Agreement, Franchisor and Area Developer shall enter into an individual Franchise Agreement for each such Center within thirty (30) days prior to the grand opening thereof, which Agreement shall be in the form of the then current Franchise Agreement offered to new franchisees; provided, however, that the royalty fees shall remain the same as those royalty fees set forth in the individual Franchise Agreement being executed currently herewith.

D. *Development Schedule*

Area Developer shall open and continuously operate the Centers in accordance with the System and the development schedule set forth in Exhibit B (the "Development Schedule"). In the event that Area Developer opens and

(continues)

Figure 6-5. *(continued)*

operates a greater number of Centers than is required to comply with the current period of the Development Schedule, the requirements of the succeeding period(s) shall be deemed to have been satisfied to the extent of such excess number of Centers. Except as otherwise provided herein, nothing herein shall require Area Developer to open Centers in excess of the number of Centers set forth in the Development Schedule, nor shall Area Developer be precluded from opening additional franchised businesses subject to the prior approval of Franchisor.

E. *Location of Centers*

The location of each Center shall be selected by Area Developer, within the Designated Marketing Territory, subject to Franchisor's prior approval, which approval shall take into account the marketing information and report provided by Area Developer. The acquisition of any proposed site by Area Developer prior to approval of Franchisor shall be the sole risk and responsibility of Area Developer and shall not obligate Franchisor in any way to approve the same. The approval of a proposed site by Franchisor does not in any way constitute a warranty or representation by Franchisor as to the suitability of such site for location of a Center.

F. *Assignment and Ownership of the Centers*

1. *By Franchisor.* Franchisor shall have the absolute right to transfer or assign all or any part of its rights or obligations hereunder to any person or legal entity.

2. *By Area Developer*

    A. Area Developer understands and acknowledges that the rights and duties set forth in this Development Agreement are personal to Area Developer and are granted in reliance upon the personal qualifications of Area Developer. Area Developer has represented to Franchisor that Area Developer is entering into this Development Agreement with the intention of complying with its terms and conditions and not for the purpose of resale of the development and option rights hereunder.

    B. Neither Area Developer nor any partner or shareholder thereof shall, without Franchisor's prior written consent, directly or indirectly sell, assign, transfer, convey, give away, pledge, mortgage, or otherwise encumber any interest in this Agreement or in Area Developer. Any such proposed assignment occurring by operation of law or otherwise, including any assignment by a trustee in bankruptcy, without Franchisor's prior written consent shall be a material default of this Agreement.

C. If Area Developer is in full compliance with this Agreement, Franchisor shall not unreasonably withhold its approval of an assignment or transfer to proposed assignees or transferees who are of good moral character, have sufficient business experience, aptitude, and financial resources, and otherwise meet the Franchisor's then applicable standards for area developers and are willing to assume all obligations of Area Developer hereunder and to execute and be bound by all provisions of the Franchisor's then current form of Area Development Agreement for a term equal to the remaining term hereof. As a condition to the granting of its approval of any such assignee or transferee, Franchisor may require Area Developer or the assignee or transferee to pay to the Franchisor its then current transfer fee as specified in Subsection F to defray expenses incurred by the Franchisor in connection with the assignment or transfer, legal and accounting fees, credit and other investigation charges and evaluation of the assignee or transferee, and the terms of the assignment or transfer. Franchisor shall have the right to require Area Developer and its owners to execute a general release of Franchisor in a form satisfactory to Franchisor as a condition to its approval of the assignment of this Agreement or ownership of Area Developer.

G. *Change in Territory*

The parties acknowledge that the development of the Designated Marketing Territory as anticipated hereunder has been determined according to the needs of the existing individuals who constitute Area Developer's targeted market in the Designated Marketing Territory, as determined by Franchisor, as of the date of execution of this Agreement. The parties agree that if there is an increased public demand for the products and services offered by Franchisor due to an increase in the number of individuals in the Designated Marketing Territory, as may be determined by a future demographic study, Franchisor shall have the right

(continues)

Figure 6-5. *(continued)*

to demand that additional Centers be established within the Designated Marketing Territory. Area Developer shall have the right of first refusal to establish any such additional Centers deemed necessary and Franchisor agrees that such additional Centers shall be established only under the following terms and conditions:

(i) Any additional Centers shall be governed by the then current individual Franchise Agreement; and

(ii) Additional Centers will only be deemed necessary if the number of individuals in the Designated Marketing Territory increases by persons.

H. *Acknowledgments*

1. Area Developer acknowledges and recognizes that different terms and conditions, including different fee structures, may pertain to different Development Agreements and Franchise Agreements offered in the past, contemporaneously herewith, or in the future, and that Franchisor does not represent that all Development Agreements or Franchise Agreements are or will be identical.

2. Area Developer acknowledges that it is not, nor is it intended to be, a third-party beneficiary of this Agreement or any other agreement to which Franchisor is a party.

AREA DEVELOPER REPRESENTS THAT IT HAS READ THIS AGREEMENT, THE OFFERING CIRCULAR, FRANCHISE AGREEMENT, AND ALL EXHIBITS THERETO IN THEIR ENTIRETY AND THAT IT HAS BEEN GIVEN THE OPPORTUNITY TO CLARIFY ANY PROVISIONS AND INFORMATION THAT IT DID NOT UNDERSTAND AND TO CONSULT WITH AN ATTORNEY OR OTHER PROFESSIONAL ADVISER. AREA DEVELOPER UNDERSTANDS THE TERMS, CONDITIONS, AND OBLIGATIONS OF THIS AGREEMENT AND AGREES TO BE BOUND THEREBY.

Structuring Subfranchising Agreements

Subfranchising agreements present a myriad of issues that are not raised in the sale of a single-unit franchise or an area development agreement, primarily because the rewards and responsibilities of the subfranchisor differ from those of the area developer or single-unit operator. In most subfranchising relationships, the franchisor will share a portion of the initial franchise fee and ongoing royalty with the subfranchisor, in exchange for the subfranchisor assuming responsibilities within the given region. The proportions in which fees are shared usually have a direct relationship to the exact responsibilities of the subfranchisor. In addition, the subfranchisor receives a comprehensive regional operations manual that covers sales and promotions, training, and field support over and above the information contained in the operations manuals provided to the individual franchisees. The key challenge for the franchisor is whether an adequate training program has been developed not just to replicate a store but rather to literally replicate him- or herself since the subfranchisee must be trained and supported to be in a position to deliver on many obligations and services as if it were the franchisor, in the United States and particularly abroad. Some of the key issues that must be addressed in the subfranchise relationship include the following:

◆ How will the initial and ongoing franchise fees be divided between the franchisor and subfranchisor? Who will be responsible for the collection and processing of franchise fees?

◆ Will the subfranchisor be a party of the individual franchise agreements? Or will direct privity be limited to franchisor and individual franchisee?

◆ What is the exact nature of the subfranchisor's recruitment, site selection, franchising, training, and ongoing support to the individual franchisees within its region?

◆ Who will be responsible for the preparation and filing of franchise offering documents in the states where the subfranchisor must file separately?

◆ What happens if the subfranchisor defaults or files for bankruptcy? How will the subfranchisees in the region be handled?

◆ What mandatory development schedules and related performance quotas will be imposed on the subfranchisor?

◆ Will the subfranchisor be granted the rights to operate individual units within the territory? If yes, how will these units be priced?

◆ What will the subfranchisor be obligated to pay the franchisor initially for the exclusive rights to develop the territory?

- What rights of approval will the franchisor retain with respect to the sale of individual franchises (e.g., background of the candidate, any negotiated changes in the agreement, decision to terminate)?
- What rights does the franchisor reserve to modify the size of the territory or repurchase it from the subfranchisor?

A subfranchisor enters into what is typically referred to as a regional development agreement or master franchise agreement with the franchisor, pursuant to which the subfranchisor is granted certain rights to develop a particular region. The regional development agreement is *not* in itself a single-unit franchise agreement to operate any individual franchise units; rather, it grants the subfranchisor the right to award and grant franchises to individuals using the franchisor's system and proprietary marks solely for the purpose of recruitment, management, supervision, and support of individual franchisees. To the extent that the subfranchisor itself develops units, then an individual franchise agreement for each such unit must be executed. Some of the key terms, conditions, and obligations that make up the subfranchising relationship include the following:

- *Grant.* The franchisor grants the subfranchisor the right and exclusive license to develop or grant franchises for the establishment and operation of franchises in a stated geographic region for a stated term (generally ten years or more).
- *Fees.* The subfranchisor generally pays to the franchisor a development fee in exchange for the grant of the right and exclusive license to operate and sell franchises in the designated region. Typically, this development fee is paid upon execution of the regional development agreement, although it may be paid in installments.
- *Development of region.* The subfranchisor is obligated to develop and operate a franchise sales, marketing, and development program for its designated region that will include advertising and promotion of the franchisor's system, the offer and sale of franchises in the designated region, and the provision of support and assistance to franchisees in the establishment and ongoing operation of their franchises.

Traditionally, a performance schedule is set in the regional development agreement for the development of the designated region. This schedule sets forth the number of franchises the subfranchisor will be required to develop and/or sell in the designated region over the term of the agreement. Generally, if the subfranchisor fails to meet the development schedule, the franchisor may do one or more of the following:

1. Accelerate the development schedule.
2. Withdraw the territorial exclusivity granted to the sub-franchisor.
3. Redefine the designated region to encompass a smaller territory.
4. Terminate the regional development agreement.

◆ *Franchisor's obligations.* Most of the obligations of a franchisor under a franchise agreement with an individual franchisee in turn become obligations of the subfranchisor to the franchisee in a subfranchising relationship. The franchisor does typically, however, have several distinct obligations to the subfranchisor, including:

1. Provision of training
2. Provision of materials, layouts, promotional items, operations, and other manuals (sometimes including a regional development manual)
3. Overseeing the subfranchisor's operations and techniques and suggesting improvements thereto
4. Promoting the business and goodwill of the franchisor's system and proprietary marks

◆ *Subfranchisor's obligations.* By far the most extensive portion of the regional development agreement is the recitation of the subfranchisor's obligations. These obligations flow to the franchisor and to the individual franchisees in the designated region. They include the obligation to:

1. Locate and maintain an office within the designated region.
2. Submit for franchisor's prior approval all proposed advertising, promotional, and sales materials that relate to the recruitment of franchisees.

3. Offer and sell franchises only to persons/entities that meet franchisor's qualifications for experience, competence, reputation, and financial responsibility.

4. Submit to the franchisor written applications for all qualified prospective franchisees for franchisor's approval.

5. Ensure the proper execution of franchise and related agreements by the franchisee.

6. Ensure that each franchise in its designated region is developed and operated in accordance with franchisor's standards and specifications.

7. Comply with all federal and state laws and all regulations enacted by appropriate regulatory bodies with respect to the offer and sale of franchises.

8. Provide ongoing support and assistance to franchisees in the designated region, including on-site supervision, inspection, training, and provision of marketing/advertising techniques and materials.

9. Submit all periodic reports required by the franchisor.

◆ *Remuneration of the franchisor and subfranchisor.* There are three categories of remuneration involved here.

1. *Initial franchise fees paid by franchisees.* Generally, the franchisor and subfranchisor split the initial franchise fee charged to and collected from individual franchisees in the designated region. Typically, at the outset (e.g., first twenty-five franchises), the franchisor is entitled to a higher percentage of the initial franchise fee. The percentages are gradually readjusted (as an incentive to stimulate sales in the region) as more franchises are sold by the subfranchisor.

2. *Royalty fees.* In addition, the franchisor and subfranchisor share the royalty fees collected from each franchisee in the designated region. Similarly, the franchisor collects a greater percentage of said royalties at the outset (e.g., first twenty-five or so franchises sold by subfranchisor), but as more franchises are sold, the subfranchisor's percentage of royalties increases.

3. *Product sales.* The franchisor may have a business format that revolves around the sale of proprietary goods and services through the franchised distribution channel. The role of the subfranchisor, if any, in this channel must be clearly defined with respect to pricing issues, warehousing and distribution issues, warranty policies, customer training, and product support. Some franchisors will view their subfranchise relationships as regional warehouses or centralized commissaries, while other franchisors would prefer to see their subfranchisor stay focused on franchise sales and support and require only minimal responsibility from the subfranchisor with respect to product distribution and support.

The relationship between franchisor and subfranchisor is unique and somewhat complicated. If the appropriate individual is chosen for this role, the relationship can be mutually beneficial. The advantages of such a relationship to the franchisor include rapid market penetration, the delegation of obligations it would otherwise be required to fulfill to each franchisee in its network, and the ability to collect a percentage of the initial franchise fee and royalty fees from each franchisee, generally without the same level of effort that would be required in a single-unit relationship.

Managing Multiparty Franchise Relationships

The management of subfranchisor relationships by the franchisor presents a host of challenges. It is in some ways akin to a set of grandparents who disagree over how their children are raising their grandchildren. Everyone is in the same family, and a balance must be struck between the needs of the system overall to ensure that the parents are not doing anything to harm or mistreat the children against the parents' need not to feel micromanaged by the grandparents. The franchisor must create a culture where the franchisor and its team, the various subfranchisees and their teams, and each individual franchisee and its staff have unified thinking and shared objectives toward the overall goals, mission, and values of the company. These common strategic objectives and operational focus will ensure that all key parties are singing from the same prayer book and that all energies are directed at serving the needs of the customer. The franchisor must be committed to keeping technol-

Figure 6-6. Managing subfranchising relationships.

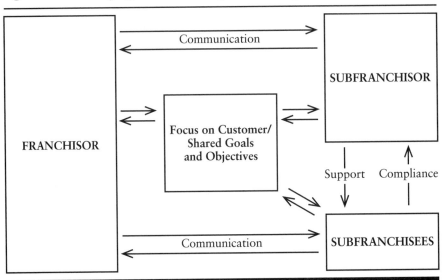

ogy-driven lines of communication open at all levels, to empowering the sub-franchisors and subfranchisees to participate in business planning and the development of shared goals, and to building systems that ensure account-ability at all levels and in all directions, as set forth in Figure 6-6.

7

Protecting Intellectual Property

At the foundation of every successful franchise system is the franchisor's intellectual property that has been developed, improved, and expanded over the years to create a unique concept, product, or service readily identifiable by consumers. The intellectual property of a franchise system consists primarily of (1) trademarks and service marks, (2) trade secrets, (3) copyrights, (4) and trade dress.

Trademarks and Service Marks

A trademark or service mark is a word, name, symbol, or device used to indicate the origin and ownership of a product or service. A trademark is used in the advertising and marketing of a product, while a service mark typically identifies a service. A trademark or service mark identifies and distinguishes the products or services of one person from those of another person.

A trademark also provides a guarantee of quality and consistency of the product or service it identifies. It assures the consumer that the products and services purchased today at one location are of the same quality as those purchased at another location. Consumer recognition of and confidence in the product or service identified by the trademark are the lifeline of a successful franchise system.

In a franchise system, the franchisor grants the franchisee a nonexclusive license to use the franchisor's trademarks in connection with the franchisee's sale of the products and services or the identification of the business that constitutes the franchise system.

Types of Marks

Not all words or phrases are entitled to trademark protection. The mark must, as a preliminary matter, identify the products or services as coming from a particular source. The goodwill and name recognition established by the franchisor is the most valuable component of the franchise for the franchisee. The mark may not, however, be generic in nature or be merely descriptive of the types of products or services it identifies. Marks that are generally protectable are coined, fanciful, arbitrary, or suggestive. In most cases, marks that are descriptive are not protectable unless certain aspects apply.

♦ *Coined, fanciful, or arbitrary.* This is the strongest category of mark that can be protected. The trademark is either a coined word, such as *Xerox,* or a word in common usage that has no meaning when applied to the goods and services in question, such as *Dove* for dish detergent or body soap. (That is, *dove* is a word for a type of bird, which has no relation to detergent or soap.) These marks are inherently distinctive for legal and registration purposes; however, as a result of the obscurity of the mark, the burden is on the manufacturer to establish goodwill.

♦ *Suggestive.* A suggestive mark requires the consumer to use some degree of imagination in determining what product or service is represented and as such is the next strongest category of mark that may be protected. Owners of suggestive trademarks are usually not required to establish "secondary meaning" (see below). Examples of suggestive marks include Seven-Up and Orange Crush, which merely suggest that they identify refreshing beverages.

♦ *Descriptive.* Trademarks that are descriptive of the goods or services they identify cannot be protected unless the manufacturer can establish distinctiveness. This requires demonstration that the public associates this particular mark with the goods of the specific producer (known as secondary meaning). This category would include names like Holiday Inn for motels, which is descriptive but nevertheless registered because it is distinctive.

The host of marks that will be refused registration include those that:

♦ Are immoral, deceptive, or scandalous.
♦ May disparage or falsely suggest a connection with persons, institutions, beliefs, or national symbols or bring them into contempt or disrepute.
♦ Consist of or simulate the flag or coat of arms or other insignia of the United States, or of a state or municipality or any foreign nation.
♦ Are the name, portrait, or signature of a particular living individual unless he or she has given written consent; or are the name, signature,

or portrait of a deceased president of the United States during the life of his widow, unless she has given her consent.

◆ So resemble a mark already registered in the U.S. Patent and Trademark Office (USPTO) as to be likely, when applied to the goods of the applicant, to cause confusion or to cause mistake or to deceive.

◆ Are primarily geographically descriptive or deceptively misdescriptive of the goods or services of the applicant

◆ Are primarily a surname.

A mark will not be refused registration on the grounds listed above if the applicant can show that, through use in commerce, the mark has become distinctive so that it now identifies to the public the applicant's products or services. Marks that are refused registration on the grounds listed above may be registered on the Supplemental Register (maintained by the USPTO), which contains terms or designs considered capable of distinguishing the owner's goods or services but which have not yet acquired secondary meaning.

Protections Afforded by Registration

Trademark rights arise from either (1) use of the mark or (2) a bona fide intention to use the mark along with the filing of an application to federally register the mark on the USPTO's Principal Register. Federal registration of a trademark under the Lanham Act is not required to protect a trademark, and a mark may be used without securing registration. However, registration does provide a number of advantages, as listed in Figure 7-1.

Figure 7-1. Advantages of registration.

---

1. The filing date of the application, a constructive date of first use of the mark in commerce, which gives the registrant nationwide priority as of that date, except as to certain prior users or prior applicants
2. The right to bring legal action in federal court for trademark infringement
3. Recovery of profits, damages, and costs in a federal court infringement action and the possibility of triple damages and attorneys' fees
4. Constructive notice of a claim of ownership (which eliminates a good faith defense for a party adopting the trademark subsequent to the registrant's date of registration)

(continues)

Figure 7-1. *(continued)*

5. The right to deposit the registration with customs in order to stop the importation of goods bearing an infringing mark
6. Prima facie evidence of the validity of the registration, registrant's ownership of the mark, and registrant's exclusive right to use the mark in commerce in connection with the goods or services specified in the certificate
7. The possibility of incontestability, in which case the registration constitutes conclusive evidence of the registrant's exclusive right, with certain limited exceptions, to use the registered mark in commerce
8. Limited grounds for attacking a registration once it is five years old
9. Availability of criminal penalties and triple damages in an action for counterfeiting a registered trademark
10. A basis for filing trademark applications in foreign countries

Registering a mark that is in actual use in commerce, but does not qualify for registration on the Principal Register, with the USPTO on the Supplemental Register does not provide the mark the same level of protection afforded by registration on the Principal Register. However, it does give the registrant:

◆ The right to sue in federal court and obtain statutory remedies for infringement
◆ A possible right to foreign registration in foreign countries whose laws require prior registration in the home country
◆ Protection against federal registration by another identical or confusingly similar mark
◆ The right to use the ® symbol on goods or with services

Registration on the Supplemental Register allows the owner of the mark to put the world on notice of his or her use and rights to the mark. Further, registration of a descriptive mark on the Supplemental Register may be advantageous for a period of time while the mark's use is increased to the point where it becomes so substantial as to acquire secondary meaning. It is at this time that the mark may qualify for registration on the Principal Register. It may be advantageous for a start-up franchisor to take advantage of registration on the Supplemental Register, if registration is denied on the Principal Register, until a few franchises are sold and the mark, through increased use, gains secondary meaning. This would bolster the marketability of the franchises much more than would an unregistered trademark licensed by the franchisor.

Overview of the Registration Process

Prior to the passage of the Trademark Law Revision Act of 1988 (TLRA), a trademark owner was only eligible for federal registration of his or her trademark if the mark had actually been used in interstate commerce. This requirement was different from that of most other countries, which generally allow a company to register a mark even if no actual use had been established. This meant that a substantial amount of time and expense might be invested in a proposed trade identity for a new product or service, with virtually no assurance that the mark could ever be properly registered and protected.

Under the TLRA, a franchisor may file an application to register a trademark based on actual use or upon a "bona fide intention" to use the mark in interstate commerce. This allows the franchisor to conduct some market research and further investigation without the need to actually put the mark into the stream of commerce as a prerequisite to filing for federal protection.

The USPTO has developed the following procedures for registration under the TLRA's "intent to use" provisions:

1. The company files application for registration, which is subject to all of the current tests for registrability (e.g., likelihood of confusion, descriptiveness). If the mark is used in interstate commerce prior to approval of the application by the examiner, an amendment to the application should be made to allege that use of the mark in interstate commerce has occurred.
2. When the application is approved by the examiner, a Notice of Allowance is issued to the applicant.
3. If actual use does not occur until after the application is approved, the applicant then has six months from the date of the Notice of Allowance to actually use the mark in interstate commerce and file a Statement of Use. The Statement of Use must be accompanied by examples of the mark as used (called specimens). Specimens may include labels evidencing use of a trademark on a product or brochures marketing services under a particular service mark. After review and approval of the Statement of Use and specimens, the mark will be registered. An applicant may request extensions of time for filing of the Statement of Use for up to four successive six-month periods. Failure to file by this deadline will result in an abandonment of the mark.

Regardless of whether a franchisor files under the "actual use" or "intent to use" provisions, an application must be prepared and filed at the USPTO for the trademark in the classification that is appropriate for the goods and services offered. A trademark examiner will then review the application to determine if it meets the statutory requirements and whether similar trademarks have already been registered in the same or similar lines of business. The examiner's concerns are usually enumerated in a formal office action. Legal counsel is then required to respond to all of the concerns of the examiner. This process continues until the application is finally either refused or recommended by the examiner for publication in the *Official Gazette,* which serves as notice to the general public. Anyone who believes that he or she would be injured by registration may file a Notice of Opposition within thirty days of publication in the *Official Gazette.* Failure of the parties to resolve any differences will result in a hearing before the Trademark Trial and Appeal Board (TTAB). The TTAB is also the appropriate body to appeal the examiner's final refusal to register.

Registration is a complex and often lengthy process (anywhere from twelve to eighteen months even if there are only minimal problems), but the commercial rewards may be substantial if the registered mark is properly used to provide the franchisor with a competitive edge. Registration under the Lanham Act is effective for ten years but may be renewed for additional ten-year terms thereafter so long as the mark is still in actual use in interstate commerce. The registration may, however, be cancelled after six years unless an affidavit demonstrating the continued use of the mark is filed with the USPTO between the fifth and sixth years of registration.

Maintaining Rights in the Trademarks

Because a trademark provides consumers with a guarantee of quality, the owner of a trademark is responsible for protecting and ensuring the quality of the products or services associated with the trademark. For a franchisor that has licensed its trademark to franchisees who are located all over the country, maintaining a certain level of quality of the products and services identified by the mark is certainly a challenge.

Along with the rights conferred as the owner of a registered trademark, there are responsibilities. The licensor/franchisor must actively police the mark to ensure that an established level of quality is maintained by its licensees/franchisees. A carefully drafted franchise/license agreement should set forth, in detail, the specific obligations of the franchisee with respect to the trademarks. The franchise/license agreement must provide the franchisor with supervisory control over the product or service that the mark represents. If such controls are not retained by the franchisor, the "naked" license of the trademarks could be found to be invalid. It is therefore imperative that a franchisor provide its franchisees with both guidelines for use of the trademarks and guidance on the level of quality and uniformity of the products and services that must be maintained.

Protecting the trademarks under the franchise agreement. Every franchise agreement should have a section devoted to the proper use and care of the franchisor's trademarks, which should at minimum stipulate the following:

- The identity of the trademarks that the franchisor licenses its franchisees to use.
- That the franchisee use only the trademarks designated by the franchisor and use them only in the manner required or authorized and permitted by the franchisor.
- That the franchisee use the marks only in connection with the right and license to operate the retail unit granted to the franchisee.
- That the franchisee identify itself as a licensee and not as the owner of the trademarks, and make any necessary filings under state law to reflect its status as a licensee; this identification must be included on all invoices, order forms, receipts, business stationery, and contracts. The franchisee must also display a notice at its locations stating its status as a licensee.
- That the franchisee's right to use the trademarks is limited to uses authorized under the franchise agreement, and any unauthorized use is an infringement of the franchisor's rights and grounds for termination of the franchise agreement.
- That the franchisee not use the license or the trademarks to incur or secure any obligation or indebtedness.
- That the franchisee not use the trademarks as part of its corporate or other legal name.
- That the franchisee comply with the franchisor's instructions and any local jurisdiction's requirements for filing and maintaining trade name or fictitious name registrations.
- That the franchisee promptly notify the franchise if it learns of any improper use of the marks.
- That the franchisee promptly notify the franchisor if litigation involving the marks is instituted or threatened against the franchisee and will cooperate fully in defending or settling such litigation.

In addition, the franchisee should be required to expressly acknowledge that:

♦ The franchisor is the owner of all right, title, and interest in the trademarks and the goodwill associated with and symbolized by them.

♦ The trademarks are valid and serve to identify the franchisor's system and those who are licensed to operate a franchise in accordance with the system.

♦ The franchisee will directly or indirectly contest neither the marks' validity nor the franchisor's ownership of the trademarks.

♦ The franchisee's use of the trademarks according to the franchise agreement does not give the franchisee any ownership interest or other interest in or to the trademarks, except a nonexclusive license.

♦ Any and all goodwill arising from the franchisee's use of the trademarks in accordance with the franchisor's system is solely and exclusively to the franchisor's benefit, and upon expiration or termination of the franchise agreement, no monetary amount will be assigned as attributable to any goodwill associated with the franchisee's use of the system or the trademarks.

♦ The license and rights to use the trademarks granted to the franchisee are nonexclusive, and the franchisor may therefore: (1) itself use the trademarks and grant franchises and licenses to others to use them; (2) establish, develop, and franchise other systems different from the one licensed to the franchisee, without offering or providing the franchisee any rights in, to, or under such other systems; and (3) modify or change, in whole or in part, any aspect of the trademarks so long as the franchisee's rights are not materially harmed.

♦ The franchisor reserves the right to substitute different names and trademarks for use in identifying the system, the franchise, and other franchised businesses operating under the franchisor's system.

♦ The franchisor has no liability to the franchisee for any senior users that may claim rights to the franchisor's trademarks.

♦ The franchisee will neither register nor attempt to register the trademarks in the franchisee's name or that of any other person, firm, entity, or corporation.

Trademark protection and quality control program. Every franchisor should develop an active trademark protection program designed to educate the franchisor's field staff, key vendors, advisers, officers, employees, and all of its franchisees as to the proper usage and protection of the trademarks. Development of a franchise agreement that imposes all of the obligations described above is a vital component of this program, but alone is insufficient to prevent misuse of the trademarks and enforce quality control standards. A Trademark Use Compliance Manual, which contains more detailed guidelines for proper trade-mark usage, grammar, and quality, also plays an important role in a successive trademark protection program. The compliance manual may comprise a section of the franchisor's operations manual and specify the following:

- ◆ Proper display of the marks (use of ®, tm, block *TM,* or *SM* symbol)
- ◆ Information and instructions regarding state filings (fictitious name registrations) required to reflect the franchisee's status as a licensee of the marks
- ◆ All documents, correspondence, and other materials on which the franchisee must display the trademarks and identify itself as a licensee
- ◆ All authorized uses of the marks and prohibited uses (e.g., they may not be used as part of a franchisee's corporate name)

In addition to a compliance manual, strategies should be developed to monitor franchisees, competitors, and other third parties in order to detect and prevent improper usage or potential infringement of the mark. A staff member of the franchisor should be designated to read trade publications, the business press, marketing materials of competitors, and in-house production, labeling, and cor-respondence to ensure that the mark is properly used by franchisees and not stolen by competitors. If an infringing use is discovered by a clipping service, company field representative, franchisee, trade association, or supplier, then the franchisor must be vigilant in its protection of the marks. This will require working closely with trademark counsel to ensure that all potential infringers receive letters demanding that such practices be immediately discontinued and infringing materials destroyed. As much evidence as possible should be gathered on each potential infringer and accurate files kept in the event that trademark infringement litigation is necessary to settle the dispute. The registrant considering litigation should carefully weigh the costs and likely result of the suit against the potential loss of goodwill and market share. It may be wiser to allocate those funds toward advertising rather than toward legal fees, especially if the likelihood of proving an actual infringement is remote.

Trademark Infringement and Dilution

The principal reason a trademark monitoring program must be maintained by every franchisor is to guard against trademark infringement or dilution. Under the Lanham Act, infringement is a demonstration by the owner of a registered mark that some third party is using a reproduction or imitation of the registered mark in connection with the offer or sale of goods and services in such a way as to be likely to cause confusion, mistake, or deception from the perspective of the ordinary purchaser.

The exact definition of the "likelihood of confusion" standard has been the source of much debate over the years. The focus has always been on whether the ordinary purchaser of the product in question is likely to be confused as to the source of origin or sponsorship. There is a wide variety of factors that the courts have listed as criteria for determining whether a likelihood of confusion exists, such as:

◆ The degree of similarity and resemblance of the infringer's marks to the registered marks (in terms of visual appearance, pronunciation, interpretation, etc.)

◆ The strength of the registered mark in the relevant industry or territory

◆ The actual or constructive intent of the infringer

◆ The similarity of the goods or services offered by the infringer and the owner of the registered mark

◆ The overlap (if any) in the distribution and marketing channels of the infringer and the owner of the registered mark

◆ The extent to which the owner of the registered mark can demonstrate that consumers were actually confused (usually demonstrated with consumer surveys and affidavits)

In addition to a federal cause of action for trademark infringement, many state trademark statutes provide owners of registered marks with an antidilution remedy. This remedy is available when a third party is using a mark in a manner that "dilutes" marks registered under the state statute or used under common law. The owner of the registered mark and the diluting party need not be in actual competition, nor must a likelihood of confusion be demonstrated. However, in order to make a claim for dilution, the trademark must have a "distinctive quality," which means that it must enjoy very strong consumer loyalty, recognition, and goodwill.

Trade Dress

Trade dress is a combination or arrangement of elements that comprise the total image of a business, usually in the context of a retail or restaurant business. Trade dress may include external building features, interior designs, signage, uniforms, product packaging, and similar features designed to build brand awareness and to distinguish one company's products or services from those of another. Trade dress may be protected by federal and state trademark laws if it has the following three characteristics:

1. A combination of features used in the presentation, packaging, or "dress" of goods and services
2. Elements, either individually or in combination, that are deemed to be nonfunctional; that is, they are an arbitrary aspect of the business used for identification, not to facilitate business operations
3. Distinctiveness of the elements that reveals to consumers the source of the goods or services being offered

For example, in the case of *Taco Cabana Int'l v. Two Pesos, Inc.,* which was affirmed by the Supreme Court, a jury found the following combination of restaurant decor features to be protectable trade dress:

♦ Interior and patio dining areas decorated with artifacts, bright colors, paintings, and murals
♦ Overhead garage doors sealing off the interior from the patio areas
♦ Festive exterior paintings having a color scheme using top border paint and neon stripes
♦ Bright-colored awnings and umbrellas
♦ A food-ordering counter set at an oblique angle to the exterior wall and communicating electronically with the food preparation and pickup areas
♦ An exposed food preparation area accented by cooking and preparation equipment visible to the consumer
♦ A condiment stand in the interior dining area proximate to the food pickup stand

This case, and others like it, suggests the increased availability of protection for nonfunctional components of a franchisor's system. The franchisor looking to enhance the strength of its image, and to gain trademark protection for its trade dress, would be wise to follow these suggestions:

♦ Adopt a combination of several features.
♦ Try to use as many unique features as possible in the combination.

♦ Avoid features that may be viewed as "functional" or necessary to better operate the business.

♦ Use the features consistently and continuously.

♦ Include trade dress features in advertising and promotional literature.

♦ Advertise as extensively as possible.

♦ Carry the "theme" of the trade dress throughout the entire business.

♦ Obtain federal registration of as many components of the trade dress as possible.

♦ Keep competitors from adopting similar combinations of features and from using features unique to your trade dress.

Trademark and trade dress rights are often the most valuable asset of a franchisor in today's competitive marketplace. The goodwill and consumer recognition that these intangible assets represent have tremendous economic value and are therefore usually worth the effort and expense to properly register and protect them. Management must also implement and support a strict trademark and trade dress compliance program that includes usage guidelines for all franchisees, as well as suppliers, service providers, and distributors.

Trade Secrets

A franchisor's advantage over its competitors is gained and maintained in large part through its trade secrets and proprietary information. A franchisor's trade secrets typically consist of its confidential formula, recipes, business format and plan, prospect lists, pricing methods, and marketing and distribution techniques.

Not all ideas and concepts are considered to be trade secrets. Courts have generally set forth three requirements for information to qualify for trade secret protection:

1. The information must have some commercial value.
2. The information must not be generally known or readily ascertainable by others.
3. The owner of the information must take all reasonable steps to maintain its confidentiality. In order to preserve legal protections for its trade secrets, a franchisor must follow a reasonable and consistent program for ensuring that the confidentiality of the information is maintained.

This presents a difficult problem in the franchising context where the franchisor, as the owner of the trade secrets, licenses sometimes hundreds (and even thousands) of people and/or companies to use its trade secrets. It is therefore important to continuously strive to maintain the confidential nature of the trade secrets in the hands of franchisees and their employees.

There are many factors, however, in addition to those discussed above, that courts have considered in deciding the extent to which protection should be afforded for trade secrets. Among those factors most often cited are:

◆ The extent to which the information is known by others outside the company

◆ The measures employed within the company to protect its secrets

◆ The value of the information, including the resources expended to develop the informatio

◆ The amount of effort that would be required by others to duplicate the effort or "reverse engineer" the technology

◆ The nature of the relationship between the alleged infringer and the owner of the trade secret

Implementing a Trade Secret Protection Program

There are some fundamental, affordable, and practical measures franchisors can readily adopt to protect the trade secrets that constitute the heart of their competitive advantage.

Steps to be taken by the franchisor and its franchisees. Even in an effort to protect trade secrets, there is such a thing as overkill. In fact, like the boy who cried wolf, if a franchisor tries to protect every aspect of its operation by classifying everything in sight as "trade secret," virtually nothing at all will likely be afforded protection when put to the test. Genuine trade secrets may be diluted if you try to protect too much.

The process of establishing a trade secret protection and compliance program should start with a "trade secret audit" to identify which information is *genuinely* confidential and proprietary. Although each franchisor has its own priorities, all types of franchised businesses should consider financial, technical, structural, marketing, engineering, and distribution documents, as well as recipes, business plans, operations manuals, and pricing techniques, to be candidates for protection. A portion of the franchisor's operations manual should identify all information the franchisor considers to be trade secrets and discuss the use and protection of those trade secrets it licenses to franchisees.

Trade secret protection must be a part of the franchisee's training program, during which a full briefing should be given on the franchisee's continuing duty and legal obligation to protect the secrets of the franchisor. Franchisees should be instructed that trade secrets should be disclosed only to employees who have a genuine need to know the information in order to perform their job. Those employees who have access to the franchisor's trade secrets should also be informed of their continuing duty and legal obligation to protect the trade secrets. For certain key employees, it may be advisable to require that the franchisee obtain a signed Confidentiality and Non-competition Agreement from them.

The critical rules of the franchisor's compliance program to which franchisees must also adhere are as follows:

◆ Ensure that adequate security measures are taken, which may include restricting access to certain proprietary documents and information (recipes, manuals); implementing log-in procedures prior to gaining access to locked desks, files, and vaults for proprietary documents; and posting signs and notices in all appropriate places.

◆ Purchase stamps to be placed on documents that are trade secrets in order to give notice to users of their proprietary status, and restrict the photocopying of these documents to limited circumstances.

◆ Designate a Trade Secret Compliance Officer to be in charge of all aspects relating to the proper care and monitoring of trade secrets.

◆ Carefully review advertising and promotional materials and press releases to protect trade secrets. Restrict access by reporters and other members of the media.

◆ Ensure that *all* key employees, marketing representatives, service providers, franchisees, prospective investors or joint venturers, customers, suppliers, or anyone else who has access to the company's trade secrets have signed a carefully prepared Confidentiality and Nondisclosure Agreement. See Figure 7-2.

(text continues on page 170)

Figure 7-2. Sample Confidentiality and Nondisclosure Agreement (for employees of a franchisee).

This AGREEMENT is made and entered into this day of _____, 19___, by and between _____, a corporation (the "Franchisee"); _____, a corporation (the "Franchisor"); and _____ ("Employee").

WITNESSETH

WHEREAS, the Franchisor and Franchisee have entered into a franchise agreement dated _____ ___, 19___, (the "Franchise Agreement"), pursuant to which Franchisee shall receive access to Confidential Information [as that term is defined in Paragraph ___ of the Franchise Agreement] and trade secrets of the Franchisor which Franchisee may, in certain instances, need to convey to Employee, in order to operate its _____ (the "Center"); and

WHEREAS, Franchisor and Franchisee desire to protect said Confidential Information and trade secrets from disclosure and unauthorized use by the Employee.

NOW, THEREFORE, in consideration of the employment of Employee by Franchisee and the mutual promises and covenants herein contained, and other valuable consideration the receipt and sufficiency of which is hereby acknowledged, the parties hereto, intending to be legally bound, hereby agree as follows:

A. *Covenant Not to Compete.*

Employee specifically acknowledges that due to its employment by Franchisee, Employee will receive valuable, specialized training and Confidential Information [as that term is defined in Paragraph ___ of the Franchise Agreement] and information regarding operational, sales and marketing methods and techniques of Franchisor and its System. Employee covenants that during the term of his employment and subject to the post-termination provisions contained herein, except as otherwise approved in writing by Franchisor, Employee shall not, either directly or indirectly, for himself or through, on behalf of, or in conjunction with any person, persons, partners, or corporation:

Figure 7-2. *(continued)*

1. Divert or attempt to divert any business, customer, or employees of the Franchisor or Franchisee to any competitor, by direct or indirect inducement or otherwise, or do or perform, directly or indirectly, any other act injurious or prejudicial to the goodwill associated with Franchisor's Proprietary Marks and the System.
2. Employ or seek to employ any person who is at that time employed by Franchisor or Franchisee, by any other franchisee or developer of Franchisor, or otherwise directly or indirectly induce such person to leave his or her employment.
3. Own, maintain, engage in, be employed by, advise, assist, invest in, franchise, or have any interest in any business which is the same as or substantially similar to that of the Franchisor or Franchisee.

Employee covenants that, except as otherwise approved in writing by Franchisor, Employee shall not, for a continuous uninterrupted period commencing upon the expiration of termination of his employment with Franchisee, regardless of the cause for termination, and continuing for ___ years thereafter, either directly or indirectly, for himself or through, on behalf of, or in conjunction with any person, persons, partnership, or corporation, own, maintain, engage in, be employed by, advise, assist, invest in, franchise, make loans to, or have any interest in any business that is the same as or substantially similar to that of the Franchisor or Franchisee and that is located within a radius of ___ miles of the Franchisee's Designated Territory, or the location of any Center operated under the System [as that term is defined in the Franchise Agreement] that is in existence on the date of termination of Employee's employment relationship with Franchisee. Employee acknowledges and agrees that these covenants will survive the termination of his employment. This Section shall not apply to ownership by Employee of less than a five percent (5%) beneficial interest in the outstanding equity securities of any publicly held corporation.

B. *Nondisclosure and Confidentiality.*

1. Franchisor and Franchisee may make available to Employee certain designated materials, operational techniques, and information pertinent to the franchise being operated by the Franchisee pursuant to the Franchisor's System and Proprietary Marks.
2. Employee acknowledges and agrees that all materials and information shall be used solely for the purposes of conducting his duties as an

employee of the Franchisee's Center.

3. Employee agrees to hold in strict trust and confidence all such materials and information that the Franchisor or Franchisee furnishes or otherwise makes available to Employee.

4. Neither the Employee nor his/her relatives, agents, or representatives will use such material or information for any purpose other than stated herein and shall not copy, reproduce, sell, reveal, or otherwise disclose any such materials and information to any persons or parties.

5. Employee shall not be subject to the restrictions imposed herein with respect to any information or data obtained by it from the Franchisor or Franchisee during his employment with Franchisee if the information or data:

(a) was known to the Employee or has been independently developed by the Employee at the time of the receipt of the proprietary materials and information thereof from the Franchisor or Franchisee; or

(b) was or hereafter is obtained by Employee from another source; however, the burden of proof shall rest on the Employee to demonstrate that such information or materials were not provided by the Franchisor or Franchisee.

C. *Not an Employment Agreement.*

Employee is being employed by Franchisee under separate arrangements that form no part of this Agreement. Franchisee is not obligated by this Agreement to continue to employ Employee for any particular time period, or under any specific terms or conditions. This Agreement does not create an employment relationship between Franchisor and Employee.

D. *Severability.*

The parties agree that each of the foregoing covenants shall be construed as independent of any other covenant or provision of this Agreement. If any or all portions of the covenants in this Section are held unreasonable or unenforceable by a court or agency having valid jurisdiction in an unappealed final decision to which Franchisor and Franchisee are parties, Employee expressly agrees to be bound by any lesser covenant subsumed within the terms of such covenant that imposes the maximum duty permitted by law, as if the resulting covenant were separately stated in and made a part of this Agreement.

Figure 7-2. *(continued)*

E. *Governing Law.*

This Agreement shall be construed in accordance with the laws of the State of ___, which law shall govern in the event of a conflict of laws.

IN WITNESS WHEREOF, the parties have signed this Agreement and affixed their seals on the day and year above written.

Employee

_____

Pro-Finders

By: _____

Franchisee

- Police the activities of former employees, suppliers, and franchisees; include post-term obligations in agreements that impose a duty on the employee to keep his or her former employer aware of his or her whereabouts.
- If trade secrets are contained on computers, use passwords and data encryption to restrict access to terminals and telephone access through modems.
- Establish controlled routing procedures for the distribution and circulation of certain documents.
- Purchase a paper shredder and use it where appropriate.
- Restrict photocopying of documents and *prohibit* photocopying of confidential operations manuals; use legends and maintain logbooks on the whereabouts of the original.
- Monitor the trade press and business journals for any news indicating a possible compromise and/or exploitation of your trade secrets by others.
- Conduct exit interviews with all employees who have had access to the franchisor's trade secrets. Remind employees of their obligations not to use or disclose confidential and proprietary data owned by the franchisor, and of the costs and penalties for doing so. In addition,

notify the future employer in writing of these obligations, especially if it is directly or indirectly competitive. Conversely, in order to avoid litigation as a defendant, remind new employees of the franchisor's trade secret policies and that they are being hired for their skills and expertise, not for their knowledge of a former employer's trade secrets.

Confidentiality provisions in the franchise agreement. An important component of the trade secret protection program is the franchise agreement. A properly drafted agreement should contain confidentiality provisions, covenants against competition (both in-term and post-termination), and obligations with respect to the use and care of the franchisor's proprietary operations manuals.

Provisions regarding the franchisor's proprietary operations manuals should contain the following:

◆ Franchisee will conduct its business in strict compliance with the operational systems, procedures, policies, methods, and requirements prescribed in the franchisor's manual(s) and any supplemental bulletins, notices, revisions, modifications, or amendments thereto.

◆ Franchisee acknowledges receipt of a copy of the franchisor's manual that has been provided on loan for the term of the franchise agreement; the franchisor should have an identifying number on each manual it distributes to franchisees.

◆ Franchisee acknowledges that the franchisor is the owner of all proprietary rights in and to the system and manual(s) and any changes or supplements to the manual(s); franchisee acknowledges that all of the information contained in the manual(s) is proprietary and confidential and franchisee shall use all reasonable efforts to maintain such information as confidential.

◆ Franchisee acknowledges, knows, and agrees that designated portions of the manual(s) are trade secrets known and treated as such by the franchisor.

◆ The trade secrets must be accorded maximum security consistent with franchisee's need to make frequent reference to them; franchisees shall strictly limit access to the manual(s) to employees who have a demonstrable and valid "need to know" the information contained therein in order to perform their position and strictly follow any provisions in the manual(s) regarding the care, storage, and use of the manual(s) and all related proprietary information; the franchisor should reserve the right to designate which employees of the franchisee shall execute confidentiality agreements, in a form provided by the franchisor.

♦ Franchisee shall not at any time, without franchisor's prior written consent, copy, duplicate, record, or otherwise reproduce in any manner any part of the manual(s), updates, supplements, or related materials, in whole or in part, or otherwise make the same available to any unauthorized person.

♦ The manual(s) at all times remain(s) the sole property of franchisor; upon the expiration or termination, for any reason, of the franchise agreement, franchisee shall return to franchisor the manual(s) and all supplements thereto.

♦ Franchisor retains the right to prescribe additions to, deletions from, or revisions to the manual(s), which shall become binding upon franchisee once mailed or otherwise delivered to franchisee; the manual(s) and any additions, deletions, or revisions thereto, shall not alter the franchisee's rights and obligations under the franchise agreement.

♦ Franchisee shall at all times ensure that its copies of the manual(s) are kept current and up-to-date, and in the event of any dispute as to the contents of the manual(s), the terms contained in the master set of the manual(s) maintained by franchisor at franchisor's headquarters shall be controlling.

♦ If one or more of the volumes comprising the manual(s) are lost, stolen, or destroyed, franchisee shall pay franchisor a nonrefundable replacement fee for replacement manual(s).

Misappropriation of Trade Secrets

The first step in protecting against the unauthorized use or misappropriation of trade secrets is to establish that those who come in contact with the information have a duty not to disclose or use it in any way not authorized and not in the best interest of the franchisor. Generally, this duty must be established and then breached before a cause of action will arise. The only exception to this rule is wrongful misappropriation by improper means such as theft or bribery, ascertained according to applicable state criminal statutes.

The simplest way to create such a duty is by agreement. In addition to the franchise agreement, the franchisor should have a written employment agreement with each of its employees who may have access to the franchisor's trade secrets. The employment agreement should contain provisions regarding the nondisclosure of proprietary information as well as covenants of nonexploitation and noncompetition, applicable both during and after the term of employment. In most states, these covenants will be upheld and enforced by a court if they are reasonable, consistent with industry norms, and not overly restrictive.

Agreements like these, as well as similar provisions in the franchise agreement, go a long way toward proving to a court that the franchisor intended to and in fact took reasonable steps to protect its trade secrets in the event of any subsequent litigation. These agreements should be only the beginning, however, of an ongoing program to make franchisees and franchisor employees mindful of their continuing duty to protect the trade secrets of the franchisor.

Proving an Act of Misappropriation

The key elements of a civil cause of action for misappropriation of trade secrets are:

1. *Existence* of a trade secret
2. *Communication* of it to the defendant
3. Misappropriation while defendant was in a *position of trust or confidence* (some duty not to disclose)
4. Information constituting the trade secrets *used* by the defendant to the *injury of the plaintiff*

In analyzing whether these essential elements are present, the court considers the following factors:

1. Was there any *relationship of trust and confidence,* either by express agreement or implied, that was breached?
2. How much time, value, money, and labor have been expended in developing the trade secret?
3. Had the trade secret reached the public domain? Through what channels?
4. Has the franchisor maintained a conscious and continuing effort to maintain secrecy (agreements of nondisclosure,

security measures, etc.)?

5. What were the mitigating circumstances surrounding the alleged breach or misappropriation?

6. What is the value of the secret to the franchisor?

Remedies for Misappropriation

The most important and immediate civil remedy available in any trade secret misappropriation case is the temporary restraining order and preliminary injunction. This remedy immediately restrains the unauthorized user from continuing to use or practice the trade secret, pending a hearing on the owner's charge of misappropriation. Prompt action is necessary to protect the trade secret from further unauthorized disclosure. If the case ever makes it to trial, the court's decision will address the terms of the injunction and may award damages and profits resulting from the wrongful appropriation of the trade secret.

Franchisors, however, should be aware that there are certain risks to evaluate before instituting a trade secret suit. The franchisor may face the risk that the trade secret at issue, or collateral trade secrets, may be disclosed during the course of the litigation. Certain federal and state rules of civil procedure and laws of evidence will protect against this risk to a limited extent. The franchisor should also consider that trade secret law is very unsettled and often turns on the facts of each case. Establishing the "paper trail" needed to prove all of the elements of misappropriation may be virtually impossible in some cases. Such lengthy litigation is likely to be prohibitively expensive for the average early-stage franchisor. This is all the more reason why preventive and protective measures are a far more attractive alternative to litigation.

Criminal Penalties for Trade Secret Misappropriation

Under the Economic Espionage Act (EEA) of 1996 , trade secret misappropriation is now a federal crime. The EEA contains a broad definition of a "trade secret," including tangible as well as intangible property, whether "stored, compiled or memorialized physically, electronically, graphically, photographically or in writing." One convicted of the theft of a trade secret under the EEA can face up to $10 million in fines and fifteen years in prison.

A violation of the EEA occurs if a person or entity: (1) steals, or takes without authorization, or by fraud or deception obtains a trade secret; (2) copies, photographs, downloads, uploads, alters, transmits, sends, mails, or otherwise communicates or conveys a trade secret without authorization; or (3) receives, buys, or possesses information knowing that is has been stolen or misappropriated. Before a violation may be found, however, it must be proved that the person or entity committed the act "knowingly," intended to convert the trade secret to someone else's economic benefit, and knew that the offense would injure the owner of the trade secret. (These requirements differ slightly when a foreign entity is involved.)

The law also prohibits attempted theft as well as conspiracy to commit a theft. Consequently, if an employee of one company goes to work for a competitor who expects that employee to bring with him or her information belonging to his or her former employer, both the new employer and the employee may be violating the EEA. This situation would apply equally to a franchisee who leaves one system and joins another. Aside from possibly violating noncompete provisions in his or her former franchise agreement, the franchisee may be accused of violating the EEA if he or she attempts to use any of his or her former franchisor's trade secrets in his or her new business. The new franchisor may similarly be liable if it knows the franchisee will bring trade secrets with him or her to use in the new business. Whether in the employment or franchising scenario, it is incumbent that corporations educate employees about the dangers in hiring employees, or in recruiting franchisees who have worked for the competition.

Copyrights

The legal basis for copyright protection is found in the U.S. Constitution, which empowers Congress to enact legislation to promote the progress of science and the useful arts by securing for limited times to authors and inventors the exclusive right to their respective writings and discoveries.

Congress, pursuant to the power granted by the Constitution, enacted the Copyright Revision Act (the "Act"), which provides protection to all "original works of authorship fixed in any tangible medium of expression." This definition includes not only literary materials but also pictorial, graphic, and sculptural works. Operations manuals, promotional and advertising materials, training films and videos, forms, architectural plans, and computer programs typically developed and used by franchisors are copyrightable work within the definition of the Act.

Protections Afforded to the Owner of a Copyright

The Act provides protection from the following to the owner of a copyright of an original work:

- Unauthorized reproduction
- Preparation of derivative works
- Distribution of entire or partial copies of the work
- Infringement

A copyright protects only the *expression of an idea,* not the idea itself. That is, a copyright protects only the original labor of the author that gave substance to the idea, not the underlying abstract idea or concept of the author. Once copyright ownership is established, it may be transferred or licensed to others.

How to Obtain Copyright Protection

Unlike trademark rights, which arise under common law based on use, copyright protection is a creature of statute. According to the Act, copyright protection arises *as soon as the work is created and fixed in a tangible medium of expression.* The work need not be registered prior to its publication; however, registration is necessary so that the author may commence legal proceedings against infringers. The right to sue for infringement includes the ability to obtain injunctive relief and damages. Therefore, materials are protected, *without registration,* provided they contain the required statutory notice of copyright (as described below). Prior to registration, it is advisable to examine whether registration would compromise the confidentiality of the trade secrets contained in the work. For example, the contents of a new marketing brochure are a natural candidate for copyright registration; however, the contents of a confidential operations manual should not be registered because of its proprietary nature.

The author of a work protectable by copyright must use a notice of copyright, which puts the world on notice that the author claims the work as a copyright. The prescribed notice consists of (1) © or the word *copyright* or the abbreviation *copr.,* (2) the year of first publication of the work, (3) and the name of the copyright owner.

Work Made for Hire

Typically the author of the work is the owner of the copyright. Works developed by someone on behalf of another, however, may be considered to be "works made for hire." The Act defines "works made for hire" as either:

1. A work prepared by an employee within the scope of his or her employment
2. A work specially ordered or commissioned for use as a contribution to a collective work, as a part of a motion picture or other audiovisual work, as a translation, as a supplementary work, as a compilation, as an instructional text, as a test, as answer material for a test, " . . . if the parties expressly agree in a written instrument signed by them that the work shall be considered a work made for hire . . ."

A "work made for hire," therefore, must either be prepared by an "employee" or fit within one of the narrow categories enumerated in item 2 above. Agreements with independent contributors should clearly set forth that the work is intended by both parties to be "work made for hire" under the Act and owned by the employer. Absent such express written agreement, under a recent Supreme Court case, the work would be presumed to be owned by the contributor, not the person who paid for its creation.

All materials used by the franchisor that constitute "original works" may be protected by the Act. Registration is advisable for all major nonproprietary works that are an integral part of a franchise system, and the appropriate notice must appear on all such products.

Intellectual Property and the Internet

Many franchisors and franchisees have established a presence on the Internet either to directly offer franchises, goods, or services or to advertise and promote these items. The increasing importance of communicating and obtaining information over the Internet by franchisors to prospective franchisees presents several unique intellectual property protection issues. For the most part, basic trademark, trade secret, and copyright principles should apply, but with the law in this area in its early stages, it is important that certain steps be taken to protect intellectual property on the Internet and to avoid misappropriating someone else's intellectual property found on the Internet.

Trademarks

The company that establishes a presence on the Internet should first and fore-most register its domain name (or the company name the makes up the domain name) as a trademark with the USPTO. This is important because merely obtaining a domain name registration does not, in and of itself, confer trademark rights. Network Solutions, Inc. (NSI), located in Reston, Virginia, currently controls the registration of most domain names in the United States (those with the .com extension). Domain names are awarded on a first-come, first-serve basis and, provided other requirements are met, are typically issued so long as no one else has an identical domain name. Consequently, it is pos-sible for someone to register someone else's trademark as his or her own domain name. NSI has established a procedure for a trademark owner to oppose the issuance of a domain name that contains its trademark. This pro-cedure is only applicable, however, *if the trademark owner has a federally reg-istered trademark.* Not even a pending application will suffice. The only way to ensure retention of a domain name, and to guard against someone else attempting to take it away, is to register it as a trademark.

The trademark infringement prevention activities established by a com-pany should be extended to the Internet. Franchisors should monitor the use of their marks on the Internet by franchisees, as well as third parties. If an infringement is discovered, notice should be immediately sent to the Webmaster of the site containing the infringement. Similarly, a company should monitor the sites linking to its pages. These links may not present the sort of image the company wants associated with its marks and, if this occurs, the owner should be asked to disengage the link.

Trade Secrets

Trade secrets should *not* be posted on the Internet under any circumstances. Once posted, a trade secret becomes part of the public domain and loses its trade secret status. A franchisor should constantly monitor its own and its franchisees' sites to ensure that the franchisor's trade secrets are not being posted.

The license of intellectual property rights is the heart of every franchise. Franchisors must constantly protect these rights by ensuring proper use of the intellectual property, proper notice of ownership of these rights, and protec-tion of these rights against misuse by others. These core requirements are essential whether dealing with trademarks, copyrights, or trade secrets and regardless of the medium in which they are used.

Copyrights

Prior to posting any information on the Internet that is subject to a copyright, a company should ensure that the material does not contain any confidential information. Copyright notices should be prominently displayed on every page of information, and ownership information and disclaimers should be provided on home pages. Franchisors should prohibit or provide strict guidelines regarding franchisees' posting of franchisor's copyrightable information on their own Websites. Protecting copyrights in today's high-tech world is increasingly difficult and should be taken into account prior to posting any information on the Internet.

8

Managing Disputes

Conflict in a franchise system between the franchisor and franchisee is inevitable. Resolving conflicts with franchisees, however, is an expensive and time-consuming process that can significantly impede the growth of a franchisor as well as distract the franchisor from the attainment of its business objectives. In my experience, protracted litigation yields no winners, only successful or unsuccessful litigants.

As a result, most franchisors prefer to engage in battle in the marketplace or in the boardroom rather than in the courtroom. Nevertheless, there are instances when an amicable resolution or settlement of a conflict seems unattainable. If a dispute with a franchisee or prospective franchisee matures into a courtroom battle, franchisors must understand the fundamental rules of litigation as well as alternate means of resolving disputes.

Problems Leading to Litigation

Inherent in the franchisor-franchisee relationship is a certain level of tension: The franchisor has invested a great deal of time, effort, and money in establishing a business format franchise. This involves quality control guidelines that must be followed. The franchisee, on the other hand, often desires to be his or her own boss and resists any such restrictions. The tension can often create an exciting and dynamic atmosphere that enables both parties to achieve their goals: growth for the franchisor and independence and satisfaction for the franchisee. In many instances, however, the tension that is part and parcel of every franchise relationship leads to conflict and strife that distract the parties from their common objectives.

Another key factor leading to many of the disputes between franchisors and franchisees is the gap between expectation and reality. In an effort to recruit franchisees, some franchisors raise the expectation level of the prospective franchisee regarding the level of training and support and other key aspects of the relationship, leading to disappointment and frustration by the franchisee when the realities of the franchisor's actual capabilities are revealed.

Ten Common Areas of Conflict

It is critical for franchisors to recognize and understand the problems that typically give rise to litigation and attempt, if at all possible, to resolve these in an effort to avoid legal action. Following are ten areas in which conflict commonly arises:

1. *Franchisee recruiting.* A franchised operation is only as strong as the franchisee operating it. The franchisor must carefully evaluate and screen prospective franchisees to ensure that only qualified individuals are accepted. Because the initial franchisees in a system set the tone for and establish the criteria for later applicants, it is essential that the first franchisees be carefully scrutinized to ensure they have the financial background and experience to successfully operate a franchise. The applicant should possess the requisite financial strength to meet the demands that can reasonably be expected to arise in a franchised business, including sufficient working capital for payroll, rent, unexpected complications, product purchases, and taxes. Ideally, the candidate should have a background in some business similar to or compatible with the franchised business or other sufficient experience as a business owner or manager. The intangible factors that contribute to a franchisee's success—such as motivation, loyalty, and commitment—are, of course, almost impossible to evaluate from a written application, and the franchisor should at a minimum speak with the applicant's references and his or her current employer, if there are any. A franchisee's level of motivation can also be evaluated by analyzing the franchisee's ownership interest or risk in the enterprise. A franchisee who is gambling with someone else's money will be far less committed to the business than the franchisee who has invested his or her own hard-earned dollars and personal savings. A franchisor can also learn a great deal about an individual simply through the initial screening process. An applicant who is hostile, contentious, and untruthful in the interview and negotiation process will in all likelihood be hostile, contentious, and untruthful as a franchisee. It is almost inevitable that such a franchisee will cause discord and dissension that may lead to litigation.

Many franchisors have discovered that claims of fraud, misrepresentation, and mistake commonly grow out of misunderstandings in the recruiting and sales process. Franchisors or their sales staff unintentionally make comments about other franchisees who have earned certain sums of money, and the prospective franchisee views this as a guarantee of a certain dollar amount. The sales staff may promise assistance and support that the franchisor does not commonly offer. These misunderstandings typically lead to litigation. In fact, a recent Indiana district court decision (which was later reversed) held that General Foods, the parent of Burger Chef, had made actionable misrepresentations to its franchisees that it planned to actively develop and promote its restaurant system, when in fact General Foods planned to sell Burger Chef to Hardee's. Such comments in the sales process may go beyond mere puffery or opinionated sales talk into the realm of fraud.

Although it is understandable that emerging franchisors are anxious to make sales, this eagerness should not be allowed to displace the franchisor's need for careful scrutiny of applicants and prudent communications with those prospective franchisees. In this regard, franchisors should take heed of the adage, "If you want it badly, that's exactly how you'll get it."

2. *Site selection and territorial rights*. Even the best franchise in the world cannot take root and flourish in a humble location. The franchise agreement typically imposes a duty on the franchisee to select a site for the location of the business. Often the franchisor lends some amount of assistance in this site selection process and invariably has the right to reject a site located by the franchisee. A franchisor should develop criteria to assist in the determination of whether a site selected by the franchisee is acceptable. Some of the factors considered by franchisors in such a determination include size of the site, suitability of the location and surrounding area for the type of business being franchised, adequate parking, costs of development, zoning and traffic patterns, proximity and access to major thoroughfares, compatibility with other businesses in the area, and proximity to competing businesses.

Franchisees often expect a great deal of assistance in site selection and are quick to demand compliance with the terms of agreements that bind the franchisors to offer that support. For example, Avis Services, Inc., a subsidiary of the rental car company, has been besieged by recent lawsuits that allege that Avis has failed to help franchisees find sites for quick-lube businesses and rejects sites found by the franchisees as being too expensive or unsuitable. In many instances the franchisees have demanded refunds and have alleged fraud and misrepresentation. Franchisors must ensure that site selection staff fulfill their obligations to find and develop suitable locations and guard against oversaturation of the market.

Typically, a franchisee is granted an exclusive area or territory within which to operate the business. So long as the franchisee performs its obligations under the franchise agreement, the franchisor will not establish any other franchises in this territory. The territory is often defined by population or some geographic criteria such as zip code or a certain radius area around the franchised business. While franchisors may be tempted to offer existing franchisees a right of first refusal to expand into adjacent or surrounding territories, such a right places burdensome restrictions on the franchisor, which is then precluded from selling in certain areas unless time-consuming and complicated notice procedures are followed. A franchisor's failure to strictly follow a right of first refusal and provide the appropriate notice to an existing franchisee who has been granted such a right will surely lead to litigation, and courts zealously and quite rightly protect these rights.

Another area of conflict is the operation of company-owned stores or businesses that invariably compete with those owned and operated by franchisees, commonly referred to as encroachment. A Kentucky Fried Chicken franchisee has sued its franchisor for allegedly opening a company-owned restaurant too close to the franchisee's store in violation of a provision in the franchise agreement that guarantees that each franchisee will have a protected radius of one-fourth mile. Unless expressly allowed by the franchise agreement, the establishment of a company-owned store in a franchisee's territory will lead to the argument by a franchisee that the franchisor has breached its duty of good faith and fair dealing and has deprived the franchisee of the benefit of its bargain with the franchisor.

Similarly, direct or indirect competition within the territory by a franchisor is subject to scrutiny. Franchisees at Haagen-Dazs ice cream stores sued Pillsbury Co., alleging that Pillsbury aggressively sold its Haagen-Dazs brand in grocery stores, competing with the franchised shops. However, the language in the franchise agreement allowed the company to distribute the ice cream products not only through the franchised shops but through other distribution methods. Because this language unequivocally gave the franchisor the right to market the products in the grocery stores, the court held that the franchisees had no reason to expect that distribution through the ice cream shops would be exclusively protected. Therefore, the language in the franchise agreement should be carefully drafted to allow a franchiser to open company-owned stores or to sell the products through other market channels if it so desires.

3. *Accounting practices and procedures.* The franchise agreement imposes various requirements on the franchisee to provide records, reports, and accounting information to the franchisor. Such records are needed to enable the franchisor to determine whether royalties are being calculated correctly, whether contributions to funds for advertising are being paid on time,

whether gross sales are accurately reported, and so forth.

A clearly written franchise agreement sets forth the manner and time of such reporting, for which the franchisor must act swiftly and efficiently to enforce the deadlines. As soon as a royalty or advertising payment is overdue or an accounting report is tardy, the franchisor should notify the franchisee and demand compliance with the appropriate provision of the franchise agreement. Repeated failures by the franchisee to pay or report and account may justify termination of the franchise agreement.

Franchisors should be vigilant in observing and documenting these defaults because they may be warning signs of a failing franchisee in need of extra supervision and monitoring. Failure to properly and promptly notify a franchisee may result in an assertion by the franchisee that the franchisor has given up or waived its right to insist on timely compliance with payment and record-keeping deadlines.

4. *Misuse of advertising funds.* Many franchisors require an advertising fee to be paid by all franchisees that is to be used for regional and/or national promotions and advertising programs. Fees paid into the advertising fund should be kept separate from the funds used by franchisors for their operating expenses and kept separate from the funds allocated toward advertising by the franchisor to attract new franchisees. Franchisors who experience temporary financial difficulties are often inclined to "borrow" from the advertising fund until their financial condition improves. Such "borrowing" can give rise to litigation based on the failure of the franchisor to use the funds for the specified purposes.

A recent California case focuses on this very issue. Thirty-six franchisees have sued Pioneer Take Out, the fast-food restaurant franchise, alleging, among other claims, that various rebates and allowances received by the franchisor when it purchased supplies and food products were not deposited into the advertising fund as required. The franchisees have further alleged that Pioneer, without informing the franchisees, has used their advertising contributions to pay advertising bills incurred by Pioneer prior to the date the franchisees purchased their franchises. The litigation is expected to be protracted and expensive. The temptation to use the advertising fund as a ready source of capital can be eliminated by establishing separate accounts and an advertising committee made up of franchisees as well as key members of the franchisor's management team.

5. *Supervision and support.* While franchisees are usually independent individuals who desire to operate a business for themselves, they are also attracted to franchising because of the guidance and support offered by a franchisor who has an established and proven business concept. A successful

franchisor not only meets the contractual commitments established by the franchise agreement but typically goes beyond the agreement to offer additional support and supervision to the franchisees. This increased support results in two bonuses to the franchisor: The supervision alerts the franchisor to difficulties a franchisee may be having, and it demonstrates the franchisor's commitment to the system (which never hurts when prospective franchisees are talking to existing franchisees). While overzealous supervision by a franchisor is usually not needed and in fact may interfere with a franchisee's ability to run the business, maintaining routine phone contact and making occasional visits to the franchisee's place of business show a willingness to assist with problems and an assurance that the franchisor is committed to the franchisee's goals.

A lack of such support often leads to conflict in the system and ultimately to litigations, as seen in the Pioneer case previously discussed and in which the franchisees have also alleged that the franchisor has diverted the chain's operating capital to other ventures and has failed to develop new products or support the franchisees. This contention is increasingly being leveled against franchisors. Franchisees are likewise alert to spinoffs, mergers, and other restructuring attempts by franchisors and view them as an abdication of the franchisor's duty to offer assistance and support. Burger King franchisees successfully blocked an attempt in 1988 by Pillsbury to spin off the Burger King franchise system as a defense against a takeover bid. Franchisees of the Diet Center system have sued the weight loss company following its leveraged buyout, which allegedly resulted in a 41 percent increase in royalty fees. When Marriott tried to sell its Straw Hat Pizza chain to Pizza Hut, many of the franchisees broke away and became their own franchisor by forming a cooperative. These disputes all arose out of a perceived lack of support and guidance by the franchisor and a fear that the franchisees would be burdened with a debt-ridden and undercapitalized new franchisor.

Support by the franchisor can be made available through regular meetings and seminars, newsletters, conventions, retraining programs, and the dissemination of published materials related to the franchised business.

Franchisors should respond promptly and in writing to specific questions and concerns of franchisees. Failure to respond to and manage the franchisees will not make the problem go away but will only compound it by creating an adversarial relationship between the parties. In this regard, franchisors should not attempt to interfere with or impede franchisees' efforts to form a franchisee association and, in fact, many states specifically declare any such interference to be unlawful.

Franchisors can also support franchisees by offering to provide management consulting services for special projects or general assistance at specified fees.

Communication between the parties and support and assistance offered by the franchisor serve not only to promote harmonious relations between the franchisor and franchisee but negate any argument that the franchisor was interested only in the initial franchisee fee and not in a long-term and mutually satisfactory relationship.

6. *Quality control.* The essence of a successful franchisor is the protection of its business format, image, and trademarks; the quality and nature of the goods and services sold; and the uniformity of its business operations. The franchisor must strictly protect and defend these interests; failure to do so results in a weakened system with no identifiable image. Franchisors with a need for increased revenues are often tempted to force a franchisee to purchase goods, services, supplies, fixtures, equipment, and inventory from the franchisor on the basis that such items are integral to the franchisor's system and cannot be obtained elsewhere. Because courts strictly scrutinize such franchisor requirements, many franchisors no longer sell supplies but rather regulate the items franchisees purchase by requiring that franchisees utilize suppliers approved by the franchisor or purchase in accordance with specifications designated by the franchisor. Many franchisors pass through to the franchisees any discounts or rebates received by the franchisor from its suppliers. This practice greatly allays any misgivings the franchisee may have that the franchisor is profiting on items that can be easily obtained from other suppliers at a lower cost. One of the issues in the Pioneer Take Out litigation was an allegation by the franchisees that the franchisor was charging an excessively high price for one of its special product mixes. Likewise, a change in the product mix of Steve's Home-Made Ice Cream has resulted in litigation by a franchisee that alleged fraud and breach of contract.

Franchisors need to be watchful to ensure that franchisees do not substitute unapproved goods or items in place of those that meet the franchisor's quality control standards. Such action by franchisees erodes the goodwill and regional or national recognition that distinguish the franchised business from other businesses, and if it is not stopped by the franchisor, it will signal to other franchisees that the franchisor is not interested in protecting their investment in the system.

7. *Unequal treatment.* While some circumstances may justify a decision by a franchisor to offer a benefit to one franchisee only, such as a grace period for the payment of royalties in the event of financial trouble, such advantages should be offered sparingly and only after a thorough analysis of the situa-

tion. Franchisees expect the system to operate uniformly, and any perceived arbitrariness or inequality in treatment can lead to resentment and hostility, especially when the favorable treatment is afforded to company-owned stores. In addition to creating an atmosphere of tension, any deviation by the franchisor from established operating procedures also raises the issue of whether the franchisor has waived or forgone the right to demand compliance with the franchise agreement.

Just as some franchisees should not be singled out for more favorable treatment than others, those franchisees who are difficult and demanding should not be subjected to any form of treatment that could be viewed as retaliatory or discriminatory. Any defaults or breaches of the franchise agreement by troublesome franchisees should be carefully documented and should be handled strictly in accordance with the franchise agreement. Franchisees who have made valid complaints against the franchisor or the system may not be subjected to any practice that a court would interpret as a reprisal for exercising their contractual rights. Such retaliatory treatment by franchisors leads only to litigation and further disruption of the system.

8. *Transfers by franchisees.* A franchisee who wants to sell the franchised business should be assisted by the franchisor because an unhappy or unmotivated franchisee is unproductive and weakens the system. The franchisor may be able to steer potential buyers to the franchisee or might even consider purchasing the location and operating it as a company-owned store until a suitable purchaser can be found. The decision to purchase a franchisee's business, however, should be carefully evaluated by the franchisor because word of the repurchase will invariably spread to other franchisees, who may believe that such a practice is the established policy of the franchisor and an absolute right of a disgruntled or noncomplying franchisee. In the event a franchisee presents a prospective purchaser to the franchisor for approval, the franchisor must ensure that the purchaser satisfies the selection criteria established for all applicants. In a recent case involving the transfer of a Baskin-Robbins franchise, the court held that a "reasonableness" requirement should be read into the franchise agreement and the franchisor should not be allowed to arbitrarily reject a transfer without reference to some reasonable and objective standards. If the purchaser fails to meet such objective standards and fails to qualify, a written notification should be provided to the franchisee that explains the rejection and its basis.

9. *Training for the franchisor's management and sales team.* Many of the problems that lead to litigation are caused by improperly trained members of the franchisor's staff. Salespeople are so eager to make a sale

that they sometimes ignore the Federal Trade Commission regulations relating to the provision of offering documents to the prospective franchisee at least ten days before the signing of the franchise agreement. On other occasions the salespeople make claims to prospective franchisees regarding anticipated earnings or bind the franchisor to a new contract term, such as a lower initial franchise fee or payment of the fee in installments. While such acts might not be directed or authorized by the franchisor, the principles of agency law may result in the franchisor being bound by such acts performed by these agents. Therefore, it is critical that the franchisor have in place a training and compliance program to instruct the management and sales team with regard to the FTC requirements and the franchisor's philosophy and goals. Often legal counsel for the franchisor participates in training and instructing the franchisor's staff. Form letters and checklists should be developed for routine transactions. Managers or salespeople who are "loose cannons" should be dealt with firmly to ensure that they do not "give away the store" in an effort to make a sale or retain a franchisee.

10. *Documentation.* While the goal of every successful franchisor is to manage the business rather than to manage disputes, when disputes arise the franchisor should be well prepared to discuss and resolve the conflict. This cannot be accomplished unless the franchisor has kept adequate records, including notes of all conversations, telephone message slips, memos reflecting understandings reached at meetings, correspondence between the franchisor and franchisee, copies of all documents provided to or received from the franchisee, and notices to the franchisee. The franchisor should develop procedures for such record keeping and file management and designate a reliable individual to assume responsibility for it. Meetings with a troubled franchisee should be attended by at least two of the franchisor's employees to verify the nature of the meeting and what was said.

Dealing With the Danger Signs

The problems described above are all areas of conflict that typically lead to litigation. It should be apparent that the common thread running through all of these problems is lack of or poor communication with the franchisee and inadequate documentation to support the franchisor's position. There are, however, several warning signs, such as those listed in Figure 8-1, which are often seen in troubled franchisees and which should be noted and managed by the franchisor before they erupt into a need for legal intervention.

Figure 8-1. Warning signs of troubled franchisees.

Danger Signal	Franchisor's Action
1. Late payment or nonpayment of royalties	Notice of default to be followed by termination, if default is not remedied
2. Cancellation of franchisee's insurance by insurance company	Notice of default and, if not remedied, procurement of policy by franchisor who assesses franchisee for said payment
3. Steadily declining royalties	Meet with franchisee to discuss problem; increase advertising; perform an audit to ensure reporting of sales is accurate
4. Complaints by franchisee's customers	Meet with franchisee; retrain franchisee and/or franchisee's staff; send "test" customers to franchisee's place of business to monitor and ensure compliance
5. Inability to contact or communicate with franchisee	Increase supervision of franchisee and make frequent unannounced visits to franchisee's business
6. Use of unauthorized products or unapproved advertising	Notice of default, retraining, and termination of franchise if default is not remedied
7. Standards of cleanliness and hygiene not followed	Notice of default and increased supervision of franchisee, including sending "test" customers to franchisee
8. Misuse of franchisor's proprietary marks	Notice of default and termination of franchise if default is not remedied after notice
9. Understaffing of franchisee's business	Increase supervision and inspections and retrain franchisee and franchisee's staff
10. Unhappy or troubled franchisee	Increase communication with franchisee and offer to meet to resolve conflict

Litigation Planning and Strategy

If and when a franchisor determines that litigation is the most sensible and efficient way to resolve a business dispute or when a franchisee brings suit, the franchisor must develop plans and strategies in light of the following principles:

- ◆ The franchisor must develop goals and objectives and communicate them to legal counsel. A broad strategy such as "kick the franchisee out" is not sufficient. Rather, counsel must be made aware of any specific business objectives, budgetary limitations, or time constraints that affect the franchisor well before the litigation is initiated.
- ◆ The franchisor must gather all documents relevant to the dispute and organize them in advance of the time that the opponent serves the first discovery request.
- ◆ The franchisor should explore alternative methods of dispute resolution, clearly define parameters for settlement, and communicate them to legal counsel.
- ◆ The franchisor should discuss with legal counsel the risks, costs, and benefits of entering into litigation.
- ◆ The franchisor should review with counsel the terms of payment of legal fees (as well as those of any experts needed).
- ◆ The franchisor should review the terms of its insurance policies with its risk management team to determine whether there is insurance coverage for its defense costs or any judgment rendered against the franchisor.
- ◆ The franchisor should develop a litigation management system for monitoring and controlling costs.
- ◆ The franchisor should maintain clear lines of communication with legal counsel throughout all phases of the litigation and should appoint a responsible individual to serve as a liaison with counsel.

While litigation of franchise disputes does not significantly differ from litigation of other matters, the decision to resolve a dispute through litigation must be based on a genuine understanding of the legal rights, remedies, and defenses available. For example, suppose that a franchisee has stopped paying royalties with the argument that payment of royalties is excused by the franchisor's failure to provide adequate field support and supervision. Before filing a complaint to terminate the agreement, the franchisor should carefully review:

- ◆ Alternative methods for resolving the dispute
- ◆ The elements of proving a breach of the franchise agreement in the jurisdiction that governs the agreement
- ◆ The defenses that will be raised by the franchisee, such as lack of field support and supervision
- ◆ The perceptions and opinions of the other franchisees regarding this litigation
- ◆ The direct and indirect costs of litigation
- ◆ The damages that may accrue if a breach is successfully established
- ◆ The probability that the location can be easily sold to a new franchisee if the franchise agreement is terminated

Only after the franchisor is satisfied that the answers to these issues indicate that litigation is a viable alternative should formal action be pursued. Similarly, if the franchisor is sued by a franchisee, it should attempt to resolve the dispute before responding with a formal answer.

Where Do We Battle: Forum Selection Clauses

Most franchisors will designate their home turf as the battle place in the event of a dispute. The franchise agreement designates a specific city or county courthouse and usually forces the defendant to incur the time and expense of doing battle in a foreign jurisdiction. However, these forum selection clauses in franchise agreements have come under attack lately by many courts, state legislatures, and state franchise administrators. For example, in *Kubis & Perszyk Associates v. Sun Microsystems, Inc.*, a New Jersey court held that forum selection clauses in franchise agreements are presumptively invalid. To overcome this presumption, franchisors must now establish that the forum selection clause was not imposed on the franchisee unfairly by means of the franchisor's superior bargaining position. To sustain its newly imposed burden of proof, a franchisor could provide evidence of negotiations over the inclusion of the forum selection clause in exchange for specific concessions to the franchisee.

The enforcement of forum selection clauses in franchise agreements has recently become more complex. The answer depends not only on the wording of the clause itself but also on factors such as:

- ◆ The state in which a proceeding is commenced
- ◆ The forum in which the determination is made (judicial or arbitral)

♦ Choice of law determinations

♦ In the case of judicial proceedings, whether the matter is commenced in federal or state court

♦ In the case of judicial proceedings, the procedural context in which the issue of the enforceability of the forum selection clause is determined

State Franchise Statutes Regulating Forum Selection

California, Connecticut, Illinois, Indiana, Iowa, Louisiana, Maryland, Michigan, Minnesota, North Carolina, North Dakota, Rhode Island, and South Dakota all have statutes, rules, or policies that regulate where franchise-related litigation and/or arbitration may occur. Iowa, Rhode Island, and South Dakota have similar restrictive statutes. Those state laws, while not uniform, essentially declare that a provision in a franchise agreement restricting venue or jurisdiction to a forum outside the state is void with respect to any claim otherwise enforceable under the state's franchise protection law.

California's Franchise Relations Act invalidates all contractual provisions restricting venue to a forum outside the state, declaring that "a provision in a franchise agreement restricting venue to a forum outside the state is void with respect to any claim arising under or relating to a franchise agreement involving a franchise business operating within this state."

The Mechanics of Litigation

The first step when beginning civil litigation is preparing and filing a Complaint, which must set forth your claim(s) against the other party. Each allegation should be set forth in a separate paragraph and written in a clear and concise manner, with any necessary exhibits attached to the end of the Complaint. Each allegation should relate to a claim upon which you are entitled to relief and to make a demand for judgment. If the complaint meets all statutory and procedural requirements, the clerk of the court will then prepare a Summons, which is served with the Compliant on the other party, the "defendant." The Summons, directs the defendant to serve an Answer upon your lawyer, usually within twenty days after service of process is made.

In lieu of answering your specific allegations, the defendant may file certain preliminary motions, which must be filed prior to the filing of an Answer or they are waived. These motions, which are essentially specific requests for the court to act, include motions to dismiss (due to a lack of jurisdiction, improper service or process, etc.), motion to dismiss due to failure to state a claim upon which relief can be granted, motions to strike, or motions for a more definite statement. Once the Answer is filed, it must contain three principal components. It must:

1. Admit the allegations contained in the Complaint which are true.
2. Deny the allegations which, in the opinion of the defendant, are not true.
3. Allege any affirmative defenses to the causes of action raised by the plaintiff.

The defendant must also file any counterclaims that it may have which may have arisen out of the same transaction or occurrence. Failure to raise such claims will usually prevent the defendant from raising them down the road. The Complaint, Answer, and any Counterclaims and Answers to Counterclaims are usually collectively referred to as the Pleadings.

Once all of the Pleadings and preliminary motions are filed, the parties are then permitted to begin the process of discovery. Discovery is a pretrial procedure for obtaining information that will be necessary for the disposition of the dispute. Discovery serves a number of important purposes, including:

◆ Narrowing down the issues that are actually in dispute
◆ Preventing surprise by allowing each party to find out what testimony and other evidence are available for each issue in dispute
◆ Preserving information that may not be available at the actual trial, such as the statement of a very ill witness
◆ Encouraging resolution of the dispute prior to trial

Despite these many benefits, discovery is also the process that tends to significantly increase the legal fees and related expenses of the company in connection with the litigation, as well as the amount of time that is necessary to resolve the dispute.

One of the key issues to consider is the permissible *scope* of the discovery. The general rule is that virtually any information is discoverable, provided that it is *relevant* and not subject to any category of evidentiary privilege. These privileges are usually limited to information exchanged between a doctor and patient, attorney and client, priest and penitent, or husband and wife.

Once the parties have completed the discovery process, the litigation will proceed to the pretrial conference, the actual trial, the appeal, and any post-trial proceedings. Although a comprehensive discussion of the mechanics of a trial is beyond the scope of this chapter, it is safe to say that this process consumes two of the most important resources to an emerging growth business: time and money. As a result, the various alternatives to litigation, which are likely to be less expensive and less time-consuming, should be considered when disputes must be resolved.

The five principal discovery devices that are available to litigants are depositions, written interrogatories, requests for production of documents, physical and mental examinations, and requests for admissions. (See Figure 8-2.)

Figure 8-2. Five commonly used discovery devices.

1. *Depositions.* A deposition generally involves the pretrial examination and cross-examination by legal counsel of a live witness (any person who has information relevant to the case, whether or not that person is a party to the action). The written record of the deposition may be admitted at trial as substance evidence and may be used to impeach a witness whose testimony at trial is inconsistent with the testimony given during the deposition. Depositions are usually the most productive discovery devices and are the most frequently used despite their cost, which may run as high as $1,000 per day of deposition testimony.

2. *Written interrogatories.* An interrogatory is a written question that one party may pose to another party, which must be answered in writing, under oath, within thirty days. Unlike depositions, interrogatories may be served only upon parties to the litigation. Most courts will limit the number of interrogatories that may be filed and the scope of the questions so that they are not overly burdensome and to prevent parties from engaging in a mere "fishing expedition." If a party objects to a specific interrogatory, then it must specify its grounds for refusing to answer, at which time the burden shifts to the proponent of the question to convince the court why an answer is necessary. An answer to an interrogatory may also include a reference to a particular business document or set of records, provided that the other party is given an opportunity to inspect the documents.

3. *Requests for production of documents or inspection of land.* A party may request another party to produce and permit inspection, copying, testing, or photographing business documents, tangible assets, financial books and records, or anything else that may be relevant to the litigation. Similarly, a

(continues)

Figure 8-2. *(continued)*

party may request entry to the business premises of another party for the
purposes of inspection, photographing, surveying or any other purpose
that is relevant and not subject to an evidentiary privilege. These requests
are limited to parties to the litigation, with the exception of a "subpoena
duces tecum," which is a demand to produce certain documents and
records in connection with the deposition of a nonparty.

4. *Physical and mental examinations.* A party may request that another party
   submit to a mental or physical examination by a physician or psychiatrist.
   The mental or physical condition of the party, however, must be relevant to
   the issues that are in dispute. The court will grant such a request only if good
   cause is shown and will usually limit the scope of the examination to the
   actual issues in controversy. This is the only discovery device that involves
   court intervention and is generally used in personal injury and paternity cases.

5. *Requests for admissions.* A party may serve a request for admission on
   another party for the purposes of ascertaining the genuineness of specific
   documents, obtaining the admission or denial of a specific matter, or confirming the application of certain law to a given set of facts. For example,
   you may want to use this procedure to confirm a set of facts in order to
   save the time and expense of having to prove them later. Failure to respond
   to a request will be deemed to be an admittance. Therefore, the party upon
   which a request has been served must deny the request, explain why it is
   unable to admit or deny, or file an objection to the request as improper
   within thirty days.

If a party refuses to comply with discovery requests, the court may impose
monetary sanctions, and in cases of willful or repeated refusals, the court may
dismiss a plaintiff's complaint or enter judgment against a defendant.

Alternatives to Litigation

Franchise dispute litigation is invariably time-consuming and expensive, and
a franchisor might be portrayed by adverse counsel in a number of unflatter-
ing ways designed to engender the jury's support and emotion: as a huge,
impersonal corporate entity with no feeling for the small and defenseless franchisee; as a greedy corporate conglomerate interested in increasing its coffers
at the expense of its loyal and diligent franchisees; as a vindictive and retaliatory entity motivated to get even with a franchisee that has merely exercised

its contractual rights; or as a poorly managed business that has mishandled its affairs to the ruin of its franchisees. Because litigation involves these drawbacks and uncertainties, many franchisors seek to resolve their disputes with franchisees through alternative methods.

There is a broad range of methods and procedures available that generally expedite the resolution of disputes without the need for litigation, broadly referred to as *alternative dispute resolutions (ADRs)*. ADR methods are also more attractive than litigation to franchisors because proprietary information, trade secrets, and the like can be protected whereas in a proceeding in the judicial system, the commercial information can result in intense efforts by competitors to misappropriate and use the information due to the right of access by the general public and news media.

The most commonly known ADR method is arbitration, which is when a neutral third party is selected by the disputants to hear the case and render an opinion, which may or may not be binding on the parties depending on the terms of the arbitration clause or agreement. In addition to arbitration, various forms of mediation, private judging, moderated settlement conferences, and small claims court are available to companies that are unable to independently resolve their disputes but wish to avoid the expense and delay of a trial.

Each method offers certain advantages and disadvantages that may make one process far more appropriate for resolving a particular dispute than another. Therefore, the procedures, costs, and benefits of each ADR method should be carefully reviewed with experienced legal counsel.

Benefits of ADR

◆ *Faster resolution of disputes.* Reducing delays in dispute resolution was one of the driving forces behind the ADR movement. As the number of civil filings continues to increase every year, it is clear that the court cannot expeditiously accommodate the influx without parties seeking alternatives to such filings.

◆ *Cost savings.* In a study by the Deloitte & Touche accounting firm, 60 percent of all ADR users and 78 percent of those characterized as extensive users reported that they had saved money by using ADR. The amount of savings ranged from 11 percent to 50 percent of the cost of litigation.

◆ *Preserving relationships.* ADR offers the opportunity for parties to resolve a dispute without destroying a relationship, whether business or personal.

◆ *Preserving privacy and confidentiality.* Traditional litigation often results in public disclosure of proprietary information, particularly in business disputes. ADR procedures allow the parties to structure a dispute resolution process while protecting confidential information.

◆ *Flexibility.* ADR allows the parties to tailor a dispute resolution process that is uniquely suited to the matter at hand. Parties can select the mechanism, determine the amount of information that needs to be exchanged, choose their own neutral arbitrator, and agree on a format for the procedure, all in a way that makes sense for the issue at hand.

◆ *Durability of the result.* Resolutions achieved by consensus of the disputants are less likely to be challenged than resolutions imposed by third parties.

◆ *Better, more creative solutions.* By giving litigants early and direct participation, ADR provides a better opportunity for achieving a resolution based on the parties' real interests. Such agreements often involve terms other than the distribution of dollars from one party to another and may well produce a solution that makes more sense for the parties than one imposed by a court.

Situations in Which ADR Is Successful

◆ *ADR contract clause in place.* The most important indicator of possible ADR success is the existence of an effective contract clause that provides for the use of ADR in the event of a future dispute.

◆ *Continuing relationships.* If a continuing relationship between the parties is possible (as with franchisors and franchisees or suppliers and customers), the chances of ADR success are greatly enhanced. It makes more sense for the parties to continue making money from each other over the duration of an agreement than severing the relationship and suffering the cost and disruption of litigation.

◆ *Complex disputes.* If a case is based on, for example, highly complex technology, there is a substantial chance that a jury and even a judge may become confused. Under these circumstances, ADR may be the best option, particularly if the proceedings are conducted before a neutral person who is an expert in the subject matter of dispute. In addition, the American Arbitration Association has enacted rules specifically designed for use in complex cases.

◆ *Relatively little money at stake.* If the amount of money in dispute is relatively small, the cost of litigation may approach or even exceed that amount.

◆ *Confidentiality an important issue.* The parties can maintain confidentiality more effectively in an ADR proceeding than in litigation. The need for confidentiality can prove to be more important than any other consideration in the dispute resolution process.

Situations in Which ADR Is Not Successful

◆ *Skeptical and mistrusting adversary.* The adversary may see the overture to use ADR after a complaint as a ploy designed to get an edge in litigation.

◆ *Parties or counsel with harsh attitudes.* When the parties or their counsel are particularly emotional, belligerent, and abusive, the chances for successful nonbinding ADR are significantly diminished.

◆ *One of many cases.* If the case at issue is just one of many that are expected to be filed, then it is highly unlikely that the defendant will be motivated to agree to the use of ADR. In such a setting, there is little if any hope for the successful use of nonbinding ADR, at least at an early stage. This also may be one of those rare situations where full-blown litigation is actually more cost-effective because of the efficiencies of consolidation.

◆ *Delays.* If a delay will benefit one of the parties, then the chances for the successful use of ADR are diminished.

◆ *Monetary imbalances.* If there is a monetary imbalance between the parties, and the wealthier party thinks it can wear down the other party through traditional litigation, then it probably will be difficult to get the wealthier party to agree to ADR.

Arbitration

There are many forms of formal arbitration. Each involves a process for the parties in dispute to submit arguments and evidence to a neutral person or persons for the purpose of adjudicating the differences between the parties. The evidentiary and procedural rules are not nearly as formal as in litigation, and there tends to be far greater flexibility in the timing of the proceeding and the selection of the actual decision makers.

Arbitration may be a voluntary proceeding that the parties have selected before a dispute arises, such as in a contract, or it may be a compulsory, court-annexed procedure that is a prerequisite to full-blown litigation. Owners and managers of growing franchisors who wish to avoid the cost and delay of litigation should consider adding arbitration clauses prior to entering into a contract. The clause should specify:

- The parties' agreement to submit any controversy or claim arising from the agreement or contract to a binding (or nonbinding) arbitration

- The choice(s) of location for the arbitration

- The method for selecting the parties who will hear the dispute

- Any limitations on the award that may be rendered by the arbitrator

- Which party shall be responsible for the costs of the proceeding

- Any special procedural rules that will govern the arbitration

However, due to the increasing battle over mandatory arbitration clauses in contracts, it is advisable not to include arbitration as a boilerplate provision in your key contracts. For example, in the August 1996 issue of the *ABA Journal,* it was reported that "Employment law has been one of the most significant sectors of ADR growth, as management lawyers have seized upon several Supreme Court decisions upholding mandatory arbitration clauses on statutory grounds." However, in the September 1996 issue, it was reported "consumer advocates are criticizing a U.S. Supreme Court decision invalidating a state law that required the prominent display of arbitration provisions in contracts." The following clause is recommended by the American Arbitration Association (AAA):

> Any controversy or claim arising out of or relating to this contract, or the breach thereof, shall be settled by arbitration in accordance with the Commercial Arbitration Rules of the American Arbitration Association, and judgment rendered upon the award rendered by the arbitrator(s) may be entered in any court having jurisdiction thereof.

Because the arbitrator selected is usually an attorney whose expertise may be negotiating rather than adjudicating, arbitration often results in "splitting the baby down the middle," not providing a clear award for one party or the other. In addition, because no jury is involved, the likelihood is reduced of recovering punitive or exemplary damages from an attorney or experienced arbitrator who is unlikely to be swayed by appeals to emotion. A key factor is whether the decision of the arbitrator will be binding or nonbinding. If the parties agree that the award will be binding, then the parties must live with the results. Binding arbitration awards are usually enforceable by the local court, unless there has been a defect in the arbitration procedures. On the other hand, the opinion rendered in a nonbinding arbitration is advisory only. The parties may either accept the result or reject the award and proceed to litigation. In a court-annexed arbitration, the court will order the arbitration as a nonbinding proceeding that is intended to work out the differences between the parties without the need for litigation. Another drawback of nonbinding arbitration is that after the award is made, the losing party often threatens litigation (a trial de novo, or new trial) unless the monetary award is adjusted. Thus, the party that wins the arbitration is often coerced into paying or accepting less than awarded simply to avoid a trial after arbitration.

There are many sources of arbitration rules. Unless the parties have specific rules and procedures in mind that will govern the arbitration, the two best known in the United States are the American Arbitration Association (212-484-4000) and the International Chamber of Commerce (212-206-1150). Both offer their rules at no cost; the fees for handling arbitration proceedings vary for these and other such organizations. Other sources include the U.N. Commission on International Trade Law Arbitration Rules and the Inter-American Commercial Arbitration Commission.

Whether arbitration is faster and cheaper than litigation really hinges on if the parties and their interests in arbitration can escalate arbitration costs and length to rival those of litigation. For example, in *Advanced Micro Devices Inc. v. Intel Corp.,* the proceeding lasted seven years, cost about $100 million, and included several rounds of collateral litigation. Intel's vice-president and general counsel describes the dispute as a basic contract dispute; however, a predispute arbitration clause routed into arbitration. Ultimately the arbitrator's ruling led the parties to settle in a mediation proceeding. (See Figure 8-3 for a sample arbitration procedures letter agreement.)

(text continues on page 205)

Figure 8-3. Sample arbitration procedures letter agreement.

[*NAME AND ADDRESS OF FRANCHISEE COUNSEL*]

Dear Sir/Madam:

The purpose of this letter is to propose for your consideration a set of basic ground rules for informal discovery regarding the relationship between Franchisee, Inc. ("FRANCHISEE"), and our client Franchisor, Inc. ("FRANCHISOR"). Please call to discuss at your earliest convenience, as it is anticipated that this letter and your response will form the basis of a Stipulation and Agreement concerning these rules and their effect.

In an effort to set the ground rules, we propose the following:

1. <u>Scope</u>. Unless otherwise modified by this agreement, the Federal Rules of Civil Procedure shall govern the manner and method of discovery. The materials produced pursuant to this agreement may be used only for purposes of settlement or in any subsequent arbitration between the parties, subject in any event to the covenant of confidentiality at paragraph 5 below.

2. <u>Definitions</u>. As used herein, a reference to "party" or "parties" means FRANCHISOR, FRANCHISEE, and the following individuals: [*list names*]. This agreement does not provide for discovery against third parties other than persons to be designated pursuant to paragraph 3(c) herein.

3. <u>Written Interrogatories and Production of Documents</u>. Each party may once seek the other party's response to written interrogatories and requests for production of documents pursuant to Rules 33 and 34 of the Federal Rules of Civil Procedure. All interrogatories and requests for production of documents shall be exchanged by close of business on [*date*]. Failure to meet this deadline shall make any response by the receiving party optional.

   a. A party receiving a set of interrogatories will be allocated one day to answer each separate interrogatory (a subpart of an interrogatory is here included as a separate interrogatory), the response to all interrogatories coming due at the close of business on the last day allocated to the last interrogatory. For example, if the interrogating party asks ten interrogatories, the tenth consisting of five subparts, the responding party shall have fifteen (15) days to respond, the response coming due close of business on the 15th day. A party may not respond to an interrogatory by a general reference to documents.

b. A party receiving a request for production of documents shall respond to it within thirty (30) days or at the time the responses to any interrogatories are due pursuant to paragraph 3(a) above, whichever is later.

c. Within fifteen (15) days of the effective date or within five days of receipt of documents produced to it pursuant to subparagraph 3(b) herein, whichever is later, a party shall designate for deposition by name or title no more than three individuals who are or who act as an officer, director, high-level employee, or other managing agent employed by or affiliated with the other party and who have knowledge regarding that party's answer to the interrogatories. There shall be no other depositions.

4. <u>Depositions</u>. Each party may take the deposition of any other party pursuant to the following:

a. Deponents shall be limited to persons identified pursuant to paragraph 3(c) hereof.

b. Depositions of the parties shall occur in [*city/state*], at the offices of [*location*] commencing fifteen (15) business days after the production of documents by all parties as described in paragraph 3(b). The parties shall agree on a schedule for all depositions consistent with this paragraph 4, and FRANCHISEE shall take the first deposition.

c. Each deposition shall be limited to four hours of examination, excluding any breaks called for by counsel defending the party-deponent, to be followed by no more than one hour of any examination by counsel defending the party-deponent, to be followed by one half-hour of any examination by counsel for the party seeking the deposition. No time may be reserved.

d. There shall be two depositions per day until all witnesses identified pursuant to subparagraph 3(c) are completed. The depositions shall be staggered so that the deposition of one party will follow the deposition of the other party until all persons designated by a party have been deposed.

5. <u>Covenant of Confidentiality</u>. This letter, all documents that may be exchanged or produced pursuant to this letter and any subsequent agreement on procedure, and all testimony that may be given in the depositions to occur pursuant to them shall be held strictly confidential by the parties and the persons designated pursuant to paragraph 3(c)

(continues)

Figure 8-3. *(continued)*

hereof. This covenant of confidentiality shall survive the termination of this agreement by further agreement or otherwise. It is expressly understood and agreed that this covenant of confidentiality is a material condition of the process described by this agreement. Each party agrees that it shall be liable to the other party for all, and not an allocable portion of, damages suffered by that other party resulting in any way, in whole or in part, from a breach of this covenant of confidentiality by the breaching party or one or more of its representatives, agents, or affiliates.

6. <u>Objections</u>. Either party may reserve the right to limit or withhold disclosure of information or material in the course of discovery contemplated by this agreement only on the basis of attorney-client privilege or to the extent that the information or material sought exceeds the scope of the dispute between the parties. There shall be no "speaking objections" at any deposition.

7. <u>No Action</u>. Except as expressed in the covenant of confidentiality herein, the parties to this agreement, its performance by any party, including party-deponents designated pursuant to this agreement, and the conduct of the parties in connection with or in any way arising out of this agreement or its performance shall not create or support any right, obligation, liability, cause of action, demand, or claim in law or equity.

8. <u>Notice and Costs</u>. Each party agrees to produce documents, answer interrogatories, and produce witnesses for deposition pursuant to this agreement without the necessity of any subpoena or other notice. Each party agrees to bear its own costs.

9. <u>Miscellaneous</u>.

   a. All deadlines may be met by providing documentation to counsel for each party via overnight delivery, ordinary mail, or facsimile as follows:

   (1) If to FRANCHISOR, to:
       [*name/address/telephone number*]
   (2) If to FRANCHISEE, to:
       [*name/address/telephone number*]

   b. The materials, including transcripts of testimony, produced pursuant to this agreement shall bear the following title only: "In Re Arbitration of Franchising Dispute in [*location*]."

c. The headings herein are for ease of reference only and do not necessarily reflect the terms of the agreement.

d. Any dispute arising in any way out of this agreement, including but not limited to any allegations of fraud, shall be subject to arbitration in the manner and place prescribed by the parties in the Agreement between FRANCHISOR and FRANCHISEE dated on or about [*date*].

e. This agreement may be signed by counsel.

Very truly yours,

[*Counsel for franchisor*]

Mediation

Mediation differs substantially from arbitration because an arbitrator renders a decision that is often binding. In the mediation process, the parties decide how to resolve their dispute by discussing their differences, with a mediator only making suggestions or recommendations to resolve the dispute. The mediation process typically consists of five stages:

1. Presentation of positions
2. Identification of interests
3. Generation and evaluation of options
4. Narrowing of options to resolve the dispute
5. Executing a written settlement agreement

A sample mediation clause in an agreement would read as follows:

Any dispute arising out of or relating to this Agreement shall be resolved in accordance with the procedures specified in this Agreement, which shall be the sole and exclusive procedures for the resolution of such disputes. Each party shall continue to perform its obligations under this Agreement pending final resolution of any dispute arising out of or relating to this Agreement, unless to do so would be impossible or impracticable under the circumstances.

Upon becoming aware of the existence of a dispute, a party to this Agreement shall inform the other party in writing of the nature of such dispute. The parties shall attempt in good faith to resolve any dispute arising out of or relating to this Agreement promptly by negotiation between executives who have authority to settle the controversy. All negotiations pursuant to this Agreement shall be confidential and shall be treated as compromise and settlement negotiations for purposes of the applicable rules of evidence. If the dispute cannot be settled through direct discussions within ___ days of the receipt of such notice, the dispute shall be submitted to [*name of mediator*] (or such substitute mediation service specified by the parties in writing prior to receiving notice of the existence of such dispute) for mediation by notifying [*mediator*] (or the specified substitute service) and the other party in writing. The notification shall specify: (1) the nature of the dispute and (2) the name and title of the executive who will represent the party in mediation and of any other person who will accompany the executive. Following receipt of the notice, [*mediator*] (or the specified substitute service) will convene the parties, in person or by telephone, to establish the mediation procedures and a schedule. If the parties are unable to agree on mediation procedures, [*mediator*] (or the specified substitute service) will set the procedures. The mediation shall be completed within seven (7) days of submitting the dispute to mediation, or such longer time as the parties may agree. Each party will participate in the mediation process in good faith, will use their best efforts to resolve the dispute within the seven (7) day time period, and will make available executives or representatives with authority to resolve the controversy to participate personally and actively in the mediation. The parties shall share equally the fees, charges, and expenses of [*mediator*] (or the specified substitute service).

Mediation costs are minimal and generally include only payment on an hourly basis to the mediator for his or her services. However, because the mediator has no authority to render a binding decision, the mediation process will only be effective if both parties are committed to achieving a voluntary resolution. The participants always have the ultimate authority in the mediation process, and they are free to reject any suggestion by the mediator and can ultimately pursue litigation.

The controversies surrounding mediation typically include how the mediator should resolve disputes and determining the ethical standards of conduct for mediators. Some experts believe mediation should facilitate the parties' own resolution of the problem by digging deep into the interests and feelings underlying the surface dispute. Others say the proper purpose of mediation is to bring to the parties into an amicable accord. Still others contend that mediators should provide subject matter expertise, acting essentially as sounding boards to help the parties evaluate the merits of the dispute or the proposed settlement. The American Bar Association's Section on Dispute Resolution, the Society of Professionals in Dispute Resolution, and the AAA, in an attempt to draft ethical standards of conduct, concluded that mediators should try only to facilitate the parties' own resolution and admonished professionals who serve as mediators (including lawyers) to "refrain from providing professional advice." Florida, Hawaii, and New Jersey are the only states that have adopted qualification requirements for mediators. Many states merely require completion of forty hours of training, while in others, being a member of a bar and in good standing are enough. Florida is the only state thus far to go the further step of implementing a disciplinary process for mediators.

In 1993, members of the International Franchise Association, working in conjunction with the CPR Institute for Dispute Resolution in New York City (www.cpradr.org), developed the National Franchise Mediation Program, which outlines the process for resolving disputes for participating franchisors and their franchisees. The program includes sample forms, agreements, and model procedures. One hundred major franchisors, including Midas, Pizza Hut, Dunkin' Donuts, 7-Eleven, Jiffy Lube, and McDonald's have agreed to try to resolve their disputes with franchises through mediation.

Private Judging

In many communities, retired judges are available at an hourly fee (often as high as $250 per hour) to hear and resolve disputes. Parties may agree in advance whether the decision will be legally binding. The disadvantages of nonbinding arbitration also apply to nonbinding private judging. While private judging costs are substantially higher than court-annexed arbitration costs, private judging is considerably more flexible. A private judge may be retained without court intervention and without litigation first being in stituted. The parties are free to select a judge and a mutually convenient date for the hearing. The hearing itself tends to be informal, and the rules of evidence are not strictly applied. The private judge often uses a settlement conference approach as opposed to a trial approach to achieve a resolution of the dispute.

Moderated Settlement Conferences

After litigation begins, a court may insist the parties participate in settlement discussions before a judge. If the court does not schedule a settlement conference, the parties can usually request one, often with a particular judge.

The attorneys are often required to prepare settlement briefs to inform the judge of each party's contentions, theories, and claimed damages. Parties, as well as attorneys, attend so the judge may explain his or her view of the case and obtain their consent to any proposed settlement. If a resolution is reached in the judge's chambers, the litigants often proceed to the courtroom so that the settlement (and the parties' consent to it) can be entered in the record to eliminate any further disputes. Because moderated settlement conferences produce no out-of-pocket costs (other than attorneys' fees), and information obtained or revealed is for settlement purposes only, they provide an excellent "last ditch effort" for resolving a dispute prior to trial.

Small Claims Matters

Matters that involve a small monetary amount (usually no greater than $2,500) are often best resolved in small claims court. Generally, litigants represent themselves and describe the dispute in an informal manner to a judge, who renders a decision at the time of the hearing. Court filing fees are moderate, and a trial date usually is set for within two or three months. Often a bookkeeper or credit manager may represent the franchisor as long as he or she is knowledgeable about the dispute and has supporting documentation. Unfortunately, it is often difficult for a successful plaintiff to actually collect the judgment. Because of this, many courts have small claims advisers who can assist litigants in collecting the money awarded.

Owners and managers of growing franchises must be committed to developing programs and procedures within the organization that are specifically designed to avoid the time and expense of litigation. Business conflicts are inevitable, but lengthy trials are not if prompt steps are taken to resolve business conflicts and legal disputes. If disputes cannot be resolved amicably, then the costs and benefits of litigation and its alternatives must be understood well before the Pleadings are filed. If litigation is, in fact, the only alternative available, then growing companies must work closely with counsel to establish specific strategies, objectives, and budgets for each conflict that matures into a formal legal dispute.

Part **Three**

Sales and Marketing Strategies

Developing Sales and Marketing Plans

At first blush, it would seem too obvious that the heart of a successful franchise program is the viability of the franchisor's sales and marketing strategies. In fact, most early-stage franchisors are quick to recruit an aggressive franchise salesforce well before they hire other key management positions, such as in the areas of operations, administration, and finance. Despite this commitment to marketing overall, if you were to ask most franchisors in the United States to show you a recent copy of their formal franchise sales and marketing plan, you would see a dumbfounded expression on their faces. When asked how they go about selling franchises, they would respond, "Trade shows and advertisements in the Thursday edition of *The Wall Street Journal.*"

These traditional approaches are simply not good enough in today's competitive and complex marketplace. Today's franchise sales and marketing plans require a genuine understanding of the needs and wants of the modern and more sophisticated franchisee (who may be a wealthy individual, a former senior executive, or a large corporation), a keen sense of target marketing, an understanding as to how technology (such as the Internet and videoconferencing) can enhance and support the marketing effort, access to sophisticated databases, a detailed and well-designed strategic marketing plan, a well-educated sales team, and an ability to truly understand the competition. Each franchisor must understand the fears, uncertainties, and doubts of the targeted candidate and then deal with those issues in the initial and follow-up presentations. *The days of the fast-talking, leisure-suited, blue-suede-shoe franchise salesman are long gone.*

Franchisors operating in different industries must also custom-tailor their marketing plans according to the demographics of the target franchisee, competitive trends, and the stage of the underlying product or service's life cycle. For example, a hotel franchisor markets to candidates very differently than a housecleaning services franchisor. A franchisor who is virtually alone within its industry group may market differently than a franchisor that is operating in a highly competitive sector like chicken, pizza, or bagels where the targeted franchisee may have up to thirty to fifty franchisors to choose from. A franchisor whose core product is late in the life cycle (e.g., cinnamon buns) may need to market differently from a franchisor whose product is in the early-stage cycle (e.g., CD-ROM retailing), which may be facing the added burden of educating the marketplace. Finally, larger franchisors may have very different strategies than their early-stage counterparts.

For the early-stage franchisor, the process of attracting qualified leads and closing the sale is becoming increasingly more difficult. Some smaller franchisors have had such a tough time attracting qualified candidates that they have abandoned franchising altogether. Among the hurdles that early-stage franchisors must overcome in the sales and marketing process are:

◆ A more competitive pool of qualified candidates who have the business acumen or financial resources to acquire some of today's "high-ticket" retail and food franchises

◆ A growing number of franchisors who are all competing to attract qualified franchisee candidates, as an increasing number of companies of all sizes and in virtually every industry launch new franchise programs each year

◆ A difficult time competing against larger and well-financed franchisors that can afford sophisticated media campaigns and marketing resources

◆ A fierce competition for quality retail sites, which is often won by the larger franchisors

◆ A reluctance by commercial lenders to extend financing to the franchisees of start-up franchisors

◆ A growing sense of prudence, skepticism, and cautiousness in the pool of qualified franchisees, as more and more reports of failing and failed franchisors (especially early-stage franchisors) find their way into the press

◆ A growing pressure to recoup the often significant sums spent for franchise development costs through franchise sales

The pressure to quickly achieve rapid franchise sales can result in a lowering of the standards initially set to qualify a lead. Such a compromise can significantly lower the franchisee's likelihood of success, resulting in damage to the franchisor's goodwill and probably in litigation. Proper franchise sales and marketing requires *patience and planning*—two characteristics not often initially found among the entrepreneurs who are the pioneers of franchise systems.

Before examining the details of each component of a franchise sales and marketing plan, let's take a look at the critical factors in understanding the discipline of marketing.

What Is Marketing?

Marketing is the ongoing process of (1) determining the level of consumer demand for the company's products and services, (2) matching the company's strengths and weaknesses with the established demand, (3) delivering the products and services more effectively and more efficiently than do competitors, and (4) monitoring changes in consumer demand; industry trends; political, social, environmental, and legal issues; technology; and competition in order to ensure that the company's products and services remain competitive and consistent with consumer demand. In the context of franchising, this must always be done on two levels: (1) marketing to the prospective franchisees and (2) marketing to the prospective consumers of the franchisor's proprietary products and services.

Academics and consultants often identify the well-known "marketing mix" as the foundation of a marketing program. This mix is made up of product, place, price, and promotion. All marketing plans and decisions stem from one or more of these components of the marketing mix. Some of the typical issues raised by each element of the marketing mix, as applied to franchising, are as follows:

Product

◆ What products and services will the franchisor offer to the consumer through its franchisees and company-owned centers?
◆ What are the various features, options, and styles that each product or service will include as being unique, of better quality, or proprietary?
◆ How will these products and services be packaged and offered to the consuming public?
◆ How will franchises be packaged to attract prospective franchisees?

Place

◆ In what manner will the franchisor's products and services be distributed to the marketplace? Dual distribution or exclusively through franchisees? Why has this strategy been selected?

♦ What are the various advantages and disadvantages of the distribution channels that are alternatives to franchising?

♦ In what geographic markets should the franchisor's products and services be offered (determined, for example, through demographics and population analysis, primary versus secondary market studies, local competitor analysis, analysis of local and regional consumer habits)? Will the franchisor be able to attract franchisees in these targeted markets?

Price

♦ What will consumers be willing to pay for the franchisor's products and services? How are prices determined? To what extent can price ranges be suggested to franchisees?

♦ What pricing policies will be developed with respect to discounts, credit terms, allowances, and introductory or special pricing schedules when products are sold directly by the franchisor to the franchisees? By the franchisees to the consumers? If the franchisor (or its franchisees) does engage in introductory or promotional pricing, have such policies been reviewed by legal counsel in connection with (1) Robinson-Patman Act considerations, (2) deceptive pricing regulations established by the Federal Trade Commission, or (3) prohibited predatory pricing practices?

Promotion

♦ What strategies will be implemented to ensure that targeted franchisees are aware of the franchisor's business format?

♦ What strategies will be implemented to ensure that the consuming public is aware of the company's products and services?

♦ What sales, advertising, and public relations plans, programs, and strategies will be adopted?

♦ How will human and financial resources best be allocated to these various advertising and promotional programs?

Key Components of the Marketing Program

The key components of a well-developed marketing program fall into three distinct stages: (1) marketing planning and strategy formulation, (2) implementation, and (3) monitoring and feedback. The balance of this chapter discusses these three stages.

Stage 1: Marketing Planning and Strategy Formulation

Effective marketing planning and strategy formulation typically falls into three distinct stages: marketing research, market analysis and segmentation, and development of the marketing plan. The activities of the management team during each stage are described below.

Marketing research. Effective marketing planning begins with the development of a database of information regarding the history of the franchisor; its products, services, and personnel; trends in its industry; the size of its total marketplace; the characteristics of its typical customers and targeted franchisees; the strengths and weaknesses of its current competitors; and the various barriers to entry for prospective competitors. This information is typically the end result of *market research* that must be conducted prior to the development of a formal marketing plan. Market research need not be an expensive and time-consuming process for companies with minimal resources to devote to collecting data about the marketplace.

There are essentially two types of data needed for conducting market research: external and internal. There are many sources of external data that are available virtually free of charge from state and local economic development agencies, chambers of commerce, trade associations such as the International Franchise Association, public libraries, local colleges and universities, and even federal agencies such as the Small Business Administration or the U.S. Department of Commerce. Internal sources of information include surveys; meetings with suppliers, customers, and staff of the company in order to collect additional information regarding industry trends; consumer preferences; and the strengths and weaknesses of current marketing efforts.

Market analysis and segmentation. The information collected during the franchisor's market research must then be properly organized in order to be effective in the planning process. Unorganized data collected in a haphazard manner have minimal benefit to the development of marketing plans and strategies. The end result of the marketing research should be a *market analysis,* which should include information on segmentation of the franchisor's targeted markets, trends within its industry, and an assessment of the franchisor's direct and indirect competitors.

One of the key objectives of the market research is *segmentation* and *targeting* of the franchisor's market, which serves as a starting point for market planning. Market segmentation is the process of dividing the total market into distinct groups of buyers based upon either demographic variables (e.g., age, income levels, gender, or race), geographic location of consumers, or even social-political trends and preferences. Market targeting is the evaluation and selection of one or more of these market segments toward which marketing efforts and resources will be directed. Once specific markets have been targeted, the franchisor must develop plans and strategies to *position* its franchise offering as well as its products and services in such a way as to attract these desired market segments. Market positioning involves manipulation of the elements of the marketing mix in order to effectively and efficiently reach the targeted consumer/franchisee.

Development of the marketing plan. A well-written marketing plan becomes the blueprint for the franchisor to follow in positioning its franchise offering as well as its products and services in the marketplace in order to meet its long-term growth objectives. The marketing plan becomes an integral part of the franchisor's overall strategic plan. And like strategic planning, marketing planning must be an ongoing process that allows the franchisor to respond to changes in the marketplace, law, or technology so that its marketing strategies do not remain static or risk becoming quickly obsolete. Even more importantly, marketing planning must be consistent with the franchisor's overall strategies and objectives. Therefore, managers of *all* departments and at *varying levels* of the company must be involved in the marketing planning process and kept informed of marketing strategies as they are developed on an ongoing basis. For example, an aggressive marketing plan that is likely to triple the company's franchise sales should not be adopted without consulting the training and field support departments of the organization. Otherwise, neglected and improperly trained franchisees are likely to cripple the company.

Key elements of the marketing plan. Naturally, the contents of a marketing plan vary for each franchisor in terms of topics to be addressed, relevant trends, extent of the market research, and resources that can be committed to the implementation of the plan. The elements of the plan vary from franchisor to franchisor, depending on the specific industry in which the franchisor operates, the total cost of the franchise, and the desired profile of the targeted franchisee. Nevertheless, the following key components can and should be included in the marketing plan of franchisors of all types and sizes:

- ◆ *Executive summary.* This section should provide an overview of the principal goals and strategies that the marketing department of the franchisor plans to adopt. This summary should be distributed to all members of the franchisor's management team for review and comment prior to time and resources being devoted to the completion of the plan.

◆ *Assessment of the current state of affairs.* This section must answer the classic planning question, "Where are we and how did we get here?" but this time from a marketing perspective. Although this section is primarily historical in nature, it is also analytical because it must do more than simply tell a story; it must also explain why the franchisor's marketing strategies have evolved and ensure that these strategies are consistent with current market trends and available technology. This will often require a *marketing audit,* which seeks to identify and assess current marketing programs and strategies. This section should describe the franchisor's current products and services, the size and growth of its marketplace, a profile of its current and targeted franchisees, and an assessment of its competitors.

The importance of competitive analysis should not be overlooked. Many entrepreneurs often make the statement, "Our product/service is so unique that we have no competition." Such a statement is very dangerous and naive because it often reveals both a misunderstanding of the market as well as the likelihood of poorly conducted market research. For example, suppose that a franchisor has developed a new form of recreational activity. To the best of the franchisor's knowledge, no other company is offering this activity to consumers or this type of business format to prospective franchisees. However, this could mean that the franchisor has not conducted sufficient market research and/or that the company has not recognized that *all* forms of recreation indirectly compete for the prospective franchisee's investment income and/or the consumer's disposable income that will be allocated for leisure activities or investment in these types of businesses. Therefore, direct and indirect competitors must be discovered through detailed market research and then described in the marketing plan in terms of size, financial strength, market share, sales and profits, product/service quality, and differentiation from the company's products and services, marketing strategies, and any other characteristics that may be relevant to the development of a comprehensive marketing plan.

◆ *Discussion of current issues and opportunities.* This section should summarize the principal opportunities and threats, strengths and weaknesses, and issues and concerns that affect the franchisor's products and services as well as the market conditions affecting its ability to sell franchises. The principal question to be answered is, "What market trends and factors should be exploited and what are the external/internal barriers that must be overcome before marketing strategies can be successfully implemented?" The "opportunities and threats" subsection should address the key *external* factors in the macroenvironment affecting the company's marketing strategies, such as legal, political, economic, or social trends. The exact impact of these trends will vary depending on the company's products and services. For example, a forthcoming recession could be a threat to automobile dealers because consumers will hold on to their cars longer (creating an opportunity for the automobile aftermarket services franchisors). Yet it could be an opportunity to a franchisor of miniature golf courses because market research has proved that consumers tend to spend even more money on low-cost entertainment during troubled economic periods, while at the same time possibly be damaging to a franchise system featuring upscale furniture or expensive clothing.

The "strengths and weaknesses" subsection should address the key internal factors in the microenvironment affecting the franchisor's marketing strategies, such as resource limitations, research and development, organization structure and politics, protection of intellectual property, distribution channels, service and warranty policies, pricing strategies, and promotional programs. Once all of the opportunities, threats, strengths, and weaknesses have been identified, the last subsection, "issues and concerns," should discuss strategies and tactics for exploiting the franchisor's marketing strengths and compensating for its marketing weaknesses.

◆ *Marketing objectives and strategies.* This section should define the goals and objectives identified by the managers of the marketing department with respect to market share, advertising/promotion expenditures, franchise sales, and promotional methods. Strategies should then be discussed, outlining the specific steps and timetables involved to achieve marketing goals and objectives. Marketing strategy is essentially the "game plan" that must be adopted to achieve with respect to targeted markets, positioning of products and services, budgets for advertising, sales and public relations, and delegation of responsibility within the organization for specific projects. Because this section also involves dealing with sales and profitability projections, the franchisor's marketing staff must work closely with the finance department to ensure accuracy and consistency. As is true for all forms of planning, the statement of marketing objectives and strategies should be clear and succinct and not leave the reader (or user) hanging as to methodology. For example, a marketing objective of increasing franchise sales revenue by 10 percent could be achieved by increasing the franchise fee, increasing the total number of franchise units with the franchise fee structure remaining at current levels, or increasing fees and unit sales volume. Marketing managers must identify which course of action will be taken, based upon information ascertained from the market research as well as data and input received from other departments within the organization.

◆ *Execution of marketing program.* This section of the plan should set forth timetables for achieving specific goals and objectives, identify the persons who will be responsible for implementation, and project the anticipated resources that will be required to meet the goals developed.

◆ *Monitoring of marketing plans and strategies.* This section should discuss the establishment and operation of management systems and controls designed to monitor the franchise marketing plans and strategies implemented by the company. The relative success or failure of these programs should be measurable, so that performance can be properly assessed. Periodic reports should be prepared by the marketing department for distribution to other key members of the franchisor's management team.

◆ *Alternative marketing strategies and contingency plans.* This final section should address the alternative strategies available to the franchisor in the event of changes in the marketplace that have been identified in the plan. The ability to predict these positive or negative changes that may occur in the marketing plan and adopt alternative strategies in the event that they occur is at the heart of effective strategic marketing planning.

Remember that the marketing plan will continue to evolve and may be changed as often as monthly or be revised for specific targeted markets. The ability to quickly respond to consumer demands and prospective franchisee investment preferences is critical.

Stage 2: Implementation of the Marketing Program

Once market research has been conducted and a marketing plan prepared, the next step in the development of a marketing program is the actual *implementation* of the franchisor's objectives and strategies. At most growing franchisors, a separate marketing department is responsible for the implementation of the marketing plan. The franchise marketing director and his or her staff must constantly interact with other departments, such as operations, finance, and administration, as well as outside legal counsel in order to coordinate marketing efforts and to keep the marketing program consistent with the overall strategic plans and objectives of the franchisor. This will require the marketing department to establish certain procedures and controls to monitor marketing performance and to take corrective action where necessary to keep the franchisor on its course of growth and development. These periodic performance audits should also aim to make the franchisor more efficient by reducing unnecessary promotional expenditures and managing advertising costs.

Early-stage and growing franchisors typically experience four distinct stages in the evolution of the department responsible for development and implementation of sales and marketing functions within the organization. At the inception of the company, all founders are responsible for sales and marketing efforts. During this initial stage, marketing plans are virtually nonexistent, marketing strategies are developed with a "whatever works" approach, and sales are to "anybody who will buy" what the franchise offered. Eventually, the founders of the company are too busy with other demands to continue the sales function, and as a result a professional franchise sales staff is developed—the second stage. As the franchisor reaches the third stage of its growth, all sales and marketing efforts must be centralized into a formal department. It is typically at this phase that formal marketing plans start being prepared by top marketing executives with guidance and input from managers of other departments. As the franchisor experiences changes in its external and internal operating environment, the marketing department experiences the fourth and final phase of reorganization, during which modifications in organizational structure are made in order to adapt and respond to these environmental changes.

Developing the Franchise Sales Plan

The responsibility for managing the franchise sales program is typically vested with the vice-president of sales or the director of franchise development. This individual is responsible for development of the *franchise sales plan,* which is a critical step in the implementation of the overall marketing plan. The sales plan identifies the specific steps and resources required to attract prospective franchisees. Different sales plans need to be developed for each type of franchise offered by the company. For example, designing a program to attract a qualified prospect to serve as a subfranchisor for the state of New York is quite different from attracting a candidate for a single-unit franchise for the suburbs of Des Moines, Iowa.

The key to developing a successful franchise sales plan is to ascertain a genuine understanding of the targeted franchisee. This requires the development of a detailed profile of the prospect, which includes an analysis of targeted age, gender, education, business sophistication, income levels, net worth, family size, health, communications skills, personality traits, hobbies, habits, and career objectives. Much of this information will be obtained through the use of a confidential franchise application and personal interviews. (See Figure 9-1 for a sample franchise application.) Many sophisticated franchisors have turned to detailed psychological testing methods as part of the qualification process for prospective franchisees. If the tests reflect a personality that resists following rules and procedures or lacks a certain attention to detail, then many franchisors will reject the candidate regardless of business acumen or financial net worth. There is a wide range of qualities and characteristics that franchisors look for in developing criteria for the appropriate type of franchisee. Naturally, the criteria vary from franchisor to franchisor and from industry to industry. Neither the know-it-alls nor the naive are likely to make very good franchisees. Those who understand the importance of rules and procedures and display a willingness to follow them are likely to make the best franchisees. The franchisor is looking to attract those individuals whose personalities and experience are more suited to serve as sergeants, and not generals.

(text continues on page 227)

Figure 9-1. Sample franchise application.

CONFIDENTIAL APPLICANT QUESTIONNAIRE

FOR PROSPECTIVE FRANCHISEES

Thank you for your initial inquiry about _____. The information you provide will help us consider your application to become a member of our franchise network. This application will be carefully reviewed by our Franchise Selection Committee, and your responses will be kept confidential. The completion of this questionnaire in no way obligates either party in any manner.

PERSONAL DATA

Applicant Name: _____

                       First   Middle   Last

Social Security No.:_____Date of Birth: _____

Marital Status: ___ Married ___ Single ___ Divorced

(continues)

Figure 9-1. *(continued)*

Home Address: _____

City:_____State: _____ Zip: _____

Home Phone: (___)_____Business Phone: (___)_____

Is Co-Applicant your spouse? ☐ Yes ☐ No

Co-Applicant's Name: _____

First   Middle   Last

Social Security No.:_____Date of Birth: _____

Marital Status: ___ Married ___ Single ___ Divorced

Home Address: _____

City:_____State: _____ Zip: _____

Home Phone: (___)_____Business Phone: (___)_____

May we contact your business number? ☐ Yes ☐ No

Best time to contact:_____

**THIS APPLICATION WHEN COMPLETED
DOES NOT OBLIGATE EITHER PARTY IN ANY MANNER**

Why do you feel you are suited for the retail food and beverage business?

_____

_____

_____

What is your philosophy regarding retail food and beverage sales?

_____

_____

_____

What experience do you have with the retail food and beverage industry?

_____

_____

_____

Do you feel that you possess the qualities necessary to:

1. Train and supervise staff members? ☐ Yes ☐ No
2. Handle the everyday ongoing problems that arise when dealing with customers and staff? ☐ Yes ☐ No
3. Handle staff scheduling in both regular and flex-time modes? ☐ Yes ☐ No

Briefly explain why:

_____

_____

_____

Who will operate the franchise? ☐ Self ☐ Spouse ☐ Other

Will one of you continue to work at your current place of employment after the franchise is awarded? ☐ Yes ☐ No

If yes, who? ☐ Self ☐ Spouse ☐ Co-Applicant ☐ Other

In what city, county, and state would you like to own a franchise?

City: _____

County: _____

State: _____

Do you have a specific mall or shopping center in mind?

_____

_____

_____

How soon would you be available to operate the Center?

☐ Immediately ☐ Within ___ months

Do you now own any other franchises or business? ☐ Yes ☐ No

If yes, please describe:

_____

_____

_____

APPLICANT'S EDUCATION HISTORY

Dates of Attendance	School/College	Major	Degree

CO-APPLICANT'S EDUCATION HISTORY

Dates of Attendance	School/College	Major	Degree

APPLICANT'S EMPLOYMENT HISTORY

Dates

From — To	Company	Position	Annual Income

(continues)

Figure 9-1. *(continued)*

CO-APPLICANT'S EMPLOYMENT HISTORY
Dates

From — To	Company	Position	Annual Income

Other business affiliations (officer, director, owner, partner, etc.):

_____

_____

Have you ever failed in business or filed voluntary or involuntary bankruptcy?
☐ Yes ☐ No
If yes, please list when, where, and circumstances, including any remaining liabilities:

_____

_____

Are there any lawsuits pending against you? ☐ Yes ☐ No
If yes, please describe:

_____

_____

Have you ever been charged with or convicted of a crime or act of moral turpitude? ☐ Yes ☐ No
If yes, please describe:

_____

_____

_____

Are you a U.S. citizen? ☐ Yes ☐ No
If no, in which country do you hold a citizenship: _____

Where will the funds come from to meet the requirements of the estimated start-up costs? Enter source and dollar amounts: _____

Do you plan to have a partner (other than your spouse or Co-Applicant)?
☐ Yes ☐ No

If you own your own home, do you plan to borrow against it?
☐ Yes ☐ No

Amount of equity $_____

Amount of loan $_____

Do you anticipate obtaining a loan to assist you in funding this franchise opportunity? ☐ Yes ☐ No

If Co-Applicant is other than your spouse, please copy the remainder of the form and have each Co-Applicant fill out the appropriate information.

DEPOSIT ACCOUNT INFORMATION

Personal bank accounts and savings and loan deposits carried at:

Bank: _____ Contact Name:_____

Account No.: _____ Phone No.: (___) _____

Bank: _____ Contact Name:_____

Account No.: _____ Phone No.: (___) _____

Bank: _____ Contact Name:_____

Account No.: _____ Phone No.: (___) _____

ASSETS

Cash in Banks:_____

Savings and Loan Deposits:_____

Investments (Bonds and Stocks):_____

Accounts and Notes Receivable:_____

Real Estate Owned (see schedule):_____

Automobiles: Year _____ Make _____

Personal Property and Furniture:_____

Life Insurance Cash Surrender Value:_____

Other Assets—Itemize: _____

_____

Profit Sharing:_____

Retirement Funds:_____

True Business NET Worth

Attach Current Financial Statement

TOTAL ASSETS:_____

SCHEDULE OF STOCKS AND BONDS

Amount or No. of Shares	Description	Marketable (actual market value)	Nonmarket Cable (unlisted securities— estimated worth)

(continues)

Figure 9-1. *(continued)*

SCHEDULE OF REAL ESTATE

Description and Location	Date of Purchase	Cost	Market Value	% of Owner	Mortgage Due To	Monthly Payment
_____	_____	_____	_____	_____	_____	_____
_____	_____	_____	_____	_____	_____	_____
_____	_____	_____	_____	_____	_____	_____

LIABILITIES

Notes Payable: Name Payee

to banks:_____

to relatives:_____

to others:_____

Installment Accounts Payable:

Automobile:_____

Other (attach separately):_____

Other Accounts Payable:_____

Mortgage Payable on Real Estate:_____

Unpaid Real Estate Taxes:_____

Unpaid Income Taxes:_____

Secured Loans:_____

Loans on Life Insurance Policies:_____

Other Debts—Itemize:_____

_____

TOTAL LIABILITIES:_____

NET WORTH (Assets – Liabilities):_____

TOTAL LIABILITIES
& NET WORTH:_____

SCHEDULE OF NOTES AND ACCOUNTS PAYABLE

Includes installment debts, revolving charge accounts, bank notes, etc. Specify any assets pledged as collateral indicating the liabilities which they secure:

To Whom Payable	Date	Amount Due	Interest	Monthly Payment	Assets Pledged as Securities
_____	_____	_____	_____	_____	_____
_____	_____	_____	_____	_____	_____
_____	_____	_____	_____	_____	_____

I certify that the information I have provided on this application is complete and correct. I hereby authorize _____ or its authorized agent to obtain verification of any of the above information, and I authorize the release of such information to _____ or its authorized agent.

Signature of Applicant: _____Date: _____

Signature of Applicant: _____Date: _____

Once an accurate and objective set of criteria is developed for identifying the "model" franchisee, a sales plan must be developed to attract this prospect. Shots should always be fired with a rifle, not a cannon. For example, if experience has demonstrated that a model franchisee for your franchise system is an executive female, college-educated, between the ages of thirty-four and forty-five, then an advertisement in *Working Woman* may be a better allocation of resources than an advertisement in *Inc.* magazine. The key elements of a franchise sales plan are as follows:

A. Introduction
  1. Description of the targeted franchisee
  2. Overview of the techniques and procedures to be implemented to generate the maximum number of leads and prospects whose characteristics match those of the model franchisee
  3. Procedures for meeting, disclosing, and closing the sale
  4. Post-closing procedures
B. State of the Nation
  1. *Why people buy franchises.* Corporate restructuring and downsizing in corporate America and abroad have led to job security reaching an all-time low. A wide variety of well-educated and financially secure executives and professionals lack the dreams and excitement they so sorely need to continue the daily grind or the loyalty or sense of security from the current employer. *Franchising offers these individuals an opportunity to be in business for themselves, but not by themselves.* It is an opportunity to be an entrepreneur, but without the risk and difficulty inherent in starting a nonfranchised business. It is an opportunity to avoid the job-loss risks of downsizing and restructuring by large corporate employers. For many of these individuals, franchising

offers a happy compromise between being a middle-level executive paper pusher and a total maverick. In short, it is an opportunity to control their own destiny.

Once you understand *why* people buy franchises, you need to figure out why they will buy *your* franchise. A common misconception is that people currently operating within their industry are the best candidates for their franchise offering. Remember that considerably more frustrated accountants have purchased quick-lube and tune-up centers than have trained mechanics. With the notable exception of conversion franchising (e.g., Century 21), those with years of training and experience in a given industry are not likely to perceive the benefits of franchising in the same light as does a novice.

2. *Why people buy your franchise.* As a general rule, people will want to buy your franchise because of one or more of the following reasons:

    a. They have an interest in your industry but lack the training skills to pursue this interest without assistance.

    b. They have a friend, relative, or business associate who is already a franchisee within your system. (Happy franchisees tend to lead to more happy franchisees.)

    c. They have been consumers or employees of a franchise (or company-owned store) within your system and were impressed by the quality and consistency of your products and services.

    d. They recognize your underlying product or service as being at the leading edge and want to take advantage of a ground-floor opportunity.

    e. They were impressed by the quality and professionalism of your advertising materials, the integrity of your sales staff, and the enthusiasm and passion of your management team.

C. Lead Generation and Qualification

    1. Selection of effective media and methods

        a. *National/regional/local newspapers and magazines.* If we undertake direct advertising in specific publications with focuses such as business, income opportunity, general interest, or topic-specific, which are the most likely to attract the model franchisee? Which publications have rates within our budgets? How do we get the "biggest bang" for the buck? What should our advertisements say about the company? What image do we want to project?

b. *Direct mail.* Which mailing lists are readily available and most likely to contain a large number of our "model franchisees"? At what cost? As for design of the marketing piece, what should the text say? What should the prospect's next step be? How often do we mail? Procedures for follow-up?

c. *Trade shows.* What is the quality of the trade show organizer and promoter? (I would strongly recommend the trade shows sponsored by the International Franchise Association.) Of the facility? Of the average attendee? How elaborate should we make our booth? What type of promotional displays should be developed? How many people should we send? What literature should be available? How often should we participate? In what regions?

d. *Public relations.* What story do we tell to the media? What makes our franchise system and company different from the competition? How often do we send press releases? To whom? Saying what? When should we hold press conferences? For what events?

e. *Internet Website.* In today's technology-driven Information Age, a steadily increasing number of prospective franchisees are using the Internet to gather data about franchising as well as to narrow the field of potential franchisors to consider. The development of an informative and interactive Website where you can exchange data with prospective candidates is a critical marketing tool that must be carefully considered. One strategic issue is whether you should develop a Website address on a "stand-alone" basis or whether you should appear as part of an "umbrella" site that features a wealth of information about franchising opportunities overall and that has a section on your specific offering alongside other franchisors, such as *centercourt.com,* which is produced and maintained by IFX International. As you may already know, merely having an address in Cyberspace is of no value if nobody comes to visit you. One advantage of these umbrella sites is that the host company will invest advertising dollars to promote the site overall, thereby increasing your visibility and the chances of attracting qualified leads on the Internet.

f. *Internal marketing.* You should develop lead generation and incentive programs from the existing network of franchisees. Distribute signs and brochures within the franchisee's facilities, and offer rewards to franchisees and employees for generating qualified leads and actual franchise sales.

g. *Miscellaneous sources of lead generation.* Leads for prospective franchisees can come from a variety of nontraditional sources such as military bases, college placement offices, local business organizations, outplacement offices of large corporations that have been downsized, charitable organizations, personnel agencies, and investment clubs.

2. Procedures for qualifying a lead and making a presentation

a. *Where and how should franchises be sold?* Avoid the motel bar; get the prospect to the franchisor's headquarters, if at all possible. Make prospects feel special once they arrive. Give them the red-carpet treatment and full-blown tour. Doors should be open, not closed. People should be smiling, not frowning.

b. *Qualities of an effective franchise salesperson and presentation.* The sales staff should be there to assist, *not pressure,* the prospect. Remember that many prospects will base their decision more on personality traits of the salesperson than on the cold, hard facts contained in the offering circular. The sales staff should listen to the needs and questions of the prospect: Let the prospect make the decision to buy the franchise. The sales staff should be confident, not pushy. Franchises are *awarded, not sold*.

    c. *Data gathering on the prospect.* All relevant historical and financial data must be collected and verified. No detail should be overlooked. Employment and credit references should be checked carefully. Aptitude and psychological tests are commonplace and recommended. Carefully study the prospect, looking for any early warning signs of subsequent failure. A premium should be placed on the sales representative's "gut feel" assessment of the candidate's likelihood of success.

    d. *Materials and tools for the sales team.* Beyond the personal presentation, brochures, flip charts, and inspection of the franchisor's facilities, audiovisual materials are strongly recommended. Many franchisors have produced fifteen-minute videotapes designed to educate the prospect and help close the sale. Legal compliance (timing of disclosures, avoidance of unauthorized or improper earnings claims, and misrepresentations concerning support and assistance, etc.) is critical. See Chapters 4 and 5.

D. Closing the Sale

    1. Stay in touch during the ten-day waiting period in order to offset the inevitable negative input, sweaty palms, and cold feet that the average prospect will be experiencing.

    2. Get all mystery and confusion regarding the rights and obligations of each party resolved *before signing the franchise agreement.*

    3. Consider the franchise closing an event, not a mere procedure. This is likely to be the biggest financial transaction of the prospect's life. Make it special.

    4. Stay in touch with the franchisee after execution of the franchise documents until formal training begins.

E. Managing the Sales Team

    1. Establishment of group and individual sales goals and objectives

2. Timing and timetable for franchise sales
3. Travel and promotional budgets to support sales efforts
4. Personal, ethical, and professional expectations from your sales team (no leisure suits, no gold chains, no lies, and no unauthorized earnings claims)
5. Reporting and record-keeping requirements (communications with prospects should be carefully documented; see Chapter 5)
6. Respect for prospect review and qualification procedures (data gathering and verification, committee approval, profile testing, etc.)
7. Ongoing sales and compliance training for the team (sales and closing methods and techniques, legal documents, etc.)
8. Coordination of efforts with other departments (operations, training, finance, legal, etc.)
9. Costs and benefits of the use of outside sales organization

Stage 3: Marketing Program Monitoring and Feedback

Once marketing and sales plans are developed and implemented, systems must be put into place that monitor the performance of the efforts of the sales and marketing department, as well as gather market and competitor intelligence. The market research division is usually responsible for acquiring data and intelligence, which are sometimes used as the first step in the development of the marketing plan and other times used in tracking the performance of marketing efforts in order to modify and refine marketing plans. Either way, systems must be developed to *gather and analyze the effectiveness of franchise sales and marketing efforts* as well as to study relevant market characteristics and trends affecting the franchisor's industry-competitive analysis and to monitor general business and economic, legal, political, and technological conditions. These intelligence-gathering systems are indispensable tools of a well-managed franchise marketing department and overall franchise organization. For example, very few franchisors actively follow up with qualified leads who arrived at the decision *not* to become a franchisee of their particular system in order to find out why and learn from it. Conversely, not enough time is spent in focus groups with franchisees who *did* select their system to also make their favorable decision a learning experience.

A comprehensive monitoring and review system helps the franchise sales department to identify strengths and weaknesses of the plans and strategies initially adopted and implemented to attract prospective franchisees, measure the performance of those efforts, refine plans to adapt to changes in the marketing macroenvironment, and totally eliminate marketing strategies and sales techniques that have been a complete failure.

The key components of an effective monitoring and intelligence-gathering system include (1) acquiring and maintaining sufficient computer equipment capability to manage and organize market data; (2) tracking the development and problems of competitors; (3) remaining active in industry groups and trade associations; (4) regularly reading trade journals and industry publications; (5) meeting with key suppliers and customers to understand industry trends and preferences; (6) buying the products of competitors to observe pricing, packaging, labeling, and features; (7) keeping track of the information that may be readily available from federal, state, and local governments; and (8) staying abreast of political, economic, social, and legal trends and developments affecting marketing plans and strategies.

Franchisors should continue to monitor their sales and marketing efforts by interviewing those prospects who chose not to acquire the franchise (to find out why they did not buy) as well as collect data from recent franchisees (to find out why they did). If the lost prospect bought a franchise from another franchisor, then it is critical to find out why. Ask the lost prospect as well as the recent franchisee what they liked and didn't like about the sales presentation and offering process. The franchise director should hold weekly meetings with his or her staff to analyze and deal with the common concerns and objections raised by the typical prospect. Tools and data should then be developed to overcome these concerns.

See Figure 9-2 for some common marketing mistakes made by all franchisors. Hopefully, you won't make too many of them too often.

Figure 9-2. Common marketing mistakes made by all franchisors.

- ◆ *Overlooking the warts.* The importance of the candidate's character and attitude is often overlooked by the overanxious franchisor who overfocuses on the candidate's personal net worth or is feeling the pressure to meet payroll costs. The acceptance of this franchisee into the system just to solve a short-term cash flow problem is in turn creating a long-term systematic or legal problem. A franchisee with a bad attitude is destined to fail and likely to bring litigation.

(continues)

Figure 9-2. *(continued)*

- *Looking for love in all the wrong places.* The failure to really understand how and where your targeted candidate will be evaluating opportunities will result in slow growth and probable failure of the franchisor. The franchisor must be *focused* in its marketing efforts and allocate resources to those marketing activities that will yield the best results.
- *Passion and a sense of teamwork.* To be successful a franchisee must have a passion and excitement level for the underlying business and enter the relationship with a proper understanding of the roles of each party. The franchisor must *screen* candidates carefully to ensure this level of passion and commitment as well as *educate* the candidate on the respective roles of each party in order to avoid any confusion (or potential litigation) down the road.
- *Consensus among decision makers.* Some franchisors spend too much time with the proposed operator and not enough time with the other decision makers (spouses, parents, investors, lenders, etc.) who may play a critical role in the final decision-making process. The failure to address the needs and questions of all critical players will often lead to a lost sale.
- *Matching experience and skills with your opportunity.* An age-old question in franchising is how much experience, if any, do you want your ideal candidate to have in your underlying industry? Some franchisors prefer to train from scratch and look for strong general attitudes and business backgrounds. Others prefer their candidates to have some direct prior experience in their core industry. Still other franchisors can really award franchises only to candidates with special technical skills, professional licenses, or personality types. Franchisors must decide on these qualifications in advance and then stay focused on their pursuit of candidates who meet these criteria.
- *Armchair marketing.* Franchisors who draft marketing plans from their armchairs and who do not get out into the field to see what competitors are really doing, to react to what candidates are really saying, or to understand what market trends will really affect their growth plans are destined to fail. Franchise marketing is a very "down in the trenches," *proactive*—not merely reactive—process.
- *The wrong person for the wrong job.* Particularly in the early stages, marketing is handled by the CEO/founder and/or a lost-soul family member in an act of nepotism. Bad idea. These competitive times require a genuine marketing professional who has trade show experience and strong interpersonal skills and who has been trained in techniques that prevent "the big fish from getting away." Today's franchise marketing

professional owns no gold chains or blue suede shoes and is experienced in dealing with sophisticated prospective multiunit operators. They are trained to develop and execute an automated multistep marketing process and follow-up system and not expect success with a haphazard advertising strategy and index card–driven follow-up system.

◆ *Reality and patience.* Another classic marketing mistake made by franchisors is the failure to carefully check the candidate's willingness to work very hard and to be patient before enjoying a return on his/her investment and efforts. The candidate who comes in to the meeting thinking that his/her location will be an overnight success with minimal effort and maximum financial returns is sorely misguided. Many franchising marketing professionals don't want to "burst the excitement bubble" and never get around to throwing a little cold water and a dose of reality on the situation until it's too late. Again, this gap between the *expectations* of the franchisee and the *reality* of the challenge and performance of the underlying franchised business is a major source of litigation between franchisors and franchisees.

10

Taking Your Franchise Program Overseas

Just as the overwhelming popularity of franchising has captured the attention of the U.S. economy during the 1990s, it has also begun recently to attract attention in the overseas markets. U.S.-based franchisors are currently operating in more than 160 countries worldwide, and many successful overseas franchisors are strongly considering penetration of the U.S. market. The reasons for this foreign expansion are strikingly similar to the reasons for domestic growth, including a greater demand for personal services, higher levels of disposable income, and an increased desire for individual business ownership. Foreign franchisees are responding eagerly to the greater levels of profitability and lower levels of risk that are inherent in the marketing of an established franchised system. (See Figure 10-1 for statistics on franchising around the world.)

Figure 10-1. Franchising around the world.

Country	Number of Franchise Systems	Number of Franchise Outlets
France	600	30,000
United Kingdom	432	18,600
Germany	390	17,000
Italy	387	19,000
Netherlands	309	11,005
Spain	213	22,700
Sweden	200	6,800
Austria	170	2,700
Norway	125	3,500
Belgium	90	3,200
Portugal	55	800
Denmark	42	500

Domestic franchisors taking their products abroad in many ways face an already receptive consumer market. The established fascination with American products and lifestyles can often pave the way for successful business operations overseas. Beyond the fundamental interest in American products, many countries, particularly the less developed ones, view franchising as a readily acceptable source of technological development and system support that introduces know-how to a fledgling business community in a cost-effective manner.

When embarking on an international expansion program, franchisors must always consider:

◆ *Language barriers.* Although it may seem simple enough at the outset to translate the operations manual into the local language, marketing the system and the product may present unforeseen difficulties if the concept itself does not "translate" well.

◆ *Taste barriers.* Franchisors marketing food products have frequently found that foreign tastes differ greatly from the American palate. These factors should be carefully reviewed with the assistance of local marketing personnel and product development specialists before undertaking any negotiations with suppliers and distributors.

◆ *Marketing barriers.* These types of barriers most frequently go to the deepest cultural levels. For example, whereas many overseas markets have developed a taste for "fast food" burgers and hot dogs, differences in culture may dictate that the speed aspect is less important. Many cultures demand the leisure to be able to relax on the premises after eating a meal rather than taking a meal to go. These cultural norms can, in turn, be affected by factors such as the cost and availability of retail space.

◆ *Legal barriers.* Domestic legislation may not be conducive to the establishment of franchise and distributorship arrangements. Tax laws, customs laws, import restrictions, corporate organization, and agency/liability laws may all prove to be significant stumbling blocks.

◆ *Access to raw materials and human resources.* Not all countries offer the same levels of access to critical raw materials and skilled labor that may be needed to operate the franchised business.

◆ *Government barriers.* The foreign government may or may not be receptive to foreign investment in general or to franchising in particular. A given country's past history of expropriation, government restrictions, and limitations on currency repatriation may all prove to be decisive factors in determining whether the cost of market penetration is worth the benefits to be potentially derived.

◆ *Business formation.* The structure that the international franchising transaction will take must be determined (e.g., foreign corporation, area developer, single-unit operators, joint venture).

◆ *Choice of territory.* A territory overseas may consist of a major city, a whole country, or even a geographic region encompassing several countries. The chosen territory may well affect sales, distribution, and the ability to expand at a later point in time.

◆ *Intellectual property and quality control concerns.* Protection of trademarks, trade names, and service marks is vital for a domestic franchisor's licensing of intellectual property overseas. The physical distance between the franchisor's domestic headquarters and the overseas franchisee will make the protection of intellectual property and the monitoring of quality control more difficult.

◆ *Marketing issues.* There is no substitute for local market research into the territory to be approached. Cultural differences even from city to city within the same country can doom a franchised program before it ever hits the streets.

◆ *Local laws.* Domestic legislation needs to be examined as well for issues arising under labor law, immigration law, customs law, tax law, agency law, and other producer/distributor liability provisions. The need for import licenses and work permits also needs to be considered.

◆ *Sources of financing.* The territory chosen may affect the ability to maintain and sustain financing for the undertaking, as well as affecting the ability to receive risk insurance both publicly and privately. The franchisees in the targeted markets must have access to the financing necessary to establish single-unit franchises.

◆ *Expatriation of profits.* This can frequently be the most decisive factor in deciding whether to enter a given market or not. If a franchisor is restricted in the ability to convert and remove earned fees and royalties from a foreign jurisdiction, then the incentive for entering the market may be completely eliminated.

◆ *Taxes.* The presence or absence of a tax treaty between the franchisor's home country and the targeted foreign market can raise numerous issues and may well affect the business format chosen.

◆ *Dispute resolution.* The forum and governing law for the resolution of disputes must be chosen. On an international level, these issues

become hotly negotiated as a result of the inconvenience and expense
to the party who must come to the other's forum.

◆ *Use of a local liaison.* It is critical for the domestic franchisor to
have a local liaison or representative in each foreign market. This
local agent can assist the franchisor in understanding cultural differences, interpreting translational problems, understanding local
laws/regulations, and explaining the differences in protocol, etiquette,
and custom. It may be advised to offer employment and equity to
these foreign nationals so that they have a vested interest in the success of your operations abroad.

Naturally, these opportunities also bring certain challenges for which
appropriate strategies must be developed. For example, the world's leading
franchisor, McDonald's Corporation, recently opened its first outlet in
Iceland, where it had to build an underground heated parking lot to attract
customers. It also recently opened in Israel, but spent months fighting with
the Israeli Agriculture Ministry over the importation of the proper strain of
potatoes for its french fries. Are problems like these insurmountable and
enough of a barrier to reconsider overseas expansions? Absolutely not. But
these examples are enough to warrant a thorough investigation of the company's readiness to expand internationally and a gathering of thorough
knowledge of the targeted markets.

The Eight Commandments of Successful International Franchising set
forth below are some basic guidelines for the development of a successful
international franchise program.

1. *Know thy strengths and weaknesses.* Before expanding to another
country, be sure to have a secure domestic foundation from which the international program can be launched. Make sure that adequate capital,
resources, personnel, support systems, and training programs are in place to
assist your franchisees abroad.

2. *Know thy targeted market.* Going into a new market blindly can be
costly and lead to disputes. Market studies and research should be conducted
to measure market demand and competition for your company's products and
services. Take the pulse of the targeted country to gather data on: economic
trends; political stability; currency exchange rates; religious considerations;
dietary customers and restrictions; lifestyle issues; foreign investment and
approval procedures; restrictions on termination and nonrenewal (where
applicable); regulatory requirements; access to resources and raw materials;

availability of transportation and communications channels; labor and employment laws; technology transfer regulations; language and cultural differences; access to affordable capital and suitable sites for the development of units; governmental assistance programs; customs laws and import restrictions; tax laws and applicable treaties; repatriation and immigration laws; trademark registration requirements, availability, and protection policies; the costs and methods for dispute resolution; agency laws; and availability of appropriate media for marketing efforts.

There may also be specific industry regulations that may affect the product or service you offer to consumers (e.g., healthcare, financial services, environmental laws, food and drug labeling laws). Many overseas franchisors have made the mistake of awarding a single master license to a company for the development of the United States or even all of North America, only to subsequently discover that they lack the resources and the expertise to adequately develop this vast marketplace, which encompasses well over 300 million people. To avoid the fallacy of the "single" master licensee in large and diverse markets, we advise our foreign clients to pursue a regional approach, more closely tied to the actual capability of the regional licensee as well as the anticipated market demand for the products and services offered by the business format within the targeted region.

3. *Know thy partner.* Experienced international franchising executives around the world will tell you that the ultimate success or failure of the program depends on three critical things: finding the right partner, finding the right partner, and finding the right partner. Regardless of the specific legal structure selected for international expansion into a particular market (discussed below), the master developer or subfranchisor in the local market should always be philosophically and strategically viewed as your "partner." And, just as there should always be a dating period before a marriage or a due diligence period before an acquisition, such is also the case in selecting an international partner. There is no substitute for face-to-face negotiations between parties, regardless of whether this individual is interested in a master development agreement or a single-unit franchise. The most promising candidates will often be those with proven financial resources who have already established a successful business in the host country. They should have experience and relationships with the local and regional real estate and financial communities, have capital and management resources, and have language and communications capabilities. They should also have knowledge of the underlying industry, contacts with key suppliers, and a working familiarity with computer and communications technology.

What systems do you have in place for recruiting and selecting the right candidates? What procedures will you employ for reviewing their qualifications? What fallback plan do you have in place if you wind up selecting the wrong person or company? These are critical issues, strategies, and procedures that should be in place to ensure that you make the right selection before embarking overseas. Beyond a certain point, however, only careful negotiating and contract preparation will provide any degree of protection for a franchisor risking entry into a new market.

4. *Know thy value.* Many franchisors entering overseas markets for the first time have grandiose ideas about the structure of the master license fee and the sharing of single-unit fees and royalties. *Reality* and *patience* are the two key buzzwords here. If you overprice, you'll scare away qualified candidates and/or leave your partner with insufficient capital to develop the market. If you underprice, you'll be lacking the resources and incentive to provide quality training and ongoing support. The fee structure should fairly and realistically reflect the division of responsibility between you and your partner. Other factors influencing the structure are currency exchange and tax issues, pricing strategies, market trends, the franchisor's availability of resources and personnel to provide on-site support, and which party will bear responsibility for translation of the manuals and marketing materials as well as adaptation of the system, products, and services to meet local demand trends and cultural differences.

Franchisors must be patient in the expectations of return on investment and profits from overseas expansion. In addition to normal economic cycles and break-even analysis, certain countries dictate legal structures that are essentially "forced joint ventures," placing restrictions on a franchisor's ability to "quickly" pull out capital from the targeted country. In structuring the actual master franchise agreement, the franchisor should carefully consider the structure of the relationship, the term of the agreement, and the scope and length of nondisclosure and noncompete clauses. These provisions and their enforceability take on increased importance when complicated by distance and differences in legal systems. Franchisors should also give careful thought to the structuring of the financial provisions of the franchise agreement. It is tempting to try to mitigate potential downstream losses by seeking a higher initial fee. This alternative, however, often results in uneasiness on the part of the prospective franchisees with respect to the franchisor's long-term commitment to the host country as a whole. In light of these considerations, a more balanced approach to fees and ongoing royalties should be considered.

5. *Know thy trademark.* As a general matter, trademark laws and rights are based on actual (or a bona fide intent to) *use* in a given country. Unlike international copyright laws, your properly registered domestic trademark does not automatically confer any trademark rights in other countries. Be sure to take steps to ensure the availability and registration of your trademarks in all targeted markets. Also be sure that your trademark translates effectively in the targeted country and native language. Many franchisors have had to modify their names, designs, or slogans because of translation or pirating problems in new targeted markets.

6. *Know thy product and service.* The format of your proprietary products or services that have been successful in your home country may or may not be successful in another country. Be sensitive to different tastes, cultures, norms, traditions, trends, and habits within a country before making final decisions on prices, sizes, or other characteristics of your products or services. Conversely, be careful not to make drastic changes to your product or service at the cost of sacrificing quality, integrity, uniformity, or consistency. There are many comical (yet expensive) lessons and stories that can be told about domestic franchisors who have learned the hard way that what works well for you at home may be very different abroad.

7. *Know thy resources.* Access to resources and experienced advice is a major factor in the success of an international franchising program but does not always require the help of expensive advisers or market research studies. In addition to the extensive resources available at the International Franchise Association in Washington, D.C. (202-628-8000), over thirty different countries have established national and regional franchise associations that may be an excellent starting point for gathering data about a targeted market. In addition, the International Trade Administration within the U.S. Department of Commerce, the U.S. Chamber of Commerce, and the economic bureaus of most embassies maintain extensive economic and political data on countries around the world.

8. *Know thy rationale.* Franchisors often have widely varying reasons for selecting a targeted country or market. Sometimes they are "pulled" into a market by an interested prospect who is familiar with their concept (often as a result of being a temporary resident, tourist, or student in the franchisor's home country), which is especially dangerous if the franchisor relies only on the assurances of the interested candidate that there is a demand for products and services. Other franchisors "push" their way into a targeted foreign market (sometimes as a result of market saturation or a lack of opportunity in their domestic market) by ranking the likelihood of their success by measur-

ing certain factors of overseas markets. These factors include language and cultural similarities, geographic proximity, market and economic growth trends, risk level, cooperative attitude, and potential return on investment.

Structuring International Master Franchising Relationships

There is a wide variety of forms that an international franchising program can take, each with its respective advantages and disadvantages. Although an extensive discussion of these issues is beyond the scope of this chapter, franchisors should consult with experienced counsel as to whether joint ventures, subfranchising, regional development, area franchising, direct franchising, direct product or service distribution strategies, or even more creative strategies or structures should be pursued.

Most international franchising transactions are structured as either: (1) an award "multiple-unit franchise" to aggressive entrepreneurs who will be responsible for the development of an entire geographic region, either through their own resources or by subfranchising to third parties, or (2) through some joint venture structure, as discussed in Chapter 18.

The Regulation of Franchising Abroad

While most countries do not encourage or discourage franchising specifically, the attitude toward foreign investors seeking to penetrate local markets through master or direct franchising is subject to a balancing of competing policy objections. On the one hand, local government is interested in attracting capital investment and creating employment, an influx of new technology, and an increased tax revenue that a new franchise system may provide. On the other hand, the local government may want to control the remittance of local currency to foreign investors, whether paid as licensing fees, royalties, or profits. The local government may also be committed to protecting local franchisees from paying the franchisor an excessive amount for the rights to operate the franchise and wants to protect the local franchisee from onerous clauses in the franchise agreement that unduly restrict the franchisee's operations. Therefore, restrictive clauses that require the franchisee to use only raw materials furnished by the franchisor, limit the franchisee's production, or prevent the franchisee from selling outside a particular geographic area may be invalid under local franchising or antitrust law.

Figure 10-2 presents information on franchising regulations in various countries around the world.

Figure 10-2. Franchising regulations in different countries around the world.

Country	Pre-Sale Disclosure or Registration Required by Governmental Agency	Pre-Sale Disclosure Recommended or Required by Trade Association as Criteria for Membership	Overview of Requirements
United States	Yes	Yes	FTC Pre-Sale Disclosure (10-day) Registration (14 states) International Franchise Association Code of Ethics
Canada	No	Yes	The Canadian Franchise Association has adopted mandatory disclosure rules for its members that mirror many significant parts of the UFOC
Brazil	Yes	Yes	Pre-Sale Disclosure (10-day) Agreements requiring foreign exchange payments must be registered with the National Industrial Property Institute
France	Yes	Yes	This is based on the French statute Loi Doubin
Australia	No	Yes	Franchise Association of Australia requires disclosure documents by its members
Italy	Yes	Yes	Pre-Sale Disclosure (15-day) The Italian Franchise Association requires its members to have tested their concept in the market for at least one year and have at least one pilot store operating before offering any franchises
Mexico	No	No	Upon execution of a franchise agreement, franchisors must record the agreement before the Mexican Institute of Industrial Property; all documents written in a foreign language must be translated to Spanish
Spain	Yes	Yes	Pre-Sale Disclosure (20-day)
Russia	Yes	No	Regulations not yet published
South Africa	No	Yes	Pre-Sale Disclosure (7-day)

(continues)

Figure 10-2. (*continued*)

Country	Pre-Sale Disclosure or Registration Required by Governmental Agency	Pre-Sale Disclosure Recommended or Required by Trade Association as Criteria for Membership	Overview of Requirements
South Korea	Yes	N/A	Specifically, the regulations: (1) require franchisors to provide necessary information about the franchise business to prospective franchisees; (2) prohibit franchisors from unreasonably requiring franchisees to purchase equipment or commodities from the franchisor or an approved source; (3) bar franchisors from unfairly restricting a franchisee's dealings in commodities, services, or assistance without rightful cause; (5) preclude franchisors' imposition of monetary burdens on the franchisee without prior consent; (6) ban franchisors' unilateral amendment of franchise agreements; and (7) prohibit the imposition of post-term noncompetition agreements without rightful cause
China	Yes	N/A	Pre-Sale Disclosure (10-day)

Part **Four**

Financial
Strategies

Business and Strategic Planning for the Growing Franchisor

Owners and managers of growing franchisors have come to understand that meaningful and effective business planning is critical to the long-term success and viability of any business and to its ability to raise capital. Before you read in Chapter 12 about the various methods of financing available to the growing franchisor, *you must understand the key elements of a business plan.* Regardless of the financing method or the type of capital to be raised, virtually any lender, underwriter, venture capitalist, or private investor expects to be presented with a meaningful business plan. A well-prepared business plan demonstrates management's ability to focus on long-term, achievable goals; provides a guide to effectively implement the articulated goals once the capital has been committed; and constitutes a yardstick by which actual performance can be evaluated.

The Business Plan

Business plans should be used by early-stage franchisors as well as established franchisors. There is no single "right way" to prepare a business plan. Each business plan must be reflective of the franchisor's own goals and objectives, management team, experience, and relevant industry trends. All business plans, whether used for internal or external purposes, must be clear and concise, timely, accurate, conservative, and comprehensive. Resist the temptation to mislead the reader or to leave out negative information. The following is a broad outline of the fundamental topics to be included in a typical franchiser's business plan.

Executive Summary

This introductory section of the plan should explain the nature of the business and highlight the important features and opportunities offered by an investment in the company. The executive summary should be no longer than one to three pages and should include (1) the company's origins and performance, (2) distinguishing and unique features of the products and services offered to both consumers and franchisees, (3) an overview of the market, and (4) the amount of money sought and for what specific purposes.

History and Operations of the Franchisor

In this first full section, the history of the franchisor should be discussed in greater detail: its management team (with résumés included as an exhibit); the specific program, opportunity, or project being funded by the proceeds; the prototype; an overview of the franchiser's industry, with a specific emphasis on recent trends affecting the market demand for the franchises; as well as the products and services offered by the franchisee. Figure 11-1 provides a list of questions to be addressed in this section.

Figure 11-1. Questions to address in the business plan section on the history and operations of the franchisor.

1. When and how was the prototype facility first developed?
2. Why has the company decided to expand its market share through franchising?
3. What are the company's greatest strengths and proprietary advantages with respect to its franchisees? Consumers? Employees? Shareholders? Competitors?
4. What are the nature, current status, and future prospects in the franchisor's industry?

Many of these issues will be described in greater detail in later sections of the plan. Therefore, each topic should be covered summarily in two or three paragraphs.

Marketing Research and Analysis

This section must present to the reader all relevant and current information regarding the size of the market for both franchisees and consumers, trends in the industry, marketing and sales strategies and techniques, assessments of the competition (direct and indirect), estimated market share and projected sales, pricing policies, advertising and public relations strategies, and a description of sales personnel. The following matters should also be addressed:

◆ *Describe the typical consumer.* How and why is the consumer attracted to patronize the franchisee's facility? What relevant market trends affect the consumer's decision to purchase products and services from the franchisee's facility?

◆ *Describe the typical franchisee.* How and why is the prospective franchisee attracted to the franchisor's business format? What factors have influenced the prospect's decision to purchase the franchise? What steps are being taken to attract additional candidates who meet these criteria?

◆ *Describe the market.* What is the approximate size of the total market for the services offered by the franchisee? The approximate market for franchisees?

◆ *Describe the strategy.* What marketing strategies and techniques have been adopted to attract franchisees and consumers? Where do referrals for prospective franchisees come from? Do existing franchisees make referrals? Why or why not? (Include sample promotional materials as an exhibit.)

◆ *Describe the performance of the typical franchisee.* Are current stores profitable? Why or why not? What factors influence their performance?

Rationale for Franchising

This section should explain the underlying rationale for selecting franchising in lieu of the other growth and distribution strategies that may be available. Discuss whether a dual distribution strategy will be pursued. Under what circumstances will company-owned units be established? Explain to the reader which method(s) of franchising will be selected. Single units only? Sales representatives? Area developers? Subfranchisees? Special risks and legal issues that are triggered by the decision to franchise should also be discussed.

The Franchising Program

This section should provide an overview of the franchising program with respect to key aspects of the franchise agreement, a description of the typical site, an overview of the proprietary business format and trade identity, the training program, operations manual, support services to franchisees, targeted markets and registration strategies, the offering of regional and area development agreements, and arrangements with vendors. A detailed analysis of sales and earnings estimates and personnel needed for a typical facility should be included. Discuss marketing strategies relevant to franchising such as trade shows, industry publications, and sales techniques. Explain the typical length of time between the first meeting with a prospect through grand opening and beyond. What are the various steps and costs during this time period (from the perspective of both the franchisor and the franchisee)? Discuss strategies for the growth and development of the franchising program over the next five to ten years.

Corporate and Financial Matters

This section should briefly describe the current officers, directors, and shareholders of the corporation. An overview of the capital contributed to the company thus far should be provided, along with an explanation of how these funds have been allocated. Discuss the anticipated monthly operating costs to be incurred by the corporation, both current and projected, not only for operating and managing the prototype facility but also for the administrative expenses incurred in setting up a franchise sales and services office. Discuss the pricing of the franchise fee, royalties, and promotional fund contributions. Discuss the payment histories of the franchisees thus far. Are they complying with their obligations under the franchise agreement? Why or why not?

What portion of these fees collected from the franchisee will be net profit? Discuss the amount of capital that will be required for the corporation to meet its short-term goals and objectives. How much, if any, additional capital will be required to meet long-term objectives? What alternative structures and methods are available for raising these funds? How will these funds be allocated? Provide a breakdown of expenses for personnel, advertising and marketing, acquisition of equipment or real estate, administration, professional fees, and travel. To what extent are these expenses fixed, and to what extent will they vary depending on the actual growth of the company?

Operations and Management

Provide the current and projected organizational and management structure. Identify each position by title, with a description of duties, responsibilities, and compensation. Describe the current management team and anticipated hiring requirements over the next three to five years. What strategies will be adopted to attract and retain qualified franchise professionals? Provide a description of the company's external management team (attorney, accountant, etc.).

Exhibits

Include exhibits of the franchisor's trademarks and marketing brochures, press coverage, as well as sample franchise agreements and area development agreements.

The Ongoing Strategic Planning Process

In a franchisor's early stages, the emphasis is on the business plan. Among the key concerns are how to properly launch the franchising program to attract qualified candidates and what resources will be needed to sustain the program. But what happens later? Once a franchisor reaches 50 to 100 units or more, the focus shifts away from mere business planning and on to strategic planning. The strategic planning process begins to look at more advanced types to ensure the future growth and profitability of the franchisor's system. For example:

- What are the our critical succcess factors, and how can they be measured?
- Have we developed a Code of Values and has it been adequately communicated to (and enforced by) our franchisees?
- What new opportunities should we be exploring?
- What diversifications to our product or service lines (either internally developed or obtained via acquisition) may be necessary for survival or to facilitate growth?
- What alternative distribution channels should or are being considered?
- Where are the major "disconnects" between our stated philosophies and our actual actions? Or between our objectives and our policy or resource constraints?
- Where is our leadership succeeding and where is it failing? Why?

All of these are questions that an early-stage franchisor is not likely to face, but must be in a position to face once a critical mass of franchises has been obtained. This process can be a "reality check" to ensure that the franchisor's growth plan is on the right track. Figure 11-2 presents key strategic planning issues.

Figure 11-2. Key strategic planning issues.

- What are the common characteristics of our top 20 percent of franchisees?
- What can we do to attract more people like this in the recruitment and selection process?
- What are the common characteristics of our bottom 20 percent of franchisees?
- How do we screen these out? What can we do to improve their performance?
- What are the five greatest strengths of our system?
- What is being done to build on these strengths?
- What are the five biggest problems of our system?
- What are we doing to resolve these problems?

In the context of franchising, strategic planning is an ongoing process that seeks to *build* and *improve* the following key areas:

- The quality and performance of the franchisees
- The quality and sophistication of the technology used by the franchisor to support the franchisees
- The quality and sophistication of the training and support systems
- The value and recognition of the franchiser's brand from a customer awareness perspective
- The development and communication of the franchise system's "best practices" throughout the system, as well as general "best practices" in franchising overall
- The exploration of new domestic and international markets
- The organization of franchisee advisory councils, supplier councils, co-branding alliances, and other key strategic relationships
- The development of strategies for multiunit franchising, alternative sites, and related new market penetration strategies
- The development of advanced branding and intellectual property protection strategies

The strategic planning process should manifest itself in periodic meetings among the franchiser's leadership, periodic strategic planning retreats, and a written strategic plan, which should be updated annually. The strategic planning meetings and retreats could be focused on a specific theme, such as brand building and leveraging, rebuilding trust and value with the franchisees, litigation prevention and compliance, international opportunities in the global village, leadership and productivity issues, financial management and per-unit performance issues, the improved recruitment of women and minorities, technology improvement and communications systems, alternative site and nontraditional location analysis, co-branding and brand-extension licensing, or building systems for improving internal communication. Any or all of these topics are appropriate for one meeting or for discussion on a continuing basis. The strategic planning meeting could be led by an outside facilitator, such as an industry expert, or by the franchiser's senior management team. A model agenda for a two-day general strategic planning retreat is set forth below.

Model Strategic Planning Meeting Agenda

Evaluating our strategic assets and relationships

1. Overview
   - Goals and objectives of the meeting
   - Key trends in domestic and international franchising
2. Assessing the strengths of our franchise relations
   - Franchising state of the union
   - Common critical success factors by and among our franchisees
3. Evaluating our team
   - Code of values: reality and practice
   - Motivating and rewarding employees
   - Protecting the knowledge worker
   - Providing genuine leadership
4. Our strategic partners
   - What do we expect from our vendors and professional advisers?
   - What can we do to enhance the efficiency and productivity of these relationships?
   - Building the national accounts program
   - Do all of our strategic relationships truly provide mutual reward and enhance our system?
5. Our targeted customers
   - Identifying and dealing with the competition
   - Customer perceptions of quality and value
   - Franchisor-customer communications

- Customer satisfaction surveys
- Exploring two-tier marketing strategies
- Asset-building strategies

1. Building and leveraging brand awareness
   - Building overall brand awareness
   - Brand leveraging strategies
   - Building an arsenal of intangible assets
2. Co-branding and strategic alliances
   - Identifying goals and objectives
   - Targeting and selecting partners
   - Structuring the deal
3. Shared goals and values
   - Enhancing intracompany communications
   - Building trust and respect
4. Role and value of technology
   - How technology is changing the way we work and consume products/services
   - The impact of technology on recruiting, training, and supporting franchises
   - The impact of technology on how our franchisees will market their products/services to targeted customers
5. Development of branded products and services to strengthen our revenue base
   - Business training and assistance resources for clients
   - Home cleaning and refinishing products
   - Co-branded products and services (e.g., securities sales, financial planning, home improvement and remodeling)
   - Affinity/group purchasing programs

The end result of an effective strategic planning meeting is to develop a list of specific action items. Some action items may be able to be implemented right away, and some may take some time. Here is a list of specific action items that may result:

- Consider the entry into new domestic and international markets. U.S. franchisors can start with Canada, Mexico, and South America; many franchisors are currently exploring opportunities in these markets because of their close geographic proximity to the United States.

◆ Reexamine your vertical pricing structures and strategies in light of the recent Supreme Court case *State Oil Co. v. Khan,*[1] which changed the ground rules for "suggested retail pricing" by applying a "rule of reason" test to vertical price restraints. The Supreme Court ruled that a manufacturer or supplier does not necessarily violate federal antitrust law by placing a ceiling on the retail price a dealer can charge for its products. It remains illegal, however, for manufacturers to impose minimum prices on dealers.

◆ Consider implementing various types of multiunit development strategies.

◆ Consider *alternative territorial penetration strategies* such as kiosks, satellites, carts, mini-units, seasonal units, limited service units, in-store units, resorts units, military base units, and related alternative site selection strategies.

◆ Consider joint ventures with other franchisors or nonfranchisors and complementary but noncompeting markets. This could include joint site developments, such as in the coffee and muffin industries or automobile mini-malls and other related operational joint ventures. Many food-related franchisors are actively developing co-branding programs as a vehicle for growth and new market penetration.

◆ Be aggressive and proactive in commercial leasing strategies. Consider subleasing and turnkey development strategies, stricter site selection criteria to improve failure rate and the financial performance of each franchisee, etc.

◆ Take a hard look at your financial management practices to avoid the possibility of liability under the *Meineke* case.[2] Make sure that advertising contributions have been segregated to avoid potential claims by franchisees and other financially related litigation prevention techniques.

◆ Reevaluate your internal and external management team. Get rid of internal deadwood, and don't be afraid to demand more and better from your outside advisers. Continue to evaluate your management team for any individuals who may be engaged in a course of action that is unproductive, hostile, or harassing to your current or prospective franchisees. Ask your outside advisers: What are you doing to help us grow, and do you truly care about the future direction of our company?

◆ Cleanse the baseless rabble-rousers and nonperformers from your franchise system. These negative influencers spread like wildfire. Put these fires out while there is still a spark and not a flame. It is important to separate the good constructive criticism and proactive franchisee from the just plain "whiners" whom you will never satisfy.

◆ Build up your arsenal of protectable and registered intellectual property (e.g., trademarks, copyrights, trade dress).

◆ Be proactive in creating franchisee advisory councils and other methods to improve franchisor/franchisee communications to maximize franchise relationships. Bear in mind that happy franchisees keep litigation costs down and new franchise sales up.

◆ Search for new markets and methods to find new franchisees. Be creative and untraditional. Try new venues and places that the other franchisors are not targeting.

◆ Venture into the world of being a product and service provider to your network of franchisees. These activities should be subject to applicable antitrust laws. It could be quite lucrative—provided that you are within legal boundaries, you are not too greedy, and you are properly structuring the economic relationships. These product and service provider relationships can be done directly or through joint ventures with third-party suppliers. New cases such as *Queen City,* 1997 WL 526213 (3d Cir.), discussed in Chapter 3, may open up a new door for you in this area.

◆ Get active in industry groups and lobbying efforts that may affect the operations or profitability of your franchisees' businesses.

◆ Use current and developing computer and communications technologies to enhance franchise sales and support, to gather demographics, to provide training, and to facilitate communication by and among franchisees. A franchiser's failure to take advantage of these developments along the information superhighway could be detrimental. These technologies include significantly faster microprocessors, robotics, smart cards, voice-activated and wearable hardware, Intranets and electronic mail, videoconferencing, private satellite networks, virtual reality, on-demand publishing, enhanced electronic commerce, and integrated digital communications, which will all permanently change the way we interact with our franchisees and the manner in which our franchisees interact with their customers.

◆ Develop an internally generated strategic growth plan. This plan should have clear and attainable objectives. Then really use it. Do not let the growth plan sit around and collect dust. Understand the common financial management pitfalls that hinder the performance of many early-stage and rapidly growing franchisors.

◆ Explore alternatives to franchising in certain situations where licensing, distributorships, joint ventures, dual distribution, or some other contractual distribution channel may be more appropriate.

◆ Motivate your internal team with stock option plans, bonus formulas, and other equity incentive programs. These programs will help enhance customer service and franchisee relations.

◆ Reread your UFOC as if you were a prospective franchisee. Do the documents convey your company's philosophies? Do the documents adequately tell your company's story? Do they convey a sense of trust, fairness, and reasonableness? Are the documents user-friendly to the reader and to the advisers of the franchisee? Would you buy this franchise? You will discover a lot about your UFOC and your ability to use the document as a marketing tool if you reread the document as if you were buying the franchise.

◆ Develop some good data-gathering system on the financial performance of your franchisees. Use these data to compile sample profit and loss statements and balance sheets of some of the strong, medium, and weak franchisees in the system. Circulate these documents—subject of course to confidentiality and earning claims regulations—among your existing franchisees to increase their performance and to point out flaws in their financial management, etc.

In sum, the strategic planning process is a commitment to strive for the *continuous improvement* of the franchise system. The process is designed to ensure that maximum value is being delivered, day in and day out, to the franchisor's executive team, employees, shareholders, vendors and suppliers, and, of course, franchisees. It is about not being afraid to ask: Where are we? Where do we want to be? What do we need to do to get there? What is currently standing in our way of achieving these objectives? It is about making sure that the company takes the time to develop a mission statement and define a collective vision and then develop a series of plans to achieve these goals. Executives must stay focused on these objectives and provide leadership to both the balance of the franchiser's team as well as to the franchisees as to how these objectives will be achieved. The focus must be on brand equity, franchisee value, customer loyalty, and shareholder profitability. The guidelines and protocols for internal communications must encourage honesty and openness, without fear of retaliation or politics.

By following the strategic planning process, franchisors can become truly successful. For what I call the seven habits of highly successful franchisors, see Figure 11-3.

Figure 11-3. The seven habits of highly successful franchisors.

1. An ability to adapt to challenges and changes in the marketplace
   ◆ How do we react to inevitable and constant changes in the environment?
   ◆ How well do we plan in advance, anticipate change, and face the reality of what's really happening in the trenches?
   ◆ Do we really listen to our franchisees?

2. A genuine commitment to the success of each and every franchisee
   ◆ A chain is only as strong as its weakest link. How strong is our chain?
   ◆ How is this commitment demonstrated?
   ◆ Is this how our franchisees truly perceive our commitment?

3. A culture committed to overcoming complacency
   ◆ Are we committed to research and development?
   ◆ What steps are in place to constantly improve and expand our systems and capabilities?
   ◆ How quickly do we abandon a failing franchisee?

4. A team ready to break old paradigms
   ◆ Are we committed to thinking outside the box?
   ◆ What recent examples do we have where creative thinking solved a problem or created a new opportunity?
   ◆ Are we using computer and communications technologies such as email, intranets, interactive computer training, and private satellite networks to help us support and communicate with our franchisees?

5. A total devotion to excellent customer service
   ◆ What systems do we have in place to ensure excellence in our interactions with targeted home and business customers?
   ◆ Do we have a procedure for gathering feedback and reacting to problems in the field?
   ◆ When is the last time we spoke directly with our franchisee's customers?
   ◆ What are we doing to educate our targeted customers on quality and product/service differentiation issues? How can we achieve "*Good Housekeeping* Seal of Approval" –type status with our customers (e.g., known as setting the standards for quality)? What can we do at the community/grassroots level to promote and enhance this image (e.g., controlling and enhancing the customer's buying experience)?
   ◆ Do we treat our franchisees as *our* customers?

6. A commitment to taking the time to truly understand and analyze the economics of the core business (by all key players in the organization, not just the CFO!)
   ◆ Does the current franchise fee and royalty structure make sense? Is it fair?

◆ How often are royalty and other financial reports truly reviewed and analyzed? Are key observations and trends shared in the field?

7. A bona fide understanding of the key factors that make our franchisees successful

◆ When was the last time we did market research or surveyed our current franchisees?

◆ What have we learned from our less-than-successful franchisees?

Notes

1. *State Oil Co. v. Khan et al.,* No. 96-871 (S.Ct. Nov. 4, 1997).

2. In *Broussard v. Meineke Discount Muffler Shops, Inc.,* 2 Bus. Fran. Guide (CCH) ¶ 11,125 (D.C. N.C. 1996), a federal judge in Charlotte, North Carolina, awarded franchisees $601 million in damages—the largest award ever in a franchisor-franchisee dispute. In this class action, the franchisees accused the franchisor of taking more than $31 million from advertising funds dating back to 1986. The franchisees contended that the franchisor took additional fees and commissions from the advertising account and negotiated volume discounts for advertising, but took the discounts for itself. The franchisees also alleged that the franchisor violated North Carolina's Unfair and Deceptive Trade Practices Act, committed fraud, and breached its fiduciary duty to franchisees by, among other things, using advertising funds for improper purposes such as settling a lawsuit, paying the franchisor's business expenses, and advertising for prospective franchisees. After a seven-week trial, the jury found the franchisor and other defendants (including three corporate affiliates and three individual principals of the companies) liable to the class of over 900 franchisees and awarded $197 million in compensatory damages. The judge trebled the damage award and added $10.1 million in interest, bringing the total award to $601 million. The parent company, GKN Plc of Britain, said although it plans to appeal the federal court's ruling, and retained special prosecutor Kenneth Starr to argue its appeal, it had already amended its 1996 earnings report by making provisions for $435 million in exceptional charges.

12

Raising Growth Capital for Emerging Franchisors

One of the most difficult tasks faced by the management team of a growing franchisor is the development and maintenance of an optimal capital structure for the organization. Access to affordable debt and equity capital continues to be a problem for the growing franchisor even though franchising has matured as a viable method of business growth.

Only recently have the investment banking and commercial lending communities given franchising the recognition it deserves. There are finally enough franchisors whose balance sheets have become more respectable, who have participated in successful public offerings, who have played (and won) in the merger and acquisition game, and who have demonstrated consistent financial appreciation and profitability. These developments have played a role in providing young franchisors access to affordable capital in recent years. Nevertheless, a growing franchisor must be prepared to *educate the source of capital* as to the unique aspects of financing a franchise company. And there are differences. Franchisors have different balance sheets (heavily laden with intangible assets), different allocations of capital (directed as expenditures for "soft costs"), different management teams, different sources of revenues, and different strategies for growth. The amount of capital potentially available, as well as the sources willing to consider financing a given transaction, depends largely on the franchisor's current and projected financial strength, as well as the experience of its management team and a host of other factors, such as trademarks and its franchise sales history.

The Initial and Ongoing Costs of Franchising

Before examining the capital formation strategies that may be available, you should understand the specific nature of the capital requirements of the early-stage and emerging franchisor. Although franchising is less capital-intensive than is internal expansion, *franchisors still require a solid capital structure.* Grossly undercapitalized franchisors are on a path to disaster because they will be unable to develop effective marketing programs, attract qualified staff, or provide the high-quality, ongoing support and assistance that franchisees need to grow and prosper.

Bootstrap franchising has been tried by many companies, but very few have been successful. In a bootstrap franchising program, the franchisor uses the initial franchise fees paid by the franchisee as its capital for growth and expansion. There is a bit of a catch-22, however, if the franchisor has not properly developed its operations, training program, and materials prior to the offer and sale of a franchise. Such a strategy could subject the franchisor to claims of fraud and misrepresentation, because the franchisee has good reason to expect that the business format franchise is complete and not still "under construction." A second legal problem with undercapitalization is that many examiners in the registration states will either completely bar a franchisor from offers and sales in their jurisdiction until the financial condition improves or imposes restrictive bonding and escrow provisions in order to protect the fees paid by the franchisee. A third possible legal problem is that if the franchisor is using the franchise offering circular to raise growth capital, then the entire scheme could be viewed as a securities offering, which triggers compliance with federal and state securities laws, as discussed later in this chapter.

The start-up franchisor must initially put together a budget for the developmental costs of building the franchise system. This budget should be incorporated into the business plan, the key elements of which are discussed in Chapter 11. The start-up costs include the development of operations manuals, training programs, sales and marketing materials, personnel recruitment, accounting and legal fees, research and development, testing and operation of the prototype unit, outside consulting fees, and travel costs for trade shows and sales presentations. Naturally, there are a number of variables influencing the amount that must be budgeted for development costs, including:

- ◆ The extent to which outside consultants are required to develop operations and training materials
- ◆ The franchisor's location and geographic proximity to targeted franchisees
- ◆ The complexity of the franchise program and trends within the franchisor's industry
- ◆ The quality, experience, and fee structure of the legal and

accounting firms selected to prepare the offering documents and agreements

◆ The extent to which products or equipment will be sold directly to franchisees, which may require warehousing and shipping capabilities

◆ The extent to which personnel placement firms will be used to recruit the franchisor's management team

◆ The use of a celebrity or industry expert to endorse the franchisor's products, services, and franchise program

◆ The difficulty encountered at the U.S. Patent and Trademark Office in registering the franchisor's trademarks

◆ The extent to which direct financing will be offered to the franchisees for initial opening and/or expansion

◆ The compensation structure for the franchisor's sales staff

◆ The difficulty encountered by franchise counsel in the registration states

◆ The extent to which the franchisor gets embroiled in legal disputes with the franchisees at an early stage

◆ The quality of the franchisor's marketing materials

◆ The type of media and marketing strategy selected to reach targeted franchisees

◆ The number of company-owned units the franchisor plans to develop

◆ The length and complexity of the franchisor's training program

◆ The rate at which the franchisor will be in a position to repay the capital (or provide a return on investment), which will influence the cost of the capital

Private Placements as a Capital Formation Strategy

Smaller and medium-size franchisors often initially turn to the private capital markets to fuel their growth and expansion. The most common method selected is the sale of a company's (or its subsidiary's) securities through a private placement. In general terms, a private placement may be used as a vehicle for capital formation any time a particular security or transaction is exempt from federal registration requirements under the Securities Act of 1933 as described below. The private placement generally offers reduced transactional and ongoing costs because of its exemption from many of the extensive registration and reporting requirements imposed by federal and state securities laws. The private placement usually also offers the ability to structure a more complex and confidential transaction, since the offeree will typically be a small number of sophisticated investors. In addition, a private placement permits a more rapid penetration into the capital markets than would a public offering of securities requiring registration with the Securities and Exchange Commission (SEC).

In order to determine whether a private placement is a sensible strategy for raising capital, it is imperative that franchisors: (1) have a fundamental understanding of the federal and state securities laws affecting private placements, (2) be familiar with the basic procedural steps that must be taken before such an alternative is pursued, and (3) have a team of qualified legal and accounting professionals who are familiar with the securities laws to assist in the offering.

An Overview of Regulation D

The most common exemptions from registration that are relied upon by franchisors in connection with a private placement are contained in the Securities and Exchange Commission's Regulation D. The SEC promulgated Regulation D in 1982 in order to facilitate capital formation by smaller companies. Since its inception, Regulation D has been an extremely successful vehicle for raising capital, with billions of dollars being raised each year by small and growing businesses. Regulation D offers a menu of three transaction exemptions, which are discussed below.

1. *Rule 504* under Regulation D permits offers and sales of not more than $1 million during any twelve-month period by any issuer that is not subject to the reporting requirements of the Securities Exchange Act of 1934 (the "Exchange Act") and that is not an investment company. Rule 504 places virtually no limit on the number or the nature of the investors that participate in the offering. *But even if accreditation is not required, it is strongly recommended that certain baseline criteria be developed and disclosed in order to avoid unqualified or unsophisticated investors.* Even though no formal disclosure document (also known as a prospectus) needs to be registered and delivered to offerees under Rule 504, there are many procedures that still must be understood and followed, and *a disclosure document is nevertheless strongly recommended.* An offering under Rule 504 is still subject to the general antifraud provisions of Section 10(b) of the Exchange Act and Rule 10b-5 thereunder; thus, every document or other information that is actually pro-

vided to the prospective investor must be accurate and not misleading by virtue of its content or its omissions in any material respect. The SEC also requires that its Form D be filed for all offerings under Regulation D within fifteen days of the first sale. Finally, a growing franchisor seeking to raise capital under Rule 504 should examine applicable state laws very carefully because although many states have adopted overall securities laws similar to Regulation D, many of these laws do not include an exemption similar to 504, and as a result, a formal private placement memorandum may need to be prepared.

2. *Rule 505* under Regulation D is selected over Rule 504 by many companies as a result of its requirements being consistent with many state securities laws. Rule 505 allows for the sale of up to $5 million of the issuer's securities in a twelve-month period to an unlimited number of "accredited investors" and up to thirty-five nonaccredited investors (regardless of their net worth, income, or sophistication). An "accredited investor" is *any person* who qualifies for (and must fall within one of) one or more of the eight categories set out in Rule 501(a) of Regulation D. Included in these categories are officers and directors of the franchisor who have "policy-making" functions as well as outside investors who meet certain income or net worth criteria. Rule 505 has many of the same filing requirements and restrictions imposed by Rule 504 (such as the need to file a Form D), in addition to an absolute prohibition on advertising and general solicitation for offerings and restrictions on which companies may be an issuer. Any company that is subject to the "bad boy" provisions of Regulation A is disqualified from being a 505 offeror and applies to persons who have been subject to certain disciplinary, administrative, civil, or criminal proceedings or sanctions that involve the franchisor or its predecessors.

3. *Rule 506* under Regulation D is similar to Rule 505; however, the issuer may sell its securities to an unlimited number of accredited investors and up to thirty-five nonaccredited investors. For those requiring large amounts of capital, this exemption is the most attractive because it has no maximum dollar limitation. The key difference under Rule 506 is that any nonaccredited investor must be "sophisticated." A "sophisticated investor" (in this context) is one who does not fall within any of the eight categories specified by Rule 501(a), but is believed by the issuer to "have knowledge and experience in financial and business matters that render him capable of evaluating the merits and understanding the risks posed by the transaction (either acting alone or in conjunction with his 'purchaser representative')." The best way to remove any uncertainty over the sophistication or accreditation of a prospective investor is to request that a comprehensive Confidential Offeree Questionnaire be completed before the securities are sold. Rule 506 does eliminate the need to

prepare and deliver disclosure documents in any specified format, if exclusively accredited investors participate in the transaction. As with Rule 505, an absolute prohibition on advertising and general solicitation exists.

The Relationship Between Regulation D and State Securities Laws

Full compliance with the federal securities laws is only one level of regulation that must be taken into account when a franchisor is developing plans and strategies to raise capital through an offering of securities. Whether or not the offering is exempt under federal laws, registration may still be required in the states where the securities are to be sold under applicable "blue sky" laws. This often creates expensive and timely compliance burdens for growing franchisors and their counsel, who must contend with this bifurcated scheme of regulation. Generally speaking, there is a wide variety of standards of review among the states, ranging from very tough "merit" reviews (designed to ensure that all offerings of securities are fair and equitable) to very lenient "notice only" filings (designed primarily to promote full disclosure). The securities laws of each state where an offer or sale will be made should be checked very carefully prior to the distribution of the offering documents.

Subscription Materials

A private offering under Regulation D also requires the preparation of certain subscription documents. The two principal documents are the *subscription agreement* and the *offeree questionnaire*. The subscription agreement represents the contractual obligation on the part of the investor to buy, and on the part of the issuer to sell, the securities that are the subject of the offering. The subscription agreement should also contain certain representations and warranties by the investor that serve as evidence of the franchisor's compliance with the applicable federal and state securities laws exemptions. The subscription agreement may also contain relevant disclosure issues addressing investment risks and operative clauses that will enable the franchisor to execute documents and effect certain transactions after the closing of the offering.

Offeree questionnaires are developed in order to obtain certain information from prospective offerees that then serves as evidence of the required sophistication level and the ability to fend for themselves in a private offering. Generally, questionnaires contain personal information relating to the prospective investor's name, home and business address, telephone numbers, age, Social Security number, education, and employment history, as well as investment and business experience. The requested financial information includes the prospective investor's tax bracket, income, and net worth. The offeror must exercise reasonable care and diligence in confirming the truthfulness of the information provided in the questionnaire; however, the offeree should be required to attest to the accuracy of the data provided.

Venture Capital as a Source of Growth Financing for the Franchisor

A rapidly growing franchisor should also strongly consider venture capital as a source of equity financing when it needs additional capital to bring its business plans to fruition but lacks the collateral or current ability to meet debt-service payments that are typically required to qualify for traditional debt financing from a commercial bank. This is especially true for franchisors, whose capital needs are often "soft costs" such as personnel and marketing, for which debt financing may be very difficult to obtain. As franchising as a method of expanding a business matures, a growing number of private investors and venture capitalists have been willing to consider a commitment of capital to an emerging franchisor.

The term *venture capital* has been defined in many ways but refers generally to the early-stage financing of young, emerging growth companies at a relatively high risk, usually attributable to the newness of the company itself or even the entire industry. The professional venture capitalist is usually a highly trained finance professional who manages a pool of venture funds for investment in growing companies on behalf of a group of passive investors. Another major source of venture capital for growing franchisors is the Small Business Investment Company (SBIC). An SBIC is a privately organized investment firm that is specially licensed under the Small Business Investment Act of 1958 to borrow funds through the Small Business Administration (SBA) for subsequent investment in the small business community. Finally, some private corporations and state governments also manage venture funds for investment in growth companies.

There have been some recent trends within the venture capital industry that may increase the chances for early-stage franchisors to obtain venture capital. For example, many venture capital firms have recently expressed an interest in smaller transactions in more traditional industries, with less risk and more moderate (but stable) returns. Many franchisors that do operate in basic industries (e.g., food, hospitality, entertainment, personal services) can meet these investment criteria. There has been a definite shift away from high-tech deals, which are largely dependent on a single patent or the completion of successful research and development, and toward investments in more traditional industries, even if it results in less dynamic returns.

Negotiating and Structuring the Venture Capital Investment

Assuming that the franchisor's business plan is favorably received by the venture capitalist, the franchisor must then assemble a management team that is capable of negotiating the transaction. The negotiation and structuring of most venture capital transactions revolves around the need to strike a balance between the concerns of the founders of the franchisor, such as dilution of ownership and loss of control, and the concerns of the venture capitalist, such as return on investment and mitigating the risk of business failure. The typical end result of these discussions is a *Term Sheet,* which sets forth the key financial and legal terms of the transaction, which will then serve as a basis for the negotiation and preparation of the definitive legal documentation. Franchisors should ensure that legal counsel is familiar with the many traps and restrictions that are typically found in venture capital financing documents.

The Term Sheet may also contain certain rights and obligations of the parties. These may include an obligation to maintain an agreed valuation of the franchisor, an obligation to be responsible for certain costs and expenses in the event the proposed transaction does not take place, or an obligation to secure commitments for financing from additional sources prior to closing. Often these obligations are also included as part of the "conditions precedent" section of the formal Investment Agreement.

Negotiation regarding the *structure* of the transaction between the franchisor and the venture capitalist usually centers upon the types of securities to be used and the principal terms, conditions, and benefits offered by the securities. The type of securities ultimately selected and the structure of the transaction usually fall within one of the following categories:

◆ *Preferred stock.* This is the most typical form of security issued in connection with a venture capital financing to an emerging franchisor. This is because of the many advantages that preferred stock can be structured to offer to an investor, such as convertibility into common stock, dividend and liquidation preferences over the common stock, antidilution protection, mandatory or optional redemption schedules, and special voting rights and preferences.

◆ *Convertible debentures.* This type of security is basically a debt instrument (secured or unsecured) that may be converted into equity securities upon specified terms and conditions. Until converted, it offers the venture capitalist a fixed rate of return and offers tax advantages (e.g., deductibility of interest payments) to the franchisor. A venture capitalist will often prefer a convertible debenture in connection with higher-risk transactions because the venture capitalist is able to enjoy the elevated position of a creditor until the risk of the company's failure has been mitigated. Sometimes these instruments are used in connection with bridge financing, pursuant to which the venture capitalist expects to convert the debt to equity when the subsequent rounds of capital are raised. Finally, if the debentures are subordinated, commercial lenders will often treat them as the equivalent of an equity security for balance sheet purposes, which enables the franchisor to obtain institutional debt financing.

◆ *Debt securities with warrants.* A venture capitalist will prefer debentures or notes in connection with warrants often for the same reasons that convertible debt is used—namely, the ability to protect downside by enjoying the elevated position of a creditor and the ability to protect upside by including warrants to purchase common stock at favorable prices and terms. The use of a warrant enables the investor to buy common stock without sacrificing the position as a creditor, as would be the case if only convertible debt was used in the financing.

◆ *Common stock.* Venture capitalists rarely prefer to purchase common stock from the franchisor, especially at early stages of development. This is because "straight" common stock offers the investor no special rights or preferences, no fixed return on investment, no special ability to exercise control over management, and no liquidity to protect against downside risks. One of the few times that common stock might be selected is when the franchisor wishes to preserve its Subchapter S status under the Internal Revenue Code, which would be jeopardized if a class of preferred stock were to be authorized.

Once the type of security is selected by the franchisor and the venture capitalist, steps must be taken to ensure that the authorization and issuance of the security is properly effectuated under applicable state corporate laws. For example, if the franchisor's charter does not provide for a class of preferred stock, then articles of amendment must be prepared, approved by the board of directors and shareholders, and filed with the appropriate state corporation authorities. These articles of amendment will be the focus of negotiation between the franchisor and the venture capitalist in terms of voting rights, dividend rates and preferences, mandatory redemption provisions, antidilution protection ("ratchet clauses"), and related special rights and features. If debentures are selected, then negotiations will typically focus on term, interest rate and payment schedule, conversion rights and rates, extent of subordination, remedies for default, acceleration and prepayment rights, and underlying security for the instrument as well as the terms and conditions of any warrants that are granted along with the debentures. The legal documents involved in a venture capital financing must reflect the end-result of the negotiation process between the franchisor and the venture capitalist. These documents will contain all of the legal rights and obligations of the parties, striking a balance between the needs and concerns of the franchisor as well as the investment objectives and necessary controls of the venture capitalist.

Debt Financing Alternatives for the Growing Franchisor

Early-stage franchisors have not had much luck with commercial banks during the 1980s and 1990s, because most lenders prefer to see "hard collateral" on the balance sheet of a borrower, which is often lacking with start-up franchisors who have only their intellectual property, a projected royalty stream, and a business plan to pledge. A second problem is that most lenders prefer to see proceeds allocated primarily to the purchase of "hard assets" (to further serve as collateral), which is the opposite of what many franchisors want to do with their capital. Most early-stage franchisors need capital for soft costs, such as the development of manuals, advertising materials, and recruitment fees. Often these banks are more interested in providing financing to the franchisees rather than directly to the franchisor. Certainly these intangible assets can be pledged; however, they are likely to be given far less weight than are equipment, inventory, and real estate. By the time the franchise system has matured to the point that a lender is willing to extend capital based upon the franchisor's balance sheet, royalty stream, and track record, no capital is likely to be required.

Despite these problems, it is likely that the optimal capital structure of a growing franchisor includes a certain amount of debt on the balance sheet. The use of debt in the capital structure, commonly known as leverage, affects both the valuation of the franchisor and its overall cost of capital. The maximum debt capacity that a growing franchisor will ultimately be able to handle usually involves a balancing of the costs and risks of a default of a debt obligation against the desire of the owners and managers to maintain control of the enterprise by protecting against the dilution that an equity offering would cause. Many franchisors prefer preservation of control over the affairs of their company in exchange for the higher level of risk inherent in taking on additional debt obligations. The ability to meet debt-service payments must be carefully considered in the franchisor's financial projections.

If a pro forma analysis reveals that the ability to meet debt-service obligations will put a strain on the franchisor's cash flow, or that insufficient collateral is available (as is often the case for early-stage franchisors who lack significant tangible assets), then equity alternatives should be explored. It is simply not worth driving the franchisor into voluntary or involuntary bankruptcy solely to maintain a maximum level of control. Overleveraged franchisors typically spend so much of their cash servicing the debt that capital is unavailable to develop new programs and provide support to the franchisees, which will trigger the decline and deterioration of the franchise system. In addition, the level of debt financing selected by the franchisor should be compared against key business ratios in its particular industry, such as those published by Robert Morris Associates or Dun & Bradstreet. Once the optimum debt to equity ratio is determined, owners and managers should be aware of the *various sources* of debt financing as well as the *business and legal issues* involved in borrowing funds from a commercial lender.

Sources of Debt Financing

Although most franchisors turn to traditional forms of financing such as term loans and operating lines of credit from commercial banks, there exists a wide variety of alternative sources of debt financing. Some of these alternatives include:

- ◆ *Trade credit.* The use of credit with key suppliers is often a practical means of survival for rapidly growing corporate franchisors. When a franchisor has established a good credit rating with its suppliers but, as a result of rapid growth, tends to require resources faster than it is able to pay for them, trade credit becomes the only way that growth can be sustained. A key supplier has a strong economic incentive for helping a growing franchisor continue to prosper and may therefore be more willing to negotiate credit terms that are acceptable to both parties.
- ◆ *Equipment leasing.* Most rapidly growing franchisors are desperately in need of the use but not necessarily the *ownership* of certain

vital resources to fuel and maintain growth. Therefore, equipment leasing offers an alternative to ownership of the asset. Monthly lease payments are made in lieu of debt-service payments. The "effective rate" in a leasing transaction is usually much less than the comparable interest rate in a loan.

◆ *Factoring.* Under the traditional factoring arrangement, a company sells its accounts receivables (or some other income stream such as royalty payments in the case of franchising) to a third party in exchange for immediate cash. The third party or "factor" assumes the risk of collection in exchange for the ability to purchase the accounts receivable at a discount determined by the comparative level of risk. Once notice has been provided to debtors of their obligation to pay the factor directly, the seller of the accounts receivable is no longer liable to the factor in the event of a default, although the factor will retain a holdback amount to partially offset these losses.

◆ *Miscellaneous sources of nonbank debt financing.* Debt securities such as bonds, notes, and debentures may be offered to venture capitalists, private investors, friends, family, employees, insurance companies, and related financial institutions. Many smaller businesses will turn to traditional sources of consumer credit, such as home equity loans, credit cards, and commercial finance companies to finance the growth of their business. In addition to the Small Business Administration loan programs, many state and local governments have created direct loan programs for small businesses.

Although all available alternative sources of debt financing should be actively considered, traditional bank loans from commercial lenders are the most common source of capital for franchisors. Franchisors should take the time to learn the lending policies of the institution, as well as the terms and conditions of the traditional types of loans such as term loans, operating lines of credit, real estate loans, and long-term financing.

Negotiating With Commercial Lenders

Negotiating the financing documents that will be executed by the franchisor in a typical commercial bank loan requires a delicate balancing between the requirements of the lender and the needs of the borrower. The lender wants to have all rights, remedies, and protection available to mitigate the risk of loan default. On the other hand, the franchisor as borrower wants to minimize both the amount of collateral given to secure the debt and the level of control exercised by the lender under the affirmative and negative covenants of the loan agreement while achieving a return on its assets that greatly exceeds its debt-service payments.

Before examining each document involved in a typical debt financing, you should understand some general rules of loan negotiation:

- *Interest rates.* A banker generally calculates the rate of interest in accordance with prevailing market rates, the degree of risk inherent in the proposed transaction, the extent of any preexisting relationship with the lender, and the cost of administering the loan.
- *Collateral.* The commercial lender may request that certain collateral be pledged that has a value equal to or greater than the proceeds of the loan. When collateral is requested, franchisors should attempt to keep certain key assets of the business outside of the pledge agreement so that they are available to serve as security in the event that additional capital is needed at a later time. Beyond the traditional forms of tangible assets that may be offered to the lender as collateral, borrowers should also consider intangibles such as assignment of lease rights, key-man insurance policies, intellectual property, and goodwill. Naturally, loss of these assets could be very costly to the franchisor in the event of default and should be pledged only as a last resort.
- *Prepayment rights.* Regardless of the actual term of the loan, the borrower should negotiate a right to prepay the principal of the loan without penalty or special repayment charges. Many commercial lenders seek to attach prepayment charges to term loans that have a fixed rate of interest, in order to ensure that a minimum rate of return is earned over the projected life of the loan.
- *Hidden costs and fees.* Many commercial banks attempt to charge the borrower with a variety of direct and indirect costs and fees in connection with the debt financing. Included in this category are closing costs, processing fees, filing fees, late charges, attorneys' fees, out-of-pocket expense reimbursement (courier, travel, photocopying, etc.), court costs, and auditing or inspection fees.
- *Commitment fees.* Many lenders also charge a fee for issuing a firm commitment to make the loan, after conducting credit reviews and obtaining credit committee approval to make the loan. Typically, all or some of this is reimbursable if the borrower actually draws the loan.
- *Restrictive covenants.* The typical loan agreement includes a variety

of affirmative and negative restrictive covenants designed to protect the interests of the lender. Franchisors should carefully renew these covenants to ensure that the implementation of the company's business plan will not be unduly impeded.

The Use of Initial Public Offerings by Growing Franchisors

An initial public offering (IPO) is a process whereby a growing enterprise opts to register its securities with the Securities and Exchange Commission (SEC) for sale to the general investing public for the first time. Many growing franchisors view the process of "going public" as the epitome of financial success and reward. And many national franchisors have successfully completed public offerings during the 1990s, including Shoney's (family restaurants), Wendy's Old Fashioned Hamburgers (fast food), TCBY Enterprises (frozen yogurt), Snelling & Snelling (personnel placement), McDonald's Corporation (fast food), Medicine Shoppes International (pharmacy stores), Ponderosa (steak houses), Postal Instant Press (printing centers), Yogen Fruz International (frozen yogurt and ice cream), The Dwyer Group (home and business services), Sylvan Learning Centers (adult educators), Sterling Visual (retail optical centers), Grow Biz International (multiconcept retailer of used and recycled goods), United Auto Group (auto and truck dealerships), and ServiceMaster (cleaning and janitorial services). However, the decision to go public requires considerable strategic planning and analysis from both a legal and a business perspective. The planning and analysis process involves (1) a weighing of the costs and benefits of being a public company, (2) an understanding of the process and costs of becoming a public company, and (3) an understanding of the obligations of the company, its advisers, and its shareholders once the franchisor has successfully completed its public offering.

Costs and Benefits of the IPO

For the rapidly expanding privately held franchisor, the process of going public presents a number of benefits, including (1) significantly greater access to capital; (2) increased liquidity for the franchisor's shares; (3) greater prestige in the financial markets; (4) enhancement of the franchisor's public image (which may have the effect of increasing franchise sales); (5) opportunities for employee ownership and participation; (6) broader growth opportunities, including the potential for merger, acquisition, and further rounds of financing; and (7) an immediate increase in the wealth of the franchisor's founders.

However, the many benefits of being a public company are not without their corresponding costs, and the latter must be seriously considered in the strategic planning process. Among these costs are (1) the dilution in the founders' control of the entity, (2) the pressure to meet market and shareholder expectations regarding growth and dividends, (3) changes in management styles and employee expectations, (4) compliance with complex regulations imposed by federal and state securities laws, (5) stock resale restrictions for company insiders, (6) vulnerability to shifts in the stock market, and (7) the sharing of the franchisor's financial success with hundreds, even thousands, of other shareholders.

Note that many franchisors have not been intimidated by the disadvantages of being publicly held, primarily because they (1) are already operating in a disclosure-oriented business, (2) are already compelled to provide audited financial statements, and (3) feel that being publicly held will increase credibility, which generally increases franchise sales.

Preparing the Registration Statement

The registration statement consists of two distinct parts: (1) the *offering prospectus* (which is used to assist underwriters and investors in analyzing the company and the securities being offered), and (2) the *exhibits and additional information* (which are provided directly to the SEC as part of the disclosure and registration regulations). The registration statement is part of the public record and is available for public inspection.

There is a variety of forms alternatives to the registration statement. The alternative form chosen depends on the franchisor's history and size and the nature of the specific offering. The most common form used is the Form S-1, which is required for all companies (unless an alternative form is available). The S-1, however, is complicated, has several requirements that must be fulfilled *before* going public, and requires the description of the franchisor's business, properties, material transactions between the company and its officers, pending legal proceedings, plans for distribution of the securities, and the intended use of the proceeds from the IPO. However, the Forms S-2 and S-3 (subject to certain requirements) are available for companies that are already subject to the reporting requirements of the Securities Exchange Act of 1934 (the "Exchange Act"), as is the Form S-4, which is limited to corporate combinations. Forms S-1 through S-4 are filed and processed at the SEC's headquarters office in Washington, D.C., by the Division of Corporate Finance.

The SEC's Small Business Initiatives

In 1992, the SEC implemented the Small Business Initiatives (SBIs), significantly modifying its special provisions for offerings by smaller companies, which may be of benefit to many emerging growth franchisors that are not already subject to the reporting requirements of the Exchange Act (Regulation S-B). The SBIs were designed to streamline the federal registration process in connection with IPOs to encourage investment in small businesses. A "small business issuer," as defined in Rule 405 of the Securities Act of 1933 (the "Securities Act"), is a company meeting all of the following criteria:

1. Has revenue of less than $25 million.
2. Is a U.S. or Canadian issuer.
3. Is not an investment company
4. If a majority-owned subsidiary, the parent corporation is also a small business issuer.

A small business issuer can use the Form SB-1 or SB-2 to register its securities to be sold for cash with the SEC.

The SB-1 can *only* be used to register up to $10 million of securities (the old predecessor S-18 had a ceiling of $7.5 million). Also, the company must not have registered more than $10 million in any continuous twelve-month period (including the transaction being registered). In addition, it allows for financial statements (which *must* be audited by an independent party) to be given in accordance with generally accepted accounting principles (commonly referred to as GAAP), and not the detailed requirements of the SEC.

The SB-2 (the old predecessor S-1 was the form typically used by small businesses prior to 1992) allows small business issuers to offer an unlimited dollar amount of securities, therefore allowing companies that meet the SEC's definition of a small business to sell more securities without having to undergo the same extensive disclosure process of larger companies. The advantages to using the SB-2 include repeated use, location of answered forms in a central depositor, and filing allowed with either the SEC's regional office (which is closely located to your company's principal location) or headquarters office in Washington, D.C., as well as those afforded by using the SB-1. These advantages have translated into economic benefits. For example, the average cost of the legal and accounting fees for small businesses registering to make an IPO went from $200,000 to a range of from $75,000 to $100,000. Imagine, the government has actually created a program to save us money!

The Key Elements of the Registration Statement

Regardless of which form is ultimately selected, there is a series of core procedural rules and disclosure items that must be addressed. The key disclosure areas of the registration statement include:

♦ *Cover page/forepart.* The SEC has very specific requirements as to the information that must be stated on the cover page and forepart of the prospectus. This includes summary information pertaining to the nature of the franchisor's business, the terms of the offering, the determination of the offering price, dilution, plan of distribution, risk factors, and selected financial information.

♦ *Introduction to the company.* An overview of the company, its business, employees, financial performance, and principal offices.

♦ *Risk factors.* This is a description of the operating and financial risk factors affecting the franchisor's business with particular regard to the offering of the securities (such as depending on a single customer, supplier, or key personnel; the absence of operating history in the new areas of business that the franchisor wants to pursue; an unproven market for the products and services offered; or a lack of earnings history).

♦ *Use of proceeds.* This is a discussion of the anticipated use of the proceeds that will be raised by the offering.

♦ *Capitalization.* This is a description of the capital structure of debt obligations, the company's anticipated dividend policy, and dilution of purchaser's (investor's) equity.

♦ *Description of business and property.* This is a description of the key assets, principal lines of business, human resources, properties, marketing strategies, and competitive advantages of the company and any of its subsidiaries for the last five years.

♦ *Management and principal shareholders.* This is a discussion of the key management team and description of each member's background, education, compensation, and role in the company, as well as a table of all shareholders who hold a beneficial interest of 5 percent or more.

♦ *Litigation.* This is a statement of any material litigation (either past, pending, or anticipated) affecting the franchisor or any other adverse legal proceedings that would affect an investor's analysis of the securities being offered.

♦ *Financial information.* This is a summary of financial information such as sales history, net income or losses from operations, long-term debt obligations, dividend patterns, capital structure, founder's equity, and shareholder loans.

◆ *Securities offered and underwriting arrangements.* This is a description of the underwriting arrangements, distribution plan, and the key characteristics of the securities being offered.

◆ *Experts and other matters.* This is a brief statement regarding the identity of the attorneys, accountants, and other experts retained as well as the availability of additional information from the registration statement filed with the SEC (such as indemnification policies for the directors and officers, recent sales of unregistered securities, a breakdown of the expenses of the offering, and a wide variety of corporate documents and key agreements).

An Overview of the Registration Process

When the initial draft of the registration statement is ready for filing with the SEC, you have two choices: either file the document with the transmittal letter and required fees or schedule a prefiling conference with an SEC staff member to discuss any anticipated questions or problems regarding the disclosure document or the accompanying financial statements.

The initial registration process is generally governed by the Securities Act, which is designed to ensure full and fair disclosure of material facts to prospective investors in connection with the offer and sale of securities. The Securities Act requires the company to file a registration statement with the SEC as well as a prospectus to prospective investors.

Once the registration statement is officially received by the SEC, it is then assigned to an examining group (composed usually of attorneys, accountants, and financial analysts, within a specific industry department of the Division of Corporate Finance). The length of time and depth of the review by the examining group depends on the history of the company and the nature of the securities offered. For example, a company that operates in a troubled or turbulent industry, which is publicly offering its securities for the first time, should expect a detailed review by all members of the examining group.

Following the initial review, a deficiency or comment letter will be sent, suggesting changes to the registration statement. The modifications of the statement will focus on the quality of the disclosure (such as an adequate discussion of risk factors or the verbiage in management's discussion of the financial performance), not on the quality of the company or the securities being offered. In most cases, the company will be required to file a material amendment in order to address the staff's concerns. This process continues until all concerns raised by the examining group have been addressed. The final pricing amendment is filed following the pricing meeting of the underwriters and the execution of the final underwriting agreement. During this period, the SEC has developed detailed regulations and restrictions on what information may be released to the public or the media (the "quiet period"), especially those communications that appear to be designed to influence the price of the shares. The registration statement then is declared effective and the securities can be offered to the public. The registration statement is declared effective twenty days after the final amendment has been filed, unless the effective date is accelerated by the SEC. Most companies tend to seek an accelerated effective date, which is usually made available if the company has complied with the examining group's suggested modifications.

In addition to SEC regulations, a company offering its securities to the public must also meet the requirements of NASD (National Association of Securities Dealers) and state securities laws. The NASD will analyze all elements of the proposed corporate package for the underwriter in order to determine its fairness and reasonableness. The SEC will not deem a registration statement effective for public offering unless and until the NASD has approved the underwriting arrangements as being fair and reasonable.

Section 18 of the Securities Act states that federal securities laws do not supersede compliance with any state securities laws; therefore, the requirements of each state's securities regulations or "blue sky" laws must also be satisfied. Although various exemptions from formal registration are often available, the state securities laws must be checked very carefully as to the filing fees, registered agent requirements, disclosure obligations, and underwriter or broker/dealer regulations for each state in which the securities will be offered.

The Closing and Beyond

Once the final underwriting agreement is signed and the final pricing amendment is filed with the SEC, the registration statement will be declared effective and the selling process begins. Throughout the selling period, wait patiently and hope that any minimum sales quotas (such as for "all or nothing" offerings) are met and that the offering is well received by the investing public.

To facilitate the mechanics of the offering process, you may want to consider retaining the services of a registrar and transfer agent who will be responsible for issuing stock certificates, maintaining stockholder ownership records, and processing the transfer of shares from one investor to another.

These services are usually offered by commercial banks and trust companies (which also offer ongoing support services such as annual report and proxy mailing, disbursement of dividends, and custody of the authorized but unissued stock certificates). Once the offer and sale of the shares to the public has been completed, a closing must be scheduled to exchange documents, issue stock certificates, and disburse net proceeds.

In addition to the obligations discussed previously, you are usually required to file the SEC's Form SR. The Form SR is a report on the company's use of the proceeds raised from the sale of the securities. *The information should be substantially similar to the discussion contained in the prospectus provided to prospective investors.* The initial Form SR must be filed within ninety days after the registration statement becomes effective and then once every six months until the offering is complete and the proceeds are being applied toward their intended use.

Ongoing Reporting and Disclosure Requirements

The Exchange Act generally governs the ongoing disclosure and periodic reporting requirements of publicly traded companies. Section 13 grants broad powers to the SEC to develop documents and reports that must be filed. The three primary reports required by Section 15(d) are:

1. *Form 10-K or 10-KSB (for small business issuers).* This is the annual report that must be filed within ninety days after the close of the company's fiscal year covered by the report. It must also include a report of all significant activities of the company during its fourth quarter, an analysis and discussion of the financial condition, a description of the current officers and directors, and a schedule of certain exhibits. The 10-K requires the issuer's income statements for the prior three years and the balance sheets for the prior two years. The 10-KSB requires the income statement for the prior two years and the balance sheet for the prior year (which can be prepared in accordance with GAAP).

2. *Form 10-Q or 10-QSB (for small business issuers).* This is the quarterly report that must be filed no later than forty-five days after the end of each of the first three fiscal quarters of each fiscal year. This quarterly filing includes copies of quarterly financial statements (accompanied by a discussion and analysis of the company's financial condition by its management) and a report as to any litigation as well as any steps taken by the company that affect share-

holder rights or that may require shareholder approval. The differences between the 10-Q and the 10-QSB are the same as that of the 10-K and 10-KSB. The 10-Q requires an issuer's balance sheet from the previous year and a report of the most recent fiscal quarter; however, the 10-QSB requires a report on the most recent quarter.

3. *Form 8-K.* This is a periodic report that is designed to ensure that *all material information* pertaining to significant events that affect the company is disclosed to the investing public as soon as it is available, but not later than fifteen days after the occurrence of the particular event (which triggers the need to file the Form 8-K).

The duty to disclose material information (whether as part of a Form 8-K filing or otherwise) to the general public is an ongoing obligation that continues for as long as the company's securities are publicly traded. An ongoing compliance program must be established to ensure that all *material* corporate information is disclosed as fully and as promptly as possible. A *fact* is generally considered to be material if there is a substantial likelihood that a reasonable shareholder would consider it important in his or her investment decision (whether to buy, sell, or hold, or how to vote on a particular proposed corporate action). The following kinds of information are examples of what is typically considered material for disclosure purposes:

- ◆ Acquisitions and dispositions of other companies or properties
- ◆ Public or private sales of debt or equity securities; bankruptcy or receivership proceedings affecting the issuer
- ◆ Significant contract awards or terminations
- ◆ Changes in the key management team

Pursuant to Section 12(g), certain companies of publicly traded securities are subject to additional reporting and disclosure requirements. For example, if a company either elects to register its securities under 12(g), or has greater than 500 shareholders and at least $5 million worth of total assets, then it will also be subject to the rules developed by the SEC for: (1) proxy solicitation, (2) reporting of beneficial ownership, (3) liability for short-swing transactions, and (4) tender offer rules and regulations.

- ◆ *Proxy solicitation.* Because of the difficulty of assembling each and every shareholder of a corporation for matters that require a shareholder vote, voting by proxy is a fact of life for most publicly held corporations. When soliciting the proxies of shareholders for voting at

annual or special meetings, special statutory rules must be carefully followed. The request for the proxy must be accompanied by a detailed
proxy statement, which should specify the exact matters to be acted
upon and any information that would be required by the shareholder
in reaching his or her decision.

◆ *Reporting of beneficial ownership.* Section 16(a) requires that all
officers, directors, and 10 percent shareholders (if any) file a statement
of beneficial ownership of securities. Filed on Form 3, the statement
must reflect all holdings (direct and indirect). Section 16(a) also
requires that whenever the officers and directors increase or decrease
their holdings by purchase, sale, gift, or otherwise, the transaction
must be reported on Form 4 no later than the tenth day of the month
following the month in which the transaction occurred.

◆ *Liability for short-swing transactions.* Section 16(b) requires that
officers, directors, employees, or other insiders return to the company
any profit that they may have realized from any combination of sales
and purchases, or purchases and sales, of securities made by them
within any six-month period. Any acquisition of securities (regardless
of form of payment) is considered to be a "purchase." The purpose of
Section 16(b) is to discourage even the possibility of directors and officers taking advantage of "inside information" by "speculating" in a
company's stock. Liability occurs automatically if there is a sale and
purchase within six months, even if the individual involved in the
transaction did not actually take advantage of inside information.

◆ *Tender offer rules and regulations.* Sections 13 and 14 generally govern the rules for parties who wish to make a tender offer to purchase
the securities of a publicly traded corporation. Any person acquiring
(directly or indirectly) beneficial ownership of more than 5 percent of
an equity security registered under Section 12 must report the transaction by filing a Schedule 13D within ten days from the date of acquisition. The Schedule 13D requires disclosure of certain material
information, such as the identity and background of the purchaser, the
purpose of the acquisition, the source and amount of funds used to purchase the securities, and disclosure of the company. If the purchase is in
connection with a tender offer, then the provisions of Section 14(d) also
apply, pursuant to which the terms of the tender offer must be disclosed
(as well as the plans of the offerer if it is successful and the terms of any
special agreements between the offerer and the target company). Section
14(e) imposes a broad prohibition against the use of false, misleading,
or incomplete statements in connection with a tender offer.

Rule 10b-5 and Insider Trading

A great deal of attention has been devoted by the business and financial press to the SEC's Rule 10b-5 and its application in the prosecution of insider trading cases. Here is the text of Rule 10b-5:

> It shall be unlawful for any person, directly or indirectly, by the use of any means or instrumentality of interstate commerce, or of the mails or of any facility of any national securities exchange to:
>
> (a) employ any device, scheme, or artifice to defraud;
> (b) make any untrue statement of a material fact or to omit to state a material fact necessary in order to make the statements made, in light of the circumstances under which they were made, not misleading; or
> (c) engage in any act, practice, or course of business which operates or would operate as a fraud or deceit upon any person, in connection with the purchase or sale of any security.

The most frequent use of Rule 10b-5 has been in insider trading cases, typically those in which an officer, director, or other person who has a fiduciary relationship with a corporation buys or sells the company's securities while in the possession of material, nonpublic information. However, Rule 10b-5 is also used in a variety of other situations, such as:

◆ When a corporation issues misleading information to the public or keeps silent when it has a duty to disclose
◆ When an insider selectively discloses material, nonpublic information to another party, who then trades securities based on the information (generally called tipping)
◆ When a person mismanages a corporation in ways that are connected with the purchase or sale of securities
◆ When a securities firm or another person manipulates the market for a security traded in the over-the-counter market
◆ When a securities firm or securities professional engages in certain other forms of conduct connected with the purchase or sale of securities

Therefore, it is imperative that all officers, directors, employees, and shareholders of publicly traded companies (or companies considering being publicly traded) be keenly aware of the broad scope of this antifraud rule in their transactions that involve the company.

Disposing of Restricted Securities

All shares of a public company held by its controlling persons—which typically include its officers, directors, and 10 percent shareholders (if any)—are deemed "restricted securities" under the Securities Act. The sale of restricted securities is generally governed by Rule 144, which requires as a condition of sale that:

1. The company be current in its periodic reports to the SEC
2. The restricted securities have been beneficially owned for at least two years preceding the sale
3. The amount of securities that may be sold in any three-month period be limited to the greater of 1 percent of the outstanding class of securities or the average weekly reported volume of trading in the securities on a registered national security exchange (if the securities are listed)
4. The securities be sold only in broker's transactions, and the notice of the sale be filed with the SEC concurrently with the placing of the sale order
5. If the sale involves 500 shares or $10,000, a report of the transaction on Form 144 must be filed

It is imperative that you and your managers understand the planning and registration process prior to pursuing a public offering of the company's securities. A substantial amount of time and expense can be saved if the process of planning begins early in the development of methods of operation and formulation of strategies for the company's growth. As with any contemplated method of capital formation, going public has its costs and benefits, all of which should be carefully weighed and understood by the franchisor's management and advisory team prior to selling the first share of stock to the public.

13

The Role of the Chief Financial Officer and Related Financial and Administrative Management Issues

As a franchisor grows and matures, its management team must also evolve to meet new challenges and solve new problems. In the early stages, the management team of the franchisor is heavily focused on sales and marketing, which is often a necessary prerequisite to building a critical mass of franchisees. But as the emphasis shifts from franchise sales to service and support, additional personnel must be recruited in the areas of operations, administration, and finance. Yes, finance. The management teams of many rapidly growing franchisors often lack experienced financial officers who can bring economic discipline to the organization. Effective financial management, reporting systems, and analysis are the keys to the ongoing success of a growing franchise system.

When a franchisor reaches that critical stage of growth when it is necessary to hire a full-time financial officer, the first reaction is typically panic—first, because the position must be added to the overhead, and second, because the franchisor doesn't know where to start looking. Even the well-respected and well-recognized executive recruitment firms that specialize in franchising admit that there is a lack of truly qualified and experienced financial managers. Many franchisors have unsuccessfully recruited from the accounting profession, which can result in the placement of an individual who is very well trained in the areas of accounting or tax planning but may lack the operational experience to truly understand the special financial dynamics of the franchisor-franchisee relationship. The ideal candidate will have had some initial training as a certified public accountant but will also have had hands-on experience as a chief financial officer or comptroller of a franchise company, or at least with a company that has a structure and method of distribution and growth similar to franchising such as dealerships, retailing, or licensing.

The overall task of the CFO is to manage the cash flow and profitability of the franchisor. The three cost areas that must be managed carefully are: (1) *recruitment costs,* such as marketing, advertising, trade shows, and marketing personnel; (2) *pre-opening costs,* such as the costs to get the franchisee up and running, including training, site selection, and other types of pre-opening assistance; and (3) *maintenance costs,* such as the various ongoing training and support costs to maintain a healthy and mutually profitable relationship. The CFO's job is to continue to study the financial model between the franchisor and the franchisee, such as the pricing of the *initial franchise fees* (which are designed to cover recruitment costs and pre-opening costs) and the rates of *royalty fees* (which are intended to cover maintenance costs), to ensure that the ongoing relationship with the franchisee is financially viable for the franchisor.

The day-to-day job tasks of a well-rounded CFO typically include the functions noted in Figure 13-1.

Figure 13-1. The typical tasks of a CFO.

◆ Development of accounting and reporting systems	◆ Development of cash flow management programs	◆ Preparation of financial statements in satisfaction of federal and state franchise laws
◆ Financial analysis and forecasting for proposed new products and services to be offered by franchisor	◆ Development of capital formation strategies	◆ Initial and ongoing analysis of franchise and royalty fee structure
◆ Development of royalty and related fee collection and reporting systems	◆ Management of banking relationships	◆ Development of accounts payable and accounts receivable management programs
◆ Federal and state tax planning	◆ Review and critique of franchisee financial reports	◆ Development and implementation of operating controls and internal budgeting/reporting systems

- ◆ Analysis of vendor relations and cooperative buying programs

- ◆ Analysis of proposed mergers and acquisitions, real estate development, and international expansion

- ◆ Careful and thorough financial due diligence on each prospective franchisee or area developer

- ◆ Liaison to outside accounting firms and law firms

- ◆ Coordination of operations, marketing, management, and other departments within the franchisor

- ◆ Financial analysis of strategic plans and growth targets

- ◆ Review of travel budgets, trade shows, and related promotional expenses

One of the continuing challenges of the chief financial officer of the start-up and growing franchisor is to avoid the more common mistakes that harm or even destroy franchisors at various critical stages in their development. If you or your company has never made them, then try to avoid them. If it is too late, then try to learn from the mistakes and avoid making them again.

- ◆ *Undercapitalization.* Lack of operating capital is the kiss of death for many early-stage franchisors. Although franchising as a method of business growth is less capital-intense than internal growth, a sufficient working capital reserve is still required for development and implementation of the franchising program as well as the ongoing costs of support.

- ◆ *Cash flow mismanagement.* Any time that the CFO needs to put pressure on the marketing staff to "close a deal so we can pay rent this month," cash flow is being mismanaged. Not only is the franchisor undercapitalized under such a scenario but also cash flow is being misdirected and mismanaged. General operating expenses and support costs should be paid for with royalty income, not franchise sales. A "robbing Peter to pay Paul" approach will result in a compromise of franchise screening and qualification standards as well as create an undue financial burden on the franchisor.

◆ *Underestimation of the costs of ongoing support and service.* Ask the average franchisors how they arrived at their prevailing royalty rate and they will answer, "From our competitors!" Ask them how much it *actually* costs to support and service each franchisee and you will get a blank stare. The royalty rate must be a reflection of a detailed analysis of the costs of maintaining support systems for the franchisees, not a number picked from the air.

◆ *Lack of adequate forecasting for the performance of the typical franchisee.* Regardless of whether or not your company chooses to provide earnings claims, the forecasting of the performance of a typical franchisee is a critical step in building a franchising program. The internal analysis of a typical franchisee's performance will help the franchisor determine the viability of the franchising program from the franchisee's perspective as well as help predict its own stream of royalty income on a per-unit, per-annum basis.

◆ *Underestimation of marketing and promotional expenses.* What is your cost per lead? What is your cost per award? Many early-stage franchisors are unable to predict or measure their actual costs in generating leads, screening prospects, and ultimately awarding the franchise to a qualified candidate. This may lead to an unpleasant surprise at the end of the quarter or fiscal year when you finally discover that franchises are being awarded at a loss or that marketing costs are running well beyond budget.

◆ *Underbudgeting for costs of resolving disputes with franchisees.* How much do you think it will cost to resolve a genuine dispute with a disgruntled franchisee? Take that number, triple it, and you are probably getting close. Litigation is costly, drawn out, and frustrating. The alternative dispute resolution techniques, such as arbitration and mediation, may be more cost-effective but still can be quite expensive. In building a franchise system, disputes with franchisees are inevitable, so it is best to begin building a "war chest" now so that a fight down the road does not unexpectedly cripple the franchisor.

◆ *Commingling of advertising resources.* Many early-stage franchisors inadvertently commingle funds received by their franchisees into a national advertising fund (which is supposed to help build brand awareness and create *more customers* for all franchisees) with the funds that are set aside to conduct marketing efforts to attract *more franchisees.* These accounting errors are not only a breach of the franchise agreement but also create franchisee resentment, tax issues, and accounting problems for the franchisor.

◆ *Miscalculation of projected Item 7 opening expenses.* Nobody likes unexpected financial surprises, especially not franchisees that are opening up a new franchised business. Your prospective franchisees will naturally rely heavily on the projected start-up costs included in Item 7 of the UFOC in doing their own financial planning and capital formation. Yet many early-stage franchisors try to keep the total figures in Item 7 as low as possible for marketing purposes on the theory that the lower the cost to open, the more franchises they will be able to award. It is far better to be on the conservative side in projecting Item 7 costs, allowing plenty of reserves for working capital. This will result in less disgruntled and unpleasantly surprised franchisees, which will only serve to help marketing efforts over the long run.

The challenge of the CFO of a growing franchisor is a continuing one. The position does not require merely collecting financial data but also regularly renewing and analyzing the data collected from the franchisee and communicating observations and tips for improvement to the franchisor's management team, to the field support staff, and to the franchisees and their managers in the trenches.

The CFO must carefully study industry trends and single-unit performance to determine the key financial ratios or benchmarks that are the most critical. For many retail and food services franchise systems, these include Pre-Royalty Cash Flow (PRCF) and Weekly Per Store Average (WPSA) measurements. These benchmarks are analyzed both at the franchisor's corporate headquarters and by the franchisees on a collaborative/peer analysis basis.

For example, select groups of Kwik Kopy franchisees gather at the International Center for Entrepreneurial Development (ICED) campus outside Houston from time to time to analyze each other's financial statements and performance, led by a trained moderator. The franchisees become financial and strategic sounding boards for each other in the areas of financial analysis, budgeting, forecasting, cash flow and profitability analysis, goal setting, and general strategic planning. The results of these meetings are used to improve overall performance as well as to provide a basis for future business and estate planning. The CFO can also use these data to develop a set of "Financial Best Practices" to disseminate this information into the field, as well as to update training programs and operations manuals. The franchisees generally respond well to this peer-driven process rather than feel that the franchisor is "dictating" a set of standards for profit and loss (P&L) statement preparation and analysis.

Steps to Improve the Franchisee's Profitability

One of the age-old critiques of the financial structure of the franchisor-franchisee relationship is that the royalties payable to the franchisor are typically based on gross sales, not net profits. Therefore, franchisees often perceive, rightly or wrongly, that the franchisor will build a culture of support and training that overfocuses on building sales but not on improving profits. Naturally, in the long run, it is in neither party's best interest if franchisees operate at a break-even or loss level on a sustained basis.

Therefore, the CFO and his or her team must communicate a commitment to the profitability of the franchisee. There must be financial management training and support programs that teach the franchisees how to prepare and analyze a P&L statement. In addition, field support personnel should have some financial analysis background and training. The field support personnel must be trained to detect "red flags" in the franchisees' P&L statements and effectively communicate tips and traps to the franchisees. The franchisor must teach the franchisee how to market, price, and deliver the underlying products and services in the system in a profitable fashion. The franchisor must also take steps to negotiate volume discounts and develop cost management training for the benefit of the franchisees, recognizing that profitability is a combination of increasing sales and controlling costs. The franchise fee and royalty structure should continue to be analyzed to ensure that it is in line with current market trends and actual store performance data.

One way the franchisor can increase its profitability is by offering certain financial management and administrative services support functions, for a monthly fee. See Figure 13-2.

Figure 13-2. Bringing services under the franchisor's roof.

Some franchisors have offered to bring certain financial management and administrative services support functions that would otherwise be performed by the franchisees or area developers and their accountants under the franchisor's roof, for a monthly fee. Franchisors may consider bringing one or more of the following functions under the responsibility of the franchisor's headquarters:

◆ Per-unit calculation of revenue and expenses by accounting category based on the franchisor's standard chart of accounts and calculation of royalty-based revenue and royalty fees (as each term is defined in the franchise agreement)

- Administration and maintenance of payroll, and administration of the processing of payroll and calculation of applicable tax and other withholdings relating to the franchisee or area developer's units, either through the franchisor's designated payroll service bureau or through in-house technology
- Administration of accounts payable (including check generation and wire transfers)
- Administration of recurring cash transfers between the franchisee's or area developer's applicable unit and corporate bank accounts
- Maintenance of lease files and compliance with reporting and disbursement obligations thereunder
- Administration and maintenance of a franchisee's or area developer's general ledger trial balance, balance sheet, income statement, and certain other corporate and unit reports by accounting category per the franchisor's standard chart of accounts and consistent with periodic reports the franchisor customarily prepares in the normal course of business to manage its financial affairs, and periodic distribution of such reports to franchisee or area developer using the franchisor's standard report distribution system
- Maintenance of all accounting records supporting franchisee's or area developer's financial statements (consistent with the franchisor's record retention program) in reasonable fashion, separate and discrete from the accounting records of the franchisor
- Preparation of period-end reconciliations and associated period-end journal entries for all franchisee and area developer balance sheet accounts
- Quarterly review and edit of the franchisee's or area developer's vendor master file for current and accurate data, including updates to the vendor master file as directed by the franchisee or area developer
- Approval and coding of invoices for disbursement
- Selection of accounting policies to be applied to the franchisee's or area developer's books and records (however, the franchisor will consistently apply the appropriate policies selected by the franchisee or area developer)
- Negotiation of terms and conditions between the franchisee or area developer and its suppliers, vendors, and others, such as remittance due dates and discounts
- Final review and approval of annual financial statements
- Cash investment activities (however, the franchisor will initiate and manage repetitive and/or fixed cash management activities as directed in writing by the franchisee or area developer)
- Preparation of budgets (except that the franchisor will develop a budget process and calendar to facilitate the preparation of annual budgets by the franchisee or area developer)

(continues)

Figure 13-2. *(continued)*

- Preparation, filing, or signing of any tax returns required to be filed by the franchisee or area developer, with the exception of sales and use tax returns, which will be prepared but not, however, filed or signed by the franchisor
- Bidding for and negotiation and establishment (but not administration) of health, dental, disability, life, and 401K benefit programs and accounts on behalf of the franchisee or area developer and for each covered employee thereof
- Bidding for and negotiation, establishment, and administration of a directors' and officers' liability insurance program annually on behalf of the franchisee or area developer, as requested
- Bidding for and negotiation, establishment, and administration of property, liability, umbrella, and related insurance programs annually on behalf of the franchisee or area developer
- Bidding for and negotiation, establishment, and administration of a workers' compensation insurance program annually on behalf of the franchisee or area developer
- Performance of claims reduction programs for each of the above insurance programs
- Setup and administration of option accounts, including option grant summaries, vesting, and option exercise bookkeeping and administration, for optionees of the franchisee or area developer
- Performance of year-end accrual analyses for health, dental, and FLEX plans on behalf of the franchisee or area developer

Additional Duties of the CFO

In many early-stage and emerging growth franchisors, the chief financial officer is also responsible for administrative and human resources issues. Many franchising executives hold the title of vice-president of finance and administration, thereby requiring a knowledge and expertise not only of the financial skills discussed above but also of current trends and developments in labor and employment laws. A working knowledge of these complex and constantly changing laws is important not only to manage an efficient and litigation-free workforce at the franchisor level but also to communicate the basics of these laws and requirements to the franchisees for the management of their staff to avoid unnecessary claims and litigation. Franchisors should include this information in the initial training program, in the operations manual, and in periodic updates and bulletins to ensure that franchisees have access to this information; at the same time, they must be careful not to cross the line into what may be perceived as interference with the day-to-day management of the franchisees' business, which may lead to vicarious liability (e.g., the franchisor being held liable for the actions of one franchisee). In recent years, employees and other injured third parties have tried to include the franchisor as a defendant in employment law–related claims against the franchisee, albeit with limited success thus far.

Understanding the Basics of Employment Law

This section of the chapter presents a basic overview of certain key aspects of employment and labor law as an administrative function at the franchisor level, and, within certain limitations, to be communicated at the franchisee level. Inasmuch as these laws are changing and evolving constantly, be sure to check with a qualified employment lawyer before developing employment policies, either for your internal use or for dissemination to your franchisees.

The employment at-will doctrine (which dates back to England's Statute of Labourers) allows for termination of employment by either the employer or the employee at any time for any reason or for no reason at all. The systems and procedures implemented by a franchisor for hiring and firing personnel trigger a host of federal and state labor and employment laws that you must understand, regardless of the size of your company. Failure to understand these laws, however, can be especially damaging to the smaller franchisor because of the extensive litigation costs incurred as the result of an employment-related dispute. Litigation between employers and employees continues to clutter U.S. tribunals. In fact, suits under federal employment laws currently make up the single largest group of civil filings in the federal court system. Federal and state legislatures have been equally active in designing new laws in the labor and employment arena, and small business groups have been quick to respond to the adverse impact of these laws.

The growing body of employment law encompasses topics such as employment discrimination, comparable worth, unjust dismissal, affirmative action programs, job classification, workers' compensation, performance appraisal, employee discipline and demotion, maternity policies and benefits, employee recruitment techniques and procedures, employment policy manuals and agreements, age and retirement, plant closings and layoffs, sexual harassment and discrimination, occupational health and safety standards, laws protecting the handicapped, and mandated employment practices for government contractors. The most comprehensive federal statutes and regulations affecting employment include the following:

◆ *Equal Pay Act of 1963*, prohibiting unequal pay based on gender
◆ *Title VII of the Civil Rights Act of 1964*, prohibiting discrimination based on race, color, religion, sex, or national origin
◆ *Age Discrimination in Employment Act of 1967 (ADEA)*, prohibiting discrimination against individuals age forty or older
◆ *Rehabilitation Act of 1973*, prohibiting discrimination against handicapped individuals by all programs or agencies receiving federal funds and all federal agencies (the act also protects reformed or rehabilitated drug or alcohol abusers who are not currently using drugs or alcohol; in addition, this law has been interpreted to cover people with AIDS and HIV infection and those perceived as having AIDS)
◆ *Vietnam Era Veteran's Readjustment Assistance Act of 1974*, requiring government contractors to take affirmative action to recruit, hire, and promote qualified disabled veterans and veterans of the Vietnam era
◆ *Pregnancy Discrimination Act of 1978*, prohibiting discrimination against pregnant women
◆ *Immigration Reform and Control Act of 1986*, making it unlawful for employers to recruit, hire, or continue to employ illegal immigrants to the United States; also contains similar nondiscrimination provisions as the Immigration and Nationality Act

Recent Federal Statutes and Regulations

◆ *Americans With Disabilities Act of 1990 (ADA)*. This law prohibits discrimination against a qualified applicant or employee with a disability, covering employers with twenty-five or more employees. The ADA is based on the Civil Rights Act of 1964 and Title V of the Rehabilitation Act of 1973. To fall within the ADA, a person's disability must be a physical or mental impairment that substantially limits at least one major "life activity." This covers a range of physical and mental problems, from visual, speech, and hearing impairments to cancer, heart disease, arthritis, diabetes, orthopedic problems, and learning disabilities such as dyslexia. HIV infection also is considered a disability. The ADA also prohibits discrimination based on a "relationship or association" with disabled persons, makes sure the disabled have access to buildings, etc., and protects recovered substance abusers and alcoholics.

As the courts begin to interpret various vaguely worded provisions of the ADA, franchisors can take comfort that in certain cases, deep pockets do not automatically equal liability. According to two federal district court decisions, a fast-food franchisor could not be held liable for violations of the Americans With Disabilities Act at franchise premises owned and operated by franchisees. In *Neff v. American Dairy Queen, Inc.,* U.S. District Court for the Western District of Texas, Civil Action No. SA-94-CA-280, and *Young v. American Dairy Queen, Inc.,* U.S. District Court for the Northern District of Texas, Civil Action No. 5:93-CV-253-C, it was uncontroverted that the franchisor could not be held liable under the ADA as an owner, lessor, or lessee of the premises. However, the lawsuits alleged that the franchisor was liable for violations as an "operator" of the premises because the franchise agreement gave the franchisor operating control over the franchises. However, according to the federal district court in San Antonio, the franchisor did not operate its local franchises "under a definition of the word." The fact that the franchisor had the right to approve all modifications to a franchise did not permit the franchisor to require an existing franchisee to make modifications to an existing structure. Furthermore, there was no showing that the franchisor exercised its approval rights in any way inconsistent with disabilities laws. A franchisor might be subject to liability for refusing to approve plans to bring a franchise into compliance with the law, the court held. However, merely possessing a veto power for structural modifications did not constitute operation of the premises for the purposes of the law. Neither decision is binding on other federal courts.

◆ *Civil Rights Act of 1991.* This recent legislation expanded the legal rights and remedies to those individuals who have experienced employment-related discrimination on the basis of their race, color, religion, sex, or national origin. Employees are now able to recover consequential monetary losses, damages for future lost earnings and nonpecuniary injuries such as pain and suffering and emotional distress, and punitive damages. The act also permits jury trials in these types of cases. Before the 1991 Act, employees' remedies were essentially limited to monetary damages for lost back pay, reinstatement or promotion, if appropriate, and attorneys' fees.

◆ *Family and Medical Leave Act of 1993 (FMLA).* The FMLA pro-hibits employers from interfering with, restraining, or denying employ-ees from taking reasonable leave for medical reasons, for the birth or adoption of a child, and for the care of a child, spouse, or parent who has a serious health condition. The leave is unpaid leave, or paid leave if it has been earned, for a period of up to twelve workweeks in any twelve months. During the leave period, the employer must maintain any group health plan covering the employee. At the conclusion of the leave, an employee generally has a right to retain the same position or an equivalent position with equivalent pay, benefits, and working con-ditions. Under the FMLA, an employer is defined as any person engaged in commerce, or in any industry or activity affecting com-merce, that employs fifty or more employees for each working day dur-ing each of twenty or more calendar workweeks in the current or preceding calendar year.

In addition to these federal laws, many state legislatures have enacted antidiscrimination laws that go beyond the protection afforded at the fed-eral level. These state laws must also be carefully reviewed in order to ensure that employment practices comply at both the federal and state level of regulation.

Preparing the Personnel Manual

A rapidly growing franchisor should develop a personnel manual and hand-book for the purposes of communicating to all of its employees the details of its management procedures and guidelines. Some of these recommended poli-cies and compliance tools should also be included in your operations manual for distribution to your franchisees.

A well-drafted personnel manual can serve as a personnel training program, a management tool for improving the efficiency of the franchisor, an employee morale builder, and a guardian against excessive litigation. The personnel man-ual should be sufficiently detailed so as to provide guidance to employees on all key company policies; however, overly complex manuals tend to restrict man-agement flexibility and lead to employee confusion and uncertainty. It is also crucial that your attorney review the manual before it is distributed to staff members, especially since some courts have recently held that the employment manual can be treated as if it were a binding contract under some circum-stances. And since the manual is also a written record of the company's hiring, compensation, promotion, and termination policies, it could be offered as evidence in employment-related litigation. Courts recently seem increasingly more willing to look at statements made in the personnel manual (or every unwritten employment policy of the company) in disputes between employers and employees. Although the exact contents of the manual vary depending on the nature and size of the franchisor as well as its management philosophies and objectives, all personnel manuals should contain the categories of information listed in Figure 13-3.

Figure 13-3. What the personnel manual should contain.

- Key goals and objectives of the franchisor
- Background of the franchisor and its founders
- Description of the products and services offered by the franchisor
- Current organizational chart and brief position descriptions
- Compensation and benefits:

    1. Hours of operation
    2. Overtime policies
    3. Vacation, maternity, sick leave, and holidays
    4. Overview of employee benefits (health, dental, disability, etc.)
    5. Performance review, raises, and promotions
    6. Pension, profit-sharing, and retirement plans
    7. Eligibility for fringe benefits
    8. Rewards, employee discounts, and bonuses
    9. Expense reimbursement policies
    10. Jury duty and medical absences

- Standards for employee conduct:

    1. Dress code and personal hygiene
    2. Courtesy to customers, vendors, and fellow employees
    3. Smoking, drug use, and gum chewing
    4. Personal telephone calls and visits
    5. Training and educational responsibilities
    6. Employee use of company facilities and resources
    7. Employee meals and breaks

- Safety regulations and emergency procedures
- Procedures for handling employee grievances, disputes, and conflicts
- Employee duties to protect intellectual property
- Term and termination of the employment relationship:

(continues)

Figure 13-3. *(continued)*

1. Probationary period
2. Grounds for discharge (immediate versus notice)
3. Employee termination and resignation
4. Severance pay
5. Exit interviews

◆ Maintenance of employee records:

1. Job application
2. Social Security and birth information
3. Federal and state tax, immigration, and labor/employment law documentation
4. Performance review and evaluation report
5. Benefit plan information
6. Exit interview information

◆ Special legal concerns:

1. Equal employment opportunity
2. Sexual harassment cases
3. Career advancement opportunities
4. Charitable and political contributions
5. Garnishment of employee wages
6. Policies regarding the award of franchises to employees or their family members

◆ Dealing with the news media and distribution of press releases
◆ Summary and reiteration of the role and purpose of the personnel manual
◆ Employee acknowledgment of receipt of manual (to be signed by the employee and placed in his or her permanent file)

Preparing Key Personnel Employment Agreements

Although employment agreements are typically reserved for employees of the franchisor who are either senior management or serve key technical functions, these documents serve as an important and cost-effective tool to safeguard confidential business information and preserve valuable human resources.

When combined with a well-developed compensation plan, both provide an economic and legal foundation for long-term employee loyalty.

There are many other reasons why employment agreements for key employees of the franchisor may be fundamental to a small franchisor's existence and growth. For example, venture capital investors often insist on employment agreements between the franchisor and its founders and/or key employees in order to protect their investment. Second, individuals with special management or technical expertise may insist on one as a condition to joining the company. Finally, it serves as an important human resources management tool in terms of the description of duties, the basis for reward, and the grounds for termination.

The essential provisions of a key employee employment agreement include:

◆ *Duration.* The crucial judgment that you must make when determining the duration is whether the arrangement best suits the employer as a temporary, trial arrangement or as a long-term relationship. Other factors that should influence the decision about the duration are the nature of the job, the growth potential of the candidate, the business plans of the franchisor, the impact of illness or disability, how the estate will be treated in the event of the death of the employee, and trends in the industry. A separate section should be added addressing what effect a subsequent merger or acquisition of the franchisor would have on the agreement. The provisions should also specify the exact commencement and expiration dates of employment, the terms and procedures for employee tenure or renewal, and a specific discussion of the grounds for early termination.

◆ *Duties and obligations of the employee.* The description of the nature of the employment and the employee's duties should include:

1. The exact title (if any) of the employee.
2. A statement of the exact tasks and responsibilities and a description of how these tasks and duties relate to the objectives of other employees, departments, and the franchisor overall.
3. A specification of the amount of time to be devoted to the position and to individual tasks.
4. Where appropriate, a statement about whether the employee will serve on the franchisor's board of directors, and if so, whether any additional compensation will be paid for serving on the board. For certain employees, such as executive and managerial positions,

the statement of duties should be defined as broadly as possible (e.g., "as directed by the Board"), so that the employer has the right to change the employee's duties and title if human resources are needed elsewhere; there should be a statement merely limiting the scope of the employee's authority or ability to incur obligations on behalf of the franchisor. This will offer a franchisor limited protection against unauthorized acts by the employee, unless apparent or implied authority can be established by a third party.

♦ *Compensation arrangements.* The type of compensation plan naturally varies depending on the nature of the employee's duties, industry practice and custom, compensation offered by competitors, the stage of the franchisor's growth, market conditions, tax ramifications to both employer and employee, and the skill level of the employee. A schedule of payment, a calculation of income, and a statement about the conditions for bonuses and rewards should be included.

♦ *Expense reimbursement.* The types of business expenses should be clearly defined for which the employee will be reimbursed.

♦ *Employee benefits.* All benefits and perquisites should be clearly defined, including:

- ♦ Health insurance
- ♦ Cars owned by the franchisor
- ♦ Education and training
- ♦ Death, disability, or retirement benefits
- ♦ Defined compensation plans
- ♦ Pension or profit-sharing plans

In addition, any vacation or sick leave policies should be included either in the employment agreement or the personnel manual (or both).

♦ *Covenants of nondisclosure.* Trade secrets owned by a franchisor may be protected with covenants that impose obligations on the employee not to disclose (in any form and to any unauthorized party) any information that the franchisor regards as confidential and proprietary. This should include, among other things, customer lists, formulas and processes, financial and sales data, agreements with customers and suppliers, business and strategic plans, marketing strategies and advertising materials, and anything else that gives the employer an advantage over its competitors. This covenant should cover the preemployment period (interview or training period) and extend through the term of the agreement into post-termination. The scope of the covenant, the conditions it contains regarding use and disclosure of trade secrets sources, the forms of information it describes, and the geographic limitations it covers should be broadly drafted to favor the employer. However, a nondisclosure covenant will only be enforceable to the extent necessary to reasonably protect the nature of the intellectual property that is at stake.

◆ *Covenants against competition.* Any franchisor would like to be able to impose a restriction on its employees so that should one leave the franchisor, he or she will be absolutely prohibited from working for a competitor in any way, shape, or manner. Courts, however, have not looked favorably on such attempts to rob individuals of their livelihood, and they have even set aside the entire contract agreement on the basis of this section. The courts require that any covenants against competition be reasonable as to scope, time, territory, and remedy for noncompliance. The type of covenants against competition that will be tolerated by the courts vary from state to state and from industry to industry, but they must always be reasonable under the circumstances. It is crucial that an attorney with a background in this area be consulted when drafting these provisions.

◆ *Covenants regarding ownership of inventions.* Questions that might arise regarding the ownership of intellectual property developed by an employee during the term of employment should be expressly addressed in the agreement. If they are not specifically addressed, basic common law rules regarding ownership of an employee's ideas, inventions, and discoveries will govern. These rules do not necessarily favor the employer, especially if there is a question of fact as to whether the discovery was made while working outside the scope of the employment or if it is established that the employee did not utilize the employer's resources in connection with the invention. In the absence of a written agreement, the common law principle of "shop rights" generally dictates that if an invention is made by an employee, if it utilizes the resources of the employer, and even if it is made outside of the scope of the employment, ownership is vested in the employee, subject, however, to a nonexclusive, royalty-free, irrevocable license to the employer.

◆ *Protection of intellectual property upon termination.* The agreement should contain provisions regarding obligations of nondisclosure and non-competition upon the termination of employment, and when an employee leaves, these obligations should be reaffirmed during an exit interview with at least one witness present. For example, a franchisor should inform the exiting employee of the employee's continuing duty to preserve the confidentiality of trade secrets, should reiterate specific information regarded as confidential, and should obtain assurances and evidence (including a written acknowledgment) that all confidential and proprietary documents have been returned and no copies retained. The name of the new employer or future activity should be obtained; under certain circumstances, the new employer should even be notified of the prior employment relationship and its scope. These procedures put the new employer and/or competitor "on notice" of the franchisor's rights and prevent it from claiming that it was unaware that its new employee had revealed trade secrets. Finally, the franchisor should also insist that the employee not hire coworkers after the termination of his or her employment with the franchisor.

Employers should nevertheless carefully consider the long-term implications of the terms and conditions contained in the employment agreement. Once promises are made to an employee in writing, the employee will expect special benefits to remain available throughout the term of the agreement. Your failure to meet these obligations on a continuing basis will expose you to the risk of litigation for breach of contract.

Structuring an Employee Recruitment and Selection Program

Based on the statutes we've looked at, the federal employment laws seek to protect each employee's right to be hired, promoted, and terminated without regard to race or gender. The agency tasked with enforcing these laws is the Equal Employment Opportunity Commission (EEOC). Under very limited circumstances, the EEOC will tolerate "discriminatory practices" in the recruitment and termination processes, but only if the criteria for making the determination are based on a "bona fide occupational qualification" (BFOQ) or a requirement reasonably and rationally related to the employment activities and responsibilities of a particular employee or a particular group of employees, rather than to all employees of the employer.

The equal opportunity laws do not require a franchisor to actively recruit or maintain a designated quota of members of minority groups; however, they do prohibit companies from developing recruitment and selection procedures that treat an applicant differently because of race, sex, age, religion, or national origin.

In determining whether a franchisor's recruitment policies have resulted in the disparate treatment of minorities, the courts and the EEOC look objectively at:

◆ The nature of the position and the education, training, and skill level required to fill the position
◆ The minority composition of the current workforce and its relationship to local demographic statistics
◆ Prior hiring practices
◆ The recruitment channels (such as newspapers, agencies, industry publications, and universities)
◆ The information requested of the candidate in the job application and in the interview
◆ Any selection criteria or testing (or related performance) measure implemented in the decision-making process
◆ Any differences in the terms and conditions of employment offered to those who apply for the same job

Anyone alleging discrimination in the hiring process would need to demonstrate that the following key facts were present:

◆ That the applicant was a member of a minority class that is protected under federal law (such as an African-American)
◆ That the individual was qualified for the job that was open
◆ That the individual was denied the position
◆ That the advertised position remained open after the individual was rejected, and the company continued to interview applicants with the same qualifications as the rejected candidate

If these facts are successfully demonstrated by the applicant, then the burden usually shifts to the company, which must then present legitimate business reasons for not hiring the particular applicant.

Preventive Measures

There are several preventive measures that you can implement to protect against discrimination claims. Ultimately these measures will prevail when and if a disgruntled applicant files a discrimination charge. First, a well-drafted job description that accurately reflects the duties of the position should be prepared before publicly advertising for the position. It should outline the skills, ability, and knowledge needed to perform the position competently; the compensation and related terms and conditions of employment; and the education, training, prior work experience, or professional certification (if any) that may be required for the position. A well-prepared job description will not only help you determine the qualities you are looking for in an employee and hire the right person; it will also serve as protection against a claim that the standards for the position were developed arbitrarily or in violation of applicable antidiscrimination laws.

Second, make sure your advertising and recruitment program meets EEOC standards by insisting that all job advertisements include the phrase "Equal Opportunity Employer." The context of the advertisement should not indicate any preference toward race, sex, religion, national origin, or age unless it meets the requirements of a BFOQ for the particular position. If employment agencies are used as a recruitment device, then inform the agency in writing of the company's nondiscrimination policy. If applicants are recruited from universities or trade schools, be certain that minority institutions are also visited. When selecting publications for the placement of advertisements for the positions, target all potential job applicants and advertise in minority publications where possible.

Third, develop a job application form that is limited to job-related questions and meets all federal, state, and local legal requirements. Questions in the application regarding an individual's race or religion should not be included. In court, the company will generally bear the burden to prove that any given question on the application—especially those relating to handicap, marital status, age, height or weight, criminal record, military status, or citizenship—is genuinely related to the applicant's ability to meet the requirements of the position. Even questions regarding date of birth or whom to contact in the event of an emergency should be reserved for posthiring information gathering.

Finally, an EEO compliance officer should be designated to monitor employment practices with the responsibility to: (1) structure position descriptions, job applications, and advertisements, (2) collect and maintain applicant and employee files, (3) meet with interviewers to review employment laws that affect the questions that may be asked of the applicant, and (4) work with legal counsel to ensure that the employment policies as well as recent developments in the law are adequately communicated to all employees.

The Interview

From a *legal* perspective, the questions asked in an interview must substantially be job-related and asked on a uniform basis of all candidates for the position. The exact types of questions that may be asked vary depending on applicable state laws, and therefore, state and local employment laws within the franchisor's jurisdiction should be consulted for further guidance. As a general rule, the following types of questions should be avoided:

◆ What is your marital status, and how many children do you have? How do family responsibilities affect your ability to meet work-related obligations?
◆ What is your religious affiliation? What religious holidays do you expect will interfere with work-related obligations?
◆ What is your national origin? Where are your parents from? What is your native language?
◆ Do you have any specific disabilities, or have you ever been treated for any diseases?
◆ Does your spouse object to your traveling or anticipated relocation? Will you be able to make child care arrangements given the long hours of this job?

In addition, there are several topic areas that are not necessarily prohibited but nevertheless should be asked about carefully to avoid an indirect claim of discrimination. These questions include those concerning the applicant's prior or current drug history, social clubs and hobbies, or the career plans of a spouse. Notwithstanding these difficult guidelines, there are still several types of questions that are legally available for screening candidates, such as:

◆ Why are you leaving your current position, and how does this new position resolve some of those problems?
◆ What was the most challenging project that you were responsible for in your last position?
◆ Do you have any physical or mental challenges that would restrict your ability to perform the responsibilities of this position?
◆ Are there any criminal indictments currently pending against you? What is the nature of these charges?
◆ What are your expectations regarding this position? How do these expectations influence your short- and long-term career goals?

Emerging Employment Law Issues: Drug Testing in the Workplace

Employee alcohol and drug abuse is considered to be among the most common health hazards in the workplace. In addition to costing companies of all sizes millions of dollars in lost productivity, employers perceive drug use by employees as a threat to corporate security and increased liability. As a result, employers are fighting back through the use of drug and substance abuse testing programs. While many of these drug-testing programs have proved successful, private employers must be cautious of the potential legal problems involved in such testing.

Private-sector employees generally do not have a constitutional right protecting them from tests conducted by private employers as a preemployment or in-term employment condition. However, to withstand legal challenges, your policies should be carefully drawn, based on *legitimate business considerations, accompanied by reasonable safeguards,* and applied in a *nondiscriminatory fashion.*

The abuse of or addiction to drugs and alcohol may be considered a protected handicap under federal or state law. Hence, when establishing a drug testing program to detect substance abuse among applicants or employees, you must consider laws that prohibit discrimination against the handicapped. The federal Rehabilitation Act includes recovered substance abusers within the act's definition of "handicapped." Although not directly applicable to private employers, the act applies to federal contractors and to some companies that provide goods or services either to the federal government or to a contractor with the federal government. The Rehabilitation Act does not protect *current* alcohol or drug abusers whose problem either prevents them from performing the duties of their job or constitutes a threat to the safety or property of others. The federal Americans With Disabilities Act, which applies to private employers with twenty-five or more employees, also protects *recovered* substance abusers and alcoholics since they are within the ADA's definition of "disabled."

In addition to federal legislation, many states have laws prohibiting employment discrimination by private-sector employers based on an individual's handicap. If you want to avoid being slapped with these laws, take the following steps:

◆ Relate any actions taken on account of drug test results to things such as overall performance, violations of rules governing being under the influence in the workplace, and the safety of the employee and other employees.
◆ Grant individuals showing signs of alcohol or drug dependence the opportunity to seek and obtain rehabilitative treatment.
◆ When accommodating these "handicaps," do not distinguish between alcohol- and drug-dependent individuals.

It is important to note that these handicap laws do not preclude employers from enforcing rules prohibiting the possession or use of alcohol or drugs in the workplace, provided that such rules are enforced even-handedly against all employees.

Defamation Considerations

Employers must be careful to communicate only information about employees that is accurate. If you publicly disclose untrue private facts to a third party that are offensive and objectionable to a reasonable person of ordinary sensibilities, you may be liable for defamation. For example, an employer was held liable for damages for stating that an employee was terminated for drug use where the company's only evidence was a polygraph result indicating that the employee lied when responding to a question concerning drug use.

Most states grant certain involved persons—such as personnel directors, supervisors, employees participating in an internal investigation, or unemployment compensation commissions—a qualified privilege to information concerning employee substance abuse problems. You can divulge such information about these people on a need-to-know basis as long as the information is not communicated with a malicious intent. This qualified privilege also applies when a prospective employer is checking references. The previous employer must supply information as long as it is completely accurate and not given for malicious purposes. It would be permissible to state that an employee tested positive on a drug test, but the employee should not be described as "an addict." To avoid problems involving this issue, you may adopt a policy that, when responding to reference checks, the company only supply the dates that former employees worked and the duties that they performed. Some companies have developed a limited waiver and release form (to release the employer against claims of defamation) if the former employee wants a more detailed reference.

Drug testing of current employees and applicants is increasing rapidly in private business. Consequently, private employers must be aware of the legal problems potentially involved when such tests are conducted. Because of the complexity of the legal issues involved, private employers should closely monitor all judicial and legislative developments relating to drug testing as they pertain to employers' current policies and procedures.

Emerging Employment Law Issues: Dealing With HIV/AIDS in the Workplace

The human immunodeficiency virus (HIV), the virus that causes the acquired immunodeficiency syndrome (AIDS), has led to great concern in the workplace in recent years. The majority of people infected with HIV/AIDS are between the ages of twenty and forty-five and are employed, many by small and midsize businesses. This raises questions regarding the measures an employer must take to accommodate these employees. Despite the ramifications of HIV/AIDS in the workplace, few companies have an established policy to guide their response to this issue.

Federal and State Legislation

At the federal level, there are two principal laws that protect individuals with HIV/AIDS. The first is the Rehabilitation Act and the second is the Americans With Disabilities Act. When making hiring or promotion decisions, you may not discriminate against an individual who is believed to be infected with HIV/AIDS. In a recent case, a New York State administrative agency found that the law firm of Baker & McKenzie (one of the world's largest law firms) discriminated against an associate attorney with AIDS when it terminated his employment, and the agency awarded the associate's estate $500,000 in compensatory damages. (The award-winning film *Philadelphia* also dramatized the plight of an attorney, played by Tom Hanks, whose services were terminated once it was discovered that he was afflicted with AIDS.)

The ADA also prohibits discrimination in places of public accommodation. This means that businesses such as restaurants and hotels may not deny goods or services to a person believed to be infected with HIV or AIDS. Many states and local jurisdictions have passed laws similar to those on the federal level prohibiting discrimination against people with disabilities. A majority of these laws also include people who have tested positive for HIV/AIDS within the definition of disabled. For example, in Minnesota a dentist was found to have violated the state's Human Rights Act (similar to the ADA) for refusing to treat a patient who had tested positive for HIV.

HIV Testing as a Condition of Employment

Several states prohibit HIV/AIDS testing as a condition of employment, while others permit HIV/AIDS testing when the employer can show a legitimate reason for doing so. To establish a legitimate reason, there must be some connection between HIV/AIDS and job performance or safety. This connection may exist when the job involves a risk of transmitting the disease. An employer who tests for HIV/AIDS without a legitimate reason may be liable for an invasion of privacy claim by the job applicant.

Rights of Coworkers

Certain federal laws allow employees to discontinue working when they have a reasonable belief that their working conditions are unsafe. Given the consensus in the medical field that HIV/AIDS cannot be transmitted through casual contact, it would be difficult for an employee to refuse to work with an HIV/AIDS-infected coworker on these grounds. The reasonableness of the employee's demand may depend on how the employer has educated employees about HIV/AIDS. If the employees have been taught that HIV/AIDS cannot be transmitted through casual contact, their refusal to work may be found to be "unreasonable," and they could be discharged.

Accommodations for Employees With HIV/AIDS

An issue has arisen with respect to whether an employer must make reasonable accommodations for an employee who has HIV/AIDS. Federal legislation not only prohibits discrimination against handicapped persons but also requires employers to make reasonable efforts to accommodate handicapped applicants and employees where obstacles exist that would impede their employment opportunities.

In addition, if your company is covered by the Rehabilitation Act and an employee has HIV/AIDS or develops it, you must make reasonable accommodations that permit the employee to continue working in the position. Such accommodations can include leave policies, flexible work schedules, reassignment to vacant positions, and part-time employment. The criteria used to determine whether an employer is making reasonable accommodations for an HIV/AIDS-infected employee include the cost of the accommodation, the size of the business, and the nature of the employee's work.

Guidelines to Consider

Through advance education and preparation, an employer can avoid many of the problems associated with an employee infected with HIV/AIDS. In 1987, the U.S. Surgeon General suggested that, when dealing with HIV issues, employers should:

◆ Adopt an up-to-date HIV/AIDS education program that discussed how HIV is transmitted and explains the company's policies regarding employees with HIV/AIDS.

◆ Treat HIV/AIDS-infected employees in the same manner that other employees suffering from disabilities or illnesses are treated under company health plans and policies.

◆ Allow HIV/AIDS-infected employees to continue working as long as they are able to satisfactorily perform their jobs and their continued employment does not pose a safety threat to themselves, other employees, or customers.

◆ Make reasonable efforts to accommodate HIV/AIDS-infected employees by providing them with flexible work hours and assignments.

◆ Protect all information regarding HIV/AIDS-infected employees' conditions.

There is a broad range of legal issues that an employer must consider when formulating its practices and responses toward HIV/AIDS. By educating your employees, you may be able to reduce the work disruption, legal implications, financial implications, and other effects that HIV/AIDS can have on your business. Because of the complexity and changing nature of HIV/AIDS, an employer should always examine the applicable laws in its jurisdiction and consult an attorney when handling HIV/AIDS issues in the workplace.

Emerging Employment Law Issues: Sexual Harassment in the Workplace

The problem of sexual harassment in the workplace has recently been brought to the forefront of national attention. According to *Training* magazine, sexual harassment is the fastest-growing topic on the workplace instruction circuit, now being offered by 70 percent of companies surveyed by the magazine. A wide range of sexual harassment claims against large and small companies has highlighted the importance of carefully dealing with this issue in the development of personnel policies. Sexual harassment lawsuits are growing in number across the United States, with some 15,549 sexual harassment complaints filed with the EEOC in 1995, up from 6,100 in 1990. The Supreme Court, in *Meritor Savings Bank,* held that sexual harassment is a form of sex discrimination prohibited under Title VII of the Civil Rights Act of 1964. Other cases have held that both men and women may be victims and both sexes have legal recourse under the statute.

The EEOC defines sexual harassment as any of the following:

1. *Unwelcomed* sexual advances, requests for sexual favors, and other verbal or physical conduct of a sexual nature

   where, either explicitly or implicitly, submission to such
   conduct is considered a term or condition of an individual's continued employment
2. Making submission to or rejection of such conduct the
   basis for employment decisions affecting the employee
3. Where such conduct has the effect of unreasonably interfering with an individual's work performance, or creates
   an intimidating, hostile, or offensive work environment

The first and second points listed above are known as "quid pro quo" sexual harassment, meaning sexual favors or conduct requested in return for job benefits or job retention. The third point above covers what is known as "hostile environment" harassment, when the conduct unreasonably interferes with an individual's ability to perform his or her job, or creates an intimidating, hostile, or offensive work environment.

It is important to note, however, that sexual harassment need not be overtly sexual in nature. Sexual harassment can encompass derogatory comments and the abuse of one's personal property. Furthermore, the victim need not be the person to whom the unwelcome sexual conduct is directed. If a person's work environment is adversely affected by sexual harassment toward a coworker, sexual harassment is present. Some recent cases have expanded the definition of sexual harassment by holding employers liable for the actions of nonemployees where the employer knew of the harassment and failed to take any corrective measures to remedy the situation. In one case, a jury rendered a $7.1 million verdict against a major law firm (the trial judge recently reduced the award to $3.5 million). In this case, the jury found that a former partner of the law firm had been guilty of sexually harassing a newly hired paralegal and that the firm had taken insufficient steps to rectify the problem and prevent its reoccurrence, in spite of the fact that it had been put on notice concerning this attorney's inappropriate conduct.

Sexual harassment is actionable when it is sufficiently severe or pervasive to alter the conditions of the victim's employment and create an abusive working environment. Thus, a request of a date or a lone sexual remark may not be sufficient to establish a sexual harassment claim because the behavior is not repeated. A single, particularly offensive remark or action may, however, be considered severe and thus constitute sexual harassment. To determine if a claim is valid, the court will first ask whether a reasonable person would find the conduct to have been severe or pervasive such that it altered the person's work environment. Second, the court will examine the conduct in light of the totality of the circumstances. Thus, an insulting comment made by a coworker during the course of an argument would be viewed differently from the same comment made by a superior during a nonconfrontational situation.

Franchisors have a duty to provide a workplace free from sexual harassment and to protect employees from unwanted, unwelcomed sexual overtures and invitations of a sexual nature, whether such conduct originates with managers, fellow employees, franchisees, customers, or other outsiders. In order to meet their responsibilities and to protect themselves against sexual harassment claims, employers should undertake the following defensive measures:

- Maintain and enforce a written policy against sexual harassment.
- Educate all employees on the company's sexual harassment policy, and be sure that they are aware of the consequences for violating the policy.
- Maintain a complaint procedure that allows the victim to file a complaint with a person other than the victim's supervisor.
- Investigate all complaints thoroughly and confidentially.
- Take appropriate action following each and every investigation.

To avoid liability for a claim, the employer *must* take prompt and effective action that is reasonably calculated to end the harassment. When deciding the case, the court will analyze the investigation made by the employer and the effectiveness of the remedial action taken. Unfortunately, the court's determination of the effectiveness of your response is often based on whether the remedial action ultimately succeeded in eliminating the harassment. To survive this type of hindsight analysis, the employer should conduct a prompt investigation of all sexual harassment complaints. The investigation should be conducted by an officer outside of the department concerned and commence within a week after the complaint is received. The investigator should then adopt the following guidelines:

1. Carefully document when and how the claim first came to the attention of the company.
2. Gather data to determine all relevant facts concerning the conduct in question.
3. Treat all claims as valid until proven otherwise.
4. Keep all discussions and information as confidential as possible.
5. Involve legal counsel as early as possible in the fact-gathering process to protect against claims of disparagement or defamation.

Once the investigation is complete, you must then take appropriate steps to remedy the situation. If the claim is substantiated, you must determine what discipline is appropriate. When the harassment occurred over an extended period of time, was severe, or the harasser had been disciplined previously for such conduct, then terminating the harasser may be appropriate. However, if the conduct was less severe and other means may remedy the situation, such as transferring the harasser to a different department, you should probably wait until a second offense before terminating the employee. This puts you in a better position to defend your action if the discharged employee subsequently sues you for wrongful discharge. If the employee is not transferred, you should monitor the situation to make sure the harassment does not recur.

The laws pertaining to sexual harassment are still evolving and can be difficult for any business owner to grasp. Recent cases and guidelines do not draw clear distinctions between permissible behavior and illegal behavior that may subject your company to legal liability. The standards of behavior will vary depending on the specific facts of each case and the perceptions of the employee who was subjected to the alleged harassment. The key to protecting your business against liability is to develop a stated policy regarding the type of conduct that will not be tolerated and maintain standard grievance procedures. All complaints should be dealt with promptly and seriously, and if harassment has occurred, remedial action must be taken.

Guidelines for Hassle-Free Firing of Employees

The decision to terminate an employee can be both emotional and frustrating. But it can also result in expensive litigation if it is not handled properly. These days, wrongful termination lawsuits are not idle threats. According to a recent study conducted by Jury Verdict Research, recently fired executives who bring such suits are winning often and winning big. In the review of 1,700 verdicts rendered between 1988 and 1995, it was found that former executive plaintiffs won wrongful termination suits 64 percent of the time, as compared with just 42 percent for general laborers. Executives are winning in court, say legal experts, because they often have strong communications skills and can afford better legal representation.

When an employee wins a lawsuit for unfair termination, the remedies for unjust dismissal have ranged from simple reinstatement to back pay and actual damages to even punitive damages for certain cases. Employers have also faced charges of discrimination or violation of federal statutes in connection with the termination of an employee. In order to successfully defend against these types of claims, you must be prepared to demonstrate that employee performance evaluations, policies contained in personnel manuals, and grounds for termination were implemented and enforced in a nondiscriminatory fashion and not as a result of any act contrary to applicable federal law. Specific, clear, and uniform guidelines should be developed for probation periods, opportunities to improve job performance, availability of training, and termination procedures.

Five Steps to Prevent Lawsuits

These steps can be taken prior to, during, and after the period when the employee has been fired:

- *Step 1.* The first step (well before the actual termination) is careful record keeping. Comprehensive records should be kept on each employee, including any formal performance appraisal or informal warnings, comments, or memos prepared by a supervisor to demonstrate the employee's poor work or misconduct. If a case ever gets to litigation, these documents and records may be the only evidence available to support that there were valid reasons for terminating the employee.
- *Step 2.* The second step prior to termination is to ensure that you have a proper basis for termination. This involves a careful review of personnel manuals, policy statements, memoranda, and related documentation to ensure that no implied representation or agreement has been made regarding the term of employment, severance pay, or grounds for termination that may be inconsistent with the company's intentions. The various grounds for termination should be clearly stated in the personnel manual, which should include among other things: (1) discriminatory acts toward employees or hiring candidates, (2) physical or sexual abuse, (3) falsifying time records or other key documents, (4) willful or negligent violation of safety or security rules, (5) violation of company policies, (6) unauthorized disclosure of the franchisor's confidential information, (7) refusal to perform work assigned by a supervisor, (8) destroying or damaging company property, (9) misappropriation or embezzlement, or (10) drug abuse or gambling on company premises.
- *Step 3.* The third step is to ensure that all alternatives to termination have been considered. An employee who has been performing poorly

should be provided with plenty of advance notice of management's disappointment with his or her performance through personal and written evaluations, warning notices, and published employment policies. Where the cause for termination involves an act of insubordination, improper conduct, or related incidents, then witness statements, accident reports, customer complaints, and related documentation should all be collected and reviewed. Even once a termination decision has been made by the immediate supervisor and the evidence supporting the case collected, there should be an independent review of the proposed dismissal by a member of management at least one level above the direct supervisor of the employee. An opportunity to cure the defect in performance should be strongly considered. The reviewer should take the time to confront the employee and hear his or her side of the story prior to making the final dismissal decision. Written records of these meetings should be placed in the employee's file. The reviewer should question the supervisor and coworkers of the employee to gather additional facts and to ensure that all company policies and procedures have been followed, especially those regarding performance appraisal and employee discipline.

◆ *Step 4.* Once the decision has been reached, the fourth step is to conduct an exit interview. It is important that the reasons for the employee's discharge be explained during an exit interview. The explanation should be candid and concise, in accordance with all available evidence, and consistent with any explanation of the termination that will be provided to the employee. You should emphasize to the employee that the reasons for termination are legitimate and are consistent with the company's past practices under similar circumstances. The employee should also be advised of what will be told to prospective employers, reminded of any covenants not to compete, and reminded of his or her continuing obligation to protect the company's trade secrets.

◆ *Step 5.* The fifth and final step is to prepare a comprehensive release and termination to further protect the company against subsequent litigation. The employee should be given an opportunity to have it reviewed by legal counsel. The release and termination agreement should: (1) be supported by valid consideration (e.g., some form of severance pay or covenants); (2) be signed by the employee knowingly and voluntarily; (3) include the grounds for termination in the recitals; (4) contain covenants against competition, disclosure, and litigation; (5) include all possible defendants in an employment action (company, officers, directors, subsidiaries, etc.); (6) avoid commitments regarding references to future employers; and (7) be checked carefully against all applicable federal and state laws.

The broad scope of federal and state antidiscrimination laws makes it imperative for owners (and their managers) to understand their obligations in structuring employee recruitment, selection, training, compensation, reward, testing, and seniority programs. Charges of discrimination may be defeated if proper documentation is maintained, such as a complete personnel file of the former employee, detailed records of complaints of supervisors and coworkers related to the cause of termination, copies of actual work produced by the employee that was unsatisfactory, a written record reflecting the race and sex of other persons dismissed or disciplined for the same or similar purposes, and the name, race, and sex of the individual replacing the discharged employee.

The welfare and motivation of the management team and employees at all levels are clearly one of the most valuable assets of a rapidly growing franchisor. If they are treated unfairly in the hiring or termination process, however, they can become the largest liability as well as be a major deterrent to franchise sales. Prospective franchisees who are perceptive will notice the culture and general satisfaction level of your staff when they come to visit your headquarters. Employees who are mistreated or confused are not likely to communicate the message to a prospect that you wish to convey. They might think to themselves, "Why should I buy a franchise from a company that can't keep even its own staff motivated and productive?" Employment agreements and personnel manuals are useful tools to define the rights and obligations of the employer and employee to each other and to ensure that your workforce is informed and motivated.

Special Issues in Mergers and Acquisitions

As the new millennium approaches, the number of corporate mergers and acquisitions appears to be ever increasing. The latest industry to grab the headlines of the business pages is the financial services industry, with a series of mergers among banks, insurance companies, investment firms, and credit card companies. Other recent headlines include mergers in the telecommunications, healthcare, pharmaceutical, and defense industries. Unlike the wave of mergers and acquisitions that occurred throughout the 1980s, however, which were primarily financially motivated, the more recent mergers and acquisitions have been primarily motivated by strategic considerations, where synergies between two or more merging companies could lead to efficiencies, competitive benefits, and improved operating margins. (For additional information on mergers and acquisitions, see Andrew J. Sherman, *Mergers and Acquisitions From A to Z*, AMACOM, 1998.)

Franchise companies also have been a part of this recent trend. One of the best examples is a company now known as Cendant Corporation, a provider of consumer alliance, travel, and real estate services. Cendant is the result of a merger of HFS, Inc. (formerly known as Hospitality Franchise Systems, Inc.) and CUC International, Inc. Before merging with CUC, HFS had acquired a host of well-known franchised brands, including real estate brokers Century 21, ERA, and Coldwell Banker; Avis Rent A Car; hotel/motel chains Days Inn, Howard Johnson, and Travellodge; and tax preparation service Jackson Hewitt. Other recent examples of franchise company mergers and acquisitions include Yogen Fruz International's acquisition of the Bresler's Ice Cream and I Can't Believe It's Yogurt franchise system, and Franchise Associates, Inc., which started with Arby's roast beef restaurants and now owns Sbarros pizza and T.J. Cinnamons. Another popular acquisition strategy, the "roll-up" (where a company with no preexisting operations raises capital to acquire a string of existing businesses), has been utilized with franchise companies also. For example, U.S. Office Products, one of the better known roll-up companies, recently acquired the Mail Boxes Etc. franchise system with its approximately 3,500 franchisees.

Because franchisors are just as susceptible as nonfranchise companies to the pressures of competition, shifts in demand and demographics, or the need to respond to changes in law or technology, mergers or acquisitions of competing or complementary franchise systems are a viable strategy for responding to these pressures. Thus, some of the most common reasons why franchisors consider a merger or acquisition with another franchisor or why nonfranchise companies consider franchise systems as viable acquisition targets include:

- The desire to add new products or services to their existing lines without the expense and uncertainty of internal research and development
- The desire to expand into a new geographic market or customer base without the expense of attracting new franchisees into these locations or developing a new advertising and marketing program
- The need to increase size to effectively compete with larger companies or to eliminate the threat of a smaller competitor
- The desire for market efficiencies through the acquisition of suppliers (backward integration) or existing franchisees or distributors (forward integration)
- The need to strengthen marketing capabilities or improve the quality of management personnel

There are numerous complex issues involved in the merger or acquisition of any company, including both legal and business considerations. This is especially true for franchisors, however, who must address not only the potential issues related to taxes, securities regulation, labor laws, employee benefits, environmental regulation, corporate governance, and bankruptcy and antitrust compliance, but who also must understand the nature of the assets of the franchise system being acquired and the unique relationship between the franchisor and its franchisees. A key component of the proposed merger or acquisition will be an analysis of how the transaction may affect the franchisor-franchisee relationship.

Analysis of One or More Target Companies

The acquiring company must begin the acquisition or merger process with a plan identifying the specific objectives of the transaction and the criteria to be applied in analyzing a potential target company operating within the targeted industry.

Once acquisition objectives have been identified, the next logical step is to narrow the field of candidates. Some of the qualities that a viable acquisition target might possess include:

- Operates in an industry that demonstrates growth potential.
- Has taken steps necessary to protect any proprietary aspects of its products and services.
- Has developed a well-defined and established market position.
- Possesses "strong" franchise agreements with its franchisees with minimal amendments or "special exceptions."
- Is involved in a minimal amount of litigation (especially if the litigation is with key customers, distributors, franchisees, or suppliers).
- Is in a position to readily obtain key third-party consents from lessors, bankers, creditors, suppliers, and investors (where required); the failure to obtain necessary consents to the assignment of key contracts or to clear encumbrances on title to material assets may seriously impede the completion of the transaction.
- Is in a position to sell so that negotiations focus on the terms of the sale, not whether to sell in the first place.

In addition to the general business issues discussed above, the following issues should be examined when examining the potential acquisition of a franchise system:

- The strength and registration status of the target's trademarks and other intellectual property
- The quality of the target's agreements and relationships with its franchisees
- The status of any litigation or regulatory inquiries involving the target
- The quality of the target franchise sales staff
- The quality of the franchisee relationships, including the regularity of the franchisor's cash flow from royalty obligations
- The strength of the target franchisor's training, operations, and field support programs, manuals, and personnel
- The existence of any franchisee association and its relationship with the franchisor
- The strength and performance of the target's company-owned units (where applicable)

Sometimes, instead of the acquiror affirmatively seeking acquisition targets, the process is reversed, and it is the target, rather than the acquiror, that is soliciting offers to be acquired. Such an acquisition candidate may offer an excellent opportunity for the acquiror, although the target's operations and financial condition should be closely inspected for any liability or potential pitfall that may be hidden behind the good intentions of the sellers.

The inspection of a potential target will be necessary regardless of who approaches whom (often referred to as the due diligence review). Preliminary due diligence may be undertaken before any offer is made, and more thorough due diligence will certainly need to be completed by the acquiror's in-house and outside business and legal advisers before completing the deal.

The Due Diligence Review

Before conducting a thorough due diligence review of an acquisition candidate, the acquiror may want to conduct a preliminary analysis. In most cases, the principals of each of the companies will meet to discuss the possible transaction. The key areas of inquiry at this stage are the financial performance to date and projected performance of the target, the strength of the target's management team, the target's intellectual property, the condition of the target's franchise system (including an understanding of the terms of the target's existing franchise and area development agreements), any potential liabilities of the target that may be transferred to the franchisor as a successor company, and the identification of any legal or business impediments to the transaction, such as regulatory restrictions or adverse tax consequences. In addition to a direct response from the target's management, information also may be obtained from outside sources, such as trade associations, customers and suppliers of the target, industry publications, franchise regulatory agencies, chambers of commerce, securities law filings if the company is publicly traded on a stock exchange or through the NASDAQ stock markets, or private data sources such as Dun & Bradstreet, Standard & Poor's, and Moody's. Some of this information may be readily available on the Internet.

Once the two companies have agreed to move forward, a wide variety of legal documents and records, where applicable, should be carefully reviewed and analyzed by the acquiring entity and its legal counsel.

The following is an illustrative list of some of the questions the acquiror and its legal and accounting representatives will be trying to answer as they begin to draft the acquisition agreements that will memorialize the deal:

◆ What approvals will be needed to effectuate the transaction (e.g., director and stockholder approval, governmental consents, lenders' and lessors' consents)?

◆ Are there any antitrust problems raised by the transaction? Will filing be necessary under the premerger notification provisions of the Hart-Scott-Rodino Act?

◆ Are there any federal or state securities registration or reporting laws to comply with?

◆ What are the potential tax consequences to the buyer, seller, and their respective stockholders as a result of the transaction?

◆ What are the potential postclosing risks and obligations of the buyer? To what extent should the seller be held liable for such potential liability? What steps, if any, can be taken to reduce these potential risks or liabilities? What will it cost to implement these steps?

◆ Are there any impediments to the transfer of key tangible and intangible assets of the target company, such as real estate or intellectual or other property?

◆ Are there any issues relating to environmental and hazardous waste laws, such as the Comprehensive Environmental Response Compensation and Liability Act (the Superfund law)?

◆ What are the obligations and responsibilities of buyer and seller under applicable federal and state labor and employment laws (e.g., will the buyer be subject to successor liability under federal labor laws and as a result be obligated to recognize the presence of organized labor and therefore be obligated to negotiate existing collective bargaining agreements)?

◆ To what extent will employment, consulting, confidentiality, or noncompetition agreements need to be created or modified in connection with the proposed transaction?

◆ What are the terms of the target's agreements with its existing franchisees? Are these agreements assignable? Do they contain clauses giving the franchisor discretion to change the system or ownership? Could any of these terms cause problems for the acquiring franchisor at a later date?

◆ Is the target currently involved in litigation with franchisees, creditors, competitors, or suppliers? Threatened litigation? Potential litigation? What is the risk of exposure to the acquiring franchisor?

◆ Have the target's registration and disclosure documents been properly filed and updated?

Some of the questions that will be analyzed by the acquiror's business and accounting representatives include:

◆ Does the target franchisor fit into the long-range growth plans of the acquiring franchisor?
◆ What are the target franchisor's strong points and weaknesses? How does management of the acquiring franchisor plan to eliminate those weaknesses?
◆ Has the acquiring franchisor's management team developed a comprehensive plan to integrate the resources of the target?
◆ What is the target franchisor's ratio of company-owned outlets to franchisees?
◆ Are the target's products and services competitive in terms of price, quality, style, and marketability?
◆ Does the target franchisor manufacture its own products? What proportions are purchased from outside sellers?
◆ What is the target's past and current financial condition? What about future projections? Are they realistic?
◆ What is the target franchisor's sales history? Has there been a steady flow of franchise sales and royalty payments?
◆ What is the target franchisor's attrition rate? Have there been many recent terminations or transfers? Have any of these been contested by franchisees as lacking good cause?

The Role of the Franchisee in a Proposed Merger or Acquisition

Unlike other types of growing companies involved in mergers and acquisitions, franchisors have existing contractual vertical distribution systems in place through their franchisees. The interests of these franchisees ought to be taken into account when the franchisor's counsel analyzes the legal consequences and potential costs of the proposed merger or acquisition. These franchisees are clearly "interested parties," whose contractual and other legal and equitable rights must be considered. Although there is no statutory or legal basis for disclosing the intent to engage in a merger or acquisition, nor is there typically a contractual requirement to obtain their approval, good "franchisee relations" practice would dictate their involvement in some fashion. The cooperation level of the franchisee networks of both buyer and seller can either greatly facilitate the transaction or virtually kill the deal, depending on how this communications problem is handled.

For example, if the franchisor acquires another franchisor in a competitive or parallel line of business, careful merger planning and negotiation will be necessary to ensure a smooth integration of the target's franchise system into the buyer's existing operations (assuming that only one system will survive after the transaction) and to avoid potential litigation or costly settlement with affected franchisees of either system. In addition, if conversion or change is planned as a result of the merger or acquisition, franchisors should expect to involve franchisees, at least to a certain extent, in the decision-making process. The acquiring franchisor should not automatically assume that franchisees in the acquired system will be willing to convert to the buyer's existing system. When change or conversion is contemplated, some attrition and/or franchisee resistance should be expected in both systems, and the impact and costs of this attrition and resistance will typically be reflected in the purchase price of the target franchisor.

On one hand, the franchisee is typically not a shareholder, creditor, employee, investor, officer, or director of the franchisor and would technically be governed only by the terms of the franchise agreement, which usually gives broad latitude to the franchisor to assign rights or modify the franchise system. Yet to ignore the fact that the franchisee is clearly an interested and affected party in any change in the franchisor's organizational structure or system is unrealistic and could result in very costly litigation that might even outweigh any anticipated benefits to the proposed merger or acquisition. Franchisees who oppose a pending franchisor have often waged war on the "selling franchisor" by calling for royalty payment strikes, launching class-action lawsuits, seeking injunctive relief to bar one franchisor, or launching public relations campaigns against the deal. To avoid these problems (which are likely to be "deal breakers"), franchisees should take steps to build concensus for the franchisor as early as possible. See Figure 14-1 for information on the legitimate concerns of the franchisee network in a merger or acquisition.

Figure 14-1. Legitimate concerns of the franchisee network in a merger or acquisition.

Clearly, the franchisee will have some legitimate questions and concerns when it first learns of the proposed transaction. The savvy franchisor will anticipate these concerns and integrate the proposed solutions into its acquisition plan and communications with the franchisees and/or the franchisee association:

◆ What are the acquiring franchisor's plans for the acquired system? Consolidation and conversion? At whose cost? Liquidation? Growth?

(continues)

Figure 14-1. *(continued)*

- What are the reputation and management philosophy of the acquiring franchisor? What are its attitudes toward field support and ongoing training?
- Will the acquiring franchisor be sensitive to the rights and concerns of the franchisees? Or will the franchisees adopt a "we'd rather fight than switch" mentality toward the new buyer in anticipation of hostile negotiations?
- What is the financial strength of the acquiring franchisor? Will the acquiring franchisor open up new opportunities for the franchisees, such as access to new product lines, financing programs for growth and expansion, product purchasing, and cooperative advertising programs?
- If the target franchisor owns real property that is leased to franchisees, will the terms and conditions of the current leases be honored by the acquiring franchisor? What about other contractual obligations? Are there any special relationships with third-party vendors that will be affected or damaged by the transaction?

Special Problems Relating to Franchisees of the Acquiring or the Acquired Franchise System

There are a number of potential issues for dispute between the acquiring or acquired franchisor and its franchisees that may arise as a result of a merger or acquisition. Whether or not these issues arise of course depends on a variety of factors, including the similarity of the businesses of the merging systems, the territories in which they operate, the terms of the contracts with existing franchisees in each system, the size and market power of the merging franchisors, the competitors (or lack of) of each of the franchisors, and most important, the plans of the surviving company. Because there is an implied obligation of franchisors to act in good faith and in a commercially reasonable manner, as well as a covenant recognized by many state courts in their interpretation of the franchise relationship, the issues to which both franchisors should pay special attention include the following:

- What is the extent of any territorial exclusivity granted to the franchisees of each system? Is exclusivity given only for a certain trademark or line of business? Is territorial exclusivity conditioned on the performance of the franchisees? Will substantially similar franchisees violate this exclusivity? What encroachment or other territorial conflicts may trigger legal claims from one franchisee on either or both sides?

◆ Will all existing franchisees of both systems be maintained, or will a consolidated distribution system result in termination of some franchisees?

◆ Will franchisees be required or requested to convert to a new business format? Who will pay the costs of building conversion and new training, products, and services? Will the franchisor finance all or part of the conversion costs?

◆ Will existing franchisees of each system be forced to add the products and services of the other? Will this present tying or full-line forcing problems?

◆ Does the acquiring franchisor have sufficient support staff to adequately service the new franchisees, or will the acquiring company's existing franchisees be ignored in order to develop and market the new acquisitions? What rights do the existing franchisees have to challenge this lack of attention?

◆ Will a new, third type of system combining the products and services of the acquiring and acquired franchisors be offered to prospective franchisees of the surviving entity? Will existing franchisees of either system be eligible to convert to this new system?

◆ Can the acquiring franchisor legitimately enforce an in-term covenant against competition when the franchisor itself has acquired and is operating what is arguably a competitive system?

◆ Do the franchisees of either franchisor have a franchisee association or franchisee advisory council? How and when should these groups be recognized? Must these groups be consulted? What duty does the franchisor have to involve these groups in merger planning? What about regional and multiple franchisees holding development rights?

◆ Does either franchisor have company-owned outlets in its distribution system? What will be the status of these outlets after the merger or acquisition?

◆ To what extent will royalty payments, renewal fees, costs of inventory, performance quotas, and advertising contributions be affected by the contemplated merger or acquisition? On what grounds could franchisees challenge these changes as unreasonable, breaches of contract, or violations of antitrust laws? How and when will these changes be phased into the system? Will the franchisees be given a chance to opt in or opt out (mandatory versus optional changes)?

◆ Will the proposed transaction result in the termination of some of the franchisees of either system as a result of oversaturation of the market, territorial overlap, or underperformance? What legal and statutory rights of the franchisee are triggered?

The Consequences of Inadequate Planning and Due Diligence

The consequences of inadequate pretransaction planning and investigation to both the acquiror and the target in a transaction combining two or more franchise systems can be financially devastating, often resulting in years of litigation while the franchise system suffers. For example, in a recent stock purchase acquisition of a food concept by another similar concept, the seller's management intentionally concealed from the buyer material information concerning certain contractual defaults and potential litigation problems. Although the buyer escrowed some of the purchase price to cover the costs of defending franchisee litigation that was disclosed, the undisclosed litigation was costing far in excess of the amount reserved. To make matters more complicated, the same management that had concealed the litigation sought indemnification from the buyer, who had agreed to limited indemnity for the sellers and their managers because of the ability under certain franchise and trade practices statutes of a claimant to sue individual officers and directors personally. Now, the buyer must address both the successor liability claim and the dispute with the former management.

In another example, the owners of a franchise system that was to be sold failed to inform the buyer of serious disagreements with the franchisees. The relationship between the seller and the franchisees had deteriorated to the point where the latter had retained a lawyer to represent them at a meeting with the franchisor. Fortunately, the buyer learned of the meeting and the problems and decided to delay the transaction pending the seller's ability to work the problem out with the franchisees.

Finally, in one other example, two publicly traded franchise companies signed a letter of intent to move forward with a combination that would be paid for in stock of the acquiror. Negotiating the basic terms of the transaction took a substantial amount of time and effort by both companies and their representatives. Finally, after agreement in principle was reached, the companies discovered serious securities law impediments, and after further expense and effort on everyone's part, they simply could not satisfy the regulators at the Securities and Exchange Commission. The deal was scrapped.

Thus, the difficult legal and strategic issues that are triggered in a merger or acquisition by and among franchisors can be resolved, and litigation avoided, with careful pretransaction planning and investigation by the acquiring and acquired franchisors, or else they can cause the deal to fail. Among the critical steps toward a successful transaction, communication with the franchisees of both systems will be of paramount importance.

Managing the Renewal and Transfer Process

One critical but often overlooked area of franchising management is the administration of the transfer and renewal process. Although the transfer of a franchise is a very different and usually more complex transaction than the renewal of a franchise, both situations highlight an important aspect of the relationship between franchisor and franchisee—namely, that *franchises are awarded and not sold,* and as a result, the franchisor has every right to impose certain conditions on approval of either event.

The renewal of the term of the franchise agreement is like a husband and wife renewing their marriage vows, each restating his or her mutual desire to continue the relationship. The renewal is the ideal time for the franchisor to impose certain conditions on the renewal of the term of the agreement and for the franchisee to make sure that it is ready to commit to another five, ten, or twenty years of meeting its obligations under the franchise agreement and operations manual.

The transfer process, on the other hand, is more akin to a divorce. The franchisee, for a variety of possible reasons such as retirement, relocation, burnout, or frustration, has decided to end its relationship with the franchisor, and a third party has been identified to assume responsibility for the operation and management of the franchised business. To protect itself against the "fear of the unknown," the franchisor must impose certain conditions on the approval or authorization of a transfer or resale. The franchisor should also stay in the middle of the transfer process in order to ensure that the transferee is viable, qualified, and capable of operating the franchised business. The franchisor must play the role of facilitator, investigator, and traffic cop in order to protect itself against misrepresentations being made by the franchisee to the prospective transferee about the obligations of the franchisor, the financial performance of the franchised unit, and the overall characterization of the franchised system.

This chapter highlights the key issues that arise in the course of these two critical transactions, with an emphasis on the types of conditions that should be imposed prior to approval by the franchisor of the proposed renewal or transfer.

Managing the Renewal Process

Franchise rights are awarded to franchisees for a specified initial term and subject to the continuing obligation to meet certain obligations and follow certain standardized systems. As the term of the agreement draws to a close, the franchise agreement should specify the obligations of the franchisee that must be met as a condition to renewal. Certain key issues, such as royalty rates, performance standards, territorial allocations, and advertising fund contributions, may need to be revisited. For obvious reasons, franchisees will resent any significant changes to the relationship, especially if the possibility of these proposed changes was not disclosed to them in their initial offering circular. Franchisees often complain when the renewal fee structure forces them to essentially "repurchase" their franchise at the commencement of each new term. Although the term *repurchase* shows an obvious misunderstanding of the nature of the franchise relationship, it does highlight a legitimate concern of the franchisee, namely, that it does not want to be unduly penalized for being successful in building up local goodwill and capturing local market share. If the renewal fee structure is not viewed as fair and reasonable or if the key terms of the franchise agreement significantly change upon renewal, then the renewal process is likely to be a source of conflict and dispute.

A well-drafted franchise agreement should impose, at a minimum, the following conditions to a renewal of the term:

1. At least six (6) months prior to the expiration of the initial term of this Agreement, Franchisor shall inspect the Franchised Business and give notice of all required modifications to the nature and quality of the products and services offered at the Franchised Business, the Software, advertising, marketing and promotional programs, necessary to comply with the Franchisor's then current standards, and, if Franchisee elects to renew this Agreement, shall complete to Franchisor's satisfaction all such required modifications, as well as adopt and implement any new methods, programs, Software updates, and modifications and techniques required by Franchisor's notice no later

than three (3) months prior to expiration of the initial term of this Agreement;

2. Franchisee shall give Franchisor written notice of such election to renew not less than three (3) months prior to the end of the initial term of this Agreement;

3. Franchisee shall not be in default of any provision of this Agreement, any amendment hereof or successor hereto, or any other agreement between Franchisee and Franchisor, or its subsidiaries, affiliates, and suppliers and shall have substantially complied with all the terms and conditions of such agreements during the terms thereof;

4. Franchisee shall have satisfied all monetary obligations owed by Franchisee to Franchisor and its subsidiaries, affiliates, and suppliers and shall have timely met those obligations throughout the term of this Agreement;

5. Franchisee shall execute upon renewal Franchisor's then current form of Franchise Agreement, which agreement shall supersede in all respects this Agreement, and the terms of which may differ from the terms of this Agreement, including, without limitation, by requiring a higher percentage royalty fee and/or National Advertising Fund contribution, increase in the Minimum Local Advertising Expenditure, and the implementation of additional fees; provided, however, that in lieu of the then current initial franchise fee or its equivalent, for such renewal period, Franchisee shall be required to pay a renewal fee of ___ percent (___ %) of the then current initial franchise fee paid by new franchisees of the Franchisor but in no event shall said renewal fee exceed ___ Dollars ($ ___);

6. Franchisee shall comply with Franchisor's then current qualification and training requirements;

7. Franchisee, its shareholders, directors, and officers shall execute a general release, in a form prescribed by Franchisor, of any and all claims against Franchisor and its subsidiaries and affiliates, and their respective officers, directors, agents, and employees provided, however, that Franchisee shall not be required to release Franchisor for violations of federal or state franchise registration and disclosure laws; and

8. Franchisee shall present evidence satisfactory to Franchisor that it has the right to remain in possession of the premises

where the Franchised Business is located for the duration of the renewal term.

In the event that any of the above conditions to renewal have not been met, no later than three (3) months prior to the expiration of the initial term of this Agreement, Franchisor shall have no obligation to renew this Agreement and shall provide to Franchisee at least sixty (60) days prior written notice of its intent not to renew this Agreement, which notice shall set forth the reasons for such refusal to renew.

Figure 15-1 provides a sample renewal and release agreement.

Figure 15-1. Renewal and release agreement.

RENEWAL AND RELEASE AGREEMENT

THIS AGREEMENT is made and entered into this _____ day of _____, 19___, by and between _____, a _____ corporation whose principal place of business is _____ _____ ("Franchisor") and _____ whose principal place of business is _____ ("Franchisee").

W I T N E S S E T H:

WHEREAS, on _____, 19___, Franchisor and Franchisee entered into a written Franchise Agreement by the terms of which Franchisee was granted a license to operate a _____ business in connection with the Franchisor's System and Proprietary Marks (the "Franchise") at the following location: _____; and

WHEREAS, pursuant to Section ___ of that Franchise Agreement, Franchisee desires to renew the Franchise for an additional ___ year period and Franchisor desires to allow said renewal.

NOW, THEREFORE, in consideration of the mutual promises, covenants and conditions contained herein and for other good and valuable consideration, the receipt of which is hereby acknowledged, the parties agree as follows:

1. <u>Renewal of Franchise Agreement.</u> Pursuant to Section ___ of the Franchise Agreement, Franchisee hereby renews the Franchise for an additional period of ___ years.

2. <u>Execution of Current Franchise Agreement.</u> Concurrently with the execution hereof, Franchisee shall execute Franchisor's current form of Franchise Agreement which agreement supersedes in all respects that Franchise Agreement executed by and between Franchisor and Franchisee on _____, 19___ and any other prior agreements, representations, negotiations or understandings between the parties.

3. <u>Renewal Fee.</u> Concurrently with the execution hereof, Franchisee shall pay to Franchisor the sum of $ ___ representing the renewal fee as provided in Section ___ of the Franchise Agreement.

4. <u>Release of Franchisor.</u> Franchisee, individually and on behalf of Franchisee's heirs, legal representatives, successors and assigns, hereby forever releases and discharges Franchisor, its subsidiaries and affiliates, their respective officers, directors, agents and employees from any and all claims, demands, controversies, actions, causes of action, obligations, liabilities, costs, expenses, attorney's fees and damages of whatsoever character, nature and kind, in law or in equity, claimed or alleged and which may be based upon or connected with the Franchise, the Franchise Agreement or any other agreement between the parties and executed prior to the date hereof, including but not limited to any and all claims whether presently known or unknown, suspected or unsuspected, arising under the franchise, securities or antitrust laws of Canada, the United States, or any state, or municipality.

5. <u>Acknowledgment of Performance.</u> Except as provided herein, the parties hereto acknowledge and agree that all conditions to renewal provided in Section ___ of the Franchise Agreement have been satisfactorily complied with or performed.

6. <u>Execution of Documents.</u> The parties agree to execute any and all documents or agreements and to take all action as may be necessary or desirable to effect the terms, covenants and conditions of this Agreement.

IN WITNESS WHEREOF, the parties hereto have hereunder caused this Renewal and Release Agreement to be executed the day and year first above written.

ATTEST: FRANCHISOR

_____   By: _____

                                               _____, PRESIDENT
WITNESS: FRANCHISEE:

_____   _____

Managing the Transfer Process

The "secondary market" for franchised businesses continues to flourish as franchising has matured. Many of the franchises initially awarded in the 1970s and 1980s are now operated by individuals nearing retirement age, and these franchisees are ready to transfer ownership. There is a wide variety of issues and obligations triggered when a current franchisee ("transferor") proposes to sell or transfer its rights under the franchise agreement to a third party ("transferee"), which must always be subject to approval by the franchisor. In addition to this increase in transfer activity from the existing franchisee's perspective, new entrants into franchising have shown an increasing preference toward the purchase of an existing location in lieu of the cost and start-up time of launching a brand-new franchised site. New franchise owners seem to be leaning toward the comfort of getting a proven location within a proven concept and an existing staff and customer base. There is also an ability to get a reliable set of financial data from prior years' operating history. Although these comforts may come at a premium, purchasers are finding it easier to obtain acquisition financing and enjoy an immediate cash flow from the business, which may be a cost worth paying for to many new franchisees. These factors have forced franchisors to take a more active role in the transfer management process. Some of the key issues in the administration and management of the transfer process include:

- *Franchisor's rights of first refusal.* Many modern-day franchise agreements provide the franchisor with a right of first refusal to essentially match the terms offered by a bona fide third party in the event of a sale or transfer by the franchisee. All of the proper notification, approval, exercise, or waiver procedures set forth in the agreement must be followed.
- *Data gathering.* Assuming that the franchisor will not be exercising its rights of first refusal, the franchisor must begin its due diligence on the proposed transferee. The franchisee and the proposed transferee must be diligent and timely in meeting all information requests of the franchisor in the areas of business experience, financial capability, employment and educational history, etc. The franchisor should *always* meet with the prospective transferee for a face-to-face interview.
- *Document control.* The franchisor should be provided with copies of all correspondence, listings, sales contracts, bulk sales transfer notices, broker agreements, and any other paperwork related to the transaction to ensure against any misrepresentations, inaccurate earn-

ings claims, or false statements about the franchisor being made by the transferor to the transferee in connection with the proposed transaction. The franchisor should play the role of document reviewer, not document validator. It may be tempting for the transferee to contact the franchisor directly to get its opinions on the fairness of the sales terms, the accuracy of the store's financial performance, or the credibility of the transferee's proposed business plan or pro forma financial statements. Franchisors should help to facilitate the process but resist the temptation of playing a role beyond the review and approval level, *unless* they serve as a direct remarketer of the franchise.

◆ *Franchise remarketing.* Franchisors must decide what role they plan to play in the transfer process and what their compensation will be for locating a qualified transferee. In recent years, some franchisors have become very active in the remarketing of their franchises, essentially serving as a broker on behalf of current franchisees who want to sell their business.

◆ *Transfer fees.* The franchisor must devote time and resources to the review and approval of a proposed transfer. Often the franchisor's attorneys must be brought in to review the terms of the proposed transfer. The transferee, once approved, must be trained and supported. All of the costs must be borne by someone, and it is typically *not* the franchisor. Therefore, the franchise agreement should provide for a transfer fee that is at least enough to cover all of the franchisor's training and administrative costs that will be incurred in connection with the transfer.

◆ *Debt assumption.* One of the typical conditions of the approval of the transfer (see below) is that the franchisee pay all of its outstanding financial obligations to the franchisor. In the case of a troubled franchisee, the transferee may be buying the business in exchange for a promissory note, leaving little or no cash for the transferor to pay its debts to the franchisor. If the franchisor will also be taking a promissory note back from the transferee, then the terms of the repayment, the security agreements, financing statements, and personal guaranties of both transferor and transferee must be prepared. Any other defaults by the transferor that must be cured as a condition to approving the transfer should be clearly explained to the transferee, especially if any of those defaults will be cured *after* the consummation of the transfer.

◆ *Disclosure of the transferee.* Regardless of specific legal requirements, good franchising practice dictates that the franchisor should provide the proposed transferee with a copy of its current disclosure document and clearly explain any new developments, obligations, or problems that may affect the proposed transferee's decision to buy the business and become part of the franchise system. Proposed transferees who are about to become new franchisees do not want to hear about major changes to the system, class action lawsuits against the franchisor, or the impending bankruptcy of the franchisor *just after* they invested their life savings into the purchase of the business.

 ◆ *Inspection and audit.* The franchisor should always arrange for its field support staff to visit the site of the proposed transfer in order to conduct an inspection and audit. This gives the franchisor insight into any unreported fees owed as well as help determine whether any refurbishment will be required as a condition to the approval of the transfer. This is also an opportune time for the franchisor to collect all copies of the operations manual and any other confidential information back from the transferor.

 ◆ *Execution of documents.* There is a wide variety of legal documents that may be prepared by the franchisor for execution by the transferor and transferee as a condition to approving the transfer. These documents may include mutual releases, guaranty agreements, representation and acknowledgment letters (for execution by the transferee that represents his or her capabilities and acknowledges his or her undertaking of certain responsibilities, etc.), lease agreements, or consent to sale agreements. (A sample transfer agreement is given in Figure 15-2.) There may also be certain "standard" documents that must be executed by the transferee, such as local cooperative advertising participation agreements, sign lease agreements, equipment leases, or inventory purchase agreements.

(text continues on page 342)

Figure 15-2. Transfer agreement.

FRANCHISE TRANSFER AGREEMENT

 THIS AGREEMENT is made and entered into this _____ day of _____, 19___, by and between _____, a _____ corporation, whose principal place of business is _____ _____ (hereinafter the "Franchisor"); and _____, whose principal place of business is _____ (hereinafter the

"Transferor"); and _____, whose principal place of business is
_____ (hereinafter the "Transferee").

W I T N E S S E T H:

WHEREAS, on _____, 19___, Franchisor and Transferor
entered into a written Franchise Agreement by the terms of which Transferor
was granted a license to operate a Center in connection with the Franchisor's
System and Proprietary Marks (hereinafter the "the Franchise") at the following location: _____;

WHEREAS, Transferor desires to sell, assign, transfer, and convey all of its
right, title and interest in and to the Franchise to Transferee and Franchisor is
willing to consent to said transfer, upon the terms and conditions in the said
written Franchise Agreement and upon the terms and conditions herein; and

WHEREAS, Franchisor has elected not to exercise its right and option to
purchase the Transferor's interest on the same terms and conditions offered to
the Transferee, as provided by Section ___ of the Franchise Agreement entered
into between the Franchisor and the Transferor.

NOW, THEREFORE, in consideration of the mutual promises, covenants
and conditions contained herein and for other good and valuable consideration, the receipt of which is hereby acknowledged, the parties agree as follows:

1. <u>Transfer.</u> Subject to the provisions contained herein, Transferor hereby
   sells, assigns, transfers and conveys all of its right, title and interest in
   and to the Franchise to Transferee and Franchisor consents to said
   transfer, upon the terms and conditions in the said written Franchise
   Agreement and upon the terms and conditions herein.

2. <u>Release of Franchisor.</u> Transferor hereby releases and discharges
   Franchisor and its officers, directors, shareholders and employees in
   their corporate and individual capacities from any and all claims,
   actions, causes of action, or demands or whatsoever kind or nature.

3. <u>Transferee's Agreement.</u> In lieu of an initial franchise fee customarily
   paid under the terms of the Franchise Agreement and upon payment of
   a transfer franchise fee to Franchisor by Transferee in the sum of
   _____ ($___), which sum is equivalent to

(continues)

Figure 15-2. *(continued)*

_____ percent (___%) of the initial franchise fee currently being charged by Franchisor to new franchisees, and concurrently with the execution hereof, Franchisor shall offer Transferee the standard form of Franchise Agreement now being offered by Franchisor to new franchisees and such other ancillary agreements as Franchisor may require for the Franchise. The term of said Franchise Agreement offered by Franchisor to Transferee shall end on the expiration date of the Franchise Agreement entered into by and between Franchisor and Transferor and with such renewal term(s) as may be provided by the Franchise Agreement entered into by and between Franchisor and Transferor. Except as provided herein, the Franchise Agreement offered by Franchisor to Transferee, if executed by Transferee, shall supersede the Franchise Agreement entered into by and between Franchisor and Transferor in all respects and the terms of the Transferee's Agreement may differ from the terms of the Transferor's Agreement, including, without limitation, a higher percentage royalty fee and advertising contribution.

4. <u>Transfer Fee.</u> Concurrently with the execution hereof, Transferor shall pay to Franchisor a Transfer Fee of _____ Dollars ($ ___) to cover Franchisor's administrative expenses in connection with this transfer.

5. <u>Training.</u> At the Transferee's expense the Transferee and the Transferee's manager shall attend and successfully complete any training programs currently in effect for current franchisees.

6. <u>Upgrades.</u> At the Transferee's expense the Transferee shall upgrade the premises referred to herein to conform to the design concepts now being used in other franchised locations and shall complete the upgrading and any other reasonable requirements specified by Franchisor and which relate to said upgrading on or before _____, 19___.

7. <u>Receipt of Documents.</u> On or before _____, 19___ Transferee shall sign an Acknowledgment of Receipt acknowledging Transferee's receipt of all required legal documents including Franchisor's Franchise Offering Circular, Franchisor's current Franchise Agreement, related agreements and documentation.

8. <u>Transferee's Obligations.</u> Transferee hereby assumes and agrees to faithfully discharge all of the Transferor's obligations under the Franchise Agreement entered into by and between Franchisor and Transferor.

9. <u>Guaranty by Transferee.</u> Transferee understands and acknowledges that the obligations of the Transferor under the Franchise Agreement entered into by and between Franchisor and Transferor were guaranteed by Transferor and Transferee hereby agrees to guaranty the full and complete performance of all such obligations and agrees to execute a written guaranty in form satisfactory to Franchisor.

10. <u>Transferor's Liability.</u> Transferor understands, acknowledges and agrees it shall remain liable for all obligations to Franchisor in connection with the Franchise prior to the effective date of the transfer and shall execute any and all instruments reasonably requested by Franchisor to evidence such liability.

11. <u>Transferor's Warranties.</u> Transferor warrants and represents that it is not granting any security interest in the Franchise or in any of its assets.

12. <u>Survivability.</u> Transferor acknowledges, understands and agrees that those provisions of Section ___ and Section ___ of the Franchise Agreement entered into by and between Transferor and Franchisor, to the extent applicable, shall survive this Agreement.

13. <u>Transferor's Obligations.</u> Transferor acknowledges and agrees that each of its obligations regarding transfer must be met by the Transferor and are reasonable and necessary.

14. <u>Transferor's Monetary Obligations.</u> Transferor understands, acknowledges and agrees that all of its accrued monetary obligations and any other outstanding obligations due and owing to Franchisor shall be fully paid and satisfied prior to any transfer referred to herein.

15. <u>Waiver.</u> The failure of any party to enforce at any time any of the provisions hereof shall not be construed to be a waiver of such provisions or of the right of any party thereafter to enforce any such provisions.

16. <u>Modifications.</u> No renewal hereof, or modification or waiver of any of the provisions herein contained, or any future representation, promise or condition in connection with the subject matter hereof, shall be effective unless agreed upon by the parties hereto in writing.

17. <u>Execution of Documents.</u> The parties agree to execute any and all documents or agreements and to take all action as may be necessary or desirable to effectuate the terms, covenants and conditions of this Agreement.

18. <u>Binding Effect.</u> This Agreement shall be binding upon the parties hereto, their heirs, executors, successors, assigns and legal representatives.

19. <u>Attorney's Fees.</u> Transferor shall pay to Franchisor all damages, costs and expenses, including reasonable attorney's fees, incurred by Franchisor in enforcing the provisions of this Agreement.

(continues)

Figure 15-2. *(continued)*

20. <u>Severability.</u> If any provision of this Agreement or any part thereof is declared invalid by any court of competent jurisdiction, such act shall not affect the validity of this Agreement and the remainder of this Agreement shall remain in full force and effect according to the terms of the remaining provisions or part of provisions hereof.

21. <u>Construction.</u> This Agreement shall be governed by and construed in accordance with the laws of the State of _____.

IN WITNESS WHEREOF, the parties hereto have hereunder caused this Franchise Transfer Agreement to be executed the day and year first above written.

ATTEST: FRANCHISOR

_____   By: _____

                             _____, PRESIDENT

WITNESS:

_____   _____

                             Transferor

_____   _____

                             Transferee

In addition to the key issues discussed above, a well-drafted franchise agreement should include, at a minimum, the following specific contractual conditions that must be met prior to the approval of a transfer:

1. All of Franchisee's accrued monetary obligations and all other outstanding obligations to Franchisor, its subsidiaries, affiliates and suppliers shall be up to date, fully paid and satisfied;

2. Franchisee shall not be in default of any provision of this Agreement, any amendment hereof or successor hereto, any other franchise agreement or other agreement between Franchisee and Franchisor, or its subsidiaries, affiliates, or suppliers;

3. The Franchisee and each of its shareholders, officers, and directors shall have executed a general release under seal, in a form satisfactory to Franchisor, of any and all claims against Franchisor and its officers, directors, shareholders, and employees in their corporate and individual capacities, including, without limitation, claims arising under federal, state, and local laws, rules and ordinances, provided, however, that Franchisee shall not be required to release Franchisor for violations of federal and state franchise registration and disclosure laws;

4. The transferee shall enter into a written assignment, under seal and in a form satisfactory to Franchisor, assuming and agreeing to discharge all of Franchisee's obligations under this Agreement; and, if the obligations of Franchisee were guaranteed by the transferor, the transferee shall guarantee the performance of all such obligations in writing in a form satisfactory to Franchisor;

5. The transferee shall demonstrate to Franchisor's satisfaction that the transferee meets Franchisor's educational, managerial, and business standards; possesses a good moral character, business reputation, and credit rating; has the aptitude and ability to operate the Franchised Business herein (as may be evidenced by prior related experience or otherwise); has at least the same managerial and financial criteria required of new franchisees and shall have sufficient equity capital to operate the Franchised Business;

6. At Franchisor's option, the transferee shall execute (and/or, upon Franchisor's request, shall cause all interested parties to execute) for a term ending on the expiration date of this Agreement and with such renewal term as may be provided by this Agreement, the standard form of Franchise Agreement then being offered to new franchisees and such other ancillary agreements as Franchisor may require for the Franchised Business, which agreements shall supersede this Agreement in all respects and the terms of which agreements may differ from the terms of this Agreement, including, without limitation, a higher percentage royalty fee, National Advertising Fund contribution, increase of the Minimum Local Advertising Expenditure, and the implementation of additional fees;

7. The transferee shall upgrade, at the transferee's expense, the Franchised Business to conform to the current specifications then being used in new Franchised Businesses, and shall complete the upgrading and other requirements within the time specified by Franchisor;

8. Franchisee shall remain liable for all direct and indirect obligations to Franchisor in connection with the Franchised Business prior to the effective date of the transfer and shall continue to remain responsible for its obligations of nondisclosure, noncompetition, and indemnification as provided elsewhere in this Agreement and shall execute any and all instruments reasonably requested by Franchisor to further evidence such liability;

9. At the transferee's expense, the transferee and its manager and employees shall complete any training programs then in effect for current franchisees upon such terms and conditions as Franchisor may reasonably require;

10. The transferee shall have signed an Acknowledgment of Receipt of all required legal documents, such as the Franchise Offering Circular and the then current Franchise Agreement and ancillary agreements; and

11. Transferor shall pay to Franchisor a Transfer Fee equal to ___ percent (___ %) of the then current initial franchise fee paid by new franchisees of Franchisor but in no event shall said Transfer Fee exceed ___ Dollars ($ ___) to cover Franchisor's administrative expenses in connection with the proposed transfer.

Part **Five**

Licensing and Other Alternatives to Franchising

16

Strategic and Structural Alternatives to Franchising

A wide variety of successful companies for one reason or another do not necessarily meet the foundational requirements needed to develop a business format franchising program. This does not mean, however, that the benefits of a contractual growth-oriented marketing strategy cannot be obtained through the use of licensing, joint ventures, distributorships, sales agencies, multilevel marketing plans, and other commonly adopted alternatives to franchising. This chapter examines many of these alternatives, with an emphasis on systems that provide a viable alternative to the capital and management costs of internal growth.

Why Are These Alternatives Considered?

There are various reasons why companies consider these alternatives to franchising:

- Some companies want to avoid the perceived obligations of being a franchisor.
- Some companies want to avoid the disclosure requirements of federal/state law for a wide variety of reasons.
- Some companies are afraid of the "perceived liability risk" of being a franchisor.
- Some companies can achieve greater distribution efficiencies or don't need (or want) the control.
- Some companies don't need or want their trademarks licensed.
- Some companies aren't truly prepared to be a franchisor or lack the proprietary foundation to truly have a system.
- International companies that are not franchisors in their home country don't want to be franchisors in the United States.

From a strategic and structural perspective, if you are prepared to offer a program that will be exempt from one or more of the definitions of a franchise discussed in Chapter 4, on what basis will you rely on the exemption? Which element of the test are you prepared to discard or sacrifice?

- Will you choose not to include a license of your trademark at the cost of the value of your goodwill?
- Will you choose not to provide significant support to your distribution channels at the cost of losing them to a more supportive competitor?
- Will you loosen the grip over the distribution channel at the risk of sacrificing quality control?
- Will you waive the initial fee at the risk of the program becoming a loss leader or worse?

These are difficult decisions. The solutions are not clear-cut from either a business or a legal perspective. There is always the risk that a regulator or a disgruntled franchisee or distributor will disagree with you. It is critical that you work with qualified counsel to identify an alternative that will have a reasonable basis for an exemption and still make sense from a strategic perspective. The balance of this chapter looks at the many alternatives currently being tested by many U.S. and overseas companies. As you can see, the lines of demarcation are not always clear. The differences among many of these alternatives may in fact be in name only. Some of these concepts are truly innovative and have not been tested by the courts or the regulators. In these borderline cases, a regulatory "no-action" letter procedure is strongly recommended. Other concepts are not very innovative at all and merely borrow from long-recognized and analogous legal relationships, such as chapter affiliation agreements in the nonprofit arena or network affiliation agreements in radio and television broadcasting. Still others are genuine alternatives to franchising, such as licensing and distributorships—our first two major topics in this area.

Chapter 17 provides an overview of the two most common forms of licensing arrangements: merchandise licensing, and technology transfer and licensing. Chapter 18 looks at joint ventures and strategic alliances. Other major alternatives to franchising are considered below.

Franchising and Other Strategic Alliances

Because franchising can be incorporated in varying degrees, what follows is a comparison of franchising with other strategic alliances: trademark licensing, product distributorships, employment relationships, partnerships and joint ventures, and agency relationships.

Franchising Compared With Trademark Licensing

Franchise rights can be characterized as "active rights" in contrast to the "passive rights" normally attendant to mere "licensing." The licensor's interest is normally limited to supervising the proper use of the license and collecting royalties. The franchisor, however, exerts significant active control over the franchisee's operations.

In licensing to others to use one's trademark, licensors generally want to limit their licensee's ability to modify the trademark or reduce its value through use in connection with symbols or products that will lessen the mark's goodwill. Franchisors who license the use of a trademark similarly impose limits upon the franchisees, but in addition, as part of the franchise relationship, franchisors normally insist that franchisees agree to a variety of other limits and requirements as to the conduct of the franchised business. Thus, unlike the mere license to another of the right to use a trademark, the franchisor not only seeks to protect the goodwill already associated with the trademark but also seeks, by franchising, to enhance the mark's goodwill.

Franchising Compared With Product Distributorship

Distributors are often selected for some of the same reasons that lead to decisions to franchise. A centrally located company that manufactures enough of a product to sell on a regional or national basis is often not equipped to deal with the variety of personalities, peculiarities, or other phenomena that characterize localities.

There is generally little control exercised over the distributor's manner of conducting business. While there may be geographic or business-line restrictions imposed on distributors as a means to keep them from competing with each other, there are fewer restrictions on a distributor's operations. The distributor is not granted a license to "use" anything. Rather than do business under one particular company's marks, distributors often handle the products of many manufacturers.

The main differences between a franchise and a distributorship are that:

◆ The franchisor assumes a larger obligation to teach the franchisee how to deal in the product (though this kind of activity occurs with distributorships too).

- The franchisee deals with just one company, while a distributor will often, though not always, distribute goods or services of many different producers.
- The franchise relationship often involves a greater community of interest (though again, not always, since a distributor of an extremely successful product may very well find its own success inextricably tied to its supplier's success or failure).
- The basis on which a franchisor is paid normally differs from the basis on which a distributor's supplier is paid.

In each of these areas, however, the parties may arrange their affairs so that a product distributorship looks like a franchise, or vice versa. For example, a franchisee with a large amount of leeway in how to run its business may look like an independent distributor. An independent distributor of an extremely successful product may be subject to many controls by the producer and may begin to resemble a franchisee.

Franchising Compared With the Employment Relationship

In many respects, the franchise relationship may resemble that between an employer and employee. Both kinds of relationships are characterized by the control that one party exercises over the other's activities. Almost any kind of control that an employer might exert over an employee can appear in the typical franchise agreement. Examples include working hours, services to be performed by patrons, behavior, appearance, and a variety of other work details.

There are several respects in which the franchise diverges from the employer-employee relationship. The most significant difference is that, unlike the franchisee, an employee does not normally make a payment to his or her employer for the right to enter into or continue the relationship. In addition, the franchisee normally makes a significant investment or promises to do so in order to establish the relationship. Perhaps more important, the franchisee seeks a significant profit potential; while employee participation in the employer's revenues or profits is not uncommon, it is still not the norm.

Franchising Compared With Partnerships and Joint Ventures

The franchisor-franchisee relationship has been likened to that between partners or joint venturers. The parties enter into an agreement establishing a relationship in which the parties conduct business for profit. Both parties' property and skills are in some sense contributed to the venture. However, even though a franchisor normally exacts a periodic royalty, the element of profit sharing is missing from the franchise relationship. Moreover, the normal franchise agreement does not authorize either party to act on the other's behalf, even though either may be affected, favorably or otherwise, by actions taken by the other. Furthermore, a joint venture is a partnership with reference to a specific venture or single transaction, while the franchise relationship is usually expected to have a longer duration and involve regular and frequent transactions between the parties and with others.

Franchising Compared With Agency Relationships

Franchise relationships also manifest some of the characteristics of agency relationships. An agent conducts some business or manages some affair on behalf of and for the account of the principal. A franchisee, however, merely publicizes its relationship with another while conducting business on its own behalf. Furthermore, unlike an agent, a franchisee has no authority to act on behalf of the franchisor.

Distributorships, Dealerships, and Sales Representatives

Many growing product-oriented companies choose to bring their wares to the marketplace through independent third-party distributors and dealerships. These dealers are generally more difficult to control than is a licensee or franchisee, and as a result, the agreement between the manufacturer and the distributor is much more informal than a franchise or license agreement. This type of arrangement is commonly used by manufacturers of electronic and stereo equipment, computer hardware and software, sporting goods, medical equipment, and automobile parts and accessories.

In developing distributor and dealership agreements, growing companies must be careful to avoid being included within the broad definition of a franchise under FTC Rule 436, which would require the preparation of a disclosure document. To avoid such a classification, the agreement should impose minimal controls over the dealer, and the sale of products must be at bona fide wholesale prices. In addition, the manufacturer must offer no more than minimal assistance in the marketing or management of the dealer's business. A well-drafted distributorship agreement should address the key issues outlined in Figure 16-1.

Figure 16-1. Key questions to consider when preparing distributorship agreements.

1. What is the scope of the appointment? Which products is the dealer authorized to distribute, and under what conditions? What is the scope, if any, of the exclusive territory to be granted to the distributor? To what extent will product, vendor, customer, or geographic restrictions be applicable?

2. What activities will the distributor be expected to perform in terms of manufacturing, sales, marketing, display, billing, market research, maintenance of books and records, storage, training, installation, support, and servicing?

3. What obligations will the distributor have to preserve and protect the intellectual property of the manufacturer?

4. What right, if any, will the distributor have to modify or enhance the manufacturer's warranties, terms of sale, credit policies, or refund procedures?

5. What advertising literature, technical and marketing support, training seminars, or special promotions will be provided by the manufacturer to enhance the performance of the distributor?

6. What sales or performance quotas will be imposed on the dealer as a condition to its right to continue to distribute the manufacturer's products or services? What are the rights and remedies of the manufacturer if the dealers fails to meet these performance standards?

7. What is the term of the agreement, and under what conditions can it be terminated? How will post-termination transactions be handled?

Distributors are often confused with sales representatives, but there are many critical differences. Typically, a distributor buys the product from the manufacturer, at wholesale prices, with title passing to the distributor when payment is received. There is usually no actual fee paid by the distributor for the grant of the distributorship, and the distributor is typically permitted to carry competitive products. The distributor is expected to maintain some retail location or showroom where the manufacturer's products are displayed. The distributor must maintain its own inventory storage and warehousing capabilities. The distributor looks to the manufacturer for technical support; advertising contributions; supportive repair, maintenance, and service policies; new product training; volume discounts; favorable payment and return policies; and brand-name recognition. The manufacturer looks to the distributor for in-store and local promotion, adequate inventory controls, financial stability, preferred display and stocking, prompt payment, and qualified sales personnel. Although the distributorship network offers a viable alternative to franchising, it is not a panacea. The management and control of the distributors may be even more difficult than that involved in franchising (especially without the benefit of a comprehensive franchise agreement), and the termination of these relationships is regulated by many state antitermination statutes.

The sales representative or sales agent is an independent marketing resource for the manufacturer. The sales representative, unlike the distributor, does not typically take title to the merchandise, maintain inventories or retail locations, or engage in any special price promotions unless these are instigated by the manufacturer.

Cooperatives

Cooperatives ("co-ops") have been formed as associations of member companies in the same or similar industries in order to achieve operating, advertising, and purchasing efficiencies and economies of scale. Typically the co-op (which is often confused with a franchise system) is owned and controlled by its members. Commonly known retail co-ops include Ace Hardware and NAPA Auto Parts. Co-ops have been especially effective in certain inventory-intense industries, such as hardware, automobile parts and accessories, pharmacies, and grocery stores. There is typically a common trade identity that each independent business may use in its advertising and promotion; however, ownership of the actual trademarks rests with the cooperative itself. Retail co-ops, if properly structured, are exempt from FTC Rule 436 and from some state franchise laws. The organization and ongoing operation of the co-op should be periodically reviewed by counsel in order to ensure that certain federal and state antitrust and unfair competition laws are not violated.

A co-op is a business owned and controlled by the people who use its services. They finance and operate the business for their mutual benefit. By working together, they can reach an objective unattainable by acting alone. These mutually beneficial services can include obtaining production supplies, processing and marketing member products, or providing functions related to purchasing, marketing, or providing a service. The co-op may be the vehicle to obtain services otherwise unavailable or that are more beneficial to members. The underlying function of the co-op is to increase member income or in other ways enhance their way of living. A co-op may or may not be incorporated and may or may not have its own staff or operate independently from its constituent members.

The four most basic operating characteristics of a co-op are:

1. *Service at cost.* The purpose of a co-op is to provide a service to its user-owners at the lowest possible cost, rather than generate a profit for investors. However, the co-op must generate income sufficient to cover all administrative costs and meet continuing capital needs. Because many costs cannot be absolutely determined before the end of the year, it is important for a co-op to charge competitive market prices or fees for services and then determine its at-cost basis at year's end.

2. *Financial obligation and benefits proportional to use.* Benefits are tied to use rather than to the amount of investment. Likewise, members are obligated to provide financing in proportion to the use that produces those benefits. Most co-ops' bylaws provide a system of returning capital contributions to maintain proportionality on a current basis. The bylaws should also include a provision that establishes the co-op's obligation to return net margins (total income from all sources minus expenses) to patrons. When the net margin is returned to members based on their use of the co-op, it is called a patronage refund.

3. *Democratic control.* Voting control is vested with the membership, either on an equal basis or according to use, rather than based on the amount of stock each member holds. Democratic control is usually expressed as one member, one vote. A few cooperatives have limited proportional voting based on use.

4. *Limited return on equity capital.* This feature means that payments for use of members' equity capital (primarily in the form of stock dividends) are limited. It does not mean that benefits realized from the co-op, monetary or otherwise, are limited. The overriding value of the co-op to its owners is in the range of services or economies of scale that it provides. Limiting the return on equity capital is a mechanism to support distribution of benefits according to use. It helps to keep management decisions focused on providing services attuned to members' needs. Limiting the payment for the use of equity capital is recognized by both federal and state laws. Some state laws require that co-ops either limit the dividends on stock or member capital to 8 percent per year or follow one member, one vote control.

Co-ops usually perform any one or a combination of four kinds of service functions, but with varying strategic emphasis. They are:

1. *Purchasing.* Co-ops provide members with consumer goods, products for resale through their members, or equipment and supplies for their business operation.

Individual co-ops may form federations of cooperatives to obtain further benefits of group purchasing.

2. *Marketing.* Co-ops market the products their members produce—crafts, agricultural products, etc. Marketing includes assembling, processing, and selling products or services in retail or wholesale markets for members.

3. *Service.* Co-ops provide services related to the production of a product or service for business or the home. These services may include credit, electricity, telephones, insurance, research, telecommunications, common management, or other shared services.

4. *Production.* Co-ops pool production and distribution resources in large-scale industries such as agricultural products or electrical utilities.

As under the FTC's trade regulation rule, a co-op that licenses marks to its members or purchases and resells private-label merchandise may be a franchisor under certain state law definitions. State definitions of a *franchise* commonly incorporate the following: (1) granting the right to sell goods or services using a mark or advertising owned by or designating the grantor; (2) payment, directly or indirectly, of a fee for the privilege of entering into or maintaining the relationship; and (3) either a grantor-prescribed marketing plan (under California's model state franchise law) or a community of interest in marketing the subject goods or services (under Minnesota's model). Some states, such as New York and Michigan, have even more inclusive exclusions for partnerships or cooperative associations. Most state administrators, however, do have authority under their respective statutes to establish exemptions by rule, although such exemption is only from the formal registration process and not from the disclosure requirements or antifraud provisions of the statutes. No state has exempted buying co-ops to date. In fact, the North Dakota Commissioner of Securities held that the Best Western motel system, organized as a retailer cooperative, was clearly a franchisor under the North Dakota Franchise Act, and subject to the registration and disclosure obligations of the act, notwithstanding the apparent exemption for such organizations under the FTC rule (Cooperative Lodgings Group's Franchise System, State Official Rules, Bus. Fran. Guide (CCH) ¶ 7708).

Multilevel Marketing Plans

Multilevel marketing (MLM) is a method of direct selling of products or services according to which distributors or sales representatives sell products to the consumer outside of a retail store context and often in a one-to-one setting. In some cases, the distributors purchase the manufacturer's products at wholesale and profit by selling the product to the consumer at retail price. In other instances, distributors sponsor other sales representatives or distributors and receive commissions on the sales made by the sponsored representative or any further representatives sponsored in a continuous "down-line sales organization." Leading merchandisers that use this form of marketing include Shaklee Corporation, Amway Corporation, and Mary Kay Cosmetics.

MLM is a method of distributing goods or services not through retail stores but rather through the efforts of independent distributors or sales agents. These distributors have a great deal of flexibility in training their own salespeople and earn money arising out of products sold by these salespeople (i.e., the down-line sales organization) as well as sales arising out of their own efforts. Because the initial cost is often minimal, multilevel marketing is increasing in popularity and is attractive to individuals interested in starting a business without a substantial capital investment.

MLM companies are regulated by numerous overlapping laws that vary from state to state. MLM programs are affected by a combination of pyramid statutes, business opportunity statutes, multilevel distribution laws, franchise and securities laws, state lottery laws, referral sales laws, the federal postal laws, and Section 5 of the Federal Trade Commission Act.

Recently, many MLM plans have been targeted for prosecution and litigation based on the above laws. To date, enforcement of statutes and regulations has been selective and arbitrary, and many regulatory officials have developed negative attitudes toward the legality of any one MLM program. Therefore, from a legal standpoint, MLM is an uncertain and speculative activity, and there is no assurance that even the most legitimate MLM program will be immune from regulatory inquiry.

Multilevel Marketing Statutes

Six states have laws specifically regulating companies that adopt multilevel marketing programs: Georgia, Louisiana, Maryland, Massachusetts, New Mexico, and Wyoming. Any MLM company operating in any of these states typically must file an annual registration statement giving notice of its operations in that state and must appoint that state's secretary of state as its agent for service of process.

A "multilevel marketing company" is typically defined by these states as an entity that sells, distributes, or supplies, for valuable consideration, goods or services, through independent agents or distributors at different levels and in which participants may recruit other participants in which commissions or bonuses are paid as a result of the sale of the goods or services or the recruitment of additional participants.

In addition to imposing the annual registration requirement, several states have placed additional regulations governing the activities of the MLM companies, such as:

- Requiring that MLM companies allow their independent representatives or distributors to cancel their agreements with the company, and upon such cancellation the company must repurchase unsold products at a price not less than 90 percent of the distributor's original net cost
- Prohibiting MLM companies from representing that distributors have or will earn stated dollar amounts
- Prohibiting MLM companies from requiring distributors to purchase certain minimum initial inventories (except in reasonable quantities)
- Prohibiting that compensation be paid solely for recruiting other participants

Business Opportunity Laws

A "business opportunity" is typically defined as the sale or lease of products or services to a purchaser for the purpose of enabling the purchaser to start a business and in which the seller represents that:

- The seller will provide locations or assist the purchaser in finding locations for the use of vending machines.
- The seller will purchase products made by the purchaser using the supplies or services sold to the purchaser.
- The seller guarantees the purchaser will derive income from the business opportunity that exceeds the price paid for the business opportunity, or that the seller will refund all or part of the price paid for the business opportunity if the purchaser is unsatisfied with the business opportunity.
- Upon the payment by the purchaser of a certain sum of money (usually between $25 and $500), the seller will provide a sales program or marketing program that will enable the purchaser to derive income from the business opportunity that exceeds the price paid for the business opportunity.

This definition (or some variation thereof) can be found in over twenty state statutes nationwide. While the first two elements do not apply to MLM companies, the third and fourth elements would in all probability relate to MLM companies that offer to repurchase sales kits and unsold inventory if a distributor discontinues selling and its sales kits exceed the amounts specified in the various state statutes. It is interesting to note that the very requirement imposed on MLM companies by many of the MLM statutes (i.e., requiring the company to buy back unused products) is an element of a business opportunity.

Business opportunity offerers are required to file a registration statement with the appropriate state agency (usually the Securities Division or Consumer Protection Agency) and a disclosure statement (similar to that required of franchisors) that would then be provided to each prospective offeree.

MLM companies are, however, often exempt from the coverage of the business opportunity laws by virtue of "sales kit exemptions" in the statutes. This type of exemption excludes from the calculation of "required payment" monies paid for sales demonstration equipment or materials sold to the purchaser at the company's cost.

Of additional interest to MLM companies is the typical exemption in the business opportunity laws for the sale of an ongoing business. This allows the sale of a distributorship or business opportunity to another without triggering the business opportunity laws. The following states have adopted business opportunity statutes:

California	Maine	South Carolina
Connecticut	Maryland	Texas
Florida	Minnesota	Utah
Georgia	Nebraska	Virginia
Iowa	New Hampshire	Washington
Kentucky	North Carolina	
Louisiana	Ohio	

Pyramid Laws

Consumers often confuse legitimate *multilevel marketing programs,* which are generally valid methods for distributing products and services to the public, with *pyramid schemes,* which are generally unlawful schemes subject to criminal prosecution in many states.

Numerous laws and regulations have been enacted in the United States to prohibit pyramid schemes. Some of the state laws enacted declare unlawful "pyramid sales schemes," "chain distributions," "referral selling," "endless chains," and the like. Pyramid distribution plans have also been declared unlawful as lotteries, unregistered securities, violations of mail fraud laws, or violations of the Federal Trade Commission Act.

Broadly speaking, a pyramid distribution plan is a means of distributing a company's products or services to consumers. Pyramid schemes generally consist of several distribution levels through which the products or services are resold until they reach the ultimate consumer. A pyramid differs from a valid multilevel marketing company in that in its elemental form, a pyramid is merely a variation of a chain letter and almost always involves large numbers of people at the lowest level who pay money to a few people at the utmost level. New participants pay a sum of money merely for the chance to join the program and advance to the top level, where they will profit from the initial payments made by later participants.

One of the most common elements of pyramid schemes is an intensive campaign to attract new participants who serve to fund the program by providing the payoff to earlier participants. Some schemes use high-pressure sales techniques, such as "go-go chants" and "money hums," to increase crowd enthusiasm. Often meetings are held in distant locations with everyone traveling to them by bus as a captive audience. These bus rides and meetings may include an emotional "pep rally"–type recruiting approach. In one New Jersey case, prospective recruits who did not sign up at the initial meeting were taken on a charter plane trip to the company's home office, during which flight—known as a go tour—they were subjected to intense pressure to sign contracts before the plane landed. On the plane, references were made to the success of others, large amounts of money were displayed amid talk of success, and at times piles of cash and contracts were dropped into the laps of prospects. The format of these meetings is often completely scripted and prepared strictly in accordance with the company's guidelines and policies. These scripts invariably make reference to the financial success awaiting those who participate. In the New Jersey case, recruits were told that they could easily become millionaires.

A pyramid scheme *always* involves a certain degree of failure by its participants. A pyramid plan can work only if there are unlimited numbers of participants. At some point, the pyramid will fail to attract new participants, and those individuals who joined later will not receive any money because there will be no new bottom level of participants to support the plan.

In order to avoid prosecution, the promoters of pyramid schemes often attempt to make their plans resemble multilevel marketing companies. Pyramid schemes, therefore, often claim to be in the business of selling products or services to consumers. The products or services, however, are often of little or no value, and there is no true effort to sell them because emphasis remains almost solely on signing up new participants who are needed to "feed the machine."

There are several ways to distinguish a legitimate multilevel marketing program from unlawful pyramid schemes:

1. *Initial payment.* Typically the initial payment required of a distributor of products and services of a multilevel marketing program is minimal; often the distributor is required to buy only a sales kit that is sold at cost. Because pyramid plans are supported by the payments made by the new recruits, participants in a pyramid plan are often required to pay substantial sums of money just to participate in the scheme.
2. *Inventory loading.* Pyramid schemes typically require participants to purchase large amounts of nonrefundable inventory in order to participate in the program. Legitimate multilevel marketing companies usually repurchase any such inventory if the distributor decides to leave the business. Many state laws require the company to repurchase any resalable goods for at least 90 percent of the original cost.
3. *Head-hunting.* Pyramid plans generally make more money by recruiting new prospects ("head-hunting") than by actually selling the products. Multilevel marketing programs, on the other hand, make money by the sale of legitimate and bona fide products to consumers.

More than twenty-five states have laws prohibiting pyramid schemes, whether as "endless chains," "chain distribution schemes," or "pyramids." Programs with the following three elements are prohibited:

1. An entry fee or investment that must be paid by the participant in order to join
2. Ongoing recruitment of new prospects
3. The payment of bonuses, commissions, or some other valuable to participants who recruit new participants

Generally, the purchase by a participant of a sales kit (at cost) is not deemed to be an entry fee or investment.

The following is a summary of other laws used to prosecute pyramid plans (the same laws are often used to regulate multilevel marketing companies):

◆ *Referral sales statutes.* More than ten states prohibit referral sales programs, which are generally defined to include the payment of some compensation to a buyer in return for furnishing to the seller the names of prospective recruits. Thus, any scheme in which the buyer is told that he or she can receive a return of the money paid if he or she provides a list of names to the seller is an unlawful referral sale.

◆ *Lottery statutes.* Many states prohibit pyramid programs as lotteries on the basis that financial success in the program is not based upon skill and judgment but upon the element of chance (e.g., that an endless stream of new participants will join the program, causing the original participant to receive a return higher than the initial entry fee paid to join).

◆ *Securities laws.* The sale of a security that is not registered is a violation of state and federal law. The Securities and Exchange Commission (SEC) has taken the position that the money paid by a prospect to participate in a scheme (with the expectation of profit based primarily on the activities of other parties) will be considered to be an investment contract or security that must be registered with the SEC.

◆ *Mail fraud laws.* Pyramid programs have been prosecuted under mail fraud laws that prohibit endless chain schemes involving the exchange of money or other things of value through use of the U.S. mail.

◆ *Federal Trade Commission Act.* Section 5 of the FTC Act prohibits unfair methods of competition in commerce and unfair or deceptive practices. This broad provision has been used to justify action by the FTC against pyramid programs. In one of its most famous cases, the FTC argued that Amway Corporation was an illegal pyramid program. The FTC ultimately determined that Amway is not a pyramid scheme because the only required "investment" was a sales kit sold to distributors at cost, Amway guaranteed it would repurchase unsold inventory, and the *sponsoring distributor received nothing from the mere act of sponsoring* but rather began to earn money only when the newly recruited distributor sold products to consumers.

Consulting and Training Services

Many veterans of a particular industry choose to share their expertise with others by charging fixed or hourly fees for consulting or training services. Instead of being licensed, this information is essentially sold to the client or seminar attendee at a fixed price. If support is needed by the client, then additional time may be purchased. This alternative creates competitors without the benefit of an ongoing royalty fee and should be considered only if the expertise to be conveyed falls short of what would be needed in a business format franchise or even in a licensing situation.

Employee Ownership and Profit Sharing

Many growth companies initially turn to franchising as an expansion alternative because of the need to develop "motivated managers" at each site. The theory is that this owner/operator has a better feel for the local market and as an owner will be more motivated to promote the franchisor's products and services. This is the model that has helped propel the growth of Kinko's over the years. But there are many ways to motivate managers and make them feel like owners, such as employee stock ownership plans, executive stock option arrangements, and profit-sharing plans. As an alternative to franchising, each unit could be separately incorporated, with a minority stock interest granted to the key individuals responsible for the operations of that unit. Such an arrangement could be done on a "per store" or regional basis. Although this results in some dilution of the ownership and control of the store or region, the managers would be expected to execute a shareholders' agreement that would place certain stock transfer restrictions as well as predetermined buy-out arrangements on the ownership of the stock. Naturally, the terms of these stock ownership and profit-sharing arrangements should be structured with the assistance of a tax accountant and securities law counsel.

17

Structuring Licensing Programs and Agreements

Licensing is a contractual method of developing and exploiting intellectual property by transferring rights of use to third parties without the transfer of ownership. Virtually any proprietary product or service may be the subject of a license agreement, ranging from the licensing of the Mickey Mouse character by Walt Disney Studios in the 1930s to modern-day licensing of computer software and high technology. From a legal perspective, licensing involves complex issues of contract, tax, antitrust, international, tort, and intellectual property law. From a business perspective, licensing involves a weighing of the advantages of licensing against the disadvantages in comparison to alternative types of vertical distribution systems.

Many of the benefits of licensing to be enjoyed by a growing company closely parallel the advantages of franchising, namely:

- Spreading the risk and cost of development and distribution
- Achieving more rapid market penetration
- Earning initial license fees and ongoing royalty income
- Enhancing consumer loyalty and goodwill
- Preserving the capital that would otherwise be required for internal growth and expansion
- Testing new applications for existing and proven technology
- Avoiding or settling litigation regarding a dispute over ownership of the technology

The disadvantages of licensing are also similar to the risks inherent in franchising, such as:

◆ A somewhat diminished ability to enforce quality control standards and specifications

◆ A greater risk of another party infringing upon the licensor's intellectual property

◆ A dependence on the skills, abilities, and resources of the licensee as a source of revenue

◆ Difficulty in recruiting, motivating, and retaining qualified and competent licensees

◆ The risk that the licensor's entire reputation and goodwill may be damaged or destroyed by the act or omission of a single licensee

◆ The administrative burden of monitoring and supporting the operations of the network of licensees

Failure to consider all of the costs and benefits of licensing could easily result in a regretful strategic decision or the terms of an unprofitable license agreement as a result of either an underestimation of the licensee's need for technical assistance and support or an overestimation of the market demand for the licensor's products and services. In order to avoid such problems, a certain amount of due diligence should be conducted by the licensor prior to any serious negotiations with a prospective licensee. This preliminary investigation generally includes market research, legal steps to fully protect intellectual property, and an internal financial analysis of the technology with respect to pricing, profit margins, and costs of production and distribution. It should also include a more specific analysis of the prospective licensee with respect to its financial strength, research and manufacturing capabilities, and reputation in the industry.

As previously stated, licensing programs offer many of the same benefits of franchising, such as more rapid market penetration through shifting the capital costs of expansion, and share many of the same risks inherent in franchising, such as the possible loss of quality control and a dependence on the skills and resources of the licensee. In addition, there has been a recent emphasis on brand-extension licensing, which is discussed later in this chapter.

The two principal types of licensing occur at two different levels in the marketplace: (1) technology licensing, where the strategy is to find a licensee for exploitation of industrial and technological developments, and (2) merchandise and character licensing, where the strategy is to license a recognized trademark or copyright to a manufacturer of consumer goods in markets not currently served by the licensor.

Technology Transfer and Licensing Agreements

The principal purpose behind technology transfer and licensing agreements is to join the technology proprietor, as licensor, and the organization that possesses the resources to properly develop and market the technology, as licensee. This marriage—made between companies and inventors of all shapes and sizes— occurs often between an entrepreneur with the technology but without the resources to adequately penetrate the marketplace, as licensor, and the larger company, which has sufficient research and development, production, human resources, and marketing capability to make the best use of the technology. The industrial and technological revolution has witnessed a long line of very successful entrepreneurs who have relied on the resources of larger organizations to bring their products to market, such as Chester Carlson (xerography), Edwin Land (Polaroid cameras), Robert Goddard (rockets), and Willis Carrier (air-conditioning). As the base for technological development becomes broader, large companies look not only to entrepreneurs and small businesses for new ideas and technologies but also to each other, foreign countries, universities, and federal and state governments to serve as licensors of technology.

See Figure 17-1 for additional information on why companies develop technology licensing programs. Figure 17-2 provides tips for the prospective licensor.

Figure 17-1. Why growing companies develop technology licensing programs.

- ◆ To match promising technology with the resources necessary to bring it to the marketplace
- ◆ To raise capital and earn royalty income (e.g., there are many entrepreneurs who have had doors slammed in their faces by commercial banks and venture capitalists, but they ultimately obtained growth capital and cash flow from licensees)
- ◆ As a defensive strategy, from one of two perspectives: (1) The licensor may want to have its competitors as licensees instead of watching as they eventually develop their own technology, or (2) the licensee may want to preempt a competitor or gain access to its confidential information by approaching the competitor to obtain a license (*Warning:* Some competitors will acquire an exclusive license to technology merely to "sit on it" so that it never enters the marketplace. Be prepared to negotiate certain performance standards or limits to exclusivity in the agreement in order to avoid such a trap.)
- ◆ To shift (or share) the product liability risk inherent in the production or marketing of hazardous or dangerous products with the licensee

(continues)

Figure 17-1. *(continued)*

- ◆ To reach new geographic markets unfamiliar to the technology proprietor, such as overseas, where the technology may need to be adapted or otherwise modified to meet local market conditions
- ◆ To make the widest possible use of the technology by licensing other applications or by-products of the technology that may be outside the licensor's expertise or targeted markets
- ◆ To avoid or settle actual or pending litigation (many litigants in intellectual property infringement or misappropriation cases wind up settling the case using some form of a cross-license in lieu of costly attorneys' fees and litigation expenses)

Figure 17-2. Tips for the prospective licensor.

- ◆ *Find the right dance partner.* The quest for the appropriate licensee should be approached with the same zeal and diligence that one would adopt in the search for a marriage partner. No stone should remain unturned either in narrowing the field of prospective licensees or in the due diligence process applied to a particular proposed licensee. The goals and objectives of each party, the financial strength of the licensee, the licensee's past licensing practices, the qualifications of the licensee's jurisdiction (other states, other countries), and the skills of the licensee's sales and marketing team *should all be examined prior to the commencement of the negotiation of the license agreement.* Access to the licensor's intellectual property should be severely restricted unless and until these criteria have been examined and met to the satisfaction of the licensor.
- ◆ *Avoid the inferiority complex.* Although a small company or entrepreneur, looking to license its technology to a larger business, often faces an uphill battle, this is not sufficient reason to merely "roll over" in the licensing negotiations. There are too many horror stories of entrepreneurs who were impressed and intimidated by the larger company's resources and lawyers and as a result "sold their soul" at far below the current or eventual market value of the technology.
- ◆ *Don't go in naked; don't be a motor mouth.* Many prospective licensors make the mistake of telling too little or saying way too much in the initial meetings and negotiations with the prospective licensee. Finding the right balance of disclosure to pique the interest of the licensee without "giving away the farm" is never easy; however, there is a commonly accepted solution, the *licensing memorandum.* The licensing memorandum, when used in tandem with confidentiality agreements, can provide the prospective licensee with the informa-

tion it needs to conduct the preliminary analysis without jeopardizing the rights of the licensor. The memorandum should contain a discussion of the technology and the portfolio of intellectual property rights that protect the technology, the background of the proprietor, the projected markets and applications of the technology, the proposed terms and financial issues between licensor and licensee, and a discussion of existing competitive technology and technological trends that could affect the future value of the license.

◆ *Things can and will change, so be prepared.* Like marriages, most licensing agreements are intended to continue over a long period of time. As a result, it is difficult to predict technological, social, economic, and political trends that will affect the rights and obligations of the licensor and licensee during the term of the agreement. Licensing agreements, like all legal documents, require a certain degree of precision to be enforceable and workable for the parties; however, the inevitability of change should result in a framework of trust and flexibility. Not every detail will be addressed nor every change in the external environment anticipated. Technologies become obsolete, governments get overthrown, rock stars lose popularity, movie sequels flop, and a corporation's personnel may be restructured, but the licensing agreement must be flexible enough to handle all of these unforeseen changes.

In the typical licensing arrangement, the proprietor of intellectual property rights (patents, trade secrets, trademarks, and know-how) permits a third party to make use of these rights according to a set of specified conditions and circumstances set forth in a license agreement. Licensing agreements can be limited to a very narrow component of the proprietor's intellectual property rights, such as one specific application of a single patent, or be much broader in context, such as in a classic technology transfer agreement, where an entire bundle of intellectual property rights is transferred to the licensee typically in exchange for initial fees and royalties. The classic technology transfer arrangement is actually more akin to a "sale" of the intellectual property rights, with a right by the licensor to get the intellectual property back if the licensee fails to meet its obligations under the agreement.

Key Elements of a Technology Licensing Agreement

Once the decision to enter into more formal negotiations has been made, the terms and conditions of the license agreement should be discussed. Naturally these provisions vary, depending on whether the license is for merchandising an entertainment property, exploiting a given technology, or distributing a particular product to an original equipment manufacturer (OEM) or value-added reseller (VAR). As a general rule, any well-drafted license agreement should address the following topics:

◆ *Scope of the grant.* The exact scope and subject matter of the license must be initially addressed in the license agreement. Any restrictions on the geographic scope, rights of use, permissible channels of trade, and sublicensing; any limitations on assignability; or any exclusion of improvements to the technology (or expansion of the character line) covered by the agreement should be clearly set forth in this section.

◆ *Term and renewal.* The commencement date, duration, renewals and extensions, conditions to renewal, procedures for providing notice of intent to renew, grounds for termination, obligations upon termination, and licensor's reversionary rights in the technology should all be included in this section.

◆ *Performance standards and quotas.* To the extent that the licensor's consideration will depend on royalty income that will be calculated from the licensee's gross or net revenues, the licensor may want to impose certain minimum levels of performance in terms of sales, advertising, and promotional expenditures and human resources to be devoted to the exploitation of the technology. Naturally, the licensee will argue for a "best efforts" provision that is free from performance standards and quotas. In such cases, the licensor may want to insist on a minimum royalty level that will be paid regardless of the licensee's actual performance.

◆ *Payments to the licensor.* Virtually every type of license agreement includes some form of initial payment and ongoing royalty to the licensor. Royalty formulas vary widely, however, and may be based upon gross sales, net sales, net profits, fixed sum per product sold, or a minimum payment to be made to the licensor over a given period of time, or may include a sliding scale in order to provide some incentive to the licensee as a reward for performance.

◆ *Quality control assurance and protection.* Quality control standards and specifications for the production, marketing, and distribution of the products and services covered by the license must be set forth by the licensor. In addition, procedures should be included in the agreement that allow the licensor an opportunity to enforce these standards and specifications, such as a right to inspect the licensee's premises; a right to review, approve, or reject samples produced by the licensee; and a right to review and approve any packaging, labeling, or advertising materials to be used in connection with the exploitation of the products and services that are within the scope of the license.

◆ *Insurance and indemnification.* The licensor should take all necessary and reasonable steps to ensure that the licensee has an obligation to protect and indemnify the licensee against any claims or liabilities resulting from the licensee's exploitation of the products and services covered by the license.

◆ *Accounting, reports, and audits.* The licensor must impose certain reporting and record-keeping procedures on the licensee in order to ensure an accurate accounting for periodic royalty payments. Further, the licensor should reserve the right to audit the records of the licensee in the event of a dispute or discrepancy, along with provisions as to who will be responsible for the cost of the audit in the event of an understatement.

◆ *Duties to preserve and protect intellectual property.* The obligations of the licensee, its agents, and employees to preserve and protect the confidential nature and acknowledge the ownership of the intellectual property being disclosed in connection with the license agreement must be carefully defined. Any required notices or legends that must be included on products or materials distributed in connection with the license agreement (such as the status of the relationship between licensee and licensor or identification of the actual owner of the intellectual property) are also described in this section.

◆ *Technical assistance, training, and support.* Any obligation of the licensor to assist the licensee in the development or exploitation of the subject matter being licensed is included in this section of the agreement. The assistance may take the form of personal services or documents and records. Either way, any fees due to the licensor for such support services that are over and above the initial license and ongoing royalty fee must also be addressed.

◆ *Warranties of the licensor.* A prospective licensee may demand that the licensor provide certain representations and warranties in the license agreement. These may include warranties regarding the ownership of the intellectual property, such as absence of any known infringements of the intellectual property or restrictions on the ability to license the intellectual property, or warranties pledging that the technology has the features, capabilities, and characteristics previously represented in the negotiations.

◆ *Infringements.* The license agreement should contain procedures under which the licensee must notify the licensor of any known or suspected direct or indirect infringements of the subject matter being licensed. The responsibilities for the cost of protecting and defending the technology should also be specified in this section.

Figure 17-3 shows how technology licensing can be used to create multiple revenue streams. In the example in the figure, a small company gets issued a new broad scope patent. It has limited capital and is focused on core technology.

Figure 17-3. Technology licensing to create multiple revenue streams.

In this example, a small company gets issued a new patent, which has a broad scope of potential applications. It has limited capital and decides to stay focused on its core business. It has the following options to earn additional revenue streams.

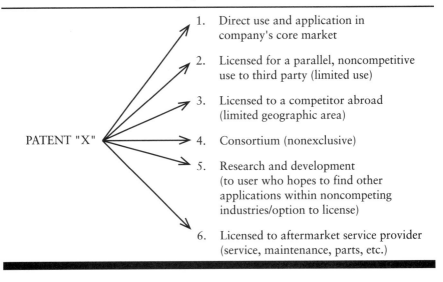

PATENT "X"

1. Direct use and application in company's core market

2. Licensed for a parallel, noncompetitive use to third party (limited use)

3. Licensed to a competitor abroad (limited geographic area)

4. Consortium (nonexclusive)

5. Research and development (to user who hopes to find other applications within noncompeting industries/option to license)

6. Licensed to aftermarket service provider (service, maintenance, parts, etc.)

Special Issues in Negotiating and Drafting Technology Licensing Agreements

There is a wide variety of special contractual issues that must be addressed in the preparation of a technology license agreement. These include:

◆ *Defined terms.* What many entrepreneurs may initially view as "legal boilerplate" is often the most hotly contested component of the license agreement. This initial section of the license agreement is intended to do much more than make the document "easier to read"; rather, it defines some of the key aspects of the relationship with respect to the specific field of the technology licensed, the territory to be covered, the milestones and objectives that must be met, the specific patents or trademarks that will be included within the scope of the license, and the nature of the compensation to be paid to the licensor.

◆ *Reports to the licensor, record keeping by the licensee.* In all licensing agreements, adequate reporting and record keeping by the licensee is critical to ensure that the licensor receives all royalty payments when due. In a technology licensing agreement, additional reports should be prepared monthly or quarterly that disclose the licensee's actual use of the technology; research studies or market tests that have directly or indirectly used the technology; the marketing, advertising, or public relations strategies planned or implemented that involve the technology; progress reports regarding the meeting of established performance objectives and timetables; reports of any threatened or actual infringement or misappropriation of the licensor's technology; and any requests for sublicenses or cross-licenses that have been made by third parties to the licensee.

◆ *Exclusivity of the license granted.* The term *exclusive* in the context of a licensing agreement negotiation is often misunderstood. Exclusivity could apply to a territory, an application of the technology, or a method of production of the products that result from the technology. Exclusivity may or may not include the licensor itself and may or may not permit the granting of sublicenses or cross-licenses to future third parties who are not bound by the original license agreement. Exclusivity may or may not be conditioned on the licensee meeting certain predetermined performance standards. Exclusivity may be conditional for a limited time period on the continued employment of certain key technical staff of the licensee. All of these issues, surrounding what on its face appears to be a simple term, must be discussed in the negotiations and ultimately addressed in the license agreement.

◆ *Technical support and assistance, dependence on key personnel.* The proper development and exploitation of the technology often depends on the availability of the proprietor and the licensor's technical team to provide support and assistance to the licensee. The conditions under which this team will be available to the licensee should be included in the technology license agreement. Provisions should be drafted to deal with scheduling conflicts, the payment of travel expenses, the impact of disability or death of the inventor, the availability of written or videotaped data in lieu of the inventor's physical attendance, the regularity and length of periodic technical support meetings, and the protection of confidential information.

Merchandise and Character Licensing Agreements

The use of commonly recognized trademarks, brand names, sports teams, athletes, universities, television and film characters, musicians, and designers to foster the sale of specific products and services is at the heart of today's merchandise and character licensing environment. Manufacturers and distributors of products and services license these words, images, and symbols for products that range from clothing and housewares to toys and posters. Certain brand names and characters have withstood the test of time, while others fall prey to fads, consumer shifts, and stiff competition.

The trademark and copyright owners of these properties and character images are motivated to license for a variety of reasons. Aside from the obvious desire to earn royalty fees and profits, many manufacturers view this licensing strategy as a form of merchandising *to promote the underlying product or service*. The licensing of a trademark for application on a line of clothing helps to establish and reinforce brand awareness at the consumer level. For example, when R. J. Reynolds Tobacco Company licenses a leisure apparel manufacturer to produce a line of Camel branded clothing, the hope is to sell more cigarettes, appeal to the lifestyle of its targeted consumers, maintain consumer awareness, and enjoy the royalty income from the sale of the clothing line. Similar strategies have been adopted by manufacturers in order to revive a mature brand or failing product. In certain instances, the spin-off product that has been licensed was almost as financially successful as the underlying product it was intended to promote.

Brand-name owners, celebrities, and academic institutions must be very careful not to grant too many licenses too quickly. The financial rewards of a flow of royalty income from hundreds of different manufacturers can be quite seductive but must be weighed against the possible loss of quality control and dilution of the name, logo, or character. The loyalty of the licensee network is also threatened when too many licenses are granted for closely competing products. Retailers also become cautious when purchasing licensed goods from a licensee if there is a fear that quality control has suffered or that the popularity of the licensed character, celebrity, or image will be short-lived. This may result in smaller orders and an overall unwillingness to carry inventory, especially in the toy industry, where purchasing decisions are being made by (or at least influenced by) the whims of a five-year-old child who may strongly identify with a character image one week and then turn away to a totally different character image the next week. It is incumbent on the manufacturers and licensees to develop advertising and media campaigns to hold the consumer's attention for an extended period of time. Only then will the retailer be convinced of the potential longevity of the product line. This requires a balancing of the risks and rewards between licensor and licensee in the character licensing agreement in the areas of compensation to the licensor, advertising expenditures by the licensee, scope of the exclusivity, and quality control standards and specifications.

In the merchandise licensing community, the name, logo, symbol, or character is typically referred to as the property, and the specific product or product line (e.g., the T-shirts, mugs, posters) is referred to as the licensed product. This area of licensing offers opportunities and benefits to both the owner of the property and the manufacturer of the licensed product. For the owner of the property, brand recognition, goodwill, and royalty income are strengthened and expanded. For the manufacturer of the licensed product, there is an opportunity to leverage the goodwill of the property to improve sales of the licensed product. The manufacturer has an opportunity to "hit the ground running" in the sale of merchandise by gaining access to and use of an already established brand name or character image.

Naturally, each party should conduct due diligence on the other. From the perspective of the owner of the property, the manufacturer of the licensed product should demonstrate an ability to meet and maintain quality control standards, possess financial stability, and offer an aggressive and well-planned marketing and promotional strategy. From the perspective of the manufacturer of the licensed product, the owner of the property should display a certain level of integrity and commitment to quality, disclose its future plans for the promotion of the property, and be willing to participate and assist in the overall marketing of the licensed products. For example, if a star basketball player were to be unwilling to appear for promotional events designed to sell his own specially licensed line of basketball shoes, this would present a major problem and is likely to lead to a premature termination of the licensing relationship.

Special Issues in Negotiating and Preparing Merchandise and Character Licensing Agreements

There are several key areas that must be addressed in the negotiation and preparation of a merchandise licensing agreement. These include: (1) scope of the territorial and product exclusivity, (2) assignability and sublicensing rights,

(3) the definition of the property and the licensed products, (4) quality control and approval, (5) ownership of artwork and designs, (6) term renewal rights and termination of the relationship, (7) initial license and ongoing royalty fees, (8) performance criteria for the licensee, (9) liability insurance, (10) indemnification, (11) duty to pursue trademark and copyright infringement, (12) minimum advertising and promotional requirements, (13) accounting and record keeping of the licensee, (14) inspection and audit rights of the licensor, (15) rights of first refusal for expanded or revised characters and images, (16) limitations on licensee's distribution to related or affiliated entities, (17) representations and warranties of the licensor with respect to its rights to the property, (18) the availability of the licensor for technical and promotional assistance, and (19) miscellaneous provisions, such as law to govern, inurement of goodwill, nature of the relationship, notice, and force majeure.

The definition of the scope of permitted use is usually accomplished with the use of schedules, illustrations, and exhibits. For example, suppose a manufacturer of children's sportswear wanted to license the likeness of basketball star Michael Jordan for a new line of clothing. Will the property consist of unlimited use of the name and likeness of Mr. Jordan, or will it be only for a specific drawing or caricature of his face? Similarly, will the licensed products be defined as virtually any style or size of children's sportswear, or will they be limited to "children's short-sleeved T-shirts up to size 20 and matching children's short pants"? Naturally, there is room for much variation and negotiation in these defined terms. In order to avoid claims and litigation over unauthorized use of the property, the licensor and licensee should clearly communicate their intent to counsel before preparation of the merchandise licensing agreement.

The key economic issue in the agreement is the section dealing with royalty payments that must be paid to the licensor by the licensee in exchange for the use of the property over a period of time. The royalty obligation is usually stated as a fixed percentage of the licensee's sales of the licensed products or as a lump sum per unit of the licensed product. Royalty rates are based purely on market forces and the negotiation skills of the parties and their counsel. This section must also address the basis for the calculation of the royalty payment (e.g., the definition of gross revenues, net sales), any minimum royalty payments that must be paid quarterly or annually by the licensee to the licensor, any adjustments to the royalty rate (which is tied to performance, inflation, a change in market conditions, etc.), royalties on noncash sales, and the licensee's obligation to prepare reports and statements to support the calculation of the royalty payment.

Brand-Extension Licensing

Over the past few years, one specific form of merchandise licensing has grown rapidly in importance, known as brand-extension licensing. This type of licensing is designed to widen the depth and the breadth of the market for the products or services identified with the owner's brand, but with the development and distribution costs at the cost of the licensed third party. Some of these transactions have proved to be natural extensions of the brand, and some have not. For example, the licensing of the Starbucks® name for a limited line of ice creams, Sunkist® for orange soda, and Hershey's® for chocolate milk were brand-extension licensing projects that have all been very successful and allowed the owners of the trademarks to enjoy instant entry into a new industry with minimal capital investment or market research. The ability to penetrate new markets, generate new income streams, build the value of the company's brand name, and increase overall brand awareness has made brand-extension licensing a very viable and profitable strategy for companies like Gerber®, which had a successful launch into the nursery monitor business through brand-extension licensing. It seems unlikely that a company like Gerber would have launched into the electronics industry without the strategic benefits of a brand-extension licensee.

It is estimated that in the United States alone, retail sales of licensed branded products surpassed $20 billion in 1992 and will reach $60 billion by the year 2000. Products born of brand-extension licensing have become staples for quality and value-driven consumers who regularly look for successful brand-licensed items. This marriage between a product and a well-recognized brand name allows trademark owners to enter into new industries without the capital investment required to actually manufacture and distribute the licensed product. Subject to strict quality control guidelines, companies with registered trademarks can penetrate new markets, build new profit centers, increase brand awareness and recognition, facilitate international expansion, and even modernize a brand's image with the appropriate brand-extension licensing strategic partners. Of course, there is a limit on what the consumer will accept. Naturally, it would do little to enhance the image or brand recognition of Ben & Jerry's® to license its name to an automobile parts manufacturer in order to produce a new line of tires. Nor will the company's "implied endorsement" be likely to enhance the sale of the tires. Yet the recent move by Starbucks to license its name for a limited line of new, prepackaged ice cream seems to have been a big hit with quality-conscious consumers who knew the Starbucks name as a symbol of quality and made a natural jump to a related product such as ice cream.

The temptation to extend the equity and value of your brand into other areas is not without its risks. You must focus on the natural zone of expansion for the brand from a consumer perspective. There are quality control issues, the risk of overbranding or misbranding from a consumer perspective, and product liability issues. The key to successful brand extension is that the brand itself must stand for something greater than the original product and that the consumer's perception of the extended brand is a natural one. The brand on a stand-alone basis must represent an attitude or a feeling or cachet that holds water when it is applied to another product. It worked well when the Gap® brand-extended a license for perfume and when Calvin Klein® brand-extended a license for eyewear, but it backfired for Harley-Davidson® when it extended its brand by awarding a license for a line of cigarettes. Although the extension seemed natural, consumers were not convinced that the motorcycle manufacturers had a brand that would lend quality and value to a pack of smokes. Even nonlicensed extensions of brand that would seem to be a home run have failed because of inadequate market research. For example, when U.S. society started eating more chicken than beef, A-1® steak sauce launched a poultry sauce that did very poorly, notwithstanding a multi-million-dollar advertising budget. Researchers missed the fact that the A-1® brand had been associated in the public mind with *steak* and not necessarily with *sauce* in general. Yet other brand-extension licensing deals have succeeded in spite of basic logic. One might think that the last thing anyone wants to smell like is a sweaty basketball player, yet the Michael Jordan line of men's cologne has sold reasonably well. This superstar's cachet has transcended this marketing challenge.

The development of an effective brand-extension licensing program involves the following components:

◆ *Discipline.* Avoid the temptation to overbrand. A key part of brand management is determining your "zone of appropriateness" and figuring out what your brand does not represent, which can be even more important than understanding what it does represent.

◆ *Market research.* It is critical to *really* understand your customers and their reasons for being loyal to your brand. An understanding of the source of that loyalty will lead to natural zones of expansion into other products and services if you listen carefully.

◆ *Due diligence.* The selection of the right brand-extension licensees who have a strong reputation in their underlying industry and the resources to execute a well-written market development plan is critical.

♦ *Quality control.* The brand owner must take a proactive role in maintaining and enforcing quality control standards in the manufacturing and distribution of the branded products or services. This includes not only direct quality issues but also indirect issues, such as the distribution channels selected and the nature of the advertising and marketing campaigns.

An effectively managed brand-extension licensing program can build brand awareness and brand equity if the company understands why consumers have an affinity toward the brand if the trust is not violated or misinterpreted. To the extent that brands can influence consumer behavior and gain consumer loyalty, they can be a very powerful marketing tool and an intangible income-producing asset.

Figure 17-4 presents a sample license agreement.

Figure 17-4. License agreement.

LICENSE AND DISTRIBUTION AGREEMENT

THIS LICENSE AND DISTRIBUTION AGREEMENT (the "Agreement") is made this _____ day of _____, 19__, by and between LICENSOR (the "Licensor"), whose address is _____, and LICENSEE (the "Licensee"), whose address is _____.

WITNESSETH:

WHEREAS, Licensor has developed and currently manufactures, markets and sells food vacuum sealers and related accessories which are primarily marketed to preparers (the "Products") and, in connection therewith, is the owner of U.S. Patent Nos. _____ and _____, patent applications, if any (the "Licensed Patents"), and certain valuable technical information, know-how and data relating to the Products (collectively with the Licensed Patents, the "Product Technology");

WHEREAS, Licensor uses the [*registered*] trademark and such related mark or other marks in marketing the Products, [*a portion/all*] of which are shown on Exhibit A, attached hereto and incorporated herein by reference (the "Licensed Marks");

WHEREAS, Licensee desires to obtain the exclusive right to use the

(continues)

Figure 17-4. *(continued)*

Product Technology and Licensed Marks in connection with the manufacturing, marketing and selling of food vacuum sealers or any product to which any application of Product Technology may be made by Licensee, which products may be sold for $_____ or less at retail, and related accessories (the "Accessories") primarily for home use (collectively, the "Home Products");

WHEREAS, Licensor desires to license the Product Technology and Licensed Marks to Licensee and allow Licensee to manufacture, market and sell Home Products pursuant to the terms hereof; and

WHEREAS, Licensee desires to license the Product Technology and Licensed Marks from Licensor and manufacture, market and sell Home Products pursuant to the terms hereof.

NOW THEREFORE, in consideration for the foregoing and the mutual covenants and agreements contained herein, the parties hereto agree as follows:

1. <u>Grant and Acceptance of License.</u> Subject to the terms and conditions in this Agreement, Licensor hereby grants to Licensee, and Licensee hereby accepts, the exclusive worldwide right and license to use the Product Technology to enable Licensee to manufacture, market and sell Home Products in the Licensed Territory during the Term (defined in Section 10 below). Licensor agrees that he shall not use the Product Technology in the manufacture, marketing and sale of Home Products or any competitive product line within the Licensed Territory during the Term nor shall he grant to any other person or entity a license or other right to so use the Product Technology. Nothing herein shall be construed to limit or prohibit Licensor from manufacturing, marketing and selling Products in the Licensed Territory during the Term. The "Licensed Territory" shall mean the entire world for purposes of this Agreement.

2. <u>Term of License.</u> Unless sooner terminated by the terms of Section 10 hereof, the license granted herein shall continue until the expiration of the Term.

3. <u>Trademark License.</u> Subject to the terms and conditions of this Agreement, and for so long as Licensee shall have the exclusive right and license to use the Product Technology (as provided in Section 1), Licensor licenses and grants to Licensee the exclusive right and license

to use any or all of the Licensed Marks in connection with the marketing of Home Products in the Licensed Territory; provided, that Licensor retains the right to use the Licensed Marks in connection with the sale of Products (including promotional materials used to promote the Products). Licensee shall have the right to use any trade names or trademarks it deems appropriate in marketing the Home Products and may register in the name of Licensee such trademarks (other than the Licensed Marks) with the U.S. Patent and Trademark Office or any state agency without the approval of Licensor.

4. <u>Distribution Arrangements.</u> Licensor hereby grants to Licensee the exclusive the right to manufacture, market and sell Home Products in the Licensed Territory. In connection therewith, Licensee shall have the right to use the Product Technology and Licensed Marks in accordance with the terms of this Agreement. Licensee agrees to use its reasonable efforts to establish a designated manufacturing facility to manufacture Home Products in commercial quantities, and to promote the sale of the Home Products within the Licensed Territory. In that regard, Licensee shall at its expense and within a reasonable time after the date hereof, begin to develop and carry out a marketing and sales program (which includes the use of direct mail, catalogs, promotional material and television commercials/infomercials) designed to promote sales of Home Products, and exert its reasonable efforts to create, supply and service in the Licensed Territory as many Home Products as is commercially practical; provided, however, nothing contained in this Agreement shall effect or limit Licensee's right to develop, manufacture, distribute, advertise, market and sell any other products and/or services. Licensee shall be solely responsible with regard to establishing a designated manufacturing facility and marketing and sales program and Licensor shall have such responsibility financial or otherwise. Subject to the quality control standards set forth in Section 6 hereof, Licensee shall have complete control with respect to the manufacturing, marketing and selling of Home Products in the Licensed Territory, including without limitation, the wholesale and retail prices at which Home Products are sold. Licensor agrees to name Licensee as an "Additional Insured" on all policies of insurance having coverage for product liability.

5. <u>Royalty Payments.</u> Licensee agrees to pay Licensor an annual royalty equal to _____ percent (_____%) [PARTIES TO DISCUSS] of Net Sales generated from the sale of the Home Products exclusive of

(continues)

Figure 17-4. *(continued)*

Accessories. Licensee agrees to pay Licensor an annual royalty payment equal to _____ percent (_____%) [PARTIES TO DISCUSS] of Net Sales generated from the sale of Accessories. Such royalty shall be paid within sixty (60) days after the end of each calendar year. During the Term of this Agreement, royalty payments shall accrue on a monthly basis. For purposes of this Agreement, Net Sales shall be defined as _____ [PARTIES TO DISCUSS].

6. Quality Control.

(a) Standards Licensee shall ensure that all Home Products it distributes (by sale, transfer or otherwise) are manufactured consistent with the reasonable and necessary quality control standards, if any, established and delivered in writing to Licensee by Licensor.

(b) Inspection From time to time and upon reasonable prior notice by Licensor, Licensor may request Licensee to submit samples of Home Products manufactured by Licensee or its designee for Licensor's approval, which approval shall not be unreasonably withheld. Unless otherwise approved by Licensor, the quality of all Home Products manufactured, marketed and sold by Licensee pursuant to this Agreement shall be of a quality at least equal to such samples. Licensee agrees to provide Licensor with requested samples of Home Products within thirty (30) days after Licensor requests such samples.

7. Technical Assistance. Licensor shall, at his sole expense and at the request of Licensee, provide technical assistance to Licensee or any of its designees during the Term of the Agreement in connection with the use of Product Technology (including, but not by way of limitation, technical assistance relating to the manufacture, design and promotion of Home Products). Licensor further agrees to fully assist and cooperate with Licensee in procuring acceptance and listing of Home Products by Underwriters Laboratories Inc. and the Canadian Standards Association. Licensor hereby agrees to provide such technical assistance initially for a minimum of four (4) hours per day until such time as Home Products can be manufactured by Licensee or its designee in commercially reasonable quantities, as determined by Licensee in its sole discretion. Once Home Products are being manufactured in commercially reasonable quantities, Licensor agrees to provide technical assistance as requested by Licensee, including that which is necessary to manufacture, market and sell new products and accessories, and implement developments and improvements relating to the Products, as provided in Section 8(a) below.

8. New Technology.

    (a) Licensor's New Products, Accessories, etc. Licensor shall promptly provide and make available to Licensee any information about new products, accessories, developments or improvements relating to the Products. Licensee shall have the right to review and research such information on a confidential basis to determine whether it is reasonably adaptable for use with or application on Home Products for such time as it deems appropriate. Further, Licensee shall have the first right of refusal to license such information from Licensor. Any such information licensed by Licensee shall, for purposes hereof, be included within the meaning of "Product Technology" and thereby subject to the terms of this Agreement.

    (b) Licensee's New Products, Accessories, etc. Any new products, accessories, developments or improvements relating to the Home Products that are developed by Licensee or any party with whom Licensee has entered in a contract, agreement or other similar arrangement during the term of this Agreement (the "New Technology") shall remain the property of Licensee. Licensee may determine whether and to what extent it desires to seek trademarks, patents or take other necessary legal steps to protect the New Technology without any interference by Licensor. In the event Licensee shall not seek trademarks, patents or take other necessary legal steps to protect any or all elements of the New Technology, Licensor shall have the right, in his discretion and at his expense, to seek trademarks or patents, or take other legal steps to protect any and all elements of the New Technology. Licensee shall reasonably assist Licensor in seeking such trademarks, patents, or such protection if requested, including securing and execution of trademark or patent applications and other appropriate documents and papers, and Licensor shall pay or reimburse Licensee for all expenses incurred by Licensee in connection with providing such assistance.

9. Claims; Infringement. Licensor represents and warrants that he has full power and authority to grant the license to Licensee as provided herein, the Product Technology and Licensed Marks are free and clear of all liens, claims and encumbrances of any nature whatsoever, and there are no governmental or regulatory proceedings, investigations or other actions pending or concluded that adversely affect the Product Technology or Licensed Marks. Licensor represents and warrants to Licensee that there are no patent, trademark or copyright

(continues)

Figure 17-4. *(continued)*

infringements with respect to the Product Technology or the Licensed Marks nor are there any threatened, pending or contemplated actions, suits or proceedings against Licensor or otherwise with respect to the same. No such infringement actions, suits or proceedings would result by reason of the transactions contemplated by this Agreement. Licensor shall promptly notify Licensor of any allegation or claim that the use of the Product Technology or the Licensed Marks infringes upon the rights of any other person or entity. Licensor agrees to defend Licensee and its directors and officers against any infringement, unfair competition or other claim respecting Licensee's use of the Product Technology or the Licensed Marks. Further, Licensor hereby agrees to indemnify, defend, hold harmless, Licensee and its directors and officers from and against any and all claims or actions, suits, proceedings, damages, liabilities, costs and expenses (including, without limitation, reasonable attorneys' fees) arising out of (a) any patent, trademark or copyright infringement by Licensor, (b) Licensor's unfair competition, misappropriation of confidential information, technology, know-how or trade secrets, and resulting from Licensor's use of the Product Technology or Licensed Marks, or (c) otherwise arising by reason of Licensee's legitimate use of the foregoing in compliance with this Agreement.

10. <u>Duration.</u> Unless sooner terminated as otherwise herein provided, the term of this Agreement shall commence upon the date hereof and shall expire on the [_____ (_____)] anniversary of that date (the "Initial Term"). Licensee shall have the right and option to renew this Agreement for term commencing on the day following the Initial Term and expiring on the [_____ (_____)] anniversary of the day following the Initial Term by giving Licensor notice of the exercise of such option at least ten (10) days prior to the end of the Initial Term. The Initial Term, along with such renewal term, if any, shall be referred to herein as the "Term."

(a) <u>Termination by Licensor.</u> In addition to any other right of Licensor contained herein to terminate this Agreement, Licensor shall have the right to terminate this Agreement by written notice to Licensee upon the occurrence of any one or more of the following events:

(i) failure of Licensee to make any payment required pursuant by this Agreement when due; or

(ii) intentional, persistent and material failure of Licensee to comply in any material respect with the quality control standards required pursuant to Section 6.

(b) <u>Termination by Licensee.</u>

(i) In addition to any other right of Licensee contained herein to terminate this Agreement, Licensee shall have the right to terminate this Agreement by written notice to Licensor upon the occurrence of any one or more of the following events:

(A) the insolvency of Licensor;

(B) the institution of any proceeding by Licensor, voluntarily or involuntarily, under any bankruptcy, insolvency or moratorium law;

(C) any assignment by Licensor of substantially all of his assets for the benefit of creditors;

(D) placement of Licensor's assets in the hands of a trustee or receiver unless the receivership or trust is dissolved within thirty (30) days thereafter; or

(E) any breach by Licensor of any representation, warranty or covenant contained in this Agreement that, if curable, is not cured by Licensor within thirty (30) days after its receipt of written notice thereof from Licensee. If such breach is not cured within such thirty (30) days period, or is not curable, then termination shall be deemed effective on the date of such notice.

(ii) If at any time following the first _____ (____) months of the Term, Licensee determines in good faith that its continued use of Licensor's Product Technology in the manufacture, marketing and sale of Home Products is commercially impracticable by reason of (A) a continued failure (after Licensee has exerted its best efforts to overcome such failure) in the performance of Home Products, or (B) Licensee's inability, after exerting its best efforts, to produce Home Products at its designated manufacturing facility, Licensee may, at its option, terminate this Agreement without further obligation to Licensor (other than payment for accrued royalties, if any) upon thirty (30) days prior written notice to Licensor.

(c) <u>Exercise.</u> Licensor or Licensee, as the case may be, may exercise the right of termination granted hereunder by giving the other party ten (10) days prior written notice of that party's election to terminate and the reason(s) for such termination. After the expiration of such

(continues)

Figure 17-4. *(continued)*

period, this Agreement shall automatically terminate unless the other party has previously cured the breach or condition permitting termination, in which case this Agreement shall not terminate. Such notice and termination shall not prejudice either party's rights to any sums due hereunder and shall not prejudice any cause of action or claim of such party accrued or to accrue on account of any breach or default by the other party.

(d) <u>Failure to Enforce.</u> The failure of either party at any time, or for any period of time, to enforce any of the provisions of this Agreement shall not be construed as a waiver of such provision or of the right of such party thereafter to enforce each and every such provision.

(e) <u>Effect of Termination.</u> Subject to the terms of Section 8 hereof, in the event this Agreement is terminated for any reason whatsoever: (i) Licensee shall return any plans, drawings, papers, notes, writings and other documents, samples and models pertaining to the Product Technology, retaining no copies, and shall refrain from using or publishing any portion of the Product Technology; and (ii) Licensor shall return any plans, drawings, papers, notes, writings and other documents, samples and models, retaining no copies, pertaining to New Technology. Upon termination of this Agreement, Licensee shall cease manufacturing, processing, producing, using, selling or distributing Home Products and shall retain no right of any kind to use anywhere in the world the Product Technology or the Licensed Marks; provided, however, that Licensee may continue to sell in the ordinary course of business for a period of one-hundred eighty (180) days after the date of termination reasonable quantities of Home Products which are fully manufactured and in Licensee's normal inventory at the date of termination and Licensee may fulfill all outstanding purchase orders received by Licensee through the date of termination (irrespective of the one-hundred eighty (180) day period) if all monetary obligations of Licensee to Licensor have been satisfied.

11. <u>Independent Contractor.</u> Licensee's relationship to Licensor hereunder shall be that of a licensee and licensor only. Licensee shall not be the agent of Licensor and shall have no authority to act for or on behalf of Licensor in any matter. Persons retained by Licensee as employees or agents shall not by reason thereof be deemed to be employees or agents of Licensor.

12. <u>Compliance.</u> Licensee agrees that it will comply in all material respects with all material laws and regulations relating to its manu-

facture, marketing, selling or distributing of Home Products and its use of Product Technology and the Licensed Marks. Licensor agrees that he will comply in all respects with all federal, state and local laws and regulations relating to the manufacture and distribution of Products and his use of Product Technology and the Licensed Marks. Licensor will not at any time take any action which would cause Licensee or Licensor to be in violation of any such applicable laws and regulations. Licensor represents and warrants that the Products comply and shall continue to comply with the requirements necessary for acceptance and listing by Underwriters Laboratories Inc. and the Canadian Standards Association.

13. <u>Definitions.</u> The following terms, whenever used in this Agreement, shall have the respective meanings set forth below.

(a) <u>"Accessories"</u> means accessory products related to the Home Products including, without limitation, bags, canisters, trays, valves and containers.

(b) <u>"Products"</u> means food vacuum sealers and related accessories currently manufactured, marketed and sold by Licensor which are marketed primarily to gourmet food preparers.

(c) <u>"Home Products"</u> means food vacuum sealers or any product to which any application of Product Technology may be made by Licensee, which sealers or products may each be sold for $_____ or less at retail, and the Accessories.

(d) <u>"Licensed Patents"</u> means U.S. Patent Nos. _____ and _____, and patent applications related to the Products, if any, owned by Licensor.

(e) <u>"Licensed Marks"</u> means the [*unregistered*] trademark and such related mark or other marks used by Licensor in marketing the Products, [*a portion/all*] of which are shown on Exhibit A, attached hereto and incorporated herein by reference.

(f) <u>"Product Technology"</u> means, subject to Section 8(a) hereof, the Licensed Patents and certain valuable technical information, know-how and data of Licensor relating to the Products.

14. <u>General and Miscellaneous.</u>

(a) <u>Governing Law.</u> This Agreement and all amendments, modifications, alterations, or supplements hereto, and the rights of the parties hereunder, shall be construed under and governed by the laws of the State of _____ and the United States of America.

(continues)

Figure 17-4. *(continued)*

(b) <u>Interpretation.</u> The parties are equally responsible for the preparation of this Agreement and in any judicial proceeding the terms hereof shall not be more strictly construed against one party than the other.

(c) <u>Place of Execution.</u> This Agreement and any subsequent modifications or amendments hereto shall be deemed to have been executed in the State of _____.

(d) <u>Notices.</u> Any notice herein required or permitted to be given, or waiver of any provision hereof, shall be effective only if given or made in writing. Notices shall be deemed to have been given on the date of delivery if delivered by hand, or upon the expiration of five (5) days after deposit in the United States mail, registered or certified, postage prepaid, and addressed to the respective parties at the addresses specified in the preamble of this Agreement. Any party hereto may change the address to which notices to such party are to be sent by giving notice to the other party at the address and in the manner provided above. Any notice herein required or permitted to be given may be given, in addition to the manner set forth above, by telecopier, telex, TWX, or cable, provided that the party giving such notice obtains acknowledgment by telecopier, telex, TWX or cable that such notice has been received by the party to be notified. Notice made in this manner shall be deemed to have been given when such acknowledgment has been transmitted.

(e) <u>Assignments.</u> Licensor shall not grant, transfer, convey, sublicense, or otherwise assign any of his rights or delegate any of his obligations under this Agreement without the prior written consent of Licensor. Licensee shall have the right to freely grant, transfer, convey, sublicense, or otherwise assign any of its rights or delegate any of its obligations under this Agreement.

(f) <u>Entire Agreement.</u> This Agreement constitutes the entire agreement between Licensor and Licensee with respect to the subject matter hereof and shall not be modified, amended or terminated except as herein provided or except by another agreement in writing executed by the parties hereto.

(g) <u>Headings.</u> The Section headings are for convenience only and are not a part of this Agreement.

(h) <u>Severability.</u> All rights and restrictions contained herein may be exercised and shall be applicable and binding only to the extent that they do not violate any applicable laws and are intended to be limited to the extent necessary so that they will not render this Agreement illegal, invalid or unenforceable. If any provision or portion of any provision of this Agreement not essential to the commercial purpose of this Agreement shall be held to be illegal, invalid or unenforceable by a court of competent jurisdiction, it is the intention of the parties that the remaining provisions or portions thereof shall constitute their agreement with respect to the subject matter hereof, and all such remaining provisions or portions thereof shall remain in full force and effect.

(i) <u>Survival of Representations and Warranties.</u> The parties hereto agree that all representations and warranties of Licensor contained herein shall survive the expiration or termination of this Agreement, and shall continue to be binding on the parties without limitation.

(j) <u>Attorneys' Fees, etc.</u> In the event either party brings any action, suit or proceeding against the other party to enforce any right or entitlement which it may have under this Agreement, either party shall, to the extent it is successful in pursuing or defending the action, and in addition to all other rights or remedies available to it in law or in equity, be entitled to recover its reasonable attorneys' fees and court costs incurred in such action.

IN WITNESS WHEREOF, the parties hereto have executed this License and Distribution Agreement as of the day and year set forth above.

Witness: "Licensor"

_____   _____

                                             "Licensee"

                                             _____

Exhibit A

Licensed Marks

18

Joint Ventures and Strategic Alliances

Joint ventures, strategic partnering, cross-licensing, co-branding, and technology transfer agreements are all strategies designed to obtain one or more of the following strategic objectives: (1) direct capital infusion in exchange for equity and/or intellectual property or distribution rights, (2) a "capital substitute" where the resources that would otherwise be obtained with the capital are obtained through joint venturing, (3) a shift of the burden and cost of development (through licensing) in exchange for a potentially more limited upside, or (4) a sharing or pooling of resources where key objectives can be met more effectively through the efforts of two or more players instead of one company on a stand-alone basis.

Regardless of the specific structure, the underlying industry, or even the actual purpose of the strategic relationship, all successful joint venture and strategic alliance relationships share a common set of essential success factors. These critical success factors include:

◆ A complementary unified force or purpose that brings and then bonds the two or more companies together
◆ A management team committed at all levels to the success of the venture, free from politics or personal agendas
◆ A genuine strategy synergy where the "sum of the whole truly exceeds its individual parts" (e.g., 2 + 2 + 2 = 7)
◆ A cooperative culture and spirit among the strategic partners that leads to trust, resource sharing, and a friendly chemistry among the parties
◆ A degree of flexibility in the objectives of the joint venture or

strategic alliance to allow for changes in the marketplace and an evolution of technology

♦ An actual alignment of management styles and operational methods at least to the extent that it affects the underlying project (as in the case of a strategic alliance) or the management of the new company created (as in the case of a formal joint venture). The general levels of focus and leadership from all key parties that are necessary to the success of any new venture or business enterprise

Joint ventures are typically structured as a partnership or as a newly formed and co-owned corporation where two or more parties are brought together to achieve a series of strategic and financial objectives on a short-term or long-term basis. Companies considering a joint venture as a growth strategy should give careful thought to the type of partner they are looking for and what resources each party will be contributing to the newly formed entity. Like in the raising of a child, each parent will be making his or her respective contribution of skills, abilities, and resources.

Strategic alliances refer to any number of collaborative working relationships where no formal joint venture entity is formed *but* where two *independent* companies become *interdependent* by entering into a formal or informal agreement that is built on a platform of: (1) mutual objectives, (2) mutual strategy, (3) mutual risk, and (4) mutual reward. These strategic types of relationships are commonly referred to as: (1) teaming, (2) strategic partnering, (3) alliances, (4) cross-licensing, and (5) co-branding.

The strategic benefits of these strategic relationships include:

♦ Development of a new market (domestic/international)
♦ Development of a new product (research and development)
♦ Development and sharing of technology
♦ Combination of complementary technology
♦ Pooling of resources to develop a production/distribution facility
♦ Acquiring of capital
♦ Execution of a government contract
♦ Access to a new distribution channel or network or sales/marketing capability

Figure 18-1 presents a comparison of joint ventures and strategic alliances.

Figure 18-1. A comparison of joint ventures and strategic alliances.

	Joint Ventures	Strategic Alliances
Term	Usually medium to long-term	Short-term
Strategic objective	Often serves as to precursor to a merger	More flexible and noncommittal
Legal agreements and structure	Actual legal entity formed	Contractual-driven
Extent of commitment	Shared equity	Shared objectives
Capital resources	Each party makes a capital contribution of cash or intangible assets	No specific capital contributions (may be shared budgeting on even cross-investment)
Tax ramifications	Be on the lookout for double taxation unless pass-through entities utilized	No direct tax ramifications

Due Diligence Before Selecting Joint Venture or Strategic Alliance Partners

Care should be taken to conduct a truly thorough review of prospective candidates, and extensive due diligence should be done on the final candidates that are being considered. Develop a list of key objectives and goals to be achieved by the joint venture or licensing relationship, and compare this list with those of your final candidates. Take the time to understand the corporate culture and decision-making process within each company. Consider some of the following issues: (1) How does this fit with your own processes? (2) What are each prospective partner's previous experiences and track record with other joint venture relationships? (3) Why did these previous relationships succeed or fail?

In many cases, smaller companies looking for joint venture partners wind up selecting a much larger Goliath that offers a wide range of financial and nonfinancial resources that will allow the smaller company to achieve its growth plans. The motivating factor under these circumstances for the larger company is to get access and distribution rights to new technologies, products, and services. In turn, the larger company offers access to pools of capital, research and development, personnel, distribution channels, and general contacts that the small company desperately needs.

But proceed carefully. Be sensitive to the politics, red tape, and different management practices that may be in place at a larger company that will be foreign to many smaller companies. Try to distinguish between that which is being promised and that which will actually be delivered. If the primary motivating force for the small company is really only capital, then consider whether alternative (and perhaps less costly) sources of money have been thoroughly explored. Ideally, the larger joint venture partner can offer a lot more than just money. If the primary motivating force is access to technical personnel, then consider whether it might be a better decision to purchase these resources separately rather than entering into a partnership in which you give up a certain measure of control. Also, consider whether strategic relationships or extended payments terms with vendors and consultants can be arranged in lieu of the joint venture.

Structuring the Joint Venture or Strategic Alliance

Unlike franchising, distributorships, and licensing, which are almost always vertical in nature, joint ventures are structured at *either* horizontal or vertical levels of distribution. At the horizontal level, the joint venture is often the first step to an actual merger, in which two companies operating at the same level in the distribution channel join together (either by means of a partnership-type agreement or by joint ownership of a specially created corporation) to achieve certain synergies or operating efficiencies. Even at the vertical level, what stands as an ordinary manufacturer-distributor relationship could evolve into a more formal strategic partnership leading to an eventual merger in order to achieve a more direct relationship with the customer or end-user. Consider the following key strategic issues before and during joint venture or strategic alliance negotiations:

◆ Exactly what types of tangible and intangible assets will be contributed to the joint venture by each party? Who will have ownership rights in the property contributed during the term of the joint venture and thereafter? Who will own property developed as a result of joint development efforts?

◆ What covenants of nondisclosure or noncompetition will be expected of each joint venturer during the term of the agreement and thereafter?

◆ What timetables or performance quotas for completion of the projects contemplated by the joint venture will be included in the agreement? What are the rights and remedies of each party if these performance standards are not met?

◆ How will issues of management and control be addressed in the agreement? What will be the respective voting rights of each party? What are the procedures in the event of a major disagreement or deadlock? What is the fallback plan?

Once all of the preliminary issues have been discussed by the joint venturers, a formal joint venture agreement or corporate shareholders' agreement should be prepared with the assistance of counsel.

Structuring Formal Joint Ventures

The precise terms of the agreement between the parties depend upon the nature and the structure of the arrangement. At a minimum, however, the following topics should be addressed in as much detail as possible:

◆ *Nature, purpose, and trade name for the joint venture.* The parties should set forth the legal nature of the relationship between themselves along with a clear statement of purpose to prevent future disputes as to the scope of the arrangement. If a new trade name is established for the venture, provisions should be made as to the use of the name and any other trade or service marks registered by the venture upon termination of the entity or project.

◆ *Status of the respective joint venturers.* The agreement should clearly indicate whether each party is a partner, shareholder, agent, independent contractor, or any combination thereof. Agent status, whether actual or imputed, can greatly affect liability between the venturers and with regard to third parties.

◆ *Representations and warranties of each joint venturer.* Standard representations and warranties will include obligations of due care and due diligence as well as mutual covenants governing confidentiality and anticompetition restrictions.

◆ *Capital and property contributions of each joint venturer.* A clear schedule should be established of all contributions, whether in the form of cash, shares, real estate, or intellectual property. Detailed descriptions will be particularly important if the distribution of profits and losses is to be based upon overall contribution. The specifics of allocation and distribution of profits and losses among the venturers should also be clearly defined.

◆ *Management, control, and voting rights of each joint venturer.* If the proposed venture envisions joint management, it will be necessary to specifically address the keeping of books, records, and bank accounts; the nature and frequency of inspections and audits; insurance and cross-indemnification obligations; as well as responsibility for administrative and overhead expenses.

◆ *Rights in joint venture property.* Growing companies should be especially mindful of intellectual property rights and should clearly address the issues of ownership use and licensing entitlements not only for the venturers' currently existing property rights but also for future use of rights (or products or services) developed in the name of the venture itself.

◆ *Restrictions on transferability of ownership interest in the joint venture.* Stringent conditions should be placed on the ability of the venturers to transfer interests in the venture to third parties.

◆ *Default, dissolution, and termination of the joint venture.* The obligations of the venturers and the distribution assets should be clearly defined along with procedures in the event of bankruptcy and grounds for default.

◆ *Dispute resolution procedures.* The parties may wish to consider arbitration as an alternative dispute resolution mechanism.

◆ *Miscellaneous.* Provisions should also be made indicating (1) the governing law, (2) remedies under force majeure situations, (3) procedures for notice and consent, and (4) the ability to modify or waive certain provisions.

Co-Branding as a Strategic Alliance

Co-branding is a form of partnership whereby two established brand names combine in order to bring added value, economies of scale, and customer recognition to each product. Companies of all sizes are realizing the cost and importance of establishing brand awareness. Campaigns and strategies to build brand recognition, brand loyalty, and brand equity have been launched by thousands of companies that recognize that a well-established brand can be the single most valuable asset on the balance sheet. This new focus on brand in the year

2000 and beyond has set the stage for a wide variety of co-branding and brand-extension licensing transactions. Companies with strong quality-oriented brands (as well as professional sports teams, athletes, and celebrities) have sought to create new sources of revenues and leverage their largest intangible asset—their reputation—to add to the strength of their income statements. To build brand awareness, companies are spending more money on media advertising and promotional campaigns and less on store displays and coupons.

Co-branding has emerged recently as a very popular type of strategic alliance. At the heart of the relationship, two or more established brands are paired and positioned in the marketplace to bring added value, economies of scale, and synergistic customer recognition and loyalty to increase sales and create a point of differentiation. Co-branding has appeared in many different forms including:

- *Financial services co-branding.* In the early 1990s, credit card companies pioneered co-branding with credit cards paired with airlines or telecommunications companies for mutual branding and shared rewards.
- *Consumer-product ingredient co-branding.* The strength of one brand appears as an ingredient in another as enhancement for sales and cross-consumer loyalty. (For example, Post Raisin Bran uses Sun-Maid raisins in its cereal, Archways uses Kellogg's All-Bran in its cookies, Ben & Jerry's uses Heath Bars® in its Heath Bar® Crunch ice cream, and PopTarts use Smuckers® fruit fillings.)
- *Implied endorsement co-branding.* The co-branded name or logo is used to build consumer recognition even if there is no actual ingredient used in the product. (Examples are the placement of John Deere on the back of a Florsheim boot, the Doritos® Pizza Craver tortilla chips that feature Pizza Hut's logo on the packaging, or Dorito®'s Taco Supreme chips that feature Taco Bell's logo on the packaging.)
- *Actual composite co-branding.* The co-branded product actually uses a branded pairing of popular manufacturing techniques or processes (e.g., Timberland boots with Gore-Tex fabric, furniture with Scotchguard® protectants, Dell or Gateway computers with Intel® inside, etc.).
- *Designer-driven co-branded products.* Certain manufacturers have co-branded with well-known designers to increase consumer loyalty and brand awareness. For example, the Eddie Bauer edition

of the Ford Explorer has been a very strong seller and product differentiation.

♦ *Retail business form0at co-branding.* This type of co-branding is growing rapidly within the retailing, hospitality, and franchising communities. Retail co-branding is being used to attract additional customers, create complementary product lines to offset different consumer tastes (such as Baskin-Robbins and Dunkin' Donuts) or consuming patterns (for example, combining a restaurant with a traditional breakfast-only consumer traffic pattern with a restaurant that has a traditional lunch-only traffic pattern), or to sell additional products or services to a "captured customer, such as in co-branded automobile services mini-malls."

Issues to Consider Regarding Co-Branding

Why and When Should a Company Think About Co-Branding as a Growth Strategy?

♦ The company may wish to leverage its own brands, and co-branding is one of four leveraging options (line extensions, stretching the brand vertically in existing product class, brand extensions into different product classes, and co-branding).

♦ It is a way of leveraging the company's intangible assets, including brand awareness and customer loyalty, by entering another product class.

♦ It can provide added value in the form of customer convenience, thereby creating a point of differentiation.

♦ It is difficult to build a strong brand since there are many internal and external impediments, including corporate bias against innovation, short-term orientation, price pressures, and competitive threats. The answer is the less risky alternative of co-branding.

♦ Over time, a company is challenged to maintain brand equity in light of competitors' new product introductions and/or declining brand awareness. Co-branding can gain visibility and create new customer interest.

♦ It can change the perception of a brand. If a company wishes to alter how its brand is now perceived, it can do so with co-branding. The company can create a new brand personality (like the use of Bart Simpson with Butterfingers) or at least update it.

◆ A company can gain access to new product categories that otherwise would have involved a significant investment of time, money, and resources.

◆ Since a brand name assists consumers' understanding of a product's characteristics, two brands may provide greater assurance about the product quality. The presence of a second brand may signal to potential customers that another company is willing to stake its reputation on the product.

◆ Reaching a new customer base usually takes three to five years, but with co-branding, you reach potential new customers far more quickly.

◆ Co-branding is a short cut to an image upgrade (as in Ford's Explorer Eddie Bauer editions).

◆ Co-branding is a way to target a key demographic.

What Key Issues Should You Consider Before Implementing a Co-Branding Program?

◆ Be aware of the fit of the brands. For example, a hypothetical Godiva/Slim Fast line of chocolate snack bars would benefit the Slim Fast brand by its association with the superior chocolates produced by Godiva. However, it would detract from Godiva's upscale brand image, and may not be viewed by one consumer as a natural pairing of brands. In this scenario, there is not a fit between the brands.

◆ Understand consumer perceptions of your product and its attributes in order to better determine whether the two brands have a common set of attributes.

◆ Examine the level of complementarity between the two brands.

◆ Rate the favorableness of each brand separately, then as a co-branded product.

◆ Explore the relative contribution each brand would make to the effectiveness of the co-branded product.

◆ Determine what types of partners would enhance your identity. Determine what types would help reduce the limitations of your identity.

Advantages of Using Co-Branding as a Growth Strategy

◆ It lets you share costs, such as those for marketing and packaging, and lets you share rent, utilities, etc., if in the same location.

◆ It enables you to expand into international markets.

◆ It is easier to get brand recognition for your brand if tied to a well-known domestic brand (in foreign markets).

◆ The additional traffic creates impulse purchases. If the consumer needs to fill up his or her tank, and there is a Dunkin' Donuts in the gas station, customers may purchase a donut or coffee. If the Dunkin' Donuts unit was on a stand-alone site, customers might pass it by.

◆ It creates conveniences for customers that can increase business for both companies. For instance, people may go to the gas station specifically to "kill two birds with one stone," getting coffee and gas in the morning. Making one stop is more convenient.

◆ It gives you market clout, with value and quality communicated to the customer.

◆ Since the idea behind co-branding is to create a product carrying two brands, it will result in double recognition, double endorsement power, and double consumer confidence.

Disadvantages of Using Co-Branding as a Growth Strategy

◆ Agreements between co-branding partners can be hard to construct and agree upon.

◆ Marketing has to be agreed upon by both parties, which can lead to loss of time of marketing to market and loss of flexibility.

◆ Bad publicity for one company can affect the other.

◆ If one brand fails to live up to its promises made to the other, co-branding relationships can dissolve.

◆ If co-branding flops, both companies feel the pain. And consumers may become confused about new products, diminishing the value of both.

Co-Branding at the Retail Level

Co-branding does facilitate complementary retail services formats that enable companies to achieve benefits in the areas of marketing and real estate expenses. For example, in the areas of gas stations and restaurants:

◆ Texaco Star Marts have teamed with Taco Bell, Pizza Hut, Burger King, McDonald's, and Del Taco.

◆ Chevron and McDonald's opened a joint operation in Marina Del Rey, California.

◆ Other gas mini-marts have teamed with Dunkin' Donuts and Subway.

Quick service restaurants have teamed up with each other to serve complementary meals. One brand finds another brand that will not compete directly against it, but will bring business in the door at a time of the day when it does not generate high consumer traffic. For example:

◆ D'Angelo's sub chain (lunch) has teamed with Pizza Hut (dinner) in over one 100 locations. (D'Angelo's is owned by Pizza Hut but maintains a distinct brand.)
◆ TCBY has teamed up with the Subway franchisee Doctor's Associates to co-locate brands and operations in one location.
◆ A Blimpie franchisee signed a co-brand agreement with Pudgie's Chicken to operate a co-brand store. This agreement was by a franchisee, not necessarily the parent.
◆ Manhattan Bagel Co. and Ranch 1 Chicken announced plans to develop twenty co-branded locations in Manhattan inside Ranch 1 restaurants.
◆ Church's Chicken and White Castle Hamburgers announced plans to develop thirty co-branded restaurants, thus sharing.

These retail co-branding trends have created a whole new specialty area of law within the general intellectual property practice, a specialty that focuses on the agreements necessary to establish and maintain these brand-extension and co-branding relationships. For example, in *Clark v. America's Favorite Chicken Co.*, 2 Bus. Fran. Guide (CCH) ¶ 10,841 (D.C. La. 1996), the federal district court in New Orleans, Louisiana, found that a franchisor's acquisition and operation of a competing franchise system, and alleged development of a dual marketing strategy for the two systems, did not breach the franchisor's agreements with several franchisees or violate the Louisiana "little FTC Act." The court found that provisions in the agreements (1) expressly reserved to the franchisor the right to "develop and establish" other systems, effectively granting it the right to operate a separate system in the franchisees' area, and (2) indicated that advertising was not intended to benefit franchisees directly. Since the franchisor was contractually authorized to develop a second system and had maintained separate marketing divisions for each system, the franchisor had not engaged in any "unethical" or "unscrupulous" acts prohibited by the statute.

Special Challenges for Co-Branding by and Among Franchisers

As discussed earlier in the chapter, co-branding by and among franchisors has dramatically grown in popularity in recent years. This trend has raised a number of special challenges that must be resolved at the franchisor-to-franchisee level as well as at the franchisee and landlord levels. These issues include:

- *Defining roles.* Who will be the "host" and who will be the "new entrant," and how will the roles and responsibilities differ from location to location? How will this paradigm differ for new locations?
- *UFOC issue.* How will the UFOCs of each system be amended to reflect the new co-branding strategy? Will all new locations of boom systems be co-branded? Or only some? How will this be determined? Will the co-branded units be awarded to one franchisee or two?
- *Scope of product or service.* The scope of products and services must be determined—for both existing lines and those that might be introduced in the future. How will overlap be determined?
- *Default and termination.* How will issues of default and termination be handled? What if the quality control standards for one system are being met but not for the other? How will subsequent requests for a full or partial transfer of the co-branded franchisee's rights be handled?
- *Encroachment and terminal issues.* How will issues of encroachment or challenges to a violation of granted terminal exclusivity be handled? How will requests for an existing location of one system to convert to a co-branded system be processed? What if the co-branding violates the franchisee's underlying commercial lease?
- *Advertising and marketing issues.* How will the co-branded units be promoted? What pro rata share should be contributed to each franchisor's respective advertising and marketing fund?
- *Uniformity within the systems.* Will the co-branding in each system be mandatory, optional or more flexible, or ad hoc and permissive? What consistency will there be throughout each system to determine how and when units must or may be co-branded?
- *Operational issues, design standards, signage, and trade dress.* There is a wide variety of operational issues (e.g., hours of operation, employee staffing, storage areas, metered utilities, entrances, dining areas, order-taking, POSs, etc.) as well as design issues (e.g., signage, trade dress, uniforms, etc.) That must be resolved in a prac-

tical, cost-effective, and customer-friendly manner at the co-branded unit level. At a macro level, franchisors may be quick to recognize the strategic and synergistic benefits of co-branded units, but also must think through the micro issues at the operating level (such as who pays which employees, how cash registers will be shared and who will be responsible for mundane issues such as the cleaning of rest rooms, the storage of supplies, and preventing theft and waste).

Resource Directory

List of State Administrations and Agents for Service of Process

California

Department of Corporations
1390 Market Street
San Francisco, CA 94102
ATTN: Greg Mangani
415-557-3787

Agent for Service of Process:
Department of Corporations
1109 Ninth Street
Sacramento, CA 95814
415-557-3787

Connecticut

Securities and Business Investment Division
Connecticut Department of Banking
44 Capitol Avenue
Hartford, CT 06106
ATTN: Cynthia Antanaitis,
    Assistant Director
860-566-4560

Agent for Service of Process:
Connecticut Banking Commissioner
Same as above

Florida	Department of Agriculture and Consumer Services
	Division of Consumer Services
	Mayo Building, 2nd Floor
	Tallahassee, FL 32399
	ATTN: Bob James, Senior Consumer Complaint Analyst
	810-922-2770

Agent for Service of Process:
Same as above

Georgia	Office of Consumer Affairs
	2 Martin Luther King Drive, S.E.
	Plaza Level, East Tower
	Atlanta, GA 30334
	ATTN: Dobbs Jordan
	404-656-3790

Agent for Service of Process:
Same as above

Hawaii	State of Hawaii
	Business Registration Division
	Department of Commerce and Consumer Affairs
	1010 Richards Street, 2nd Floor
	P.O. Box 40
	Honolulu, HI 96810
	ATTN: Susan Lee, Securities Examiner
	808-586-2744

Agent for Service of Process:
Director
Department of Commerce and Consumer Affairs
Same as above

Illinois

Franchise Division
Office of the Attorney General
500 South Second Street
Springfield, IL 62706
ATTN: Chief
217-782-4465

Agent for Service of Process:
Same as above

Indiana

Securities Commissioner
Indiana Securities Division
Room E 111
302 West Washington Street
Indianapolis, IN 46204
317-232-6681

Agent for Service of Process:
Indiana Secretary of State
201 State House
200 West Washington Street
Indianapolis, IN 46204
317-232-6531

Iowa

Iowa Securities Bureau
Lucas State Office Building, 2nd Floor
Des Moines, IA 50319
ATTN: Dennis Britson, Supervisor of
   Regulated Industries Unit
515-281-4441

Agent for Service of Process:
Same as above

Kentucky

Attorney General's Office
Consumer Protection Division
1024 Capitol Center Drive
Frankfort, KY 40602

ATTN: Beth Willis
502-573-2200

Agent for Service of Process:
Same as above

Louisiana

Department of Urban and Community
  Affairs
Consumer Protection Office
P.O. Box 94455 Capitol Station
Baton Rouge, LA 70804
ATTN: Ida Washington
504-925-4401 (general information)
504-925-4405

Agent for Service of Process:
Same as above

Maine

Department of Business Regulations
State House—Station 35
Augusta, ME 04333
ATTN: Karen L. Bossie
207-298-3671

Agent for Service of Process:
Same as above

Maryland

Office of the Attorney General
  Securities Division
200 St. Paul Place, 20th Floor
Baltimore, MD 21202
ATTN: Peggy Jones, Franchise Examiner
410-576-7044

Agent for Service of Process:
Maryland Securities Commissioner
200 St. Paul Place, 20th Floor
Baltimore, MD 21202
410-576-7044

Michigan

Michigan Department of Attorney General
Consumer Protection Division
Antitrust and Franchise Unit
670 Law Building
Lansing, MI 48913
ATTN: Marilyn McEwen, Franchise
  Administrator
517-373-7117

Agent for Service of Process:
Michigan Department of Commerce
Corporations and Securities Bureau
Same as above

Minnesota

Minnesota Department of Commerce
133 East Seventh Street
St. Paul, MN 55101
ATTN: Ann Hagestad, Franchise Examiner
612-296-6328

Agent for Service of Process:
Minnesota Commissioner of Commerce
Same as above

Nebraska

Department of Banking and Finance
1200 N Street, Suite 311
P.O. Box 95006
Lincoln, NE 68509
ATTN: Sheila Cahill, Staff Attorney
402-471-3445

Agent for Service of Process:
Same as above

North Carolina

Secretary of State's Office
Securities Division
Legislative Annex Building
300 Salisbury Street
Raleigh, NC 27602

919-733-3924
Agent for Service of Process:
Secretary of State
Secretary of State's Office
300 Salisbury Street
Raleigh, NC 27602

North Dakota

Office of Securities Commissioner
600 East Boulevard, 5th Floor
Bismarck, ND 58505
701-224-4712

Agent for Service of Process:
North Dakota Securities Commissioner
Same as above

Ohio

Attorney General
Consumer Fraud & Crime Section
State Office Tower
30 East Broad Street, 15th Floor
Columbus, OH 43215
ATTN: Rick Sheffield, Chief;
   Rita Brown, Investigator
614-466-8831, 800-282-0515

Agent for Service of Process:
Same as above

Oklahoma

Oklahoma Securities Commission
2915 Lincoln Boulevard
Oklahoma City, OK 73105
ATTN: Sonya Singer, Faye Morton
405-521-2451

Agent for Service of Process:
Same as above

Oregon

Department of Insurance and Finance
Corporate Securities Division
Labor and Industries Building
Salem, OR 96310
ATTN: Laurie Skillman
503-378-4387

Agent for Service of Process:
Director
Department of Insurance and Finance
Same as above

Rhode Island

Division of Securities
233 Richmond Street, Suite 232
Providence, RI 02903
ATTN: Thomas Corrigan,
    Securities Examiner
401-277-3048

Agent for Service of Process:
Rhode Island Attorney General
233 Richmond Street
Providence, RI 02903

South Carolina

Secretary of State
P.O. Box 11350
Columbia, SC 29211
ATTN: Carolyn Hatcher
803-734-2166
(Federal Express address:
Capitol Complex
Wade Hampton Building, Room 105
Columbia, SC 29201)

Agent for Service of Process:
Same as above

South Dakota	Department of Commerce and Regulation
	Division of Securities
	118 West Capitol
	Pierre, SD 57501
	ATTN: Joe Bjerke, Franchise Administrator;
	Debra Bollinger, Director of Securities
	605-773-4013
	Agent for Service of Process:
	Director of South Dakota Division of
	Securities
	Same as above
Texas	Attorney General's Office
	Consumer Protection Division
	P.O. Box 12548
	Austin, TX 78711
	512-463-2070
	Agent for Service of Process:
	Same as above
Utah	Utah Department of Commerce
	Consumer Protection Division
	160 East 300 South
	P.O. Box 45804
	Salt Lake City, UT 84145
	ATTN: Francine A. Giani
	801-530-6001
	Agent for Service of Process:
	Same as above
Virginia	State Corporation Commission
	Division of Securities and Retail
	Franchising
	1300 E. Main Street, 9th Floor
	Richmond, VA 23219
	ATTN: Stephen W. Goolsby,
	Chief Examiner

804-371-9051 (phone)
804-371-9911 (fax)

Agent for Service of Process:
Clerk of the State Corporation Commission
State Corporation Commission
1300 E. Main Street
Richmond, VA 23219
804-371-9051 (phone)
804-371-9911 (fax)

Washington

Department of Financial Institutions
Securities Division
P.O. Box 9033
Olympia, WA 98507
ATTN: Deborah Bortner
360-902-8760
(Federal Express address:
General Administration Building
Securities Division
210 11th Street S.W., 3rd Floor West
Olympia, WA 98504)

Agent for Service of Process:
Same as above

Wisconsin

Commission of Securities
101 E. Wilson Street, 4th Floor
Madison, WI 53702
ATTN: James R. Fischer,
  Franchise Administrator
608-266-1365

Agent for Service of Process:
Wisconsin Commissioner of Securities
Same as above

International Franchise Organizations

Argentina
Argentine Franchise Association
Santa Fe 995, Piso 4
Buenos Aires 1059, Argentina
ATTN: Richard Rivera, President
(54) 1-393-5263 (phone)
(54) 1-393-9260 (fax)

Australia/New Zealand
Franchisors Assn. of Australia & New Zealand
Unit 9, 2-6 Hunter Street
Parramatta, NSW 2150, Australia
ATTN: Berridge Hume-Phillips, Executive Director
(61) 2-891-4933 (phone)
(61) 2-891-4474 (fax)

Austria
Austrian Franchise Association
Nonntaler Hauptstrasse 48
Salzburg 5020, Austria
ATTN: Waltraud Frauenhuber
(43) 662-83-21-64 (phone)
(43) 662-83-21-64 (fax)

Belgium
Belgische Franchise Federatie
 Groot Molenveldlaan 52
1850 Grimbergen, Belgium
ATTN: President
(32) 2-253-27-12 (phone)
(32) 2-253-40-37 (fax)

Brazil
Brazil Franchise Association
Rua Professor Ascendino Reis, 1548
Sao Paulo 04027-000, Brazil
Attn: Bernard Jeger, President
(55) 11-5711303 (phone)
(55) 11-5755590 (fax)

Bulgaria
Bulgarian Franchise Association
25 A Ochrid Street
9000-Varna, Bulgaria
ATTN: Lubka Kolarova, President
(359) 52-256-891 (phone)
(359) 52-256-891 (fax)

Canada
Canadian Franchise Association
5045 Orbitor Drive, Suite 201, Building 12
Mississauga, Ontario L4W 4Y4, Canada
ATTN: Richard B. Cunningham, President
(905) 625-2896 (phone)
(905) 625-9076 (fax)

Chile
Association de Franchising de Chile (AFICH)
Hernando de Aguirre 128, of. 704
Providencia, Santiago, Chile
ATTN: Carlos Fabia
(56) 2-234-4189 (phone)
(56) 2-232-7759 (fax)

Colombia
Association Colombiana de Franquicias
Apartado Aereo 25200
Cali, Colombia
ATTN: Francisco J. Patino, President
(57) 2-331-1086 (phone)
(57) 2-331-7138 (fax)

Czech Republic
Ceska Asociace Franchisingu
Rytirska 31, P.O. Box 706
11000 Praha 1, Czech Republic
ATTN: President
(42) 2-242-30-566 (phone)
(42) 2-242-30-566 (fax)

Denmark
Danish Franchise Association

Amaliegade 37
Copenhagen K 1256, Denmark
ATTN: Peter Arendorff, President
(45) 33-156011 (phone)
(45) 33-910346 (fax)

Europe
European Franchise Federation
50, rue La Boetie
Paris 75008, France
ATTN: Michel Micmacher, Chairman
(33) 1-5375-2225 (phone)
(33) 1-5357-2220 (fax)

Finland
Finnish Franchising Association
P139
Helsinki, SF 08501, Finland
ATTN: Antti Wathen, Executive Officer
(358) 12-334-584 (phone)
(358) 12-334-542 (fax)

France
French Franchise Federation
60, rue La Boetie
Paris 75008, France
ATTN: Chantal Zimmer, Executive Director
(33) 1-5375-2225 (phone)
(33) 1-5375-2220 (fax)

Germany
German Franchise Association
Paul Heyse Str. 33-35
Munchen 80336, Germany
ATTN: Felix Peckart
(49) 89-53-50-27 (phone)
(49) 89-53-13-23 (fax)

Hong Kong
Hong Kong Franchise Association
22/F Unit A United Centre,
95 Queensway
Hong Kong

ATTN: Charlotte Chow, Senior Manager
(852) 2529-9229 (phone)
(852) 2527-9843 (fax)

Hungary
Hungarian Franchise Association
Secretariat: c/o DASY
P.O. Box 446
Budapest H-1537, Hungary
ATTN: Istvan Kiss, Secretary General
(361) 212-4124 (phone)
(361) 212-5712 (fax)

Indonesia
Indonesia Franchise Association (AFI)
J1. Pembangunan 1/7
Jakarta 1030, Indonesia
ATTN: Anang Sukandar
(62) 21-3802449 (phone)
(62) 21-3802448 (fax)

Ireland
Irish Franchise Association
13 Frankfield Terrace, Summerhill
South Cork, Ireland
ATTN: John Neenan, Director
(353) 21-316080 (phone)
(353) 21-316080 (fax)

Israel
Israel Franchise & Distribution Association
P. O. Box 3093
Herzeliya 46590, Israel
ATTN: Michael Emery, Chairman of the Board
(972) 9-576-631 (phone)
(972) 9-576-631 (fax)

Italy
Italian Franchise Association
Corso di Porta Nuova, 3
Milano 20121, Italy
ATTN: Michele Scardi, General Secretary

(39) 2-29003779 (phone)
(39) 2-6555919 (fax)

Japan
Japan Franchise Association
Elsa Bldg. 602, Roppongi, 3-13-12, Minato-ku
Tokyo 106, Japan
ATTN: Sigeyuki Ochiai, Executive Managing Director
(81) 3-34010421 (phone)
(81) 3-34232019 (fax)

Malaysia
Malaysian Franchise Association
Lot 8 Plaza Putra dataran, Merdeka, Jalan Raja
Kuala Lumpur 50050, Malaysia
ATTN: Ishak B. Che Long, Director
(60) 3-294-7055 (phone)
(60) 3-294-7033 (fax)

Mexico
Mexican Franchise Association
Insurgentes Sur 1783, #303, Col. Guadalupe Inn
Mexico City, DF 01020, Mexico
ATTN: Adolfo Crespo, Director General
(52) 5-661-0655 (phone)
(52) 5-663-2178 (fax)

Middle East
Middle East Franchise & Distribution Association
P.O. Box 3093
Herzeliya 46590, Israel
ATTN: Michael Emery, Chairman of the Board
(972) 9-576-631 (phone)
(972) 9-576-631 (fax)

Netherlands
Netherlands Franchise Association
Boomberglaan 12
Hilversum 1217 RR, Netherlands
ATTN: A. W. M. Brouwer, General Secretary
(31) 35-24344 (phone)
(31) 35-249194 (fax)

Norway
Handelen Hovedorganisasjon
Postboks 2483, Solli
Oslo 2 0202, Norway
ATTN: Per Reidarson, President
(47) 22-558220 (phone)
(47) 22-558225 (fax)

Poland
Polish Franchise Association
Krolewska 27
00-670 Warsaw, Poland
ATTN: Jolanta Kramarz, Chairman
(48) 22-27-78-22 (phone)
(48) 22-27-78-22 (fax)

Portugal
Associacao Portuguesa Da Franchise
Rua Castilho, n 14
Lisbon 1000, Portugal
ATTN: Pascale Lagneaux, Directora General
(351) 1-315-1845 (phone)
(351) 1-315-1845 (fax)

Romania
Romanian Franchise Association
Calea Victorieri Nr. 95, Et. 4, AP. 16, Sect. 1
Bucharest, Romania
ATTN: Violeta Popovici, Chief Executive
(401) 3126889/6180186 (phone)
(401) 3126890 (fax)

Singapore
Singapore International Franchise Association
71 Sophia Road
0922 Singapore
ATTN: Tan Thuan Seng
(65) 334-8200 (phone)
(65) 334-8211 (fax)

Southern Africa
Franchise Association of Southern Africa

Kenlaw House, 27 De Beer St., P.O. Box 31708
Braamfontein, 2017 South Africa
ATTN: Jack Barber, Executive Director
(27) 11-4033468 (phone)
(27) 11-4031279 (fax)

Sweden
Swedish Franchise Association
Box 5512-S., Grevgatan 34Stockholm 11485, Sweden
ATTN: Stig Sohlberg, Chief Executive Officer
(46) 8-6608610 (phone)
(46) 8-6627457 (fax)

Switzerland
Swiss Franchise Association
Lowenstrasse II, Postfach CH-8039
Zurich, Switzerland
ATTN: Werner Kieser, President
(41) 41-225-4757 (phone)
(41) 41-225-4777 (fax)

Turkey
Turkish Franchising Association (UFRAD)
Istiklal Cad No: 65, Emgen Han, 80600 Beyogl
Istanbul, Turkey
ATTN: Temel Sahingiray, Chairman
(90) 212-252-5561 (phone)
(90) 212-252-5561 (fax)

United Kingdom
British Franchise Association
Thames View, Newton Road, Henley-on-Thames
Oxon RG9 1HG, United Kingdom
ATTN: Brian Smart, Director
(44) 1491-578-049 (phone)
(44) 1491-573-517 (fax)

Yugoslavia
Yugoslav Franchise Association (YUFA)
21000 Novi Sad
Mokranjceva 28, Yugoslavia
ATTN: Zdravko Glusica, President
(381) 21-614-232 (phone)
(381) 21-614-232 (fax)

Federal Agencies

Export-Import Bank (Eximbank)
811 Vermont Avenue, N.W.
Washington, DC 20571

Offers financing assistance for potential exporters and companies of all sizes interested in doing business abroad.

Federal Trade Commission (FTC)
Bureau of Public Affairs
Washington, DC 20852

U.S. Department of Commerce (DOC)
Herbert C. Hoover Building
14th Street & Constitution Avenue, N.W.
Washington, DC 20230
202-482-2000

Offers a wide variety of programs and services relating to economic development, international trade, and minority business. The U.S. Patent and Trademark Office (800-786-9199) is a division of the DOC that processes federal patent and trademark applications and publishes various resources on the protection of intellectual property.

U.S. Small Business Administration (SBA)
409 Third Street, S.W.
Washington, DC 20416
800-827-5722

Offers a wide variety of financing programs, workshops and seminars, management and technical assistance, etc. — typically through its many district offices.

In addition to the agencies above, all major federal departments and agencies have an Office of Small and Disadvantaged Business Utilization (OSDBU), which is responsible for ensuring that an equitable share of government contracts are awarded to small and minority-owned businesses. Some sample OSDBU phone numbers within selected agencies include:

Agency for International Development
703-875-1551

Department of Agriculture
202-720-7117

Department of Defense
703-614-1151

Department of Justice
202-616-0521

Office of Personnel Management
202-606-2180

State Agencies

Although a comprehensive state-by-state directory is beyond the scope of this chapter, virtually every state has at least one office or agency that is responsible for coordinating programs and assistance for small and minority-owned businesses. These various state programs offer a wide range of services, from technical assistance to advocacy to financial support. Each state "houses" the small business division in a slightly different place, but a safe place to start is with a call to the state's Department of Commerce or Department of Economic Development. A few states—such as California (916-324-1295), Connecticut (860-258-4200), Illinois (217-524-5856), and Minnesota (800-657-3858)—have a stand-alone Office of Small Business. Many states offer training programs, seminars, publications, and even tax breaks to foster and encourage the growth of small businesses. The chambers of commerce in each state are also an excellent starting point for determining the availability and extent of small business development programs in a given region.

Trade Associations

There are literally thousands of trade associations, networking groups, venture clubs, and other organizations that directly or indirectly focus on the needs of small business owners, entrepreneurs, growing companies, women-owned businesses, minority-owned businesses, importers and exporters, and virtually every other group that shares common interests. Some of the more established groups with a genuine nationwide presence and solid track record include:

Alliance of Independent Store Owners and Professionals (AISOP)
P.O. Box 2014, Loop Station
Minneapolis, MN 55402
612-340-1568

AISOP was organized to protect and promote fair postal and legislative policies for small business advertisers. Most of its 4,000+ members are independent small businesses that rely on reasonable third-class mail rates to promote their businesses and contact customers in their trade areas.

American Entrepreneurs Association
2392 Morse Avenue
Irvine, CA 92714
800-482-0973

The American Entrepreneurs Association was established to provide small business owners with benefits and discounts that are generally reserved for big businesses, such as express shipping, health insurance, and long-distance telephone rates.

American Small Business Association (ASBA)
1800 North Kent Street
Suite 901
Arlington, VA 22209
800-ASBA-911

ASBA's membership base consists of small business owners with twenty or fewer employees. ASBA members have access to the same advantages that larger corporations enjoy through member benefits and services.

International Franchise Association (IFA)
1350 New York Avenue
Suite 900

The IFA serves as a resource center for current and prospective franchisees and franchisors, the media, and the government.

Washington, DC 20005
202-628-8000

National Association for Female
Executives (NAFE)
30 Irving Place, 5th Floor
New York, NY 10003
212-477-2200

National Association for the
Self-Employed (NASE)
2121 Precinct Line Road
Hurst, TX 76054
817-683-1601

National Association of Development
Companies (NADCO)
4301 N. Fairfax Drive
Suite 860
Arlington, VA 22203
703-812-9000

National Association of Investment
Companies (NAIC)
1111 14th Street, N.W.
Suite 700
Washington, DC 20005
202-289-4336

National Association of Manufacturers
(NAM)
1331 Pennsylvania Avenue, N.W.
Suite 1500 North
Washington, DC 20004
202-637-3000

The IFA has promoted pro-
grams that expand opportunities for women and minorities
in franchising.

Through education and networking programs, NAFE helps
women share the resources and
techniques needed to succeed in
the competitive business world.

NASE helps its members
become more competitive by
providing over 100 benefits that
save money on services and
equipment. NASE's members
consist primarily of small business owners with few or no
employees.

NADCO is the trade group of
community-based, nonprofit
organizations—known as
Certified Development
Companies (CDC)—that pro-
mote small business expansion
and job creation through the
SBA's 504 loan program.

NAIC is the industry association for venture capital firms
that dedicate their financial
resources to investments in
minority businesses.

NAM serves as the voice of the
manufacturing community and
is active on all issues concerning
manufacturing, including legal
system reform, regulatory
restraint, and tax reform.

National Association of Small Business Investment Companies (NASBIC)
1199 N. Fairfax Drive
Suite 200
Alexandria, VA 22314
703-683-1601

NASBIC is an association of SBA-chartered small business investment companies that provide equity and commercial debt financing to small and emerging growth businesses.

National Association of Women Business Owners (NAWBO)
1100 Wayne Avenue
Suite 830
Silver Spring, MD 20910
301-608-2590

NAWBO uses its collective influence to broaden opportunities for women in business. It is the only dues-based national organization representing the interests of all women entrepreneurs in all types of business.

National Business League (NBL)
1511 K Street, N.W.
Suite 432
Washington, DC 20005
202-737-4430

NBL is primarily involved in business development among African-Americans and serves as a voice for black business on Capitol Hill and in the federal government.

National Federation of Independent Business (NFIB)
53 Century Boulevard, Suite 300
Nashville, TN 37214
600 Maryland Avenue, S.W.
Suite 700
Washington, DC 20024
800-634-2669
800-552-6342

NFIB disseminates educational information about free enterprise, entrepreneurship, and small business. NFIB represents more than 60,000 small and independent businesses before legislatures and government agencies at the federal and state level.

National Small Business United (NSBU)
1155 15th Street, N.W.
Suite 710
Washington, DC 20005
202-293-8830

The NSBU is a membership-based association of business owners that presents small businesses' point of view to all levels of government and the Congress.

National Venture Capital Association
1655 Fort Myer Drive
Suite 700

The National Venture Capital Association's mission is to define, serve, and promote the

Arlington, VA 22209
703-351-5269

interests of the venture capital industry; to increase the understanding of the importance of venture capital to the U.S. economy; and to stimulate the flow of equity capital to emerging growth and developing companies.

U.S. Chamber of Commerce
1615 H Street, N.W.
Washington, DC 20062
202-659-6000

The U.S. Chamber of Commerce represents 215,000 businesses, 3,000 state and local chambers of commerce, 1,200 trade and professional associations, and 72 American chambers of commerce abroad. It works with these groups to support national business interests and includes a Small Business Center (202-463-5503).

U.S. Hispanic Chamber of Commerce
1030 15th Street, N.W.
Suite 206
Washington, DC 20005
202-842-1212

The Hispanic Chamber advocates the business interests of Hispanics and develops minority business opportunities with major corporations and at all levels of government.

In addition to the above, there is a wide variety of special-purpose or industry-specific trade associations or foundations. These include:

American Electronics Association
1225 I Street, N.W.
Suite 950
Washington, DC 20005
202-682-9110

American Farm Bureau Federation
225 W. Touhy Avenue
Park Ridge, IL 60068
847-399-5700

American Financial Services Association
919 18th Street, N.W. 3rd Floor
Washington, DC 20006
202-296-5544

American Society of Association Executives (ASAE)
1575 I Street, N.W.
Washington, DC 20005
202-626-2723

Association of American Publishers
1718 Connecticut Avenue, N.W.
Suite 700
Washington, DC 20009
202-232-3335

Council of Growing Companies
8260 Greensboro Drive
Suite 260
McLean, VA 22102
800-929-3165

Information Industry Association
555 New Jersey Avenue, N.W.
Suite 800
Washington, DC 20001
202-639-8262

National Association of Convenience Stores
1605 King Street
Alexandria, VA 22314
703-684-3600

National Association of Wholesaler-Distributors
1725 K Street, N.W.
Suite 300
Washington, DC 20006
202-872-0885

National Foundation for Teaching Entrepreneurship to
Handicapped and Disadvantaged Youth, Inc. (NFTE)
120 Wall Street, 29th Floor
New York, NY 10005
212-232-3333

National Restaurant Association
1200 17th Street, N.W.
Washington, DC 20036
202-331-5900

National Retail Federation
325 Seventh Street, N.W.
Suite 1000
Washington, DC 20004
202-783-7971

Opportunity International
360 W. Butterfield Road
Elmhurst, IL 60126
630-279-9300

Young Entrepreneurs' Organization (YEO)
1321 Duke Street, Suite 300
Alexandria, VA 22314
703-519-6700

Resources in Cyberspace

Over the past few years, hundreds of Websites have been developed to provide resourceful support to franchisors and entrepreneurs. Websites come and go quickly and change often, so it's probably best to use one of the popular search engines and enter key words that will narrow the scope of your search or particular resource need. Next time you are surfing the Net, here are some Websites worth visiting:

Name/Internet Address	*Main Features*
1. American Association of Individual Investors http://www.aaii.org	Offers a basic guide to computerized investing and articles from the *AAII Journal* and *Computerized Investing.*
2. American Society of Association Executives http://www.asaenet.org	
3. "Ask the Lawyer" http://www.fairmeasures.com	A new Website that offers practical advice for complying with employee law and preventing lawsuits.
4. BusinessLink On-Line http://www.buslink.com	
5. *Business Journal* http://www.amcity.com (home page) http://www.amcity.com/toolstogrow	The second site features expert advice for small businesses on topics such as sales and marketing, technical issues, business financing, and tips on shopping for business products and services.
6. CareerMosaic http://www.careermosaic.com	Offers a database of national job offerings.
7. CareerPath http://www.careerpath.com	Launched by the *Boston Globe, Chicago Tribune, Los Angeles Times, New York Times, San Jose Mercury News,* and *Washington Post,* it divides hundreds of listings by journal and by field of interest.

8. Dun & Bradstreet Information
   http://dbisna.com

   A comprehensive source of financial and demographic information.

9. EDGAR
   htpp://www.sec.gov/edgarhp.htm

   A database that contains all corporate annual and quarterly reports (and exhibits) filed with the Securities and Exchange Commission.

10. E-Span
    http://www.espan.com

    Used by human resources professionals to post jobs worldwide; provides reference materials for human resources practitioners.

11. *Herring Magazine*
    http://www.herring.com

12. IdeaCafe
    http://www.ideacafe.com/
    welcome.html

    Small business meeting place.

13. IFX International
    http://www.centercourt.com

    Articles and information on franchising.

14. *Inc.* Online
    http://www.inc.com

    Allows users to (1) build their own Websites; (2) read the current issue or browse through *Inc.* magazine's extensive archives; and (3) interact with other entrepreneurs, experts, and *Inc.* editors.

15. *Income Opportunities Magazine*
    http://www.incomeops.com

16. Info Franchise News, Inc.
    http://www.infonews.com/franchise

17. Interbiznet
    http://www.interbiznet.com/ibn/top25.html

    Lists top twenty-five recruiting sites.

18. International Franchise
    Association
    http://www.franchise.org

    Offers *IFA's Franchising Opportunities Guide, Franchising World*, bulletin boards, calendar of events, and more for franchisors and franchisees.

19. The Internet Mall
    http://www.internetmall.com/
    4mplymntsrvcs.htm

    Offers links to résumé services, city job banks, career counseling, and publications.

20. Investment Brokerages Guide
    http://www.cs.cmu.edu/%7Ejdg/
    invest_brokers

    Offers links to full-service and discount and online brokerages worldwide.

21. Invest-O-Rama
    http://www.investorama.com

    Offers a directory of investment-related information such as the stock market, brokerage firms, mutual funds, and dividend and reinvestment plans.

22. JobHunt
    http://www.rescomp.stanford/
    edu/jobs

    A commercial site that distributes electronic résumés.

23. Legaldoc
    http://legaldocs.com

    Low-cost legal forms.

24. Let's Talk Business Network
    http://www.ltbn.com

    Offers a wide variety of resources on entrepreneurship and franchising.

25. *Marketing Tools Magazine*
    http://www.marketingtools.com

26. Monster Board
    http://www.monster.com

    Offers a variety of issues, from hiring to staffing to other related topics for human resources executives.

27. NetMarquee Family Business
    Net Center
    http://www.nmq.com/fambiznc

    Offers articles and newsletters covering management issues of family-owned businesses.

28. NETworth
    http://networth.galt.com

    Offers information and links to mutual fund companies and online access to fund prospectuses.

29. OfficeNET
    http://www.officenet1.com

    Offers administrative, secretarial, and professional support services.

30. Online Career Center
    http://www.occ.com

    A nonprofit consortium for corporations posting job openings.

31. SBA Women in Business
    http://www.sba.gov/
    womeninbusiness

32. SHRM (Society for Human   Lists a variety of services and
    Resource Management)   products for human resources
    http://www.shrm.org   professionals.

33. Small Business Express
    http://www.gnn.com/gnn/met.a/
    finance/smallbus/index.htm

34. Small Business Resource Center   Offers dozens of tips to help
    http://www.webcom.com/   make a small business a success.
    ~seaquest

35. Span Link Communications
    http://www.spanlink.com

36. Switchboard
    http://www.switchboard.com

37. Venture Capital Institute   Wide range of venture capital
    http://vcinstitute.org   resources.

38. *The Wall Street Journal's*   Allows users to access news and
    Interactive Edition   financial information about spec-
    http://www.update.wsj.com   ified companies.

Index

absentee ownership and management, 89

accounting
 franchise agreement requirements for, 184–185
 franchisor services for franchisees, 292–294
 generally accepted accounting principles (GAAP) in, 278
 technology and, 50
 for technology transfer licensing agreements, 369

accounts receivable, factoring, 274

accredited investors, 267–268

Ace Hardware, 353

acknowledgments
 in area development, 146
 of receipt of documents, 93, 94, 135

active rights, 349

actual composite co-branding, 395

Adcom Express, Inc. et al. v. EPK, Inc., 47

administrative staff, 17

Advanced Micro Devices Inc. v. Intel Corp., 201

advertising programs, 8
 claims concerning, 76, 77
 co-branding, 400
 compliance requirements, 115–118
 disclosure requirements for, 86–87, 95, 100
 franchise agreements and, 125
 quality control and, 50–51
 in recruiting franchisees, 228–231
 see also cooperative advertising funds

Age Discrimination in Employment Act of 1967, 296

agency relationships, franchising versus, 351

alcohol testing, 307–309

Allied Domecq PLC, 10

all or nothing offerings, 281

alternative dispute resolution (ADR), 196–208
 advantageous situations for, 198–199
 arbitration, 127, 193, 197, 198, 199–205, 290
 benefits of, 197–198
 disadvantageous situations for, 199
 disclosure requirements for, 90, 98
 in international franchising, 239–240
 mediation, 205–207, 290
 moderated settlement conferences, 208
 private judging, 207
 small claims matters, 208
 trademark and service mark use, 158

American Arbitration Association (AAA), 198, 200, 201, 207

American Bar Association, 207

Americans with Disabilities Act of 1990 (ADA), 296–297, 308, 310

Amway Corporation, 356, 361

antitrust law, 258
 pricing and, 58–60, 257
 Sherman Antitrust Act, 56, 58–59, 60
 tying arrangements and, 52–57

arbitration, 127, 193, 197, 199–205, 290